Fodor's

EIGHTH
New
EDITION

Korea

D0684567

Fodor's Travel Publications, Inc.
New York and London

Korea

Fodor's Korea

Editor: Julie Tomasz
Area Editors: Robin Bulman, Young-Ho Lee
Senior Writers: Edward B. Adams, Juliellen Sabalis
Editorial Contributors: Steve Doherty, Caroline Liou, Marcy Pritchard
Drawings: Ted Burwell
Maps: Burmar
Cover Photograph: Jean Kugler/FPG International

Cover Design: Vignelli Associates

Edward B. Adams (Introduction to Korea), Headmaster and founder of Seoul International School, has lived in Korea for over 25 years. He has authored over 30 books on Korea, among which are Korea Guide, Kyongju Guide, Art Treasures of Seoul, Korea's Pottery Heritage, Korea's Folk Art and Craft, Palaces of Seoul, and over 10 children's folktales.

Juliellen Sabalis (Facts at Your Fingertips, Exploring Korea), a freelance journalist and consultant, and longtime Seoul resident, is currently living in Argentina.

Special Sales

Fodor's Travel Publications are available at special discounts for bulk purchases
(100 copies or more) for sales promotions or premiums. Special editions,
including personalized covers, excerpts of existing guides, and corporate
imprints, can be created in large quantities for special needs. For more
information, write to Special Marketing, Fodor's Travel Publications, 201 East
50th Street, New York, NY 10022. Inquiries from the United Kingdom should
be sent to Merchandise Division, Random House UK Ltd. 20 Vauxhall Bridge
Rd., London SW1V 2SA.

MANUFACTURED IN THE UNITED STATES OF AMERICA
10 9 8 7 6 5 4 3 2 1

CONTENTS

FOREWORD

While every care has been taken to assure the accuracy of the information in this guide, the passage of time will always bring change, and consequently the publisher cannot accept responsibility for errors that may occur.

All prices and opening times quoted here are based on information supplied to us at press time. Hours and admission fees may change, however, and the prudent traveler will avoid inconvenience by calling ahead.

Fodor's wants to hear about your travel experiences, both pleasant and unpleasant. When a hotel or restaurant fails to live up to its billing, let us know and we will investigate the complaint and revise our entries where the facts warrant it.

Send your letters to the editors of Fodor's Travel Publications, 201 E. 50th Street, New York, NY 10022.

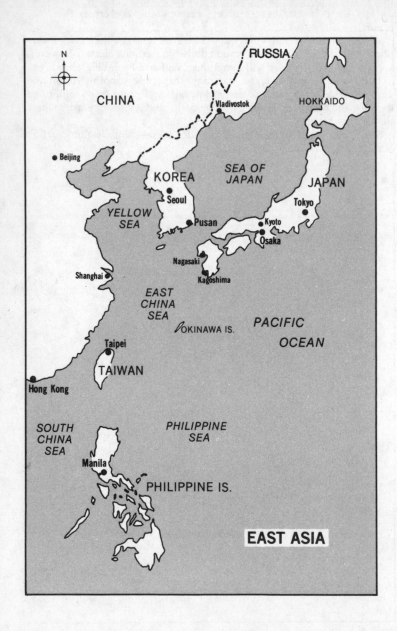

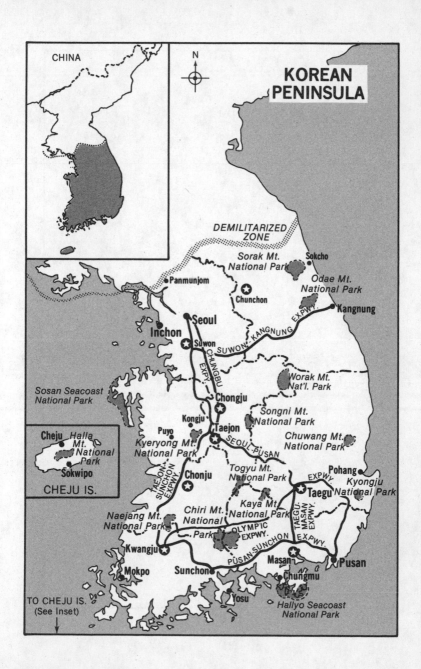

INTRODUCTION

During the centuries when the rulers of Korea shunned foreign contacts, the monarchy was spoken of as the Hermit Kingdom. Later the country was called the Land of Morning Calm, from the Korean *choson,* the title of the last dynasty under the Yi (Lee) family rulers. The Yi Dynasty came to a close at the turn of the last century; today, in Korea's modern era, the mist of morning calm has dissipated and the nation might well be known as the Land of Cultural Contrasts.

Though many of the people, especially in Seoul, have generally become quite Westernized, they still follow the old customs and traditions.

The name Korea comes from the word *koryo,* meaning high and clear—an apt description of the country's clear blue skies, rugged mountains, and rushing streams, which have earned the Korean peninsula the nickname Switzerland of Asia.

The East Sea (Sea of Japan) and Korean Straits separate the Korean peninsula from Japan to the east, while the Yellow Sea lies between Korea and the People's Republic of China to the west. The 600-mile Korean peninsula, which borders Russia and China to the north, varies from 130 to 200 miles in width. The northern boundaries of the Republic of Korea were established by the Armistice Agreement signed after the Korean War in 1953. Today this barrier, called the Demilitarized Zone (DMZ), lies only 30 minutes from Seoul.

Foreign tourists are often surprised to learn that the city of Seoul, a modern metropolis of 10 million people and the capital of the Republic, was founded one hundred years before Christopher Columbus discovered the Americas. But when compared to Korea's history of five thousand years, the capital city is relatively new.

1

Today Korea is an emerging industrialized nation. Its remarkable progress over the last several decades has not been accomplished by chance. The Koreans are a hardworking, industrious people who have always had a fierce loyalty to their nation and pride in their cultural heritage.

Over the centuries the Korean people have persistently held to one language, one culture, and an ancient tradition. Only recently have outside influences brought dramatic changes to the people and the nation. Generally speaking, the Koreans are more familiar with Western cultures than the average Westerner is with the Korean way of thinking. Thus the Korean people are among the friendliest toward Westerners. Their keen sense of humor is balanced by an earthy common sense.

Korea's proximity to China has permitted a reciprocal flow of people along with their ideas and skills over its 5,000-year history. There has also been a predominantly one-sided cultural and racial flow from Korea to Japan since ancient times. Historical documentation points to an immense Korean contribution to Japan's cultural and social development over the last 2,000 years.

Traditionally, Korea has had a fairly rigid class structure wherein a man could attain a position of influence only through education in the Confucian classics, which defines correct social behavior. At the turn of the century, American Presbyterian missionaries established Korea's first modern Westernized educational institutions.

Academic achievement is still considered an important step to top positions and social distinction, although wealth has now become an important factor in class structure. The old class system has had to adjust to the wealthy businessmen and skilled workers in Korea's industrialized society. Today the literacy rate in Korea is one of the highest in the world.

A recent phenomenon in Korea's modernizing process is the changing status of women and the impact it has had on the family structure. The shift has been most dramatically away from Confucian concepts as many well-educated women search for equality in what has been traditionally a male-dominated society. Korean women are actively contributing to their country's progress and developing democracy.

In September 1981, Seoul City won its bid to host the 1988 Summer Olympic Games, thus becoming the second nation in Asia to have this honor. Koreans proudly embraced the opportunity, and the two-week event represents one of the most important milestones in the Republic's history.

Seoul City developed an impressive Sport Complex, many of whose facilities were used for the Asian Games of 1986. The capital's substrata were filled with over 72 miles of subway lines, and expressways moved vehicular traffic conveniently throughout the city and farther south. During the Olympic period Korea also hosted an ambitious Festival of Arts and Culture.

Because of the Olympics of 1988, Korea has made phenomenal strides in the tourism industry. All aspects of travel to Korea, including transportation, hotels, recreation, and sightseeing, have been scrutinized and improved. Tourism has much to offer, and the government is taking an active interest in tapping the nation's cultural resources.

The tourist attracted by Korea's heritage and culture will encounter absorbing and fascinating things, from trails to mountain temples to city palaces and museums, from picturesque villages to tombs of royalty who died hundreds of years ago. Even those in search of a restful holiday will find that Korea has much to offer—from excellent beaches to wooded mountains and the enchanting island of Cheju in the south.

Visitors to Korea find it an extraordinary country of simple grandeur and amazing contrasts, a country rich in history and culture, a country of varied and often spectacular landscape.

The best time to come is spring and fall, as the weather is clear and bright. In spring the hills are aflame with the azalea blooms against the light green of new growth, and autumn brings a kaleidoscope of colors.

Touring Korea in Brief

If you have only a few days in Korea, there is much to do and see in Seoul and its vicinity. If it is shopping that you want, it is best to move away from the hotels to the department stores, South Gate or East Gate markets, or the famous Itaewon area, which is a well-known foreign enclave. Almost all proprietors in Itaewon speak fairly good English, and prices are negotiable. The shopping arcade called First Avenue between the hotels Lotte and Chosun is highly recommended—though prices are usually higher, the quality is good. Nearby Myongdong is the center of high fashion and consists of a maze of narrow lanes. It is Seoul's equivalent of Tokyo's Ginza.

The new (1986) National Museum located in the old capitol building is worth a visit. The excellent displays carry English descriptions. Daily tours are conducted through Changdok-kung Palace and the Secret Garden. In Kyongbok Palace and the Toksu Palace, tourists can wander about at their own pace and enjoy the historical remains. Don't miss the Folk Art Museum.

Spend an afternoon at the refurbished Changgyong-kung Palace, which contains some of the oldest palace buildings (bring your camera) in Korea. The dance performances conducted almost nightly at Korea House are an excellent introduction to Korea's music and dance heritage, and you can enjoy the buffet Korean meal prior to the performance. You should, of course, have a Korean meal; with many excellent restaurants, Seoul has become an eating paradise for its citizens.

Many of the numerous art galleries in Seoul will be found in and around the district of Insadong, famous for its antiques stores. Some 200 exhibitions are held in Seoul each year. Information on dates is usually given in both of Korea's two local English newspapers, the *Korea Herald* and *Korea Times.*

If you have extra time, there are plenty of one-day trips outside of Seoul. A visit to Korea's Folk Village near Suwon, this country's version of Williamsburg, Virginia, is recommended. Located only 45 minutes from Seoul, this cultural Korean village includes almost everything that is uniquely Korean from days gone by. Be certain to try the traditional Korean food in the village market.

The Korea Tourist Bureau and the United Service Organization conduct tours to Panmunjom, where the DMZ represents the impasse in the Korean War of 1950–1953.

Farther out from Seoul is Yongin Family Land with the excellent Hoam Museum, which specializes in ceramics and paintings, both modern and traditional. Yongin Family Land has a Disney-like appeal; it includes a zoo and is especially popular with the young folks. North Fortress and South Fortress near Seoul are popular tourist attractions as well as Kanghwa Island, west of Kimpo. The fortress walls and gates add a special charm to the mountainous landscape.

An hour-and-a-half drive south of Seoul will take you to Onyang and Korea's most comprehensive and unusual Folk Art Museum. This is one of the best in the country; its exhibits are exceptionally well done. While at Onyang, also visit the National Shrine to 16th-century Admiral Yi Sunshin, Korea's foremost military hero and naval strategist.

An hour's drive south of Seoul near Ichon you'll find many pottery kilns where visitors can actually see the traditional as well as modern ceramic wares being made. The potters often have showrooms where ceramic pieces can be purchased, usually for less than you would pay in Seoul. With special permission the working artisans will be photographed.

Travel in the countryside is becoming easier; most roads are now paved and adequate hotel accommodations with baths are usually available near tourist sites. Intercity air-conditioned buses and trains are economical, comfortable, and punctual. Even domestic air transportation is not unduly expensive.

If you have a few days to spend outside Seoul, your first choice should be a trip to Kyongju, the ancient Silla capital. This can be done on your own by purchasing a train ticket directly to the historic capital. It is about a four-hour trip. Walk around the downtown area or hire a bicycle or taxi. Kyongju was the cradle of Silla culture and the dynasty's capital from 57 B.C. to A.D. 935. Miraculously, the area escaped destruction during recent wars. Royal tombs, temple sites with weathered stone pagodas and Buddhist reliefs, and fortress ruins are scattered throughout the valleys and hills. You should visit the National Museum of Kyongju, Tomb Park, and the monastery of Pulguksa.

Only one of the several hundred royal tombs in the vicinity has been turned into a museum. This is the famous Heavenly Horse Tomb (Tumulus 155) located in Tomb Park. Thousands of fifth- and sixth-century treasures taken from this tomb and several others, which have been excavated over the years, are on display in the national museums of Kyongju and Seoul. Also, the recently constructed exhibition hall at the National Museum, which houses the excavations from Anap-ji, is worth attention for those interested in archaeology.

Built on a series of stone terraces 10 miles from Kyongju is Pulguksa, Korea's most famous and one of the oldest surviving monasteries in the country. Though Pulguksa is not typical of most Korean Buddhist monasteries, which still manage to maintain an aura of calm serenity, to tour Kyongju and not visit this famed temple of Silla's "golden age" would nevertheless be unthinkable.

To view Korea's most classic example of Silla stone sculpture, visit the stone-cave hermitage called the Sokkuram, located on Toham Mountain behind Pulguksa. Here in this grotto is found the distinctive quality of Korean art, namely, earnestness matched with dignity and grandeur, classic and idealistic naturalism, simple interpretation of form.

Probably the best known of all of Korea's ancient remains is the stone astronomical observatory located in the heart of Kyongju. This 29-foot tower, believed to be the oldest observatory in the world, is one of the oldest man-made structures in the country. It was built in 634 during the reign of Silla Queen Sondok.

Cheju, the largest and most famous of the 3,000 islands of Korea, is approximately 60 miles from the southern coast. This island of wind, rocks, and women has become the vacationland of the nation. The mystic volcanic peak of Hallasan rises 6,400 feet above the citrus orchards. It is a popular region for newlyweds, one where honeymoon couples gaze wistfully out to sea from snug villas along the rocky coasts. Though ferryboats are available, we recommend flying to the island.

Cheju has had a turbulent history, and the distant waves of many cultures, including a Dutch shipwreck in the seventeenth century, have washed ashore, making this island in many ways fascinating and different from the Korean culture of the mainland. The future of Cheju Island is bright for tourism, for the government has developed it into a recreational region, which appeals to Korean tourists as well as to foreign visitors.

If you consider Korea's hundreds of temples and have time to visit only one, we recommend that you make it the monastery of Haeinsa. You will need at least two days, but three would be preferable. In size it is one of the three major historic temples of the country, but the mountainous scenery alone will awe any tourist. Haeinsa is the repository of Korea's famous 81,258 *Tripitaka* woodblocks, which are the oldest (thirteenth century) and most complete Buddhist scriptures in the world.

As cooler temperatures come to the Korean peninsula and autumn foliage begins to turn to crimson red and golden yellow, the scenic spires guarding the valleys of Sorak Mountain beckon to Korean and foreign tourists alike.

The wooded wonderland of Sorak Mountain, which is part of the east coast Diamond Mountains, is considered one of the world's most spectacular natural wonders. Cascading streams, which tumble over cataracts and drop from precipices to form fleecy waterfalls, as well as awesome sawtooth cliffs and monolithic rock formations jutting into the blue skies, give this area an unparalleled beauty and popularity.

FACTS AT YOUR FINGERTIPS

FACTS AT YOUR FINGERTIPS

Travel Information

FACTS AND FIGURES. Korea is a peninsula, suspended from the Asian mainland at its northern end (Manchuria and Siberia) and projecting southward into the waters of the western Pacific. This 600-mile-long peninsula faces eastward across the Sea of Japan (which the Koreans call the East Sea), only 120 miles from the Japanese island chain. Westward across the Yellow Sea (the West Sea to Koreans) lies China. At its widest point, Korea is only 130 miles across.

The Republic of Korea, or South Korea, has an area of about 38,000 square miles—approximately the size of Virginia or Portugal. A range of mountains, called Taebaeksan, runs down through the peninsula, a spiny backbone somewhat closer to the east coast. This range effectively divides South Korea into eastern and western halves. In many parts of the country the view is one of unending rugged terrain, and it is said that there is nowhere in the country one can stand without seeing at least one mountain. In sharp contrast to the hills are vast fields of rice paddies that are flat for long stretches, for South Korea was the "rice bowl" of the once-unified country, whereas North Korea was the industrial half.

In the east, the mountains drop sharply into the sea, making a rough but beautiful coastline, with many rocky islets lying just off the shore. In the south and west, the land merges more gently into the sea, creating many bays and harbors and forming some excellent swimming beaches. The 1990 census indicated a population of around 43 million in South Korea, with almost 10 million living in the area of the capital city, Seoul.

The country is administratively divided into nine provinces, plus a special city (Seoul), and five other cities (Pusan, Taegu, Inchon, Taejon, and Kwangju) that each enjoy the status of a province directly under the central government. There are 67 cities (shi) and 137 counties (gun) in the nine provinces. The counties are subdivided into 183 towns (up), and almost 1,260 villages (myon).

TRAVEL ARRANGEMENTS. The best source of information on all things Korean is the **Korea National Tourism Corporation** (KNTC), the state-run organization now over 20 years in operation. The head office is in Seoul, in the Tourism Center Building, 10, Ta-dong, Chung-ku, Seoul (Tel. 757–6030; Telex KOTOUR K28555; Fax. (02) 757–5997); C.P.O. Box 903, Seoul, Korea.

The KNTC has over 20 offices or appointed representatives worldwide, all of which will assist with current details on the country's vacation opportunities.

In the United States

Chicago
205 N. Michigan Ave., Suite 2212
Chicago, Illinois 60601
Tel. (312) 819–2560
Fax. (312) 819–2563

Hawaii
1188 Bishop St., Century Sq.
PH 1, Honolulu, Hawaii 96813
Tel. (808) 521–8066
Fax. (808) 521–5233

Los Angeles
3435 Wilshire Blvd., Suite 350
Los Angeles, California 90010
Tel. (213) 382–3435
Fax. (213) 480–0483

New York Area
Two Executive Dr., 7th Fl.
Fort Lee, New Jersey 07024
Tel. (201) 585–0909, (212) 688–7543
Fax. (201) 585–9041

Seattle
c/o Ehrig and Associates
4th Vine Bldg.
Seattle, Washington 98121
Tel. (206) 441–6666
Fax. (206) 441–9135

In the United Kingdom

London
Vogue House, 2d fl.
1 Hanover Sq.
London W1R 9RD
Tel. (071) 409–2100
Fax. (071) 491–2302

In Australia

Sydney
Tower Bldg., Suite 1714
Australia Sq., George St.
Sydney 2000
Tel. (02) 252–4147/8
Fax. (02) 251–2104

In Asia

Hong Kong
Rm. 506, Bank of America Tower
12 Harcourt Rd., Hong Kong

Tel. 523–8065
Fax. 845–0765

Singapore
24 Raffles Pl., No. 20–03
Clifford Centre, Singapore 0104
Tel. 533–0441/2
Telex KOTOURS RS21673
Fax. 534–3427

A growing number of overseas tour operators are developing Korea vacation programs, either featuring Korea as a destination in itself or linked with visits to other countries in Asia and the Far East. Today there is therefore a number of practical alternatives in planning a Korea vacation—either joining an organized tour from your own country, or setting up your own itinerary in a combination of set programs and "do-it-yourself" arrangements.

The majority of visitors will arrive in Korea by air, and the most likely arrival points are the airports of Seoul, in the northwest corner of the country and Pusan, in the southwest. You can arrive and leave through the same gateway, of course, but we'd like to suggest a different approach—arriving at either Seoul or Pusan and working your way through the country to depart from the other main gateway.

For a stay of around two weeks, here's a sketch of a possible itinerary: Arrive in Seoul and spend a couple of days in and around the capital. Next, take a bus tour to the Mt. Soraksan National Park in the East Coast area; then return to Seoul and complete your explorations there. Start south by bus or train into the West Plain/Coastal Area, spending at least one day each in Kongju and Puyo. From here you can make a side trip into the Central Area, and continue south, perhaps pausing at Taejon, to Taegu. You should stay here long enough to make side trips to the Haeinsa Temple and the ancient city of Kyongju, an important cultural area. Finally, work your way southward from Taegu (or Kyongju) to Pusan, where you can visit the sights of the city, cruise the Hallyo Waterway for a day, explore the beaches, and, if you have time, head over for a couple of days on Cheju Island. You can fly out of Pusan, or take the ferry over to Japan.

Note that you can introduce a variation in this touring plan by continuing south through the West Plains/Coastal Area, rather than traveling into the center, and head for the city of Kwangju, turning east to Pusan for the final portion of the trip. In this case, you should plan at least a two-day trip by bus or train north to Kyongju; it's only an hour's ride from Pusan.

The overland plan works equally well from the opposite direction, starting in Pusan and ending in Seoul. But don't think of this plan as a long meandering trip that might leave you stranded in some small town. It is very easy to move from city to city, making reservations in advance as you go. There are times to be cautious, however, as special holidays and local festivals (such as cherry-blossom time at Chinhae) can stretch available accommodations. Bear in mind that distances are not great, and bus or train services are wonderfully frequent (the entire trip, nonstop, from Seoul to Pusan by bus, for example, is just over five hours), and you will find it easy to move from one town to the next.

WHEN TO GO. One of the meteorological labels for Korea is "monsoonal," which is an indication that the summer pattern is often two or three rainy days followed by three or four days of clear weather. Visitors from the United States often compare the summers with New York, and the winters with Boston. Pusan, on the southern tip of the peninsula is more like the Baltimore-Washington, D.C. corridor in midsummer (July and August)—hot and humid. North of Pusan, summer weather can be a little milder, and along the shore there are sea breezes.

Looking at the seasons, March shows the earliest signs of spring, as temperatures begin to rise and trees begin to bud. Spring truly arrives in April, with the blossoming of the cherry trees, along with azaleas, magnolias, forsythia, and lilacs. In May, farmers prepare their fields for the planting of rice and other crops.

There is a monsoon-induced rainy season in late June and July, during which half of the annual rainfall is recorded. July and August are the traditional vacation times for Koreans, and city dwellers head for the beaches and mountain resorts.

Fall brings warm days, cooler nights, and refreshingly lower humidity. Conditions are ideal for exploring the country—particularly the forested areas, which become a riot of autumn colors. Many of Korea's liveliest festivals take place during this period.

The winter's air is crisp and chilly, and the skies are brilliantly clear and blue. Snow begins to fall in the mountains in late November, in Seoul a little later. City streets are cleared very quickly and there are few problems in getting around. The coldest months are December, January, and February, with the ski season usually running through the middle of February.

Climate

Below is a chart of maximum and minimum temperatures and average rainfall in Seoul over a 12-month period. For Pusan and the rest of the southern coastal areas, you can anticipate slightly higher temperatures, both in winter and summer, but tempered by sea breezes along the shore. Temperatures are given on the Fahrenheit scale; rainfall in inches and tenths.

	Jan.	Feb.	Mar.	Apr.	May	June	July	Aug.	Sept.	Oct.	Nov.	Dec.
MAX.	37°	32°	47°	62°	72°	80°	84°	87°	78°	67°	51°	37°
MIN.	15°	20°	29°	41°	51°	61°	70°	71°	59°	45°	32°	20°
RAIN	1.2	0.8	1.5	3.0	3.2	5.1	14.8	10.5	4.7	1.6	1.8	1.0

You will see that the midsummer period of July and August is not only the hottest but the wettest time of year in Seoul—and you can take both the heat and rainfall up a couple of notches for Pusan and the South Coast.

WHAT IT WILL COST. A recent survey by the Korea National Tourism Corporation indicates that spending per visitor during 1991 amounted to an average of $237 per day. This was broken down into 31 percent for accommodation, 18 percent for meals, inside and outside hotels, 13 percent for entertainment, 27 percent for shopping, and 12 percent for sightseeing, local transportation, and miscellaneous expenses. It should be noted that this is an indication of average spending, taking all nationalities and all types of visitors—students to businessmen—into account.

As visitors from North America tend to spend at the high end of the scale, here are some approximate costs for a mixed collection of goods and services (at press time the exchange rate was around 800 won to the U.S. dollar):

One-night hotel accommodation, at a deluxe hotel, based on one person, sharing a twin room	W90,000
American breakfast	W 8,000
City tour, half day	W18,000
Lunch, hotel coffee shop	W10,000
Taxis, to a sightseeing attraction, shopping district, and back to the hotel	W10,000
Dinner, Continental menu, top-hotel restaurant	W35,000
Bottle of local white wine, at hotel	W12,000
Bottle of imported wine, medium brand	W32,500
Bottle of good French champagne	W72,500
Bottle of local beer, at hotel bar	W 2,300
Glass of spirits, at hotel bar	W 4,500

The above prices do not include service charges or taxes, and meal prices do not include drinks.

There are many ways to cut down on expenses, such as eating at the many fast-food restaurants or small Korean rice-and-noodle shops, using the hotel's free shuttle services to the most popular shopping areas rather than taking taxis, getting around by subway or bus (if you can find someone to translate the bus routes for you), shopping in the markets instead of in the air-conditioned stores (it's more fun, too), and exploring palaces and other places of interest with a map and guidebook, avoiding the expense of an organized tour.

TRAVEL DOCUMENTS. You must have a valid passport, but you do not need to obtain a Korean visa if your stay is to be less than 15 days and you have a confirmed ticket for departure.

If you plan to stay longer than 15 days, you should obtain a tourist visa from a Korean embassy or consulate abroad. In the United States, the embassy is in Washington, D.C., and consulates are maintained in Anchorage, Atlanta, Chicago, Honolulu, Houston, Los Angeles, New York, San Francisco, and Seattle. In Canada, the embassy is in Ottawa with additional consular services in Montreal, Toronto, and Vancouver. All Korean consular services for the United Kingdom are handled out of the embassy in London. Note that under a special agreement, visitors from the United Kingdom can stay up to 90 days in Korea without a visa. Remember, people of most other nationalities, including the United States and Canada, need to obtain visas for stays of longer than 15 days.

A tourist visa is good for a stay of up to 90 days.

It is against Korean law to engage in any remunerative activities while holding a tourist visa. Entry for employment requires a special permit from the Ministry of Justice.

Immigration Offices. For information and assistance regarding your visa or length of stay while you are in Korea, you can contact an immigration office in any of the following cities:

Seoul: 319–2, Sinjung 6-dong, Yangpyong-ku, Seoul; Tel. (02) 653–3041.

Inchon: 1–17, 7–ka, Hang-dong, Chung-ku, Inchon; Tel. (032) 882–0544.

Pusan: 17–26, 4–ka, Chungang-dong, Chung-ku, Pusan; Tel. (051) 463–7161/6.

Cheju: 673–8, Konip-dong, Cheju, Cheju-do; Tel. (064) 22–3494/5.

There are also immigration offices at **Kimpo International Airport** in Seoul, at **Kimhae International Airport** in Pusan, and at **Cheju International Airport** in Cheju.

Vaccinations. None are specifically required for entry into Korea, but it is recommended that if you travel from or through areas infected with cholera or yellow fever, you take the precaution of vaccinations.

Animals. Cats and dogs must be left in quarantine on arrival in Korea for a period of 10 days, and you are also required to produce a valid certificate of inoculation against rabies. For details, call the National Animal Quarantine Service, (02) 635–5036.

Plants. All plants and plant products must be declared on arrival and a Phytosanitary Certificate, issued by the plant-quarantine organization of the country of export, must be shown. For details, call the National Plant Quarantine Office of Korea, (02) 664–3841.

WHAT TO TAKE. The first rule is, as always, travel light. Seasoned travelers already know about lightweight luggage and wash-and-wear clothing, and how to make each item in your vacation wardrobe serve two functions. For Korea, here's what you'll need, according to the time of year.

March–May: Lightweight clothes. Add a sweater or jacket, as it's windy, and temperatures can get cool early and late in the day.

June–August: Definitely short-sleeved shirts, sports clothes, swimwear, light raincoat, and an umbrella. Prepare for the heat, but remember that your indoor time will just about always be air-conditioned.

September–November: Light clothing again, but prepare for chilly days and evenings.

December–February: This is the time when the pattern is three cold days followed by four warmer ones, but it's still very cold. You'll appreciate thermal underwear, warm boots, and down jackets. Korea offers a wonderful selection of cold-weather gear, such as down jackets and ski-wear, so you can always buy what you need when you're there.

Regarding **clothing etiquette,** Koreans take a dressy approach to all city activities—suits for men and dresses for women—and a more casual approach to sightseeing and recreation. Shorts are confined to the beach. Slacks are acceptable for women, and are recommended for touring, but dresses are favored for most social occasions.

INFORMATION FOR DISABLED VISITORS. Facilities for the disabled in Korea are woefully inadequate, but the situation is improving, slightly and slowly. Some of the top Seoul hotels, for example, have special rest rooms in public areas, and there are also toilet facilities at the main airports. Getting around is a problem. Curbs end abruptly at street crossings—there are no ramps—and in the downtown areas most of the passageways across busy roads are underground, involving lots and lots of stairs. There is one rumor that this is how the Koreans keep fit; simply by having to cross the road.

For the disabled, Korea is not an easy place to visit unassisted.

Getting to Korea

BY AIR. At our press time, 25 scheduled international airlines served Seoul, providing some 420 direct or nonstop flights per week between Seoul and major cities in North America, Europe, the Middle East, and Asia. Korea has two national flag carriers, the well-established Korean Air and the newer Asiana Airlines, which has begun to expand its international flights. Other on-line services for passengers are provided by Aeroflot, Air France, Alitalia Airlines, All Nippon, British Airways, Cathay Pacific, China Airlines, Continental Airlines, Delta, EVA Air, Garuda International, Japan Air Lines, KLM, Lauda Air, Lufthansa, Malaysian Airline System, Northwest Airlines, Philippine Airlines, Qantas Airways, Royal Dutch Airlines, Saudi Arabian Airlines, Singapore Airlines, Swissair, Thai International, and United Airlines. The Korean government is also discussing reciprocal flights with several other countries.

The country has three international airports: Kimpo International (around 11 miles west of downtown Seoul), Pusan's Kimhae International (17 miles northwest of the southern port city), and Cheju International (just 2½ miles from downtown Cheju, on the island province off Korea's southwest corner). All three are equipped with modern air-traffic-control facilities and support systems, and all have restaurants, gift shops, information desks, hotel reservation counters, duty-free shops, and other services you would expect from an international airport facility. A fourth international airport is scheduled to open at Taegu at the end of 1993.

Your arrival in Korea by air is most likely to be through Kimpo in Seoul unless you are traveling from Japan, which would give you the choice of Seoul, Pusan, or Cheju as your arrival point.

To give you an idea of flight times, from the East Coast of the U.S. it takes 18 hours; from Midwest cities, 15 hours; from the West Coast (Los Angeles), 13 hours, and from Seattle, 10 hours; from Europe it takes around 19 hours. From Japan it takes just one or two hours, depending on your point of departure. From the United States, several of the services are nonstop—out of Chicago, Hawaii, Los Angeles, New York, Portland (Oregon), and Seattle.

BY SEA. An increasing number of cruise ships are stopping at Pusan, offering passengers tours of the environs of Pusan and the ancient center of Kyongju. But the port of Pusan is also providing a gateway for tourists entering Korea from Japan. With adequate time and a love of sea voyages, you can do this on an established sailing schedule. A large sea-going ferry sails daily from Shimonoseki, Japan (on Honshu Island), carrying over 900 passengers, plus cars. Departure time is 6 P.M., arriving in Pusan at 9:30 A.M. the following morning. The reverse journey, Pusan to Shimonoseki, is also from 5 P.M. to 8:30 A.M. Fares per person: "A" first-class, one-way (two-person cabin)—$90; "B" first-class, one-way (four-person cabin)—$80; second-class, 6–10 persons with tatami sleeping facilities—$65; and economy class, nonsleeping, open cabin—$55. The charge for a car is $160, one-way. It is possible to arrange for car transportation only for Shimonoseki–Pusan–Shimonoseki, not the reverse. Hydrofoil service is also available. Daily departures are 9:30 A.M. from Shimonoseki and 1:40 P.M. from Pusan; fares are $62–$80. For bookings and further information, call (02) 738–0055 in Seoul, (051) 463–3161 in Pusan, (0832) 24–3000 in Shimonoseki, (03) 3567–0971 in Tokyo, and (06) 345–2245 in Osaka.

Another ferry service, by the good ship *Kukjae,* links Osaka, Japan, with Pusan. It leaves Osaka every Wednesday and Saturday at noon and arrives in Pusan the following day at 9 A.M. From Pusan, departures are at 5 P.M., every Monday, Wednesday, and Thursday, arriving in Osaka at 2 P.M. the next day. Fares are $100–$250, depending on class of travel. For information, call (02) 754–7786 in Seoul, (051) 463–7000 in Pusan, and (06) 266–1111 in Osaka.

Arriving in Korea

IMMIGRATION FORMALITIES. On arrival in Korea, you will be given a length of stay according to your visa status. Those traveling without a visa will need a confirmed onward ticket for a 15-day stay; those with a tourist visa will be permitted to stay up to 90 days. (Visitors from the United Kingdom traveling for pleasure, however, are entitled to stay 90 days without obtaining a visa.) All arriving passengers fill out an Arrival Card, and a copy of this is kept in your passport until departure. Additional details, as well as information on immigration offices within Korea, are outlined in the earlier section on Travel Documents.

CUSTOMS PROCEDURES. An oral declaration is sufficient for hand baggage. You should declare all expensive jewelry, cameras, fur coats, and similar luxury items. The following items can be brought in duty-free: necessary personal items, clothing and toiletries; 400 cigarettes, 50 cigars, ½ lb. of pipe tobacco, and 3 ½ oz. of other tobacco, the total quantity not to exceed 1 lb., 2 oz.; two bottles of liquor (1.520 cc); 2 oz. of perfume; and gifts up to the value of W300,000 (approximately $375 at press time).

Excess amounts are subject to duty payments. However, if you place such items in bond at the customs office on arrival, you escape the duty and can reclaim the goods on departure.

Prohibited items include firearms, gold or silver bullion, two-way radio equipment and articles or literature that are considered subversive, pornographic or in opposition to government interests.

Import of Currency. Foreign currencies equivalent to more than US$5,000 can be brought in without limit, provided the amount is declared on arrival. You do not need to declare anything less than $5,000. Only up to W2,000,000 in local currency may be imported, or exported.

Staying in Korea

MONEY MATTERS. The unit of Korean currency is the *won,* usually written as a simple capital W preceding the amount, as W1,000. As coins, the won is minted in 1-, 5-, 10-, 50-, 100-, and 500-won denominations; as banknotes, it is issued in 1,000-, 5,000-, and 10,000-won bills.

To Purchase Won. Foreign currency and traveler's checks can be converted into won at airport foreign-exchange counters, foreign-exchange banks, and major tourist hotels.

Exchange Rate. As with most currencies around the world, the won exchange rate fluctuates, but at press time the rate was around 800 won to the U.S. dollar.

Banking Hours. Banks are open 9:30 A.M. to 4:30 P.M. Monday through Friday, and 9:30 A.M. to 1:30 P.M. on Saturday. Banks are closed on Sunday.

Re-exchanging Won. Upon departure, you may change won back into dollars, or other foreign currencies, at any of the exchange places listed above. Remember to keep your exchange receipts; you will need to show them when you reconvert your extra won. However, you may reconvert up to US$100 without an exchange receipt. These restrictions can change, usually with little advance notice.

Traveler's Checks. These may be cashed for won at banks and major tourist hotels. Bear in mind that some hotels are reluctant to change traveler's checks for those who are not guests of the hotel, so use your own hotel's facilities or head for an exchange bank.

Credit Cards. These are now widely accepted, however more so in Seoul than in other parts of the country. The credit card companies have been most active in building up their lists of participating establishments, including hotels, department stores, restaurants, souvenir shops, and many of the smaller stores in areas frequented by overseas visitors. The most commonly accepted are Visa, American Express, MasterCard, and Diner's Club.

ACCOMMODATIONS. Over the past few years there has been a surge of hotel construction in Korea, mainly in preparation for the hosting of the summer Olympics that took place in 1988. Today in Seoul, for example, there is a wide selection of deluxe hotels (several operated by international chains), and many more in the first-class and economy-class categories. Occupancies can be high, especially at the top hotels, and during the popular holiday seasons. October and early November can be particularly crowded at the deluxe properties—it's not only a fine time for touring Korea, it's also one of the most popular seasons for business visits, buying missions, trade shows, and conferences.

Outside Seoul, the major cities and resorts have their share of good hotels as well, and again accommodations can be tight at peak seasons.

Looking at approximate costs, a double or twin room at a superior deluxe or deluxe hotel will cost from W100,000 to W190,000 per night; first-class, W60,000 to W80,000; second-class, W40,000 to W60,000; and third-class, W30,000 to W40,000 per night.

As you will note in the sections of this guide describing each of the four major areas of the country, and in the separate sections on major cities, the better hotels offer a range of services that you might find anywhere. These include one or more bars and cocktail lounges, restaurants with a range of cuisines, on-site recreation facilities such as tennis courts, swimming pools and health clubs, game rooms, gift shops, barbershops and beauty salons, full laundry services, and round-the-clock room service. In each section, hotels are divided into groups by price: Superior Deluxe (where applicable), Deluxe, 1st class, 2d class, and 3d class. The price ranges are given in each section.

Korean Inns. Most foreigners who live in Korea for any length of time and travel about the Korean countryside will tell you that the best accommodation bargains are to be found in the Korean inns, or *yogwan*. Although some of the comforts you've learned to expect from hotels may be absent, there are many features that the adventurous and the economy-minded will appreciate.

Traditionally, the yogwan offered you a small bedroom, clean but sparse, with sliding doors covered with rice paper and hard-paper floors (called *ondol*), which you walked on in stockinged feet. With virtually no furniture, your hosts rolled out a mattress, called a *yo,* at bedtime and provided a quilt *(ibul)* and a hard pillow (filled with wheat husks)—a *pyogae.* In chilly weather, the room would be heated by the ondol system, a series of hot-air ducts passing under the floor. Bathroom facilities may or may not have been inside.

Today, while some do retain the traditional ways of hospitality, most of the yogwan, especially in Seoul, have added regular beds, inside bathrooms with hot water, and even color television. In preparation for the 1988 Olympics, around 280 yogwan throughout the country passed an extensive examination of their facilities and service to become designated as lodgings suitable for foreign tourists. The lack of full facilities (often no restaurants at all, for example) is well compensated for by the cost savings. The charge for one night ranges from W12,000 to W30,000.

Youth Hostels. For those who want something even cheaper, there are around 20 youth hostels in Korea. The basic idea, of course, is maximum economy through minimum space and privacy, usually in a bunk-room holding six to eight people. Double and twin rooms are also offered. The youth hostels are open to members only, but you can join at any hostel for a reasonable fee. Nightly accommodation rates range from W3,500 to W7,500. Specific hostels are listed in the area chapters in the *Exploring Korea* section.

DINING. For a small country, Korea has a good array of restaurants. The best variety is within the deluxe hotels, which often have specialty restaurants for Western (including French and Italian), Korean, Chinese, and Japanese meals as well as general coffee shops. Outside the hotels, the choice is more limited, especially away from the capital city. Fast-food restaurants have really sprung up in Seoul over the past couple of years, and there are many Korean versions of the American hamburger, as well as famous names such as McDonald's, Burger King, Wendy's, Kentucky Fried Chicken, Shakey's, and Pizza Hut. Winchell's, Dunkin' Donuts, and Baskin Robbins have also found their places.

What will it cost? The price range is very wide, as low as W3,000 for a simple dish at an inexpensive Korean or Chinese restaurant, up to W30,000 for a three-course meal at a deluxe Western restaurant (excluding drinks), and as high as W75,000 for a Korean lunch or dinner in the grandest native style. Here are a few examples of costs per person, in the various categories (drinks, service charges, and taxes are excluded):

Deluxe: Top hotel breakfast, American style, W8,000; buffet lunch in a specialty restaurant, W20,000; dinner at outside French restaurant, W40,000.

Moderate: 2d class hotel breakfast, American style, W4,500; lunch at a Western coffee shop, W8,000; dinner at hotel specialty restaurant (Chinese or Japanese), W15,000.

Inexpensive: 3d class hotel breakfast, American style, W3,500; lunch of Pibimpap (rice topped with assorted vegetables) at a street-side restaurant, W4,500; dinner at hotel restaurant, W10,000.

It is possible to economize on food, even at the better hotels. Many offer excellent international buffets, along with lunch and dinner specials at each of the restaurants.

Outside the capital, prices for Western food tend to be about the same as those in Seoul, but Korean, Chinese, and Japanese dishes can cost a little less.

Information on restaurants is also included in the area chapters in the *Exploring Korea* section.

TIPPING. Tipping is not the custom in the Far East. Asians in general and Koreans in particular find this practice offensive. The suggestion that a tip is necessary to ensure good service can cause a loss of face. In hotels and restaurants, a 10 percent service charge is added to your bill. Taxi drivers do not generally expect tips unless they help with luggage. Porters at terminals are paid according to a posted schedule. A tip in a beauty parlor or barbershop is more customary, but wherever you see a "No Tipping" sign, heed the advice. Our suggestion is that you consider tipping taxi drivers the spare change and at least W1,000 when going to or from the airport; food service people need not be tipped at all.

KOREA TIME. The country lies in the international time zone, 17 hours ahead of U.S. West Coast time; 14 hours ahead of Eastern Standard time, and nine hours ahead of Greenwich time. That means when it's 7 P.M. Tuesday in California, it's noon Wednesday in Korea.

Unlike most other places in the world, Korea no longer follows the daylight-saving time schedule. This should be taken into account when calculating time differences, and it also has a seasonal effect on some international transportation schedules.

The standard working day is 9 A.M. to 6 P.M. (including government offices), although some Korean companies start at 8:30 A.M. and close at

6:30P.M. (with employees often working even later). Many offices, along with the government offices, are also open on Saturday morning, from 9 A.M. to 1 P.M. Banks are a major exception; they open at 9:30 A.M. and close at 4:30 P.M. on weekdays and operate from 9:30 A.M. to 1:30 P.M. on Saturday.

The large department stores are open from 10:30 A.M. to 7:30 P.M., and most of them close one day a week. Smaller stores and markets generally open earlier and close later, and are open every day of the week.

FOREIGN MISSIONS IN KOREA. The **United States Embassy** in Seoul is at 82, Sejongno, Chongro-ku; Tel. 732–2601. There is also a **consulate** in Pusan, at 24, 2-ka, Taechong-dong, Chung-ku, Pusan; Tel. (051) 264–7791.

The **Embassy of the United Kingdom** in Seoul is at 4, Chong-dong, Chung-ku; Tel. 735–7341/3, and there is an **Honorary Consul** in Pusan, at Yoochang Building, 12th floor, 25-2, 4-ka, Chungang-dong, Chung-ku, Pusan; Tel. 463–0041.

The **Canadian Embassy** is on the 10th floor of the Kolon Building, 45, Mugyo-dong, Chung-ku, Seoul; Tel. 753–2605/8.

KOREAN CULTURAL ORGANIZATIONS. Korea House. Located near Toegyero at the northern foot of Seoul's Namsan Mountain, Korea House is operated by the nonprofit Foundation for the Preservation of Cultural Properties. It is open six days a week (closed Sundays and public holidays) from noon to 9:30 P.M. Buffet or à la carte lunches and dinners of Korean specialties are offered, and a small 200-seat theater stages one-hour programs of Korean classical music and dance in the evenings, usually around 8:30–9:30 P.M. There are also showrooms with handicraft items on sale. Reservations for dinner and the theater are necessary; call (02) 266–9101.

The **International Cultural Society of Korea.** This nonprofit organization offers cultural programs and services to all foreigners in order to promote mutual understanding and friendship. The ICSK arranges seminars and symposiums on cultural topics in conjunction with foreign institutions. For further information, call (02) 753–3463.

Royal Asiatic Society RAS. The RAS is the most active cultural society in Korea for those interested in tours, publications, and lectures. The society arranges a variety of tours all over the country, usually on weekends, during the spring and fall, and will provide a listing on request. The RAS also offers the largest selection of books on Korea in English, call (02) 763–9483 (C.P.O. Box 255, Seoul, Korea).

LANGUAGE. The Korean language is a highly inflected, polysyllabic tongue which belongs to the Altaic family. It has its own distinctive alphabet, *Hangul,* developed by King Sejong and scholars of the Royal Institute in 1443 and commemorated every year with a national holiday on October 9. There are 14 consonants and 10 vowels. Before the creation of Hangul, written communication relied on Chinese characters. These are difficult to learn, and thus education was very much limited to the upper classes. Easy to read and write, Hangul has represented a vital means of communication for the masses. It is interesting to note that today, about 90 percent of the country's youth graduate from high school, and among the 42 million people there is a literacy rate of over 95 percent.

Language problems have been cited by visitors as the major difficulty in getting around in Korea, and steps have recently been taken to provide solutions. In Seoul, the campaign has been particularly successful. For example, streets have been more clearly marked, now in both English and Korean, and subway maps and destination signs are given in the two languages. The hosting of the 1988 Summer Olympics was the biggest incentive for the improvement of all services to visitors, and one of the emphases was on the development of English-language skills of all people active in the tourist trade. Seoul taxi drivers have been given English-language courses, and the results have been impressive.

These days, you are not likely to encounter many language difficulties around the major hotels, resorts, and tourist attractions, but while you're exploring outside these areas you will need to be patient. On the street, you'll find Koreans very willing to assist if you're lost, and you'll solve many problems by having your destination written out in the Korean language. Your hotel information staff can help you here.

The Spelling of Korean Place Names. As you read this guide, study your tourist map, or browse through brochures in your travels through Korea, you may find yourself becoming confused. You'll read a paragraph about some interesting place and won't be able to find it on a map. You have to use your imagination and look for something that seems or sounds similar. Korea used to use two methods of "romanizing" its words into English. The internationally accepted McCune-Reischauer system is used in most Korean publications and promotional literature. However, street signs and maps often used the different system of the Ministry of Education. In 1983, this alternative system was dropped in favor of the McCune-Reischauer version, but it is taking time for everything to be synchronized.

For example, the sound for K may be replaced by G, as in yokwan ME yogwan (the word for inn). Or the sound for T may be replaced by D, as in Taegu ME Daegu. The sound for P may be replaced by B, as in Pusan ME Busan. Further, the sound for CH may appear as J, as in Cheju ME Jeju. Finally, R may be represented by L, as Soraksan ME Seolaksan. This last one reveals another variation in spelling, a simple O being replaced by EO.

Similarly, there are suffixes that indicate meaning, such as *sa* (temple), *kang* (river), *shi* (city), *do* (island or province), *san* (mountain), and *won* (park). For example, Haeinsa is the Haein Temple, but for the sake of clarity we have referred to it as Haeinsa Temple. In most cases, we felt it best to leave the name as it is commonly known to Koreans, while also indicating to you that it is a temple, a river, a city, etc.

Confusing? Yes, it can be. But by applying a little imagination, you'll be able to find any place you're looking for.

MAIL, TELEGRAPH, AND TELEPHONE. Mail. Postal services are provided at all post offices (9 A.M. to 5 P.M. weekdays, and 9 A.M. to 1 P.M. Saturday), but the easiest way is simply to give cards and letters for mailing to your hotel desk. The cost of an airmail letter (up to 10 grams) to North America or Europe is W440. An express mail service is also available. In Seoul, the International Post Office is in the Sinchon district, near

Yonsei University, but the Central Post Office is more accessible, opposite Shinsegae Department Store downtown. You can mail parcels from here, and there are many packers in the small lane outside who will also provide the documentation you need. Most hotels also have a packing and wrapping service.

There are a number of courier services operating in Korea. Recommended is DHL (Tel. 716–0001 for information), which also offers a small packet service.

Telegrams. Three types of telegraph services are available: ORD (Ordinary), which takes 12 hours; LT (Letter Telegram), which takes 24 hours; and URGENT, which takes 6 hours. You can send a telegram by dialing 115, but it's better to write it out at a telegraph or post office to avoid any miscommunication.

Telex. Telex services are available at the business centers of the major hotels and are usually available only during normal business hours.

Facsimile. Again, this is a service often provided by hotels, but the Seoul Central Post Office can also help. There are at least 20 countries that share this service with Korea, including the United States and Great Britain, and the cost per page is W6,000 to any of the destinations.

Telephones. Local calls can be made anywhere in Korea from red or green-gray phones located in most large buildings and on street corners. You need two W10 coins to make a local call, and you can talk for only three minutes before the line is automatically cut. You hear a warning beep, but you can extend your call by adding more coins if, and only if, you are at a gray (stainless steel) phone.

Long-distance calls can be made through the gray public pay phones. Make sure you have a good collection of W10 and W100 coins; many of the telephone areas of hotels, railway stations, and bus terminals have automatic money changers.

Direct distance dialing (DDD) will connect you with a number in another city or town, provided that you know the proper prefix (Seoul 02, Pusan 051, Taegu 053, Inchon 032, Kyongju 0561, Cheju 064). As you talk, a digital display atop the phone keeps ticking, indicating how much money you have left for the call. If you want to continue talking, make sure you add more coins before the display reaches zero. For operator-assisted intercity calls, you dial 101 anywhere in the country.

Overseas Calls. International calls can be made either with operator assistance or by international subscriber dialing (ISD). More than 100 countries are already served by ISD and more countries are being added all the time. For ISD service, you dial an international access code (001), country code, and area code before the desired individual number. For operator-assisted calls, dial 0077; if you need additional assistance placing an international call, dial 004. Overseas operators speak excellent English and are very helpful.

To give you an indication of costs, a three-minute, operator-assisted call to the U.S. or Canada, station-to-station, is W5,100; person-to-person,

W6,370. A three-minute call to the U.K., station-to-station, is W4,650; person-to-person, W5,810. ISD calls are a little cheaper.

It is possible to make ISD calls from the gray magnetic card phones available at hotels, airports, and several stadia. You can also make local and long-distance calls by simply inserting the card into the telephone. The cards can be purchased at post offices and many newsstands.

NEWSPAPERS, MOVIES, TELEVISION, AND RADIO. There are two English-language dailies, the *Korea Herald* and the *Korea Times.* Neither is published on Mondays. Price, W200. Your hotel bookstore will usually have a good collection of English-language books and magazines. Korea has five television networks, all broadcasting in Korean, and there is also the Armed Forces Korea Network (AFKN) operated by, and for, the U.S. military. Reception for AFKN outside the Seoul area is not always good.

The Korean stations do broadcast the English-language soundtracks, in addition to a Korean translation, of many overseas films, but television sets need to have been specially adapted to receive them. The daily papers have television schedules for all channels, with indications of what films are to be broadcast in dual language. Regarding VCRs, Korea follows NCST standards for television broadcasting.

There are also six major radio stations (plus an AFKN U.S. military station) and many affiliated stations throughout the heavily populated areas.

Locally produced and overseas films are a highly popular form of entertainment, and with the relaxation of import regulations many of the latest American releases are being shown. Such films are in English, with Korean subtitles. Every main town has a good collection of cinemas, and admission is around W3,500 to W4,000.

ELECTRIC CURRENT. The electricity in Korea has been mainly 100 volts, sufficient to run appliances rated for 110 volts. Most hotels, and many homes, in Seoul have outlets for both 110 and 220, but outside the capital 220 is more common. Check before you plug in a hairdryer or shaver.

HEALTH AND MEDICAL SERVICES. Your best reference for any kind of medical attention is your hotel. Most tourist hotels have established a relationship with a nearby hospital or clinic for guest emergencies, and will also be able to recommend doctors and dentists who speak English. Pharmacies (not drugstores in the American sense) are plentiful and the range of over-the-counter medicines is enormous. Koreans are addicted to such patent medicines, and typically ask the neighborhood pharmacist to diagnose and treat them. Most of the larger hotels have a pharmacy, usually part of the gift-and-book store, and you will easily be able to purchase such things as aspirin, cold remedies, antiseptics, and sanitary supplies. Tampons can be hard to find, but most larger supermarkets and pharmacies sell western brands and the local brand, Tempo.

Additional information about available medical services is given under "Useful Addresses and Telephone Numbers" in each of the area chapters.

Drinking Water. Water is piped into the cities from reservoirs after being filtered and is considered safe for drinking, though most Koreans still boil drinking water. Major hotels also have their own filtration systems. However, outside the hotel and while you're exploring the countryside, drink bottled water to be safe. It's readily available and comes in plastic 1-liter bottles.

Swimming. Avoid swimming in any freshwater river, including the Han downstream from Seoul, even though a major clean-up project has been completed. It's also advisable to keep out of lakes, reservoirs, and major harbors (such as Inchon, Ulsan, Masan, and Pusan) because of industrial pollution and discharge of sewage. Away from busy harbors and the river mouths, such as on the East Coast, at the beaches west and north of Pusan, and on Cheju Island, the beaches are beautifully clean and the water is safe.

CIGARETTES AND TOBACCO. Korea is a cigarette manufacturer and exporter, blending imported tobaccos with the locally produced leaf. The top brands of local cigarettes are priced at W600 or W700 for a pack of 20. A variety of American and other foreign brands are also available for about W800 per pack, at hotels, tourist stores, some entertainment establishments, and designated dealers throughout the country.

An active antismoking campaign (although Korea still has one of the world's highest percentages of smokers) has resulted in many offices and government buildings allocating special smoking areas. Major restaurants are often divided into smoking and no-smoking areas, and some hotels have introduced no-smoking floors.

SECURITY. Seoul is a remarkably safe city to stroll around in, but you should take the usual precautions against petty theft and pickpockets. Use your hotel's security services for your valuables and travel documents, and don't carry large amounts of cash.

When you're out sightseeing, it's a good idea to keep a hotel card handy, with the name, address, and telephone number (in Korean) of where you're staying. You can then return by taxi with no mix-up about where you want to go. It's also a good idea to jot down the telephone number of your embassy.

Police stations are on all major streets and can be identified by a yellow lighted sign. Police officers will try to be helpful in an emergency, but language problems can occur.

Complaint Center. The Korea National Tourism Corporation has a complaint center in Seoul that you can call not just to complain but also to ask for advice and assistance. The number is (02) 735–0101. Outside the capital, the tourist-administration sections of the provincial governments deal with such matters, and you call 0101 prefixed by the pertinent area code. The exceptions to this are: Taegu (053) 422–5611 and Chongju (0431) 52–0202. Send letters to KNTC Complaint Center, CPO Box 903, Seoul.

NATIONAL HOLIDAYS AND FESTIVALS. Korea's public holidays and festivals represent an unusual blend of the past and the present. The country officially follows the Gregorian Calendar, but many of its national holidays originated centuries ago and are based on the Orient's ancient lunar calendar. Lunar New Year, for example, commonly known as Chinese New Year, is called Folklore Day in Korea and has only recently been designated an official holiday.

The most celebrated of all the lunar festivals is *Chusok,* the Korean "Thanksgiving," which falls on the 15th day of the 8th moon, sometime in September or October. It is observed by all families all over Korea and is just about the only time of year that all stores, businesses, and markets are closed.

There are 14 national public holidays, when banks, government offices, and businesses are closed. In addition, there are over a dozen major festivals during the year, celebrating heroes and heroines, famous castles, great ruling dynasties, and local arts and culture. Since many of the festivals are not national but regional, you have to be there at the right time to enjoy them.

Here is a list of the public holidays and major festivals for 1993. More details of the festival events are covered elsewhere in this guide, in the descriptions of the major areas in which they occur.

National Holidays

January 1—New Year, a two-day public holiday when Koreans visit hometowns to pay respect to their elders.

January 23—Folklore Day, the Chinese New Year according to the lunar calendar. This is a three-day holiday.

March 1—Independence Movement Day, celebrating the anniversary of the Korean uprising against the Japanese in 1919.

April 5—Arbor Day, when people all over the country plant trees as part of a vast reforestation program.

May 5—Children's Day, the successor to a former "Boys' Day," is to honor Korean youth and to focus attention on the importance of the family institution. On this day, children are often dressed up in traditional costume and taken on holiday excursions to parks and children's centers. Parents' Day is on May 8, but is not a public holiday.

May 28—Buddha's Birthday, which always falls on the eighth day of the fourth lunar month, also known as the "Feast of Lanterns." Elaborate rituals and candlelight processions take place at most Buddhist temples.

June 6—Memorial Day, when the nation pays tribute to its war dead.

July 17—Constitution Day, commemorating the creation of the Republic of Korea on July 17, 1948. Ceremonies are held in all major cities.

August 15—Liberation Day, to mark the anniversary of the end of 35 years of Japanese occupation in 1945.

September 30—Chusok, the Korean Thanksgiving. This is celebrated by everyone, all over the country. The occasion is marked by a three-day public holiday and is the only time of year when all offices, and just about all shops and markets are closed. It is also a time when it seems that the whole nation is on the move—the Seoul railroad stations and bus terminals are crammed with people heading to their hometowns. It is a good time to stay in Seoul if you're a visitor.

October 1—Armed Forces Day, marked by military parades and special ceremonies around the country.

October 3—National Foundation Day, commemorating Tangun, the legendary founder of Korea.

October 9—Hangul Day, celebrating the anniversary of the Korean written language, created by King Sejong in 1443.

December 25—Christmas Day.

Festivals

At the time of preparing this guide, not all festival dates had been confirmed. You can check with the KNTC Tourist Information Center in Seoul (Tel. (02) 757–0086) for final details.

February 25—Sokchonje. Held twice a year, in the second and eighth lunar months, in the "Hall of the Great Sages" on the Sungkyunkwan University campus in Seoul. This is one of the capital's two major Confucian rites, to honor Confucius, his disciples, and great Korean and Chinese sages. There are performances by a traditional court orchestra and a number of rituals presided over by officials in full court regalia. Starting time is 10 AM. The rites are held again on September 23.

March or *February*—Unsan Pyolshin Ritual. By tradition, the events are performed in a shrine just outside Unsan (West Plain and Coastal Area) to honor the spirits of legendary generals who fought for independence during the Paekje Kingdom. The festival is Korea's Intangible Asset No. 9.

April—Cherry Blossom Festival. During the first two weeks of April the town of Chinhae (in the southeast), the headquarters of the Korean navy, celebrates the navy's inauguration and the victories of the famous Admiral Yi. The thousands of blossoming cherry trees attract over a million visitors. (Needless to say, accommodations are scarce.) The Korea National Railways has special fares out of Seoul during the festival period.

April—Kossaumnori Festival. The spectacular "Loop Battle" of two competing teams which each comprise a commander, guards, and pushers (all men), and one woman, who controls the "tail." Held at Kwangsan-ku, Kwangju (West Plain Area), and an unforgettable visual experience. The date is not confirmed.

April or May—Yongdung Festival at Chindo. A lively celebration held at the time of an annual "miracle" when a stretch of water separating two villages at Chindo Island (West Plain and Coastal Area) is parted to make a sandy walkway. The date is unconfirmed, but the event is usually held early in the third lunar month.

May 2—Chongmyojerye. The other major Confucian ceremony, to pay homage to the royalty of the Yi, or Choson Dynasty. Chongmyo, in Seoul, is the ancestral shrine of the Yi Royal House, and the buildings and inner court are open to the public especially for this occasion. The rituals are traditionally held on the first Sunday in May; starting time is around 10 A.M.

May—Ghinnam Festival. Held in Yosu (in the Southeast Area), the festival honors Admiral Yi Sun-Shin, with a costume parade, folklore exhibitions, and various cultural contests.

May—Tano Festival. Held at a shrine on a mountain in Kangnung (East Coastal Area), this is an ancient ritual to pray for a good harvest. The major event is a procession of Shamans, followed by a presentation of masked dance and drama. Traditionally held from the third to the seventh day of the fifth lunar month.

May 28—Buddha's Birthday. (See National Holidays, above.)

May—Chunhyang Festival. Held in Namwon (in the southern sector of the West Plain Area), this festival commemorates Chun Hyang, a heroine of ancient times regarded as the shining example of feminine virtue. Her birthday is said to be the eighth day of the fourth lunar month. Highlight of the festivities is a Pansori contest to determine the best singer of a traditional narrative song.

September—Halla Cultural Festival. A wonderful festival of the arts on Cheju Island, featuring music and dance and the unique folkloric arts of the island.

September—Paekche Cultural Festival. Held in Puyo (West Plain and Coastal Area) to commemorate the glories of the ancient Paekche Kingdom in music and dance. The date is not confirmed.

September—Andong Folk Festival. In Kyongsangbukdo Province (Central Area), this is one of Korea's most vibrant celebrations, featuring the Chajonnori, or "War of Wagons," designated as Korea's Intangible Asset No. 24. Other cultural events are also featured. The date is not confirmed.

September—Silla Cultural Festival. Held in Kyongju (Southeast Area), the ancient capital of the Silla Kingdom, the celebrations revive the spirit and cultural activities of the era.

September 23—Sokchonje. The second of the two-part Confucian rite at Sungkyunkwan University in Seoul.

September 30—Chusok. (See National Holidays, above.)

September to October—Sorak Festival. Held in the Sokcho area of the East Coast, to honor the spirit of the mountain with a variety of colorful displays, processions, and cultural events.

October 5—Pusan Citizens' Day. Celebrated mainly at Sajik Stadium in the southern port city, with traditional music and dance.

October—Chongson Arirang Festival. In Chongson, Kangwon Province (East Coast), this is Korea's most famous folk-song contest, and there is also a competition for the liveliest farmers' dance. The date is not confirmed.

October—Moyang Castle Festival. In Kochang (central West Plain and Coastal Area), this is the only castle festival in Korea; it celebrates the completion of Moyang Castle, which was built only with female labor. More than 5,000 women and girls parade in traditional costume on top of the castle wall, more than a mile around. The date is not confirmed.

October—Hansan Victory Festival. At Chungmu, on the Hallyo Waterway (Southeast) to commemorate the victory of Admiral Yi Sun Shin at Hansando Island. A variety of traditional dances is performed, along with other cultural displays and contests.

November—Kaechon Art Festival. Held in Chinju (West Plain and Coastal Area) to promote and recognize local cultural activity. There are many contests in poetry and calligraphy, as well as music and drama performances. The date is not confirmed.

SPORTS. The Korean people like outdoor activities, so you'll find lots to do along athletic lines, and plenty to watch if you're a spectator.

The Korean traditional sports date back centuries, having evolved from the skills developed in the art of war, and they provide some entertaining contrasts to the sports of today.

Taekwondo. A form of self-defense martial art that originated in Korea and is now practiced in 80 countries around the world. The literal translation is "art of hand-and-foot fighting," with emphasis on blows by the feet. This dates back to the era of the Three Kingdoms (57 B.C.–A.D. 668), and many ancient wall murals show warriors practicing this form of combat sport. The world headquarters of the Taekwondo Federation is in Seoul, and you can call the organization for information on watching competitions. Tel. (02) 566–2505.

Ssirum. A Korean style of wrestling, this equally ancient sport is still popular, especially in the rural areas. To win, you don't pin your opponent; you merely have to throw him to the ground or cause him to touch the ground with any part of his body other than his feet. The traditional prize for the winner was an ox, but nowadays cash is more popular. For information call the Korea Amateur Sports Association in Seoul at (02) 420–3333.

Yudo. Similar to Japanese judo, this form of wrestling is older by centuries and is said to have shaped the development of judo. Matches in Seoul and other cities are frequent.

Archery. While the Japanese are famous for their swordsmanship and the Chinese for their skill with the spear, Koreans have a centuries-old reputation for excellence with the bow and arrow. The traditional Korean bow is much shorter than European or other Asian models, but shoots arrows much farther—due, it appears, to the double curvature of its configuration. Today, however, Koreans are conforming to the European style of bow and continue to perform outstandingly in international competitions. For information call the Korea Amateur Sports Association in Seoul at (02) 420–3333.

Baseball. Korea's modern sports include professional baseball, consisting of seven teams. There are high-school and college teams in vast numbers and it is easy to find a game under way during the spring, summer, and fall months.

Soccer. This sport, introduced by the crew of a British warship in 1882, is the most popular in Korea. There are a number of professional teams with enthusiastic support, and there is a national team which represents the country in international competitions.

Tennis. This dates back only to the 1930s and has soared in popularity over recent years. Several of the major hotels have their own courts, and there are public courts available, but in all playing seasons reservations are essential. Your hotel will be able to help.

Hiking. Backpacking is extremely popular among Koreans, but if you want to enjoy nature without the crowds, plan your trips for weekdays. There are a good many mountain hikes with well-marked trails within the vicinity of Seoul, and at the many national parks. For information on hiking tours, usually organized for weekends, call (02) 757–8765, or the KNTC Information Center in Seoul (02) 757–0086.

Swimming. Most major hotels have swimming pools, and large cities have public pools (usually open from mid-July to the end of August), which are often very crowded. The section on beaches will provide some details on saltwater swimming.

Table Tennis. Korea is recognized as one of the leading Ping-Pong competitors in the world, always in close competition with mainland China and Japan in international matches; in fact Korea beat China in table tennis gold medals during the 1986 Asian Games. If this is your sport, it's easy to find a place to play; table-tennis halls abound, tables and paddles can be rented for modest fees, and it's easy to find someone to play against you.

Golf. Golf is another sport that has been growing even more in popularity over recent years. There are more than 50 courses; 29 of them in or near Seoul, 2 in Pusan, and others in or close to main centers, such as Taejon, Taegu, Kyongju, and Cheju Island. In addition, many major resort hotels either have their own courses or access to a nearby country club. Caddies, usually female, are available. The cost to play is around W45,000 on weekdays, W59,400 on weekends, plus W20,000 caddy tip. Most of the clubs are for members only, but the hotels are usually able to make arrangements for visitors.

Korean Air has introduced a package tour especially for golfers, called the "Sky Green Tour," that is available through some 16 travel agencies in Seoul. The tour arranges play on three courses, including Cheju Island.

For details on golf courses, you can call the Korea Golf Course Association in Seoul (02) 783–8271.

Fishing. Surf casting from a beach and deep-sea fishing from a boat are available; the two principal areas for these are the Hallyo Waterway (Southeast Area) and Cheju Island. Hotel information or tour counters can provide information on arranging fishing trips to lakes and reservoirs.

Hunting. From November to February, visitors are permitted to hunt on Cheju island and Koje Island for game including boar, elk, rabbit, cock-pheasant, turtle doves, duck, and snipe. In addition, Kangwon Province on the mainland has been opened as a special hunting area. The Korea Safety Engineering Association of Explosives & Guns will provide details and can assist with the security and customs clearances of guns and ammunition. With one month's notice, the association will also arrange guides and hunting dogs. The address is: Korea Safety Engineering Association of Explosives & Guns, 541–11 Shinsa-dong, Kangnam-ku, Seoul Tel. (02) 515–2343.

On Cheju, there is also a year-round hunting ground, operated by the Daeyu Hunting Club at Chungmun Resort in the south of the island. The area is stocked with wild pigeon and pheasant. Hunting equipment, rifles and dogs can be rented for W110,000 per person per day. The telephone number is (02) 544–0432 in Seoul; (064) 32–0500 in Cheju.

Sports Organizations. The Korea Amateur Sports Association (KASA) is located at 888, Oryun-dong, Songpa-ku, Seoul; tel. (02) 420–3333. Other associations are responsible for baseball, basketball, boxing, cycling, fencing, ice hockey, rowing, ice skating, swimming, volleyball, wrestling, badminton, bowling, canoeing, gymnastics, handball, judo, tennis, archery, equestrian sports, hockey, roller skating, rugby, shooting, skiing, table tennis, taekwondo, and weight lifting. KASA will be able to provide details.

BEACHES. The West Coast provides the best places for saltwater swimming because here the land merges gently into the sea and creates wonderful shelving beaches. When the tide goes out, it leaves miles of exposed sea bed for beach strollers, and the waters of the Yellow Sea tend to be mild in temperature. Beaches are officially open from early July until early September. There are often special ceremonies held at the sea-resort areas with the authorities and local merchants resolving to provide the visitor with exemplary attention. Following is a list of the best beaches in Korea.

West Coast Beaches. Mallipo, at the western tip of Chungchongnamdo Province, about two hours from Seoul by car or bus. **Taechon,** about two and a half hours from Seoul, near the superhighway west of Puyo. **Pyonsan,** in Pyonsan Provincial Park, Chollapukdo Province, northwest of Chongju.

South Coast Beaches. Haeundae, about 11 miles northeast of Pusan, is probably the best-developed beach-resort area in Korea and is certainly the one most used to catering to foreign visitors. The beach is lined with all types of restaurants and hotels, including a couple from international chains. You would be well advised to make bookings in advance of the summer season. Haeundae marks the beginning of its summer business with a pageant of yacht races, rituals to the sea god for the safety of swimmers, and fireworks displays. Another good South Coast beach is **Namildae,** on Namhae Island at the western end of the Hallyo Waterway; in addition to the warm waters that the southern beaches provide, this one has magnificent seascapes.

East Coast Beaches. Here the shore is rockier, and the waters cooler, especially at the northern end. Starting at the southern end of the area, not far from Kyongju, there are: **Pohang,** a protected harbor; **Kyongpo-da,** about four miles north of the town of Kangnung; **Naksan,** about 12.5 miles south of Sokcho, the large town near both Mt. Odaesan and Mt. Soraksan national parks.

SPAS. Hot springs or spas have been favored throughout the ages as cure-alls for whatever ails you. Korea has a number of popular spas, with the waters cooled or heated depending on the water temperature of the source. The area chapters will provide details.

WINTER SPORTS. The northeastern corner of Korea has a number of good **ski resorts** that cater to foreign visitors. The slopes are excellent, facilities include snow machines, chair lifts, and T-bars, and instructors are available for group or private lessons. Unquestionably, the best known and biggest is the Dragon Valley Ski Resort. It lies just off the Suwon-Kangnung express highway, about 15.5 miles short of the East Coast.

Another excellent resort is Alps, located farther north near the Sorak Mountains. Three ski resorts closer to Seoul (less than an hour away in fact) are Yongin Farm Land (south), Chonmasan (northeast), Bears Town (also northeast of Seoul), and Muju, the newest (southwest of Seoul).

Since skiing has become a highly popular pleasure for Koreans and the country's foreign residents, reservations at all resorts should be made well in advance.

Ice skating is also popular, although there are few indoor rinks. However, winter outdoor skating facilities have blossomed all over the country—iced-over rice fields or tennis courts—and the user's fee is around W1,000.

TEMPLES. No guide to Korea would be worthy of the name unless it made particular mention of Korea's temples, the architectural core of the country's roots in the Buddhist religion. If you were to see all of them—and there are several hundred—you would enter structures whose building dates may span more than 500 years. And although the basic themes that animated their original construction flowed from the single impetus of the Buddha, the size and shape from temple to temple, the interior and exterior decoration detail, and the treatment of them as to setting, paths, foliage, statues, and flowers, vary widely. Korean temples will provide some of your most memorable impressions of Korea, and, of course, the photographic opportunities are magnificent.

PARKS. There is a profusion of parks scattered all over the country, especially national parks of scenic distinction. Not only are the Korean people lovers of the outdoors, but some of their minor religions find their spiritual connections with the deity through the many forms of nature. Many aspects of nature—trees, rocks, mountains, streams—are believed to be the direct creations of shamanistic deities and thus these objects are held to have deep spiritual significance. Hence the special regard for nature and the loving attention given to protecting its beauty. There is an expression promoted in Korea, which translates as "Love trees, love your country."

The Korean government has designated 17 scenic areas throughout the country as national parks. Within the boundaries of the mountain parks are many temples set in beautiful surroundings. While the parks are managed by the central government, facilities near them are run privately. In addition to the national parks, over 20 provincial parks also have ancient Buddhist temples, hiking trails, waterfalls, and splendid mountain scenery.

The national parks are as follows:

Mt. Pukhansan. Just a 30-minute drive north of downtown Seoul. At 2,700 feet provides good hiking and rock climbing, and exploration of a Yi Dynasty fortress.

Mt. Soraksan. East Coastal area. Near the coastal city of Sokcho and considered to be the most beautiful mountain in Korea. The highest point is 5,600 feet, and the park is famous for granite peaks, green valleys, old temples, caves, and waterfalls. The tourist facilities here are very well developed.

Mt. Odaesan. East Coastal area. This is the home of the Woljongsa Temple, with a nine-story pagoda dating to the year 645. The highest point is 5,100 feet.

Mt. Chiaksan. Central area. Seven miles southeast of Wonju, Mt. Chiaksan is a mountain shrouded in legend. The Kuryongsa Temple houses and preserves many ancient documents relating to the mountain's history. The highest point is 4,220 feet.

Mt. Woraksan. Central Area. Three hours southeast of Seoul, Mt. Woraksan is close to hot springs and beautiful lake reservoirs.

Mt. Songnisan. Central area. This is most famous for its Popchosa Temple, with Korea's tallest Buddha statue. It is a popular spot for hiking and picnics.

Mt. Chuwangsan. East Coastal area. At 2,365 feet, this is an area of moderately easy hiking, and there are several temples, hot springs, and other tourist attractions in the area.

Mt. Kyeryongsan. West Plain area. About 30 miles west of Taejon, this mountain (2,780 feet) has some 20 peaks in a row, with many beautiful temples.

Kyongju. Southeast area. In the eighth century, this was the capital of the Silla Dynasty, and the area is now a vast outdoor museum. It is covered in a separate chapter of this guide.

Mt. Togyusan. Central area. Ninety miles southeast of Taejon, Mt. Togyusan (5,300 feet) is famous for two historical temples.

Mt. Kayasan. Central area. Forty miles west of Taegu, Mt. Kayasan (4,690 feet) is the smallest of Korea's national parks. It is the home of the country's best-known temple, Haeinsa, which houses more than 80,000 ancient wooden printing blocks.

Mt. Naejangsan. West Plain and Coastal area. Located between the towns of Chonju and Kwangju, this is a famous area for autumn foliage and the temple of Paegyangsa.

Mt. Chirisan. Southeast area. This is the first and largest national park of Korea, covering 169.5 square miles. About 85 miles northeast of Kwangju, Mt. Chirisan itself (6,280 feet), the second-highest mountain in the country, is best known for its Hwaomsa Temple, which contains many national treasures.

Sosan Sea Coast. West Plain and Coastal area. This is a maritime park with many bays, beaches, and rocky outcrops.

Tadohae. West Plain and Coastal area. On the southwestern tip of the peninsula, this is another maritime park with a variety of beaches and islands.

Hallyo Waterway. Southeast area. This is a stretch of water some 93 nautical miles long, running from Hansando Island, south of Pusan, to Yosu in the west. The park is made up of some 400 islands in a total area of 184 square miles.

Mt. Hallasan, Cheju Island. At 6,398 feet this is the highest mountain in Korea, an extinct volcano famous for its unusual flora and fauna.

SHOPPING. Korea may be one of the world's best-kept secrets as a place of low prices for certain quality goods. Of course, you have to know where to look. You can practice your bargaining skills in great open-air markets, underground shopping arcades, or the rows of tiny sidewalk shops that all seem to offer the same articles for a whole block at a stretch, or you can enjoy the security of price tags in the department stores. A good idea is to check the prices in such stores, then head out into the markets knowing the top price you should pay.

The individual places mentioned below are in Seoul, certainly the biggest bargain center of the country. Other places of shopping interest are mentioned in the area chapters of this guide.

Fabrics. For the widest and most colorful collection of cottons, wools, silks, synthetics, and blends, try the Tongdaemun Market, particularly the second floor of the fashion fabrics building that runs between Chongno 4-ka and Chonggyechon 4-ka. Here also you'll find all the beautiful fabrics used in Korea's national costumes.

For hand-printed silk, try the Koryo store on the lower level of the Chosun Hotel. It ranges from around W20,000 to W25,000 a yard.

Furs. Seoul is the home base of the famous **Jindo.** This is one of the world's largest fur factories, which sells its luxury fur garments directly to visitors at duty-free prices. Pelts are imported and crafted here, and such fur items are delivered to customers at the airport on their departure. Jindo and other fur manufacturers have large showrooms in Itaewon, the major shopping district for Seoul visitors. (More about wonderful Itaewon later.)

Tailoring. Custom-made clothes are well made and cheaper than just about anywhere in the Orient. Most foreign women in Seoul buy fabric at Tongdaemun market and take it to a dressmaker, along with a picture or sketch of what they want made. Men's tailors carry wide selections of fabrics, both Korean-made and imported. Treat yourself to at least a tailored shirt (around $15 in Itaewon), if not a suit or tuxedo. Allow time for two fittings if you can. Any major hotel arcade has a tailor and dressmaker, but cheaper prices can be found elsewhere. A man's wool suit, tailored in Itaewon, for example, costs in the range of $180 to $250, depending on the weight. In the area of the Lotte Hotel, prices are higher but tailoring is more elaborate. The dressmakers in Itaewon are familiar with Western women's sizes and tastes. Many places here will make jogging suits or ski outfits in 24 hours or so, but there's also plenty of such gear available ready-made. Custom-made leather clothing has also become popular, as has ultrasuede, with the fabric either local or imported.

Ready-made clothes. This is where Itaewon comes into its own. Until recent years the street was a collection of small, run-down stores and stalls spilling out onto the pavement, catering mainly to American soldiers from the U.S. Army headquarters nearby. Recently, major reconstruction has modernized and tidied up the area dramatically. While some say the charm has been lost, the bargains are still very much in evidence. Sneakers, running shoes, sweaters, T-shirts, blue jeans, skirts, shorts, tops, silk and synthetic dresses galore. There are a lot of export rejects (famous names, and copies of them abound) so inspect carefully before you buy. Itaewon has also become the center for eelskin, in shoes, handbags, wallets, and briefcases. Prices average around W35,000 for a medium-size handbag and W30,000 for shoes.

Another small shopping street that has become popular among foreign residents for ready-made clothes (again you'll find many famous brands) is known as Gate 19. It runs from the Yongsan Post Office to Gate 19 of the U.S. Army garrison.

Tongdaemun and Namdaemun markets (the latter near the center of town) also have plenty of ready-made clothes at excellent prices. But be careful about sizing; Koreans are slim in the hips and short in the arms.

And while we're discussing clothes, Myongdong should be mentioned. This is an area being promoted as an exclusive shopping district; a showplace of Korean quality and high fashion. It is a downtown maze of narrow streets in the area opposite the Lotte Department Store, featuring boutiques, shoe stores, and a variety of fast-food restaurants.

Jewelry. Korea is not the place for pearls or diamonds (although there are some duty-free diamond outlets), but it is the place for semiprecious amethyst, smokey topaz (actually smokey quartz), and beautiful pale green or white jadeite. Mined here, each is available in any size in almost any design. If you want a special design, the jeweler will do it for minimal labor cost. You pay for the quality of the stone and the weight of the gold or silver setting. Store clerks tend to call any green stone jade, so be careful because Korea does not mine precious green jade. Korea's jadeite comes exquisitely carved as pendants or earrings, which are surprisingly cheap. Shop in any of the hotel or underground arcades or, again, in Itaewon.

Antiques or reproductions. Korea is justly famous for its long history of excellent ceramics—the Silla earthenware, Koryo celadon, and Yi blue-and-white porcelain. It is still possible to buy authentic examples of these wares, but one cannot take them out of the country without written approval from the Cultural Properties Preservation Bureau of the Ministry of Culture and Information. Some items will already be marked with red stamps to show that they have been so approved. Authentic pieces of good quality are not cheap; in addition, many fakes exist and they're difficult to detect. Fine modern reproductions are widely available. Those signed by modern masters are also expensive, but cheaper good reproductions can also be found. Most fail to capture the original Koryo color, but the Yi-style blue-and-whites are quite beautiful. Be sure to keep the receipt to prove to customs officials on departure that your purchase is new. All the above advice also holds true for Korean wooden chests and Yi paintings, whether classical or folk art. One of the best places to browse is Insadong (commonly known as Mary's Alley), which is well known for its collection of arts and crafts (Sun and Moon is one of the better stores here for chests and other antiques). Changang-dong, in the eastern district of Seoul, has an antiques market of over 150 stores, and you'll also see plenty of examples along the upper end of Itaewon and in the underground arcades.

Lacquerware and brassware. Black lacquerware inlaid with shimmering mother of pearl is a traditional Korean specialty, as are heavy brass rice and soup bowls that ring for minutes when they're struck with a mallet ("bell brass"). Nowadays, lacquerware is made for all sorts of uses—cigarette, jewelry, and candy boxes; small and large tables; and huge free-standing closets. Brassware has become a decorative item in almost any shape you can imagine, including brass beds, of which Korea does a lively export trade. Lacquerware prices depend on size and design. A piece made by a master will be expensive, but most are rather reasonable, especially the smaller items. For old bell brass, the antiques stores are best. For modern brass, go to Itaewon, and for lacquerware, to the underground and hotel arcades, and to Tongdaemun market.

Ginseng. The medical panacea of the Orient has been making inroads in the West. Valued for its reputed power to prevent illness and rejuvenate the weary, ginseng is available as a powder, liquid extract, tea, an ingredient in soap and cosmetics, and in its natural root form, often immersed in a jar of liquor. Ginseng comes in two varieties: Red, the more valued of the two, is processed and sold under a government monopoly; white is privately produced. Shops specializing in ginseng products are everywhere. You may take out of the country 1,200 grams of red ginseng and 1,200 grams of white, plus restricted amounts of tablets, drinks, and extracts. Take your purchase receipts to the airport.

Souvenirs and final advice. Buy dolls in Korean costume, eelskin wallets, silk beads strung in necklaces, objects of carved wood or soapstone, wall hangings, cushion covers, embroidered purses, Korean-style slippers, and novelty key rings. None of these is expensive, and all can be found in just about any shopping arcade or department store. Don't overlook goods sold on the literally thousands of street tables. The price is always right and you might be surprised at what you find.

A word about what not to buy: foreign-made products are subject to high customs duties and are thus very expensive in Korea. Bring a camera, but buy your film here. Buy liquor duty-free before you come. As mentioned earlier, American cigarettes are available, but they are more expensive than local brands.

Practice your bargaining. Outside the department stores, be prepared to haggle, and enjoy it. But take your time, don't appear too eager to buy, and leave your jewelry and furs at home. Look affluent, and the price is guaranteed to be high. Start low in your bartering—50 percent, for example. This is not a sign of cheapness, only an indication of good sense and appreciated aggressiveness.

Itaewon is still the best place to go, although discounts nowadays from the asking price are quite small, certainly no more than 10 or 20 percent, depending on what you're buying. Most sales clerks speak English, and you can use dollars or won.

Don't worry if you tend to overbuy; excellent luggage is available at ridiculously low prices to carry your added weight. Have fun.

Taxes. A Value Added Tax (VAT) is levied on most goods at a standard rate of 10 percent. VAT is also levied at a standard rate of 10 percent on services you receive in hotels and tourist facilities. (This is in addition to the usual 10 percent service charge.) However, foreign visitors do not have to pay any VAT on hotel bills. This means that all services within your hotel, billed to your hotel room account, will be exempt from the VAT. Check the bill when you pay. Goods and services that you purchase outside the hotel, for which you pay cash (or use a credit card), however, will be taxed.

Foreign visitors are eligible for refunds of VAT, Special Excise Tax, and Defense Tax when shopping at authorized tax refund stores. The system is a little complicated, but here's how it works. When you make a purchase at an authorized store, present your passport or other form of ID and complete a Tax Refund Form. Two copies of a Certificate of Selling Goods, and a postage-paid envelope addressed to the store will be given to you. These must be given to the customs officer at your point of departure, and you will also need to show him the goods you purchased. If you have already mailed the goods, you should show the post-office receipt or shipping document. The customs officer will verify your purchases and give you back a copy of the selling certificate. The other copy will be mailed back to the store. A refund, less service and handling charge, will be sent to you within 30 days. Note that goods must be taken out of the country within three months of the date of purchase, and that the price of each item must exceed W50,000.

At press time, the tax-refund system applied to about 15 shopping centers in Seoul, plus stores in Yongin, Taejon, Chongju, Kyonju, Taegu, Pusan, and Cheju. Tax Refund Stores are indicated in the information sections of each area chapter.

NIGHTLIFE AND ENTERTAINMENT. Korea offers the visitor a variety of nightlife. You can find sophisticated nightclubs with floor shows, beer halls, wine houses, cocktail lounges, theater-restaurants, discos, and gambling casinos. You can feel comfortable on the streets at night, but do take the normal precautions against petty theft and pickpockets. Many of the better known night spots are located in the major hotels, yet if you wish to wander and explore there are hundreds of clubs and cabarets in Seoul, particularly in the districts of Myongdong and Shinsadong. For foreigners, Seoul's Itaewon probably offers the best collection of evening entertainment; there are plenty of small bars specializing in jazz, country and western, or rock, plus a number of neon-signed discos. You'll find whatever you're looking for.

The area chapters within this guide will give you an outline of what's available in different places, but here's a general idea of the highlights:

Nightclubs and Discos: The more well known, and most expensive, are located in the major hotels. The floor shows are good, but drinks are sky-high (W40,000 per four-person table, which includes four beers and a side dish). The discos are often affiliated with international chains, and match their Western counterparts in dazzle and effects.

Bars and Cocktail Lounges: The fanciest are in the hotels, where you pay around W3,500 for a local bottle of beer, W4,500 for spirits. Often there will be a pianist or a small band. Outside the hotels, in Itaewon for example, drinks run around W3,000 (or less) for a beer, W3,500 for spirits, depending on the type of bar and entertainment. There are locally blended gin, vodka, and whiskey, so you'll often pay more for imported brands.

Beer Halls and Wine Houses: These are the favorite night spots of the Korean male. The intake is often high. Beer halls serve only beer, and you are expected to buy a dish of snacks. Prices are lower than at nightclubs. The wine houses are inexpensive but rowdy. These establishments generally serve Makkolli, a milky-white liquor brewed from rice, and Soju, a potent distilled drink made from potato. The eating and drinking will be easy on one's wallet, and there's an abundance of local color and activity.

Theater-Restaurants: These, like their Western counterparts, charge a flat rate per person, offering a set number of drinks (usually two), dinner, and an elaborate musical revue of either Korean or Western theme. Extra food and drinks are pricy, so sticking to the package deal is the only way to economize.

Gambling Casinos: If your pleasure is games of chance, there are several government-designated places in Korea where you can buck the odds. All are plush casinos offering roulette, blackjack, poker, and other games of chance. They are staffed by trained and experienced casino personnel. In addition, most tourist hotels have "game rooms" devoted to slot machines.

The casinos are located in Seoul, Inchon, Kyongju, Mt. Songnisan, Mt. Soraksan, Cheju, and Pusan. Look under the area chapters for details.

Music and Dance: For the visitor, Seoul offers most of the highlights, with the exception of festival times in other cities. Korea's traditional music and dance is seen in such places as Korea House and the National Theater, and there are also outdoor performances at a couple of *Madang*— open-air arenas. A dozen all-purpose theaters present various kinds of performing arts—plays, operas, traditional and contemporary dance, concerts, and recitals. The best source of information is the "What's On" columns of the English-language daily newspapers. Here you'll find details not just on the current performing arts, but also on museum and gallery exhibitions, women's group meetings, cultural tours, and special-interest lectures and seminars.

Travel in Korea

Here is a general picture on getting around in Korea. More details of services are given in the practical information sections of each area chapter.

BY AIR. Korean Air and Asiana Airlines handle all domestic routes. The head office for Korean Air is in Seoul, 41–3, Sosomun-dong, Chung-ku, Seoul; Tel. (02) 751–7114. Ticket reservations and advance purchases are available from travel agents or directly at the following Korean Air reservation offices:

Seoul, (02) 756–2000
Pusan, (051) 463–2000
Cheju, (064) 52–2000
Kwangju (West Plain), (062) 222–2000
Taegu, (053) 423–2000
Yosu (Southeast), (0662) 41–2000
Sokcho (East Coast), (0392) 32–2000
Chinju (West Plain and Coast), (0591) 57–2000
Ulsan (Southeast), (0522) 71–2000
Kangnung (East Coast), (0391) 43–2000
Pohang (East Coast), (0562) 72–2000

Asiana Airlines's head office is at 10–1, Hoehyon-dong 2-ka; Tel. (02) 758–8114. Reservation offices are:
Seoul, (02) 774–4000

Pusan (051) 465–4000
Cheju, (064) 43–4000
Kwangju, (062) 226–4000
Taegu, (053) 421–4000
Yechon, (0584) 52–4000

All the above destinations outside the capital are served from the Kimpo domestic airport in Seoul with varying frequencies. More flights are added for key destinations during peak seasons.

Fares are reasonable (W31,500 for the 50-minute flight to Pusan, for example), and planes are modern and comfortable.

BY SEA. Since Korea has water to its west, east, and south, car ferries and hydrofoils make frequent runs between the mainland and outlying islands. There are regular services between Pusan and Cheju Island, Pusan and Yosu (through the pretty Hallyo Waterway), Wando Island and Cheju, Mokpo and Cheju, and between Pohang and Ullungdo Island off the East Coast.

BY RAIL. The Korean National Railroad maintains an extensive and well-organized network of railways connecting just about the entire country. The Saemaul superexpress train now operates on the Seoul-Pusan (Taejon, Taegu) line to the south; Seoul-Mokpo (Taejon, Nonsan, Iri, Chongju, Kwangju) line to the West Plain and Coast; Seoul-Yosu (Taejon, Chonju, Namwon, Sunchon) line to the Southeast; and from Seoul to the ancient capital of Kyongju, in the Southeast, via Taejon and Taegu.

Apart from the superexpress, there are air-conditioned express (Mugunghwa) and ordinary express (Tongil) trains connecting cities and small towns in all areas of the country.

Distances are short (the Saemaul service between Seoul and Pusan takes just four hours, 15 minutes) and fares reasonable (W16,400 economy, W21,000 in first class for the Seoul-Pusan service). Special package fares are available.

Ticket reservations and advance purchases are available from travel agencies and the train stations. Several stations have special ticket counters for foreigners, where staff speak English and can assist with service information. You can telephone the counters in Seoul, (02) 392–7811; Taejon, (042) 23–7788; Taegu East, (053) 955–7789; Pusan, (051) 463–7551; Kyongju, (0561) 43–8053; and Yongju, (0572) 2–1330.

BY BUS. Fast and reliable highway bus services connect virtually all major points. The Seoul Express Bus Terminal is the main bus depot and is divided into two terminals: the Kyongbu-son Terminal (Tel. (02) 535–4151), which operates services to the east and southeast, and the Yongdong-son Terminal (Tel. (02) 591–3402), which handles services to the west. Tickets go on sale three days in advance.

In addition, many tour companies operate express luxury coach services to most well-known destinations. Ask any travel agent for details.

BY CAR. For 10 hours with unlimited mileage, the self-drive rental-fee ranges from W29,150 to W101,200; for a 24-hour period the charge ranges from W41,800 to W115,500, depending on the make of car.

Cars are Korean models and charges include insurance coverage (but you'll need to pay extra for collision-damage coverage).

Chauffeur-driven cars are also available, and are recommended for people unused to Seoul traffic. It should be noted here that the general standard of driving is not high, and that Koreans tend to be hasty and aggressive behind the wheel. Including a driver, car hire fees run from aroundW52,000 to W72,000 for 3 hours; W74,000 to W158,000 for 10 hours. One-way rentals are possible, but the drop-off charges are high.

Driving is on the right, but you'll sometimes wonder if it is optional. The watchword is to be careful; the Korean accident rate is very high. Another note about driving safely is to be extremely careful in small villages. Country people (and their city fellows, too) are simply not used to cars, and don't practice even the rudiments of pedestrian safety. Be especially watchful of children—they often play in the streets.

The speed limit on the major highways is 55 mph. Most expressways are toll roads. You tell the toll keeper your destination as you enter in order to get a ticket for the right exit.

The law says that seat belts must be used by the driver and front-seat passenger on expressways.

More details about hiring cars are in the practical information sections of the area chapters of this guide.

ORGANIZED TOURS. Although we have so far talked about getting around only on your own, and will shortly list the sights of special interest that you can find by yourself, many visitors will prefer to see Korea on an established tour with an English-speaking guide. A range of organized programs is operated by some two dozen or so agents, and there are even fewer agents which have had experience in catering to the American, Canadian, or English visitor. While there are over 90 travel agents registered with the Korea Tourist Association, many of these handle other special market groups, such as the Japanese, or are primarily concerned with inexpensive programs for the domestic market.

Arranged tours in and around the capital are covered in the Seoul section of this guide, and the area chapters will give you an idea of programs available in different tourist centers of the country. Looking at package tours out of Seoul, however, there are a few that are especially popular and can be arranged for a minimum of just two people. For private groups the system is much more flexible, of course, and any of the recommended agents would put together an itinerary tailored especially to that group's interests.

The most common tour programs for individuals traveling outside Seoul are to Kyongju for one night/two days (around W165,000 per person); Kyongju and Pusan for two nights/three days (around W250,000); the Mt. Soraksan area for one night/two days (around W130,000); Yosu, Pusan, and Kyongju for three nights/four days (around W280,000); and Cheju Island for one night/two days (about W300,000) or two nights/three days (about W380,000). The programs include travel by train and bus (also air where Cheju is concerned), overnight accommodations, some meals, and visits to the major sights in the particular areas.

While it is not always necessary to make reservations well in advance, you would be advised to book ahead if your visit is in a peak season, or is to coincide with a major festival event.

The airlines and their agents also put together package tours of Korea, covering the airlines' domestic destinations and special-interest activities such as golf. The airlines' offices will be able to give you details of programs and reservations.

Here are the names and Seoul contact addresses of some recommended tour operators in Korea.

Global Tours, Ltd.
186-43, Tonggyo-dong, Mapo-ku
Seoul, Korea
Tel. (02) 335–0011;
Telex K27683;
Fax. (02) 333–0066

Samhee Travel Service, Inc.
148-1, Karibong-dong, Nowon-ku
Seoul, Korea
Tel. (02) 755–9251;
Telex SAMTRVL K26188;
Fax. (02) 773–2596

Korea Travel Bureau, Inc.
1465-11, Socho-dong, Socho-ku
Seoul, Korea
Tel. (02) 585–1191;
Telex KTBLTD K27360;
Fax. (02) 585–1187

Korea Travel Co., Ltd.
112-6, Sogong-dong, Chung-ku
Seoul, Korea
Tel. (02) 777–5661;
Telex KTCSEL K25346;
Fax. (02) 757–8452

Dong Yang Express Travel Service, Inc.
75, Sosomun-dong, Chung-ku
Seoul, Korea
Tel. (02) 753–0931/3;
Fax. (02) 752–6333

Aju Tourist Service Co., Ltd.
5–2, Sunhwa-dong, Chung-ku
Seoul, Korea
Tel. (02) 753–5051;
Telex AJUTOUR K24103;
Fax. (02) 774–0028

Hanjin Travel Service Co., Ltd.
132-4, 1-ka, Pongnae-dong,
Chung-ku
Seoul, Korea
Tel. (02) 777–0041;
Telex HJTRVLS K24734;
Fax. (02) 752–3882

Korea Travel International, Inc.
58-17, Sosomun-dong,
Chung-ku
Seoul, Korea
Tel. (02) 771–31;
Telex KOTRAVL K28458;
Fax. (02) 755–0849

Lotte Travel Service, Ltd.
27-1, Supyo-dong, Chung-ku
Seoul, Korea
Tel. (02) 265–4151/5;
Telex LOTTETS K26350;
Fax. (02) 274–6472

Korea's organized tour industry shifted into high gear for the 1988 Summer Olympics with a wide variety of new routes and packages that promise to continue pleasing foreign tourists.

Royal Asiatic Society Tours. The Korea branch of the society puts together an excellent range of cultural and special-interest tours for the spring and fall months, with one- or two-day trips mostly on weekends. For information on the programs, write to C.P.O. Box 255, Seoul; (02) 763–9483.

Tour Guides. What if you don't want to follow the set pattern of the tours you've investigated? You can hire your own English-speaking guide in any of the major tourist areas, for a half day or a full day, or for longer trips. These approved guides have passed a national examination and are certified by the government as qualified. They can be reached through local travel agents—make inquiries at hotel tour desks.

Goodwill Guides. The Korea National Tourism Corporation introduced its Goodwill Guide Program in 1983 and now has over 12,000 people registered in major cities and resorts where foreigners visit. The volunteers include students, office workers, and housewives who can communicate in a foreign language. They can be identified by the distinctive Goodwill Guide badge.

Leaving Korea

DEPARTURE FORMALITIES. Before your departure you should fill out the final details on the card that was stapled into your passport on arrival. This card will be kept by the immigration official as you leave.

If you are leaving by air, the **airport tax** is W6,000 per person.

Your **unused Korean currency** can be changed back to dollars, or another foreign currency, provided you have the original exchange receipts. (Without a receipt, you can change back up to $100 only.)

Cultural Properties: Remember that a Cultural Properties Preservation Law prevents the export of valuable crafts, paintings, and sculptures. If there is any doubt about the authenticity or value of any item, you should first take it to the Art and Antiques Assessment Office, Tel. (02) 662–0106, for evaluation. If the article is judged to be of no cultural value, export will be permitted. Otherwise export is forbidden.

Wildlife. To take out live or stuffed animals, you need a permit from the Forestry Office.

Limits on Other Items. The limit on red ginseng is 1,200 grams; the same for white ginseng. You can take out only five ladies' wigs and three men's. There are also limits on false eyelashes, cuttlefish, and phonograph records. The latter are good value here; you pay around W2,500 for local pressings, under license, of both classical and modern LPs. The export limit is $100.

CUSTOMS RETURNING HOME. American residents who are out of the U.S. for at least 48 hours and have claimed no exemption during the previous 30 days are entitled to bring in duty-free up to $400 worth of items for their own personal use. Each member of a family is entitled to this exemption, regardless of age, and exemptions among family members can be pooled.

The duty-free allowance is based on the retail value of the goods. You must list all items purchased and the items *must* accompany you when you return to the U.S. Keep all your receipts handy along with the list and try to pack all purchased items in the same suitcase. This will help the customs inspection to go as quickly and smoothly as possible.

One liter of alcoholic beverages, up to 100 non-Cuban cigars, and up to 200 cigarettes can be included in the exemption if you are 21 years of age or older. Alcoholic beverages in excess of one liter are subject to customs duty and internal revenue tax. Only one bottle of perfume trademarked in the U.S. may be brought in duty-free unless you get permission from the manufacturer. Other perfumes are limited by weight and value.

You do not have to pay U.S. duty on art objects or antiques over 100 years old provided that you have documentation establishing the age of the item. Be sure to ask the dealer for a certificate. Remember that Korea's Cultural Properties Preservation Law forbids the export of objects deemed to be of cultural value.

It is illegal to bring foreign agricultural items (meats, fruits, plants, soil, etc.) into the U.S. without individual permission because they can spread destructive plant or animal pests and diseases. For more information, read the pamphlet *Customs Hints,* or write to the Department of Agriculture, Federal Center Bldg., Hyattsville, MD 20782, and ask for Program Aid No. 1083 entitled "Traveler's Tips on Bringing Food, Plant and Animal Products into the United States."

You may (and should) register with U.S. Customs all your furs, jewelry, watches, cameras, tape recorders with serial numbers that you take with you as they might be mistaken as items purchased abroad. If you do not, you may obtain a registration at the U.S. Customs Office at your departure airport. Otherwise, you may have to pay duty when you return, and then file for a refund once you can provide proof of purchase in the U.S.

The U.S. Customs Service publishes a multitude of pamphlets and brochures on its procedures and on other related travel information. Write to the U.S. Customs Service, Customs Information, 6 World Trade Center, Room 201, New York, NY 10048, and request their free tourist brochures.

British citizens may import duty-free: (1) 200 cigarettes or 100 cigarillos or 50 cigars or 250 grams of tobacco; (2) two liters of table wine with additional allowances for either one liter of alcohol over 22% by volume or two liters of alcohol under 22% by volume; (3) 60 milliliters of perfume and ¼ liter of toilet water; and (4) other goods up to a value of £32.

PORTRAITS OF KOREA

THE HISTORY OF KOREA

Although present-day Korea is a modern industrial state, a new manufacturing marvel of the Far East, the country still shows many signs of its ancient past. Recent archaeological discoveries have established that primitive peoples inhabited the peninsula at least a half million years ago. Precisely who they were is lost in the mists of antiquity, but a murky picture emerges of Mongol nomads who drifted into the northern reaches of Korea from Siberia and Manchuria.

The cave dwellers lived by fishing, hunting, and gathering wild fruits. They had developed rudimentary pottery making, and carvings of animals, birds, fish, and human faces made with bone and shell have been unearthed.

Ancient Choson

Korean myths tell of the legendary Tangun, born of a heavenly father and a mother from the Bear Clan, who became ruler of the "eastern bowmen or barbarians" in 2333 B.C. and who ruled ancient Choson for a thousand years. Though Korea claims a 4,000-year history, for our brief survey we must pick a later starting point.

One glance at a map reveals why war shaped Korea's destiny from ancient times. Korea is a 600-mile-long pendant of land (about the size of Utah or the United Kingdom), extending southward from the underside of Manchuria into Pacific waters. In ancient times its situation was precarious. To the west, beyond the Yellow Sea, lay China; to the east, across the Sea of Japan, lay the Japanese Islands; and to the north, across the

Yalu River (her natural border), lay a land of restless, warlike Mongol tribes. On all sides were potential and eventual enemies.

Within the peninsula, warfare was a way of life. Fighting ranged from small tribal clashes for local ascendancy, lasting a few weeks, to months-long wars of large provincial armies of professional soldiers battling to determine the supremacy of one feudal lord over another, to massive invasions by foreign armies, in campaigns lasting decades, for total conquest of Korea.

The Korean people of today are descended from Tungusic tribesmen, whose language was related to the Altaic tongue spoken in eastern Siberia and northern Manchuria.

The Age of the Three Kingdoms

For convenience, we can divide Korean history into four major periods, starting with 57 B.C. These eras are: Age of the Three Kingdoms—700 years; Rule of the Silla Kingdom—300 years; the Koryo Dynasty—450 years; and the Yi Dynasty—500 years. These four periods span a bit more than 2,000 years, up to the early 20th century.

Chinese invaders in the second century B.C. established several colonies in Korea. The Lolang colony at the site of present-day Pyongyang City lasted until the fourth century A.D. when it was overwhelmed by the horse-riding warriors of Koguryo. Pyongyang, the ancient capital of Tangun, became the Koguryo capital.

For seven centuries the peninsula was basically ruled by three major kingdoms that gradually formed themselves during the first century B.C. First in the south was the Silla Kingdom (57 B.C.). Next, about 37 B.C., was the Koguryo Kingdom in the north and finally, about 18 B.C., the Paekche Kingdom emerged in central Korea. Over the years Paekche was pushed farther south by Koguryo from Seoul to Kongju until it finally established its last capital in Puyo. The Silla capital remained in what is now called Kyongju for almost one thousand years.

The Great Silla Period

In the seventh century Silla was able to unify the peninsula by defeating the Koguryo and Paekche kingdoms with the help of the Chinese armies. The Chinese intended to turn on Silla, their ally, and put the Korean peninsula under Chinese control. Munmu (30th king of Silla), with the aid of the famous General Kim Yushin, was able to lead the Silla nation to victory and unification (A.D. 668).

For over two and a half centuries the Silla Dynasty reached a peak of influence and prosperity unequalled in most parts of the world. Freed from domestic conflicts and foreign conquests from China, this era was marked by peace and prosperity. Korea benefited from the dynamic culture of Tang China and rapid development occurred in all areas of the arts, religion, commerce, and education. Today one speaks of this period as Korea's "golden age."

Buddhism became the state religion and, along with the Confucian influence of the scholars, reached and affected all aspects of Korean life. Silla's capital, which is now the city of Kyongju, reached a population of over 1 million inhabitants (10 times its present size) and was the fourth-largest city in the world during the eighth century (Baghdad, Constantinople, and Changan were larger).

By the ninth century, the ruling class was living a life of luxury and self-indulgence. Silla had lost the vitality that had brought it to power during the seventh century. Peasant revolts against brutal taxation were common throughout the countryside. Several rebel leaders were even able to sack the capital without reprisal. One rebel leader, General Wang Kon, finally became so powerful that the last Silla ruler, realizing that he had no alternative, abdicated in 936. Thus began the third great era, called the Koryo Kingdom, which was an abbreviated form of Koguryo and would later give rise to the name of *Korea*.

Koryo: The Centralized State

Wang Kon opened his reign wisely. He married a Silla princess to forge a link with the former royal family, placated the magistrates, protected the Buddhist monks, freed slaves, and started a civil service system. Under Wang Kon and later Koryo kings, a new cultural flowering began, especially in literature. But it was the growing influence of Confucian precepts that gave structure to the society and unified the people under a commonly felt national identity. And amid this progress came another war.

As the tenth century turned into the eleventh, an alliance of Mongol tribes, called the Liao, invaded Korea and sent the Koryo royal family fleeing the capital at Pyongyang. This situation had barely stabilized when another Mongol league, calling itself the Chin Empire, attacked the Liao and defeated it in a 10-year war. In 1238, a third Mongol invasion—a war lasting 30 years—put Korea under Mongol domination for the next century.

By the middle of the fourteenth century, however, Mongol power was on the wane, itself a victim of internal dissension. In China, the Ming Dynasty grew in power, defeated the Mongol armies in 1368, and reclaimed the throne for a Chinese ruling family. A period of peace, trade, and culture permeated the Orient. In Korea, however, cracks began to appear in the apparently smooth surface of society. The humanist, family-oriented teachings of Confucian philosophy had begun to clash with the ascetic demands of the Buddhist religion. This conflict would intensify for ages.

Scholars of the late Koryo period could see the violation of Confucian principles and were concerned that the throne was being dominated by Buddhism. Corruption was rampant and various factions were demanding reform. The stage was set for another strong leader to appear. General Yi Song-gye had distinguished himself in a series of successful military engagements and had been wise enough to stay out of court politics.

In 1388, General Yi Song-gye was ordered to take his armies north to drive out Ming forces that were occupying former Mongol fortresses. He knew that the Ming forces were too strong and that continued allegiance to the Mongols was sheer folly. While at the Yalu River, General Yi was placed in the same position as Caesar at the Rubicon.

His wise decision was to change the entire course of history. General Yi and his armies returned to the capital, overpowered its defenders, and exiled the royal family. He then began land reform and in 1392 declared himself king, becoming the first of 27 rulers.

Choson: The Confucian State

General Yi started his rule brilliantly: He moved the capital from Song-do to Seoul. In this single deft move he turned the old capital into a backwater. Thereafter, the old power cliques had to travel to his city when appealing for royal favor.

Under the Choson Dynasty (usually called the Yi Dynasty by Western historians), the last of four great eras, Confucianism became the guiding principle and pragmatism became the modus operandi for an extensive reorganization of society. Royal support brought great progress: land reform, scholarship, education, and inventions—such as movable type for printing, for example. In 1442, the pluviometer (a device for measuring rainfall) was perfected, nearly 200 years before its invention was claimed by the Italian Gastelli.

The stability of the Yi Dynasty government was finally secured during the enlightened reign of the fourth monarch, Sejong (1418–1450), grandson of Yi Song-gye (King Taejo). One of the world's greatest literary achievements was the royal development of the phonetic alphabet called *Hangul,* a precise and scientific system of writing that is used today. Considered the dynasty's greatest king, Sejong initiated impressive developments in music, science, and technology.

Invasions of Korea

Korea's foremost military hero and one of the world's outstanding naval strategists was Admiral Yi Sun-shin. In terms of importance, he is often compared with Sir Francis Drake and Lord Nelson of England. When the Japanese fleet defeated the Russian navy in 1905, the victorious admiral was quoted as saying, "You may wish to compare me with Lord Nelson but do not compare me with Korea's Admiral Yi as he is too remarkable for anyone."

When the Japanese Hideyoshi armies invaded Korea in 1592, the Korean navy, though outnumbered, was able to completely dominate the sea routes. Admiral Yi developed the world's first ironclad warship, which was called the "turtleboat," and engaged the Japanese fleet in a series of brilliantly executed naval operations that defeated the enemy every time.

Using matchlock muskets that far outclassed Korean weapons, Japanese troops marched up the peninsula and reached Seoul within two weeks. The worried Chinese finally sent troops to assist and eventually drove the Japanese back. In a final battle with Japanese troops that were fleeing the peninsula, Admiral Yi was fatally wounded by a stray shot. Korea's most important shrine is Hyonchungsain, dedicated to honor Admiral Yi. A replica of the famous "turtleboat" can be seen there.

Ironically, Japan, the loser, quickly entered a period of peace, prosperity, and progress. The Ming Dynasty in China had suffered such a financial loss by supporting Korea that it was almost on its knees. And Korea was left with a devastated countryside and a decimated civilian population.

At the start of the seventeenth century, China was forced to open her ports to European commerce, while Korea's agricultural surpluses—rice, wheat, and millet—drew avaricious Western traders like magnets. When the rising Manchu Dynasty in China attacked the weakened Mings, Korea sent aid to her old ally. For this costly act of loyalty—the Ming Dynasty fell—the new Manchu emperor demanded complete Korean fealty to China's new regime. When the Korean king refused, the Manchus invaded Korea, conquered the peninsula, and held it under "pagan" domination for more than a century. In this dire period, Koreans withdrew into themselves, nurturing and perfecting their own culture and earning the name the Hermit Kingdom in the outside world.

Close of the Yi Dynasty

As the Industrial Revolution spawned a powerful merchant class in Europe, the needs of mercantilism—raw materials for manufacturing and markets for finished products—brought uninvited warships and merchant vessels into Korean waters with insistent demands that she open her ports and grant trade concessions to the West. In 1876, Korea could no longer resist the pressure and signed a trade treaty with Japan. This was the open door Japan had been seeking. With the silent approval of the West, which feared the imperialist designs of czarist Russia from her Siberian base, Japan set the stage for conquest.

Defeating China in the Sino-Japanese War of 1894–1895, and Russia in the Russo-Japanese War of 1904–1905, Japan became, overnight as it were, a world power. First, it sent troops into Seoul to "protect" its legation. Then Japan's resident-general engineered the assassination of Korea's Queen Min—an international atrocity that was met with silence from the West. Each time Korea was forced to relinquish another royal prerogative to Japan, it was made to sign yet another treaty to "legalize" the new concession for the world. In 1905, right after defeating Russia, Japan made Korea a protectorate. Finally, in 1910, Japan unashamedly annexed Korea outright, installing a puppet Korean "ruler" to appease world opinion.

Japanese Occupation

The occupation of Korea by Japan from 1910 to 1945 was the worst period of Korean history. Japan first dominated and then completely absorbed every aspect of Korean life: banks, law courts, the educational system, religion, industry, agriculture. The Korean language was replaced with Japanese in the schools, newspaper censorship was imposed, and a network of spies was installed to betray Korean patriots. Despite this total domination, a Korean army of independence fought on against the enemy until 1915, and a government in exile was established in Shanghai.

With the start of World War II, Japan turned Korea into an arsenal-factory-farm for the support of the Japanese war effort, even drafting Korean youth into its army. But even upon the Japanese surrender in 1945, Korea was denied its pre-Japanese status as a unified nation. Instead, it was divided at the 38th parallel into two trusteeships, the northern half under the Soviet Union, the southern half under the United States.

Korea's Most Recent War

The Soviets refused to permit national elections that might have reunited the two halves of Korea, and the result was that north and south fell into a bitter ideological dispute that pitted one against the other. In 1948, the U.S. withdrew its occupation troops, and Dr. Syngman Rhee was elected president of the south, now the Republic of Korea.

Then, on June 25, 1950, North Korean forces launched an unprovoked attack across the 38th parallel and drove the surprised South Korean army into a small perimeter around the southern port city of Pusan. When Korea appealed to the United Nations for help, a United Nations army was formed under the command of American General Douglas MacArthur. After defeating the North Korean forces in a brilliant flanking maneuver—the Inchon landing—MacArthur drove northward. In October 1950, the Chinese Communists, fearing that MacArthur would cross the Yalu River into China, sent several armies into North Korea and drove the United Nations army back toward the Han River, capturing Seoul for the second time.

In January 1951, the United Nations army counterattacked, and by March 1951 a military stalemate was reached approximately at the 38th parallel. Negotiations for a cessation of hostilities began in July 1951 and dragged on until July 1953, when a truce was finally signed.

Postwar Reforms

Since the uneasy peace of 35 years ago, the Republic of Korea has made phenomenal economic progress to overcome the disadvantages of being separated from the northern industrial half of the peninsula. The first modern government under the democratic presidential system began in 1948 under President-elect Syngman Rhee. When President Rhee was elected for a fourth term in a fraudulent election in 1960, nationwide student demonstrations caused him to resign. Yun Po-son was elected as president with Chang Myon as prime minister in Korea's second republic. In 1961, General Park Chung Hee led a military revolution. In another general election, General Park was elected president in 1963. Social and economic changes began to take place; Park's aim was to "Koreanize" democracy while completing the task of national revival and achievement of Korea's economic goals.

In October 1979, President Park was assassinated. Martial law was declared and many months of political unrest followed. Eventually Chun Doo-hwan emerged. Under his tenure Korea has grown into an economic powerhouse. Chun In 1987, however, also managed to set off some of the most violent riots in Korea in years with his plan to install a political ally, Roh Tae-woo, as his successor. To quell the violence, Chun agreed instead to hold a democratic free election and to institute several democratic reforms, all before the end of his seven-year term in the spring of 1988 just prior to the Olympics. In February of 1988, Roh Tae-woo was inaugurated president of the Sixth Republic of Korea, following an election that was generally believed to be fair. Roh came into office with a plurality win and a handful of promises to democratize Korean society. Roh's democratically elected successor is due to take office in February of 1993.

RELIGIONS OF KOREA

The religions practiced in Korea today are a unique blending of traditions that reach back some 5,000 years to shamanistic myths. Later Buddhist and Confucian beliefs, influenced by Chinese characteristics, seasoned Korea's religious palate. Today religious liberty is a right guaranteed to all citizens of the country.

Korea's more ancient religions are shamanism, Buddhism, and Confucianism. These faiths have played an important role in shaping the nation's cultural development. Still practiced in many rural areas, shamanism is Korea's indigenous religion, and it has persisted for centuries. Buddhism and Confucianism were introduced to the peninsula from China during the Three Kingdoms period. One has provided a code of morality and behavior, while the other has bequeathed to the nation an artistic legacy. Christianity as well as several additional native religious movements were introduced in Korea at the end of the nineteenth century, while the Islamic faith entered the country following the Korean War.

Koreans tend to be pragmatic and will try anything once. A Korean's evaluation of a belief is determined by whether it works for one in a pinch. An early American missionary, Homer B. Hulbert (1863–1949) wrote in 1906 that "as a general rule we may say that the all around Korean will be a Confucianist when in society, a Buddhist when he philosophizes and a spirit worshipper [shamanist] when he is in trouble. Now when you want to know what a man's religion is, you must watch him when he is in trouble. It is for this reason that I conclude that the underlying religion of the Korean, the foundation upon which all else is mere superstructure, is his original spirit worship."

51

One trait that characterizes Koreans is their incessant search for harmony in life, a national preoccupation that transcends all existing systems of faith. This is probably one reason why Christianity initially, when proclaiming exclusive possession of the truth, did not achieve harmony with the traditions of the existing faiths, especially Confucianism.

Shamanism

Spirit worship is Korea's oldest belief and is based on the premise that humans are not the exclusive possessors of spirits, as they also reside in inanimate objects and forces of nature. Most of these spirits are not friendly. The shaman priestess, or *mudang* in Korean, is the sorceress who attempts to mediate with these spirits or appease them in preventing disasters and curing illnesses. The mudang is able to resolve conflicts and tensions that might have existed between the living and the dead. Thus serving as a spiritual medium, the mudang can communicate between the living and departed souls of ancestors.

Korean shamanism encompasses the worship of thousands of spirits and demons. This includes rocks, trees, mountains, and streams, as well as celestial bodies.

Koreans think of a shaman ceremony, or *koot,* more as a religious festival than as a serious service. It is a ritual that combines dramatics with music and dance. A good Korean mudang is an actress, a dancer, an acrobat, and a magician all in one. This results in a ceremony that is generally lively and enthusiastically received by the public. Often spectators join in the dancing portion of the ritual. A highly talented performer, the mudang gains supernatural powers once she becomes possessed by a spirit in the course of the koot. These are demonstrated in acrobatic feats, such as dancing barefoot on a pair of knife blades without shedding blood, or walking a bridge of thin paper without breaking it. The mudang will display a long knotted piece of cloth, which is symbolic of the psychological wounds sustained by the departed person when alive. This former suffering should be dissolved and untied. A shaman ritual may take several days.

Buddhism

Korea has over a thousand temples, most of which are nestled in the country's mountainous landscape. Many of the temple sites are more than a thousand years old. Buddhism arrived in Korea in A.D., 372 according to the officially accepted date, when it was brought to Koguryo by Sundo, a Chinese Buddhist priest. Twelve years later Buddhism reached the Paekche Kingdom through the missionary efforts of Marananda, an Indian priest, who had come by way of China.

The new faith spread like wildfire through the Koguryo and Paekche kingdoms as it received royal patronage. By the sixth century, Korean priests and religious artisans were migrating to Japan with scriptures and artifacts to form the basis of the early Buddhist culture on the island kingdom.

The Silla Kingdom in the southeast corner of the Korean peninsula was extremely resistant to Buddhism. After 155 years of rejection, the religion was finally adopted owing to an alleged miracle and martyrdom of the court official Echadon in 527. As he prophesied, his blood ran white after he was beheaded. The royal family stepped down from the throne and entered a monastery.

For 1,000 years, Buddhism was the greatest influence on Korea's art, inspiring its architecture, sculpture, painting, textiles, and ceramics. The footprints of this creative activity can still be seen across the countryside. Buddhism is a highly disciplined philosophic religion which stresses personal salvation through the renunciation of worldly desires. This prevents an endless cycle of reincarnations and brings about the absorption of the soul of the enlightened into Nirvana, a paradise without want or desire. Arriving in Korea nine centuries after its humble beginnings in India, this Mahayana (greater cycle) form gave rise to an elaborate and complex hierarchy of deities, saints, and guardians. This religion blended the various Buddhist sects brought from China, absorbed the indigenous shaman beliefs, and accepted Taoist principles and deities.

As Silla succumbed to Koryo during the tenth century, Buddhism remained politically powerful with over 80,000 temples in active operation. Buddhism continued to have an enormous influence on Korea's literature, art, and culture. Numerous religious books were published, including what was probably the greatest accomplishment in Korean history—the production of the *Tripitaka Koreana* during the thirteenth century. Today this work remains the world's oldest and most complete set of Buddhist woodblock scriptures.

However, Buddhist political power and corruption in court resulted in dramatic changes and the eventual decline of Koryo. When General Yi Song-gye established his kingdom in 1392, the Buddhist clergy was banished from the capital and the religion fell into disfavor. Confucianism was established as the state religion. Many temples were abandoned and sacred Buddhist objects destroyed. When Japan annexed Korea in 1910 unsuccessful attempts were made to amalgamate Japanese Buddhism with Korea's Buddhist tradition.

Buddhism has experienced a strong revival since the Korean War. Probably one-third of the nation's population is considered Buddhist. The income from land owned by temples has been used for modern education, social services, and the spread of Buddhist teachings through mass media.

Buddhism has blended well with other religions over the centuries. Almost every temple has evidence of shamanistic, Confucian, and Taoist beliefs. The biggest celebration for Buddhist believers is the "Feast of the Lanterns," which honors Buddha's birth. This national holiday falls on the eighth day of the fourth lunar month, which is usually April or May. Elaborate and solemn rituals are held at many temples across the country, while lanterns are carried in parades through the streets and hung in the temple courtyards.

Most Buddhist temples are open to visitors and photography is permitted. Larger temples have several entrance gates, with the first being the *ilju-mun,* or single-pillar gate. The name plaque of the temple is on this gate. A larger gate, the *sach'onwang-mun,* houses the four heavenly kings who guard the four cardinal directions of the universe. Occasionally there is another gate, one which honors the Bodhisattvas (attendants of Buddha) Munsu and Pohyon—one rides a tiger and the other rides an elephant. In front of the main courtyard there is a study hall. Opposite this courtyard is the main hall, often titled *taeung-jon* and housing the Sokkamoni, the historic Buddha, with two Bodhisattva attendants. If the main hall carries the title of *kuknak-jon* it houses the popular image of the Amitabul, Buddha of Western Paradise. Other Buddha deities, though not as common, are *Piroch'ana, Nosana,* and *Yaksa-yorae.* Bodhisattva, or Buddha attendants, are usually seen on either side of the main altar. These are second-rank deities who have not entered Nirvana (paradise) and have chosen to stay behind to help others. The most popular Bodhisattva in Korea is the *Kwanseum-posal,* or Goddess of Mercy.

Larger temples have one building called the *myongbu-jon* or Judgment Hall. This shrine contains the Bodhisattva *Chijang* and ten judges, who determine one's fate after death. Vivid murals depict the punishment for the sins of life. Another building, the *yongsan-jon,* houses Buddha with his many disciples, or *nahan* in Korean. The number of disciple images (including some women) can range from 16 to 500.

The shaman influence on all Korean temples can be found in the main hall or side shrines. The most popular shaman figure is the *sanshin,* or Mountain Spirit, with the tiger companion. Another popular spirit is *chilsong,* or Seven Star Spirit, which represents the seven stars of the Great Dipper constellation. A third spirit is *toksong,* the lone disciple or sage.

At more historic temple sites there are often many stone monuments. Tablets and stupalike monuments may have been erected to honor famous priests of the past. Called *tap* or *pudo* in Korean, these monuments are often bell- or pagoda-shaped. Ashes from cremation, *sarira,* and personal articles belonging to deceased priests were interred in these stone monuments.

Other stone sculpturing that might be seen on the temple grounds are stone-banner pillars, cisterns, turtle bases, decorative steps, lanterns, or simple lotus-patterned foundation stones that were once used for the building's pillar supports.

Traditionally five musical instruments are used at temples. These include a large bronze bell, a drum, a bronze gong, a carved wooden carp, and a wooden clacker, called a *moktak.* The hollow belly of the wooden carp is struck inside with sticks. The moktak is used by monks to keep the rhythm while chanting.

Historically, there have been many Buddhist sects but today there are only two major ones—the larger celibate sect, called *chogye,* and the smaller group of married priests called *taego.* The latter group consists of about 20 percent of Korea's priestly population. The chogye sect controls all of the major temples of the country.

Confucianism

Confucianism is not a religion in the strict sense of worshiping a divine power but a code of morals and conduct that has formed the standards of ethical behavior in Korean society. Confucian thought originally had no place for the supernatural, but as time passed Confucius and his disciples (both Chinese and Korean) have been deified.

Confucius (550–478 BC), a Chinese scholar and statesman, set up an ethical-moral system to ideally govern all relationships in the family, community, and state. Though Confucius never held a government post, his successors were instrumental in creating a monarchal form of government based on Confucian principles.

The exact date that Confucianism entered Korea is not known. No doubt it arrived with the first examples of written Chinese materials. All societies of the Three Kingdoms have left records that indicate an early existence of Confucian influence. Both the Koguryo and Paekche kingdoms established Confucian universities during the fourth century. The southeastern kingdom of Silla was the last to adopt this foreign influence in 503. But during the seventh century, when Silla conquered both Koguryo and Paekche, its interest in Confucianism along with other aspects of Chinese Tang culture rapidly increased. Though Buddhism was the state religion of Silla, Confucianism formed the philosophical backbone of the monarchy.

In 1392, Confucianism became the state religion, while Buddhism was relegated to a position of lesser importance. Study halls, called *sowon,* were established throughout the countryside with Songgyungwan, the Confucian University in Seoul, becoming the center of Confucian thought and study. Education at the time meant learning the Confucian classics.

During the next 500 years, Confucianism was accepted in Korea so eagerly and in such an autocratic form that the Chinese themselves regarded Korean adherents as more virtuous than themselves. In Korea, Confucianism meant a system of education, ceremony, and civil administration.

Confucius taught that society was made up of five relationships—those between ruler and subjects, husband and wife, father and son, elder brother and younger brother, and between friends. The chief virtue was filial piety, a combination of loyalty and reverence, which demanded that a son show respect to his father and fulfill the demands of his elders.

From this belief stemmed the practice of ancestor veneration. Members of a family would always be very careful not to breach etiquette or perform any act that would bring disrespect or discredit upon their ancestors. However, during the time of the Yi Dynasty divergences in doctrinal interpretation quickly led to political power struggles that eventually weakened the government.

In modern Korea, the tight family system has become fragmented and the previously ingrained Confucian concepts are becoming less influential. But though the Confucian educational system has disappeared as a basis for government administration, Koreans have not really discarded the customs, thought patterns, and habits derived from the Confucian tradition. Social stability, respect for learning, and reverence for age are still practiced. Korea's Confucian heritage is still very much in evidence in society.

Christianity

The first Western clergy in Korea is believed to have been Father Cespedes, a Jesuit priest who accompanied a Japanese invasion force as chaplain in 1592. He had virtually no contact with Koreans. In 1785, another Jesuit, Peter Grammont, secretly crossed the northern border and began baptizing believers. In 1795, a Chinese Catholic priest, James Chou, became the first foreign missionary to enter Seoul, but because of repression of the new doctrine, he was executed in 1801. Yet the Christian faith persisted.

The initial Protestant Western contact with Korea was in 1832, when the Reverend Carl A. F. Gutzlaff, a German missionary to China, landed along the west coast of Korea. For about a month he served as an interpreter while investigations were being made to open trade relations. Tracts and Bibles were distributed to the people. In 1836, the first Western resident missionary, a French Catholic priest named Pierre Maubant, entered Korea in disguise. Other Western missionaries soon followed.

Several years later, persecution of Christians broke out anew. The Western priests were captured and with over 80 Korean converts were executed on the banks of the Han River outside of Seoul. In 1845, the first ordained Korean priest, Father Andrew Kim, returned from China but was soon arrested and executed. However, the number of converts continued to increase and within the next 15 years there were 12 foreign priests and a Catholic population estimated at 23,000.

During the rule of the boy Kojong, his father and regent, *Taewon-gun,* ordered a severe persecution in 1866. As a strict Confucianist, the regent was fearful of the infiltration of Western ideologies. Nine of the 12 foreign priests were martyred, while the remaining three escaped to China. Thousands of Catholic Korean converts were also martyred for their faith.

During the 1866 Christian persecution, an American merchant ship, the *General Sherman* sailed up the Taedong River near Pyongyang. The ship was loaded with salable goods. Aboard the *General Sherman* was a Scottish missionary from China, Robert J. Thomas, who was making his second trip to Korea and served as a translator.

A message was sent to the governor requesting permission to trade with the city. The frightened governor refused and ordered the ship to leave. However, the crew took the Korean head of the delegation into custody and continued up the river until the vessel ran aground. The uneasy crew, fearful of attack, shot several Koreans. In anger the Koreans, who had thought the ship was coming to retaliate against the bloody anti-Christian killings, burned the ship. As the 24 crewmen swam ashore, they were massacred. It is believed that when Thomas reached shore he presented a Bible to the man who executed him, thus becoming Korea's first Protestant martyr. For many years the anchor and chain of the *General Sherman* hung in the south gate of Pyongyang as a symbol of the country's isolation policy.

It wasn't until 16 years later that a diplomatic Treaty of Amity and Commerce was signed between Korea and the United States on May 22, 1882, and Lucius H. Foote, the first American envoy, arrived in Seoul. Protection was now provided for foreign residents. Dr. Horace N. Allen, who was first assigned to China, requested to go to Korea. He arrived on May 24, 1884, and was warmly accepted as the American Legation badly needed a doctor.

Dr. Allen's efforts in saving the life of Min Yong-ik—a high-ranking official and nephew of Queen Min, who was seriously injured in an attempted coup—served to improve the image of the missionary movement in the eyes of the court. This provided a new impetus for the Christian movement.

The Protestant missionaries found a deep desire among young Koreans for Western education, seen as a tool that would help them in their struggle for badly needed social reforms. Western missionaries introduced modern education, establishing schools and hospitals as well as churches. They quickly became identified with progressive movements and the introduction of democratic ideals.

Early missionaries arranged for advanced education abroad for many of Korea's potential leaders and stood shoulder to shoulder with Korea's patriotic independence movement. Of the 33 signers of the 1919 Declaration of Independence, almost half were Christians. By 1980, it was estimated that Korea had over 7 million Protestants (one out of every five Koreans) and 1.5 million Catholics. There are an estimated 25,000 Christian churches, one of which has the largest church membership in the world.

Though Korea is not predominantly a Christian nation, many of its twentieth-century ideals have been drawn from the Christian church. In 1989, the Pope visited Korea and canonized many Catholic martyrs of the past. As a result, Korea now has more saints than any other country except Italy.

Other Religions

Several indigenous religious movements emerged in Korea during the nineteenth century. The largest of these was the *tonghak,* or Eastern Learning movement, founded by the martyr Choe Che-u in 1862. The name was later changed to *chondogyo.* Its objectives also changed from political to purely religious-nationalistic ones. Its membership is over 1 million.

Another powerful religious force, prominent first in the United States, is the Unification Church led by the Reverend Moon Sun-myung, a self-declared reincarnation of Christ. His heresy has spread widely throughout the United States and the church's tentacles, with vast sums of money, have reached into many aspects of both Korean and American societies.

Other groups are the colonies of the "Olive Branch" faith led by a Rev. Park, and *taejonggyo,* a revival of an ancient creed based on Korea's legendary founder, Tangun.

The Islamic religion received its impetus following the Korean War, when Turkish troops arrived. In 1966, a Federation of Korean Islamic Churches was established and the first mosque was built. There are now seven mosques throughout the country and approximately 20,000 registered Korean Muslims.

CREATIVE KOREA

Korea, lying between Japan and China, was destined from its earliest centuries to have cultural ties with these neighbors. However, Korea emerged early in Asian history as a highly creative force in its own right, with an artistic vision focused on its own history, religion, and worldly viewpoint.

Art connoisseurs from around the world now realize that Korean art forms, techniques, and designs are unique and fresh compared with the sometimes overornate and occasionally pattern-ridden artifacts of other Asian nations. The 5,000 Years of Korean Art exhibition, which had its debut at the Asian Art Museum of San Francisco in May 1979, provided the Western world with a rare view of the wealth and diversity of one of Asia's more important—and too-little-understood—cradles of art history.

Korean art reveals an intimacy with nature, and familiar sights of daily life are often incorporated into the art forms. Shamanistic beliefs survived side by side with Buddhism and Confucianism, and this intensified the Korean's already strong link with nature. Pride in Korea's artistic achievements has emerged as changes have been made in government regulations and renovations have been completed at many historic sites.

Recent archaeological discoveries have revealed that a paleolithic culture existed on the Korean peninsula. Over the last decade, tomb excavations conducted in the Silla and Paekche capitals have unearthed artifacts that substantiate the unique skills and high level of development of early Korean craftsmen. We now know that art forms that developed through Buddhist zeal and Korean folk traditions returned to China with renewed inspiration and then traveled eastward to Japan, where they had a profound impact on early Japanese art and culture.

Painting

A major contribution of Korean art is in the field of painting. Tomb wall paintings from the seventh century are some of Asia's oldest extant art. The world's oldest Buddhist painting (A.D. 755) decorated the Korean case that once held the oldest handwritten Buddhist scriptures.

With the beginning of the Yi Dynasty in 1392, a cultural explosion swept Korea as the country moved from Buddhist domination to the widespread influence of Confucianism; this transition is quite evident in the development of Yi paintings. Though these Yi paintings contain influences from China, most reveal indigenous techniques characterized by a simple and humble beauty. However, the native fervor for creativity was restrained by Confucian formalism.

Generally speaking, the paintings of the Yi era can be classified into two periods, separated by the devastating Japanese Hideyoshi wars of 1592. The first period was dominated by the Sung and Mongol cultures, whereas the painters of the later era were influenced more by the Southern School of the Ching Dynasty of China.

During the early nineteenth century, genre paintings came into great vogue. Probably the greatest practitioners of this style were two artists—Kim Hong-do and Shin Yun-bok. These genre paintings revealed detailed aspects of customs in Korean everyday life as well as employing uniquely Korean painting techniques.

Until recently, Korean folk-art paintings have been ignored by art historians outside Korea. Unconventional and unorthodox, the folk-art paintings of Korea date from ancient times and are referred to as *minhwa*. Bearing no signatures, these anonymous creations were intended to serve the lives of the people without the need to credit the artist. Serious or amusing, imaginary or real, *minhwa* art depicts deep religious convictions or themes of life's realities. Colorful and vivid, the compositions are free and unbound by Confucian restraint, and they often employ impressionistic techniques.

Ceramics

Another major aspect of Korean art is the slow development of ceramics to a high level of perfection—beginning with earthenware produced during the Neolithic period. Silla Dynasty tombs have produced a vast amount of gray stoneware pottery, which can be described as unassuming, sturdy, and straightforward while exhibiting a pleasing and spontaneous ingenuity.

The celadon wares of the Koryo Dynasty, produced in the eleventh and twelfth centuries, surprised even the highly cultured Chinese. Koryo celadons are now praised as one of those rare types of art in which the chemistry and creative spirit of the Korean people were completely harmonized. Koreans were the first to develop the inlay technique on celadon.

The thirteenth-century Mongol invasion of Korea disrupted the political as well as the artistic aspirations of the nation. Under the influence of the Mongol culture, changes appeared in shapes, decorative patterns, and firing methods. Though the fourteenth century saw the end of Koryo celadon, the dynamic impact of the new Yi Dynasty stimulated a spiritual revival in ceramic work, as seen in the refreshing *punchong* pottery and white porcelain.

Yi ceramics have a straightforward, solid masculinity and are characterized by a heavy potting approach and seemingly slipshod techniques. These aspects may seem coarse and humble to us today; yet it was precisely these qualities that the Japanese tea masters admired when they took captive potters to the island nation, where they gave birth to the vast ceramic industry of Japan. The special creativity revealed in the decorations used is the hallmark of Yi potters and unmistakably connects them with the unpretentious traditions of the earliest Korean ceramists. This ceramic art legacy is one of Korea's unique accomplishments.

The Buddhist Influence

As in ancient Chinese (as well as Japanese) art forms, the central stimulus of Korean art is Buddhism, from the fourth century to modern times. Buddhist art was further accelerated by Silla unification of the country in the seventh century, which introduced the renaissance or "golden age" of Korean art—a period spanning two centuries. During this Silla era the capital had a population of more than 1 million (and was the fourth largest city in the world). The culture of this period paralleled the great culture of Tang China.

Korean Buddhist sculpture can be grouped historically into two categories, gilt-bronze and stone. Most extant sculpture does not date earlier than the sixth century. Since granite is plentiful in Korea, sculptors often worked in stone. What is probably the most outstanding sculptured monument found anywhere in Asia, the Buddhist grotto called Sokkuram, lies behind the monastery of Pulguksa near Kyongju City.

In this grotto are found certain distinctive qualities of Korean art. Dignity and grandeur are revealed in the classic and idealistic naturalism and the combination of simplicity with modest and unobtrusive interpretation of form. During this period of Tang assimilation, Silla not only accepted the traditions of its teachers but in the case of the Sokkuram, ennobled it and provided the world with a classic example of Buddhist cave-temple art. A new tradition was born.

Other Arts and Crafts

The quality and distinction of Korean bell-making have won worldwide recognition and must be ranked among the proudest achievements of Korea's artistic impulse. Unfortunately, the technique used in casting temple bells during the Silla period (eighth century) has been lost. However, the bells' superior tonal quality speaks volumes for the technical sophistication of artisans of that period. Artifacts unearthed from Silla tombs during the past few decades also reveal a society sophisticated in the use of silver and gold.

Artisans of the Yi Dynasty period were skilled in the design and construction of wooden furniture, often with remarkable results. Their craft is characterized by simple and sensitive designs, using wrought iron and both white and yellow brass fittings. Fine lacquerware inlaid with mother-of-pearl and ox horn also reveal a range of decorative talent. Old furniture made as a folk art is increasingly hard to find, and what survives falls into the category of collector's items.

Song and Dance

There is no doubt that the Korean people have been fond of singing, dancing, and drinking from earliest times. As a result, a wide range of song, dance, and drama has evolved. Music and dance can be divided broadly into two types—court music and folk music.

Court music, which was standardized during the fifteenth century and preserved within it many characteristics taken from China's Tang and Sung dynasties, was later passed on to Japan. Today court music has become nonfunctional and is preserved only through the National Classical Music Institute.

Folk music, dance, and drama contain many Buddhist and shamanistic elements. Since Korea was basically an agricultural nation, most of its folk songs relate to the rural environment. Possibly the oldest of Korea's folk expressions is the farmers' band music and dance, which originated during the Three Kingdoms period and was intended to appease the spirits of the earth and to ensure good harvests.

Korean dance and drama portray symmetrical beauty and exotic motion, creating for the spectators an inner spiritual awareness. Dance drama has its origin in the religious rites of prehistoric Korea. The mask dances are believed to be central Asian in origin and were initially introduced with Buddhism. The evolution of the mask-dance drama is best seen as an aspect of Korean folk art and its relationship to early spiritual beliefs. Later, such drama served as a vent for the many grievances of the common people against the prevailing social restrictions imposed upon them by the nobility.

The exuberant folk tradition, together with the disciplined and elegant court tradition, help bring to light the complex and intriguing spirit of the Korean people.

FOOD AND DRINK

A wide variety of Korean dishes have gained popularity among international gourmets in recent years. Generally, Korean food tends to be less oily than Chinese food and not as bland as Japanese cooking. The Korean dishes that are hot and spicy are laced with red pepper; yet there are many milder dishes.

Kimchi, Korea's most traditional dish, will always be served at any meal—in one of several different forms. The basic Korean meal is simple: a bowl of rice, meat or fish soup, kimchi, and perhaps other vegetables. To make kimchi, hot ground red peppers and salt are used to prepare cabbage for fermentation. Then large white turnips, radishes, cucumbers, and other vegetables, also pickled in brine, are added to complete the dish. Weeks of slow, controlled fermentation bring the blend to perfection.

Winter kimchi is prepared in the late fall and stored in large sealed earthenware jars, which by tradition are buried in the ground with only the mouths of the jars above the surface. The preparation of winter kimchi is a monumental family project each autumn. Mountains of cabbages are seen in the market places as they are brought in from the countryside for *kimjang* (kimchi making). During November a friend will ask not about your health but whether you have finished your kimjang yet.

During warmer weather in the past, a summer kimchi was usually made on a day-to-day basis. Today, with modern refrigeration, this is no longer necessary. Bright red peppers, which are used in making kimchi and many other dishes, are frequently seen drying on mats in courtyards and occasionally on the thatched roofs of farmhouses in late fall.

For foreigners, one of the most popular Korean meals is *pulgogi,* which consists of strips of marinated beef charcoal-broiled over a brazier at the table. Also, *kalbi* (short ribs) are roasted in the same manner after being marinated in soy sauce, sesame, and spices. *Sinsollo* is a regal casserole of vegetables, eggs, and strips of meat and fish, mixed with pine and gingko nuts. Only a century ago, this exotic dish was prepared exclusively for royalty.

Other everyday Korean dishes worth trying include the following:

Kalbitang (갈비탕) . A rich soup, with chopped boiled beef ribs added.

Saengson chigye (생선찌개) . A tasty stew of vegetables and tender chunks of fish.

Pibimpap (비빔밥) . Rice with assorted vegetables and cooked egg.

Naengmyon (냉면) . A bowl of cold noodles with vegetables; eggs, and pieces of beef.

Maeuntang (매운탕) . A hot-spicy fish soup with lots of vegetables.

Kungjung chongol (궁중전골) . A variety of shellfish, fish, meat, and vegetables cooked in a broth. Called a "palace dish."

Manduguk (만두국) . A soup with meat dumplings.

Hanjongsik, (한정식) means "meal of the day." If you are staying at a Korean inn and you wish to eat in your room, this is what you would order. Dishes will vary.

After walking into a Korean restaurant and being served an elaborate array of fish, meat, and vegetable dishes, you will be surprised to find that the bill is reasonably modest. Many restaurants are now combining Korean and Western dishes on their menus. Especially in the larger cities, Korea has become a gourmet's paradise—at reasonable cost.

Cocktail houses are a recent phenomenon in Korea and run the full range from pleasant to rip-off. Usually it's best to go with someone who knows his way around. Most establishments have bars and private rooms in which patrons may have the services of hostesses. A tip for a hostess might run $75 or more, just for an evening of chatter. Prestige drinks are unbelievably expensive. Highball prices vary from $7 to $10. *Always* ask for a menu or price list before ordering.

Beer halls are cheaper and also offer a lively entertainment. There are two types of Korean beer, OB and Crown. Draft beer can be ordered at most places. The cost is about $2 per drink, and you will be expected to order a side dish of snacks, which might consist of mixed nuts, dried fish, or fresh fruit. These dishes are usually overpriced. You are not required to tip the waitress. Some beer halls feature continuous stage shows with well-known talent.

In a class all their own are the *makkolli,* or wine houses, of Korea. If you wish to indulge in an evening of less elegance but more adventure, we recommend them. This is the common man's drinking place, where the native rice brew is milky white but has a pleasant enough taste. Though it appears mild, this drink is actually quite potent, so sip slowly. The side dishes served at the makkolli (막걸리) houses are even more interesting and impressive than those found in the other eating establishments. You can also order *pindaedok* (빈대떡) , a vegetable pancake, or *maeuntang* (매운탕) , hot fish soup. Such an evening can be fun and not too hard on your wallet. Foreigners find the locally produced white wine, *majuwang,* exceptionally good.

Korean Kisaeng

Many foreigners who arrive in Korea have heard about Korea's *kisaeng,* and many have been royally entertained by these attractive women. For the average foreign male, the flood of feminine attention is almost overwhelming. However, the expense of kisaeng recreation can cost literally hundreds of dollars, so be prepared.

Actually, the true kisaeng disappeared from the Korean scene at the turn of the century, but the lure and excitement of this traditional form of entertainment lingers on. Most foreigners know little of the cultural origins and training of these historical kisaeng. The food served in kisaeng restaurants is exceptionally good.

At the other end of the spectrum is the *tabang tashil* (다방, 다실) (tearoom). Barley tea *(poricha)* is always served and is free; refills keep coming. Besides tea and coffee you may order ginseng tea, ginger tea, walnut tea, and a variety of cold drinks. A poached egg may be served, and occasionally fruit in season will be available. Foreigners are always welcomed and are usually escorted to the better seats if the place is not overcrowded. Cheaper drinks are about $3.

EXPLORING KOREA

SEOUL

At first sight, Seoul will be a shock to those who expected an East Asian city. The 1988 Olympic City, the Korean capital shows the results of a nationwide commitment to industrialization and the achievements of a highly educated, highly motivated work force.

To the casual visitor to Seoul, therefore, Korean tradition and culture may seem buried beneath the surface of Western influence. It appears that here East meets West in a manner familiar to Western visitors. But this is not so. The strong forces of a culture not yet eroded by outside influences are ever present, with the ways of the West often in conflict with Korean standards and the Confucian approach to life.

Everywhere one meets the unexpected. Unimpressive office buildings tower over palaces that have been the pride of gracious dynasties since the fourteenth century. Men in grey suits and girls in prim office uniforms hurry down a street bedecked with Buddhist lanterns. A farmer herds his goats through an underpass of computer stores and ginseng showrooms. And a sidewalk vendor sells imported bananas next to Gucci bags made in Korea. All this is in downtown Seoul, where the landscape is in constant change and the people flow with the times.

These scenes and many more are the threads that make up the fabric of a vibrant city. After all, Seoul has a population pushing 10 million—a population that has mushroomed by some 80 percent over the past 15 years or so, through a rising birth rate and heavy migration from the countryside. Today's statistics show that 65 percent of South Koreans live in an urban environment, and that over 50 percent of the total population is under 25. With almost a quarter of all South Koreans living here, Seoul is an exciting example of how fast things happen and how successful the country has been in its pursuit of rapid economic development.

However, one must accept that Seoul is crowded. The air is not always clear. The traffic is hectic and noisy. People are not always polite. Walking down city streets or browsing through department stores and markets does require some agility and forbearance. Koreans seldom stroll; they stride with purpose and little regard for anyone in their way. They're really not discourteous, far from it. Rather, getting bumped and doing some hustling and bumping of your own are the simple realities of life in this busy city, and do not require apology.

You will recall that Seoul has literally risen from the ashes of the Korean War, which ended with a truce in 1953. All the modern buildings with a few exceptions—the National Museum, City Hall, Seoul Station, the Bank of Korea, Myondong Cathedral, the Anglican Cathedral, and a few others here and there—were built during the past 30 years. The rise of Seoul into the modern capital it is today is nothing short of phenomenal.

Seoul has not yet finished rejuvenating itself; it probably never will. One of the major fields of development has been underground. The Seoul subway system with a total of over 72 miles is the seventh longest in the world. The system, which is new, modern, and efficient, is now being expanded. Some of the stations have been elaborately decorated, others feature arcades of boutiques and the ubiquitous ginseng stores, and some now have escalators as well.

Line 1, finished in 1974, runs through the center of the city under Chongno Street, connecting Seoul's two most important railway terminals—Seoul Station and Chongnyangni Station, beyond East Gate. This rail line emerges aboveground and branches off to Suwon in the south, Inchon on the west coast, and Uijongbu to the north. Line 2 runs a circle route around Seoul, crossing the Han-gang River to the south. Called the "loop line," it serves the Seoul Sports Complex and also stops at some of the city's major universities—Seoul National, Ewha Women's (Yonsei and Sogang are nearby), Hanyang, Konkuk, and Hongik.

Line 3 runs from the northwest to the southeast and connects both sides of the Han-gang River through the heart of downtown. Line 4 is a mirror opposite, running northeast to southwest.

The major impetus behind much of the reconstruction of the city was the selection of Seoul as the site of the 1988 Summer Olympic Games. Competition in 11 of the 23 total sports events took place either in the Seoul Sports Complex or the Olympic Park, both on the south side of the Han-gang River. The Seoul Sports Complex (site of the 1986 Asian Games) comprises two gymnasiums and the Olympic Stadium, site for the opening and closing ceremonies. This stadium can seat 100,000 people. The Olympic Park is four kilometers from the Seoul Sports Complex and contains the major athletic facilities, the Olympic Village, Olympic Hall (control center for the Games), and a spacious park with historical sites and recreational facilities.

These Olympic facilities are laid out along the southern banks of the Han-gang River, which has itself undergone massive redevelopment. The large-scale project transformed a 36-kilometer stretch of riverbanks into parks, sports fields, and other recreational areas. The river bed has been dredged to accommodate cruise boats, and these now operate on a number of routes between Yoido and Chamshil, the major Olympic area.

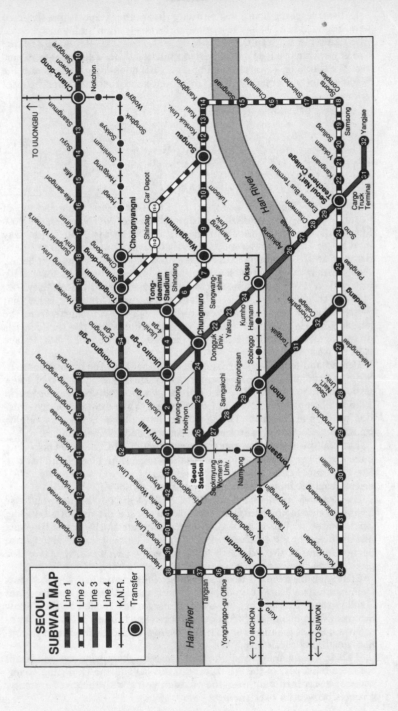

In these respects, Seoul is a new city. In another respect, it is far from new. Founded in 1394 as the capital of the newly risen Yi Dynasty, Seoul (the name means "capital") is nearly 600 years old. Reminders of the dynasty—which ended in 1910 with occupation by the Japanese—still survive. Toksu-kung, Kyongbok-kung, and Changdok-kung palaces and the Namdaemun and Tongdaemun (Great South and East gates) are the most visible.

Exploring Seoul

An Overview from Seoul Tower

To see how the city is laid out, try a bird's-eye view from the top of Seoul Tower, which rises 500 feet from the peak of Mt. Namsan, the 900-foot saddle-backed mountain in the middle of the city. The easiest way up is by taxi, but there is a special bus that leaves from the children's park halfway up the mountain. Until the explosive growth of modern Seoul, Namsan marked the city's southernmost boundary. From its foot, a 10-mile wall of earth and stone circled northward around the old city.

From the tower, you'll see Namdaemun, one of the nine gates that pierced the old city wall. A busy 10-lane highway runs north from the gate to City Hall Plaza, a fountained circle from which the traffic swirls off in five directions. City Hall is on the plaza's north, and Toksu Palace is at its west.

Behind and to the west of Namdaemun you'll see the bronze dome of Seoul Station, one of the city's major rail terminals. Construction of a new station building, behind the old red-and-white structure, was begun in 1986 and completed before the 1988 Olympics (like most major construction projects in the city). The new 26-story building houses a shopping center, hotel, an exhibition hall, sky lounge, and business offices.

The 360° from Mt. Namsan to Namdaemun Gate, to Kyongbok-kung Palace, to Changdok-kung Palace, to the Tongdaemun Gate, and back to Mt. Namsan circumscribe most of the area of the old walled city. We'll discuss each of these landmarks in later paragraphs.

Due north from Namsan across the bowl of the city center, you'll see a ridge of mountains, and may even be able to see the roof of a building perched atop it. This is a tearoom and restaurant on the Pugak Skyway, just the place for a spectacular view of the city looking south, and of some of the remains of the old north wall. It's easily accessible by taxi and is often a scheduled stop on organized tours of the city.

Clearly visible from the tower is Samillo, the elevated highway that runs from downtown halfway to Seoul's eastern edge. You can see, too, that Seoul's urban area stretches west until it merges into Inchon on the Yellow Sea coast. Part of Samillo Street curves south and tunnels under Mt. Namsan itself, one of the three tunnels that burrow under the mountain to connect north and south Seoul.

Walk in a semicircle around to the tower's southern windows and you'll see the newest part of the city sprawled out beyond the Han-gang River. Most of it has been built over the past ten years, with the most dramatic changes being seen over the past four.

Immediately identifiable to the west is the dome of the National Assembly Building on Yoido, an islet in the Han-gang River. The area is a ruled grid of high-rise apartments and office buildings. A landmark on Yoido, the "Golden Tower" Daehan Life Insurance Building (DLI 63), completed in 1985, rises 63 stories and is one of Asia's tallest buildings.

Most of the city south of the river consists of rows of high-rise apartment buildings interspersed with shopping centers. Many of the areas have recently become "trendy" places to live in, with the result that supermarkets, popular fast-food restaurants, and exclusive boutiques have followed. The well-known designer Andre Kim, for example, now has his showroom south of the river, in the Yongdong area just over the Songsu Bridge.

From your tower lookout, you will see lots and lots of bridges. At the last count there were 19, one of them double tiered—but now with a bump in the lower level to let the cruise boats pass underneath. One of the bridges, the Hannam Grand Bridge, leads to the Kyongbu Expressway, the country's major north–south artery, which ends at the port city of Pusan. The Chungbu Expressway, opened in 1987, joins it, linking Seoul with Taejon and passing by Chongju on the way.

Closer at hand, on Namsan's southwest slope, you'll see the mirrored facade of the Hyatt Hotel. Just below and to the right are the white minarets and onion dome of the mosque, built with funds donated by Saudi Arabia for Korea's followers of Islam.

The mosque stands over one of the city areas most popular with foreigners—Itaewon, playground of American soldiers from the nearby army base and a wonderful shopping center for tailor-made clothes, sports shoes, brass beds, jewelry, and ready-made clothes of all descriptions. Most of the city's foreign population explores Itaewon for bargains, and it has become popular with tourists, too. The clothes are not only cheap, they're in Western styles and sizes. There's an excellent collection of American fast-food restaurants, doughnut shops, and ice-cream parlors for when you need a break from shopping. (Look under "Shopping" in the *Facts at Your Fingertips* section for more details.)

Across the river to the east lies the Chamsil area, with the Seoul Sports Complex and nearby Olympic Park.

Now that you've had an overview of Seoul, it's time to give you details on the major tourist entertainments.

Toksu Palace

To the west of City Hall Plaza, Toksu-kung (Palace of Virtuous Long Life), originally built during the fifteenth century, is the site of the Yi Dynasty's final days. Forced to abdicate in 1907, King Kojong retired here. He was a witness to his son's loss of the throne, his country's annexation by the Japanese, and the end of his family's dynasty after ruling for more than 500 years. The palace's main gate still stands. So does the audience hall with its gate and flagstone courtyard, where the king's courtiers once waited in ranks to greet him, advance their petitions, and offer advice.

The most prominent buildings now, however, are two large Western-style ones, designed by the British architect H.W. Davidson in 1901 and completed in 1909. Today they serve as annex buildings of the Museum of Modern Art, the main center of which was moved from here to the suburb of Kwachon in 1986. These annex buildings are closed on Mondays.

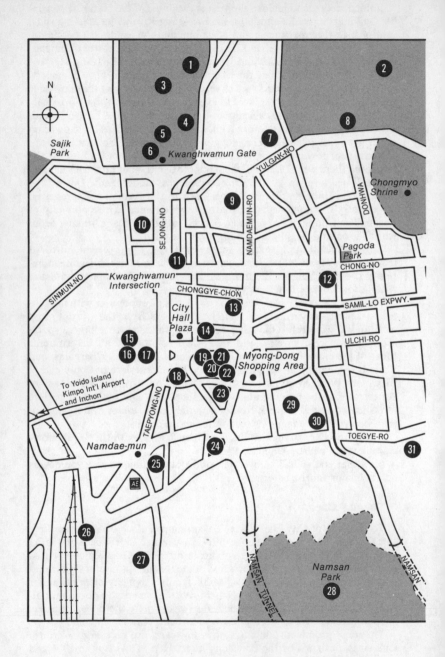

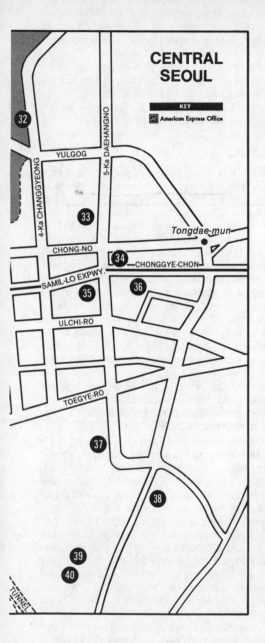

CENTRAL SEOUL

KEY

[AE] American Express Office

Points of Interest

Ambassador Hotel **37**
Anglican Cathedral **15**
Changdok-kung Palace **8**
Changgyong-kung Palace **32**
Chogyesa Temple **9**
Chosun Hotel **20**
Hilton Hotel **27**
Hotel Lotte **21**
Hotel Shilla **38**
Hyangwon Pavilion **3**
King Sejong Hotel **30**
Korea House **31**
Korea National Tourist Corp. **13**
Kwanchondae Observatory **7**
Kyongbok-kung Palace (entrance) **4**
Lotte Shopping Center **22**
Main Audience Hall **5**
Midopa Dept. Store **23**
Myong-dong Cathedral **29**
Namdaemun Market **25**
National Folklore Museum **1**
National Institute of Classical Music **39**
National Museum **6**
National Museum of Modern Art Annex **16**
National Theater **40**
Pangsan Market **35**
Pigak Pavilion **11**
Piwon (Secret Gardens) **2**
Poshingak Belfry **12**
President Hotel **19**
Pyonghwa Market **36**
Royal Asiatic Society **33**
Sejong Cultural Center **10**
Seoul Plaza Hotel **18**
Seoul Station **26**
Seoul Tourist Information Center **14**
Seoul Tower **28**
Shinsegae Dept. Store **24**
Toksu-kung Palace **17**
Tongdaemun Market **34**

Open daily to the public for a small fee, the palace grounds are a favorite resting place for Seoul's pedestrians. The peony gardens are in full bloom in May and June. In the late fall, the grounds are ablaze with a riot of chrysanthemums and the brilliant gold of gingko trees, a delight for painters and photographers.

Watching over Toksu-kung's visitors is a statue of King Sejong, the fifteenth-century monarch best known for introducing Hangul, the Korean written alphabet. North of Toksu Palace is a small street leading to the Anglican Cathedral (built in 1926), the British Embassy, and the British Ambassador's residence. The latter two date from 1980.

The Area of Kwanghwamun

The 10-lane highway, which begins at the Namdaemun Gate and runs along City Hall Plaza, ends at the great Kwanghwamun gate (Gate of Transformation by Light), which stands before the National Museum, formerly the capitol building. Between City Hall Plaza and Kwanghwamun is an intersection with a statue of Admiral Yi Sun-shin, a sixteenth-century naval commander who invented the ironclad "turtle ships" that defeated the Japanese war fleets in a 1592 invasion. (You'll see a lot of this famous admiral; he's featured in pageants, monuments, and museums throughout the country.) From this intersection northward to the gate, the boulevard is called Sejongno (after the king). Southward, back to Namdaemun, it's called Taepyongno (Great Peace Street). To the east, the street is called Chongno, and to the west it's Sinmunno (New Gate Street).

The name of the intersection itself is Kwanghwamun, the same as the gate, which used to be here before being moved a block north. This is confusing, but be comforted by the fact that this is the only place in Seoul where streets change names as they cross.

On the west side of Sejongno is the Sejong Cultural Center, a major venue for traditional and modern performing arts, and on the east side is the American Embassy. A little to the south of the embassy is the Kyobo Building, a useful landmark. It houses a number of international banks and business offices (such as Westinghouse and Du Pont), has the city's best stationery store in the basement, and also has an excellent French restaurant, one of the few good Western restaurants outside the top hotels.

Chongno was once the main shopping street of the old city, and it runs all the way eastward to the Tongdaemun Gate, near the most wonderful market areas of the city. Just a couple of blocks east of the Kwanghwamun intersection on Chongno is the Chonggak intersection, with a famous belfry, Poshingak. The original bell was rung at dawn and sunset during the Yi Dynasty to signal the opening and closing of the city gates. After Korean liberation, the bell was rung at midnight on the last day of each year by the mayor of Seoul. A developing crack in the 500-year-old bell caused concern. The bell was rung for the last time on December 31, 1984, and moved to the National Museum for preservation in 1986. A new bell now replaces the old one in the belfry.

Kwanghwamun, the gate, is distinguished by a plaque written in Hangul (and in the late President Park Chung-hee's own calligraphy) instead of in the traditional Chinese characters. It is guarded by a pair of stone haetae, mythical animals said to prevent fire. From the fifteenth century onward, their job has been to protect not only the gate but also Kyongbok-kung Palace, whose extensive acreage lies beyond the former capitol building.

The National Museum

The collection of the National Museum is now housed in the former capitol building. It was built by the Japanese, who wished to symbolize the replacement of the old dynasty with the new colonial authority after annexation in 1910. The total exhibition space is large enough to show only less than a tenth of the museum's collection, which totals around 120,000 pieces. These represent over 5,000 years of life on the Korean peninsula.

Displayed are fine examples of prehistoric pottery, Silla Dynasty earthenware and glittering gold crowns, the Koryo Dynasty's famed celadon, Yi Dynasty porcelain, Buddhist sculpture in bronze and granite, and many beautiful old paintings. The museum is open from 9 A.M. to 5 P.M. every day except Monday.

Kyongbuk-kung Palace

Surrounded by walls, the grounds of Kyongbok-kung (Palace of Shining Happiness) are entered through one of two gates in the east wall. One gate leads visitors into the palace grounds proper, the other into the garden of the National Folklore Museum in the northeast corner. Small admission fees are charged at each. Before it was moved to the renovated capitol building nearby, the National Folklore Museum used to display the collection of the National Museum. The Folklore Museum's galleries feature a wealth of objects for daily use: for work (farming, cooking, hunting, weaving), play (games, cards, toys), entertainment (musical instruments, mask-dance costumes), ceremony and religion (shamanistic, Buddhist, and Confucian ritual artifacts), education, medicine, and commerce.

Kyongbuk-kung itself was first built in 1395 by the founder of the Yi Dynasty, King Taejo, but was burned during the Japanese invasion of 1592—to be left in ruins until 1868, when it was rebuilt by the regent Taewon-gun for his second son Kojong, the 26th Yi ruler (who retired to Toksu-kung Palace after his abdication).

Many historic stone pagodas and monuments were placed on the grounds during the Japanese occupation (1910–1945), including a 13-story pagoda from the Koryo Dynasty period of the fourteenth century, located near the east-gate entrance.

Two lotus ponds have been preserved on the palace grounds, one with a large two-story open pavilion in the center, Kyonghoe-ru (the Hall of Happy Meetings), where kings used to hold elaborate banquets. The other does actually bloom with lotus in late July and has a small wooden pavilion (Hyangwon-jong or Lotus Pavilion) built on an artificial islet connected to the shore by a graceful wooden bridge. School art classes are brought here in the fall to try out their brushwork on the scene of pavilion, bridge, and turning leaves.

The other major building of Kyongbuk-kung Palace is the Throne Hall, directly behind the National Museum, where many Yi kings were crowned and official audiences held for Korean and foreign dignitaries.

Changdok-kung Palace

Traveling east from the Kwanghwamun gate along Yulgokno, you will come to a large, leafy walled-in area that blooms pink and white in spring with cherry and dogwood blossoms, and turns to orange, red, and gold in autumn. This is the area of Changdok-kung (Palace of Illustrious Virtue), which has what is probably the oldest gate in Seoul, Tonhwamun. This gate escaped the ravages of the Japanese invasion of 1592, when major portions of the palace were burned.

Dating from the fourteenth century, Changdok-kung Palace is not as large as Kyongbok-kung, but it is now the residence of the surviving royal family. Their private quarters, Naksonjae, are closed to the public, but the palace's audience halls, reception rooms, and former living quarters offer intriguing glimpses into a now-vanished royal way of life. Near the entrance is the royal garage, containing Korea's first motor vehicle.

Piwon, the Secret Garden

A section of Changdok-kung Palace, Piwon comprises 78 acres of rolling woodland where once royalty retired to relax and disport themselves among streams, ponds, and pavilions. Within Piwon is Pandoji, a pond that is contoured roughly like the Korean peninsula and has a small fan-shaped pavilion on its shore. Altogether, there are some 44 pavilions scattered in the area, and this is considered one of the most charming outdoor spots in Seoul. Entry to Piwon is only by guided tour. An excellent commentary is given in English.

A

Changgyong-kung Palace

East of Piwon is Changgyong-kung (Palace of Glorious Blessings), which reopened to the public in early 1987 after three years of extensive restoration. It is now claimed to be one of the finest displays of the life and arts of the ancient royal family.

The palace was originally built during the Koryo era and became the residence of King Taejo, founder of the Yi Dynasty, when he came to Seoul. After he moved to Kyongbok-kung Palace, Changgyong-kung was allowed to fall into disrepair and was rebuilt by King Songjong during the late fifteenth century. Although Changgyong-kung was a detached palace, it was combined with its neighbor Changdok-kung during the seventeenth century to form one royal compound.

An impressive double-roofed entrance, Honghwamun (the Gate of Vast Transformation), on Changgyong-kungno Street (opposite Seoul National University Hospital), leads across a small stone bridge to the main halls Munjongjon and Myongjong-jon, the main throne hall and the oldest in the city. Other halls have the delightful names of Hwangyongjon (Hall of Happiness), Kyongchunjon (Hall of Spring), and Tongmyongdang (Hall of Clear Thinking), all with displays of royal sedan chairs and other court relics.

At the far north end of the grounds is a very beautiful botanical garden, lovely all year but particularly spectacular in spring, when the cherry trees blossom.

Chongmyo Shrine

Across the street from Changdok-kung Palace is another small parklike area, Chongmyo, the Royal Ancestral Shrine, where two long pillared halls house the ancestral tablets of all 27 Yi kings and their queens. The forested grounds are open every day, but the main shrine buildings are open only on the first Sunday in May with the reenactment of an ancient Confucian ritual. Court music and stiff, formalized dance, both dating from the fifteenth century, accompany the movements of celebrants who offer wine, incense, and respect to each of the departed spirits. Formerly an all-day affair, the ceremonies now take only six hours, and the public may attend. It is a rare opportunity to see the costumes, hear the music, watch the movements, and sample the atmosphere of an elaborate court ritual born in another age.

The entrance to Chongmyo is from Chongno Street, behind a large parking lot between Chongno 3-ka and Chongno 4-ka. The entrance can also be reached through a side street off Chongno 4-ka itself. There is a small admission fee.

Namdaemun, the Gate and Market

The Great South Gate of Seoul, Namdaemun, was originally built in 1398 as part of the construction of a wall to fortify the newly proclaimed capital. Although it is now commonly known as the Great South Gate, the name written on its signboard is Sungnyemun, the "Gate of Exalted Ceremony," which is much more evocative. It is now designated as National Treasure No. 1.

A minute's walk away, to the gate's southwest, is the Namdaemun Market with basement shops, open stalls, and buildings with floors and floors of all manner of merchandise—from silk and china souvenirs to fresh flowers and camping goods. And, of course, lots and lots of ready-made clothes. It all appears very haphazard. Down one ramp and you're in the fish market. Down another, it's children's clothes (wonderful bargains here!); and down another to see rows and rows of American foods—the "ghost market" that goes through cycles of high and low visibility, depending on how the authorities feel. You'll find people here specializing in foreign exchange—the rate may be better than the banks', but it's always a risk and is quite illegal.

Tongdaemun, the Gate and Market

This gate is the other surviving main gate to the city, now in the center of a busy traffic rotary at the end of Chongno Street. Like Namdaemun, its name has been simplified—the formal name is Hunginjimun, the "Gate of Uplifting Benevolence."

Apart from the sight of the gate, why would you want to go there? Simply to wander around one of the largest indoor-outdoor markets in the world. It is many blocks square, and everything is sold: produce from land and sea; textiles, especially gorgeous silk brocades; ready-made clothes for young and old; housewares and furniture; sports and camping equipment; even dogs and birds . . . whatever you might need. If you're hungry, stop at one of the "snack bars"—trestle counters and tiny stools right in the midst of the shoppers—where marketgoers pause for a bowl of noodles or a plate of squid accompanied by varieties of the fiery kimchi. You can at least have a cold soft drink or a beer. Watch out for the men carrying chigye (A-shaped wooden frames) on their backs; and for pushcarts piled high with bolts of cloth. Be wary with your camera; the market people are generally sensitive about having their pictures taken.

There are several other major markets in the district, but the Tongdaemun area, the south side of Chongno back from the gate toward the 4-ka intersection, is probably the most interesting for a visitor. Unless you're interested in electronics. Between the 4-ka and 3-ka intersections, again on the south side of Chongno Street, is what is known as the Chonggye Electronics Market, which displays an incredible collection of Korean-made appliances and electronic equipment. You'll see the top local brands of computers, microwave ovens, televisions, audio equipment, home appliances, and electric and electronic gadgets galore—and the prices are far cheaper than those in the dealers' stores. However, bear in mind that cheaper doesn't necessarily mean cheap. You'll pay far more in Korea than you would at home for the same brand, same model. Also, whatever you buy here will have markings and instructions in Korean.

Chogyesa Temple

This is the only important Buddhist temple in or near downtown Seoul, and it is the headquarters of the official chogye sect, serving some 1,500 affiliated temples throughout Korea. The temple is located between Chongno and Yulgokno streets, off an alley on Ujonggukno Street northwest of the Poshingak Belfry. As it is in the middle of the city, Chogyesa is rather atypical of how temples usually look and feel. The gilded Buddha on the main altar is sheltered in a glass case, and a piano may be standing in the worship hall ready for use during services. As a headquarters, the temple is often busy with monks, laymen, and worshipers passing through the gate and misses most of the tranquillity normally associated with Buddhist temples. As you enter or leave, pause at the shops at the alley entrance; they specialize in Buddhist ritual objects—rosaries, wooden gongs, Buddhist images, incense, and candles.

The temple area is very pretty at the time of Buddha's birthday, the eighth day of the fourth lunar month (May 28 in 1993), when the surrounding streets are decorated with lanterns. There is a candlelight procession in the evening.

The Daehan Life Insurance Building

Known as the "Golden Tower" or simply "DLI 63," this is one of Asia's tallest buildings and the headquarters of the Daehan Life Insurance Company. It is the most distinctive landmark to the east of Yoido Island. We have included it here as a noted attraction because there are a number of activities available that are of interest to foreign visitors. The observation platform is on the 60th floor, reached by a high-speed elevator (the ride costs W3,000 per person) or an exterior glass elevator if you have a head for heights. The view is indeed spectacular. You look out over Seoul and beyond, as far as the port city of Inchon to the west, and, on a very clear day, over the border to North Korea. The observation deck is open daily from 10 A.M. to 10 P.M. The upper floors have elegant restaurants, but the food is not as spectacular as the views of the city. The ground floor features an American-style shopping mall, with Korean, American, and Japanese fast-food bars—the food values here are better.

Also on the ground floor is one of the few IMAX theaters in the world, where films are projected on a screen 10 times larger than usual, giving you the feeling of being part of the action. Sometimes there are presentations of a film called *Beautiful Korea;* at other times you see views of the American Grand Canyon. The first screening, daily, is at 10 AM.

For those who enjoy fish of all types and sizes, DLI 63 offers Seaworld 63, with over 20,000 freshwater and saltwater marine animals. There are frequent shows in the largest tank, with dolphins, stingrays, sharks, octopuses, and other marine creatures. The entrance fee is W3,500. You can find out more details from the building's information desk (call 789–5670).

Seoul Grand Park

This has been a major recreational development project, partially opened in 1984 and fully completed before the 1988 Olympics. Located off the Seoul-Pusan Expressway at the foot of Chonggyesan Mountain, the park covers more than 1,600 acres and features a zoo, botanical gardens, youth culture center, and amusement park.

The zoo has more than 4,000 animals of some 450 species, making it fifth in size among world zoos. The animals are well cared for and some are kept in imaginatively designed cages. Giraffes and zebras, for example, share a large compound with deer and antelope. The enclosure has sculpted "cliffs" of foliage so the giraffes can eat as they would naturally. Electric trains circle the major areas, and there is also a very popular dolphin show.

The botanical gardens are arranged in two separate sections: a greenhouse and a forest in which birds and other animals are also displayed. The 14,000 plants of over 3,000 species are impressive and well worth seeing.

The amusement park is a Korean version of Disneyland and has been constructed in two phases. The first opened in late 1986, and the second opened in about the middle of 1988. Four theme areas—Land of the Future, Land of Fantasy, Garden of Samcholli (the Korean peninsula), and Village of the World—provide a variety of displays.

The entrance fee to the zoo is W1,000, with another W300 for the dolphin show. The easiest way to get there is by taxi (around W6,000 from downtown). You can also catch a green bus, No. 90, outside the Sejong Cultural Center, at Kwanghwamun intersection, but green buses run infrequently.

Cruising the Han

Taking a boat cruise along the Han-gang River is Seoul's newest sightseeing entertainment, a result of the massive redevelopment and "clean up" of the river and its surroundings. The riverbanks have been landscaped into parks and sports fields, the river has been extensively dredged, and new floodgates have been built to control the water level.

There are eight boats altogether with spacious upper and lower decks, and they operate on five routes. Route 1 is a 15-kilometer course from

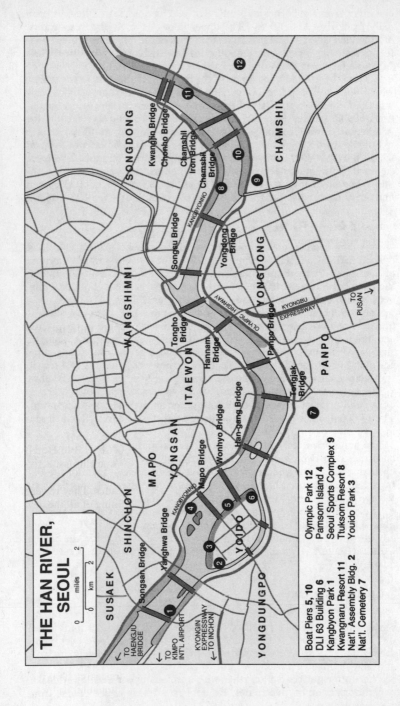

THE HAN RIVER, SEOUL

miles
0   2
km
0   2

Boat Piers 5, 10
DLI 63 Building 6
Kangbyon Park 1
Kwangnaru Resort 11
Nat'l. Assembly Bldg. 2
Nat'l. Cemetery 7

Olympic Park 12
Pamsom Island 4
Seoul Sports Complex 9
Tuksom Resort 8
Youido Park 3

the landing in Yoido to Chamshil, near the Seoul Sports Complex. Route 2 is the journey in reverse, from Chamshil to Yoido. The third route, of 13 kilometers, is a round-trip between Yoido and the Tangsancholgyo Bridge, via the Pamsom bird sanctuary. Seasonal visitors to this islet include white-tailed sea eagles, white-naped cranes, whooper swans, kestrels, and various types of ducks. Route 4 of the river cruises is another round-trip, from Chamshil to the Tongho Bridge, and route five is between Ttuksom and Tongho Bridge.

Fares are W3,500 for Routes 1 and 2, each of which takes 90 minutes, and W3,000 each for the three other routes, taking 60 minutes. The first cruise of the day is at around 10 AM; the last departs at around 7:15 PM. Schedules do change with the seasons, so check operating times before you leave the hotel. For more information on scheduled or private cruises, call the Semo Company at 785–4411.

Live Korean pop music is played at some of the piers during the day, making them a nice place to stroll before or after your trip.

Walking Tours

The easiest way to explore downtown Seoul is on foot. You'll have to go up some pedestrian overpasses and down lots of pedestrian underpasses (very few main streets have zebra crossings), but it's well worth the exercise. You can put together some good combinations of walking, riding the subway, and taking taxis. Buses are best avoided unless you know for sure which number to catch, in which direction. Bus signs are unfortunately all in Korean, and available maps are not very helpful. Before you set out, make sure you have the name of your hotel written in Korean so you won't have a difficult time getting home.

Let's start at City Hall—it's an easy landmark—and from here you'll have several choices. You can cross underground to the west, to Toksukung Palace; take a subway to Tongdaemun (Line 1, four stops, W250) to explore the market; stroll north to Kwanghwamun (the intersection and then the gate) to visit the National Museum and Kyongbok-kung Palace; or head east (crossing underground in the direction of the Lotte Hotel) to tour the department stores and Myongdong. We'll look at this last activity since the other attractions have already been covered.

But first a word about underground passages and arcades. They're very confusing. Since so many of them are new, with the opening of all the new subway stations, the Koreans themselves are often bewildered. If you're lost, take the next staircase up to find your bearings. A happy note these days is that most of the direction signs are written both in Korean and English, and besides, there'll always be someone to show you the way.

The department stores: Start at the main Lotte Hotel (an annex building was completed around March of 1988) and head for the lower shopping floor. This will lead you to the basement of the Lotte Department store, Seoul's largest, which is open on Sunday and closed on Tuesday. It's sure to be crowded, especially on weekends when hordes of schoolchildren and office workers use their little free time to browse. There is a supermarket in the basement, a miscellaneous collection plus excellent leather items on the ground floor, and then floors of men's, women's, and children's clothing, china, and household goods. There are few bargains here, but it's fascinating to see what is considered chic and fashionable.

On the eighth floor is a duty-free store for foreign visitors (anything you buy, and it will be expensive, is delivered to you at the airport on your departure).

The ninth and tenth floors are devoted to eating, and are excellent places to try out Korean, Chinese, and Japanese foods. Each small restaurant, often crowded, displays its selection in showcases, with prices clearly marked. And the prices are reasonable.

Leave the department store underground by taking the escalator downstairs to the basement and turning left, following an arcade of shops out into the underground Sogong shopping area. After turning left, you can make a right turn off into the Midopa Department Store (not as elaborate as Lotte), but do return to the arcade and continue. When you climb above-ground to the street again, you'll be in Myongdong, a series of streets and alleys behind the banks and office blocks opposite the main entrance to the Lotte Department Store. The area stretches south to Toegyero Street.

Myongdong is considered to be the center of fashion and entertainment. Fashion is certainly served, judging by the plethora of shoe and dress shops, tailoring establishments, jewelry boutiques, and the like. (There are also a number of fast-food restaurants.)

After work, the area's alleyways are thronged with people indulging in a bit of window shopping before they pop into one of the small drinking houses that serve *soju,* a cheap liquor made from potatoes, and *anju,* snacks that always accompany drinking in Korea. Window displays of steaming bean pancakes, wriggling eels, and sizzling pigs' feet lure hungry customers.

As the evening wears on, these drinking houses become noisier, hazy with cigarette smoke, and brimming with good cheer. Invariably someone bursts into song. Korean men love their singing and drinking—which leads some to say that the Korean national pastime is *not* hiking.

Some after-work revelers prefer to listen to others entertain, and there are plenty of Myongdong places with live performers to sing pop songs and folk music from Korea and the West.

If you forego all these temptations and continue straight up Myongdong's main street, you'll reach the foot of the hill on which Myongdong Cathedral stands. Built in the 1890s, it is the seat of Roman Catholicism in Korea. The cathedral was once the tallest structure in the city. When it was being built, some historians say, there was much debate at court about allowing a building to stand on ground higher than the palace.

Go across the street leading out of Myongdong, actually following the pedestrian overpass that crosses under the Samillo elevated highway, down a block and a turn to the right, and you'll be at Yongnak Presbyterian Church, a large granite building.

Christianity is a strong minority religion in Korea but one fragmented into many sects—some orthodox, some not. Despite the churches, most Koreans profess no religion at all. One often quoted saying goes, a Korean is a Buddhist in philosophy, a Confucian in society, a Shamanist in trouble. Because of its visibility on almost every neighborhood street corner, Christianity may seem more pervasive than it really is.

Anyway, that's Myongdong, the area that the tourism authorities are promoting as quite the "in" place in Seoul. It's always entertaining.

More walks: The Changdok-kung and Changgyong-kung palaces are side by side, so you can head there by taxi, explore the major halls and gardens (including Piwon), and wander toward Chongno Street to visit the Chongmyo Shrine. If you have time and energy left, take the subway two stops from the Chongno 3-ka station along to Tongdaemun and check out the market area. Return to your hotel by taxi, or subway if you're staying near a station.

For strolling around antiques, art stores and small galleries, go to Insa-dong, occasionally called Mary's Alley. You can take the subway to Chonggak Station on Chongno Street (site of the Poshingak Belfry) and head northward down Ujonggukno Street to the first street off to your right, which will lead you into the main area of Insa-dong. The Chogyesa Temple is in the same area, down an alley off the west side of Ujonggukno, so you could visit here first. Near Insa-dong, also, is Pagoda Park, on the northeast corner of Chongno and Samillo streets. This small park has a new shrine to recent history, commemorating the place where the Korean Declaration of Independence was proclaimed on March 1, 1919, setting off nationwide peaceful demonstrations against the Japanese. Here, too, is the Wongaksa Pagoda, the only remains of the Wongaksa Temple built in 1464 and destroyed in 1512 during an anti-Buddhist purge. Pagoda Park has lots of shady trees and benches and is a common place to see elderly Koreans in traditional costume.

Another "street of culture" is Daehangno, literally meaning University Street, a tree-lined boulevard which runs off the end of Chongno 5-ka to the Hyehwa Rotary. Among Koreans, this is known as the street of "teeny-boppers" as it's a favorite hangout of high-school students. There are plenty of sidewalk cafes (and a Kentucky Fried Chicken restaurant), plus galleries, stamp markets, and areas for the display of paintings and pottery and for the presentation of dance performances and poetry readings.

There are several tape and record stores here, also, and it's a good place to browse for both popular and classical recordings. You'll pay only about W3,000–W5,000 for a record or tape; they're made in Korea under license from major international companies.

To promote the cultural activities of Daehangno, the road is closed to traffic between 6 PM and 10 PM on Saturday; and from noon to 10 PM on Sunday. You can get there by subway (Hyehwa Station on Line 4; transfer at Tongdaemun if you're coming from downtown by Line 1).

Day Trips Out of Seoul

TO THE NORTH

Mt. Pukhansan National Park

The north fortress Pukhansan-song dates from the Paekche Kingdom, around A.D. 132, but it was of little strategic importance until after the Hideyoshi Wars of the 1590s and the Manchu invasions of the 1630s. The Yi King Sukchong sought a safe refuge north of the capital, and in 1659 an earthen fortress was erected within the area of the present fortifications, which were constructed around 1711.

The length of the wall is around 5 ½ miles, and its height ranges from three feet on some of the higher mountains to 18 feet on level stretches. Seven peaks are enclosed within the wall, which these days is not continuous, and the clean air, plant and animal life, temples, and other historical sites have made hiking trips in the area popular. There are also challenging spots for rock climbing.

Pukhansan-song has been declared a national park, but plans to add resort-type facilities, such as a cable car and funicular railway, have, happily, so far not been approved.

There are a number of established hiking trails, departing from different points around the fortress, taking from around three to six hours each. The *Discovering Seoul* guidebook produced by the Royal Asiatic Society, tel. (02) 763–9483, has details, or you can contact the Korean Alpine Federation at (02) 782–5539 for assistance. The Pukhansan park is about a 30-minute drive from downtown Seoul.

Panmunjom

Site of the continuing United Nations Military Armistice Commission (MAC) talks with North Korean and Chinese negotiators, Panmunjom straddles the Military Demarcation Line in the Demilitarized Zone (DMZ) that bisects the Korean Peninsula. Ever since the truce agreement was signed in July 1953, talks have been held whenever either side has a complaint to lodge or a point to make. Though seemingly of little real importance, the talks have served to defuse potentially serious confrontations between the two sides. For the American soldiers stationed at the truce camp under the heavy scrutiny of their North Korean counterparts only 100 yards away, the duty is tense. They never know when tempers might flare, as happened in 1976 when two American soldiers were killed by North Korean troops in an incident over pruning a tree. All the American soldiers stationed there are volunteers for the job, and all meet strict physical and psychological qualifications.

When meetings are held between North and South Korea, representatives from both sides gather in a simple building that is half below and half above the Military Demarcation Line. The table they sit at has one end decorated with the Republic of Korea's flag, the other with the North Korean flag. The press must peek through the windows to hear and photograph proceedings.

No visitors are allowed when the Military Armistice Commission is meeting, but on other days the Korea Tourist Bureau runs tours from Seoul with English-speaking guides. It is not possible for Korean nationals to visit the Demilitarized Zone.

The tour bus leaves from the Lotte Hotel. The 30-mile drive takes about an hour and a half, due largely to the time spent getting out of city traffic. Once out of the city area, the bus runs up the Tongillo (Unification Highway), curving north past rice paddies and rural villages. There are stops made at a memorial for Philippine troops killed during the Korean War and at Unification Park, which features a memorial to the fallen Korean soldiers. There is also an interesting monument here to all the newspaper correspondents killed while covering the war. On the way, the guides fill you in on Korean War history; some guides get emotionally carried away with their own descriptions.

Once you've crossed Freedom Bridge and reached the truce camp, visitors are given a general briefing before being escorted by U.S. military guards as well as a spokesman to the MAC conference room and then to Freedom House, from which you can gaze into sealed-off North Korea. Some 60,000 people have visited here from the South Korean end, but only 5,000 or so from North Korea have done so. Under the close supervision of your soldier guide, you may be permitted to walk to the North Korean side of the negotiating table, where you will stand briefly in North Korea— but this is possible only in the MAC conference room. Visitors are instructed not to make any gestures at the North Korean soldiers, and to always conduct themselves in a subdued and polite manner. The general atmosphere does not invite levity.

After lunch at the army cafeteria, you will begin the return journey to Seoul, stopping on the way at the third infiltration tunnel, which was discovered in 1978. This tunnel, like the two previously discovered, heads toward Seoul and cuts through bedrock approximately 240 feet deep. It could move a full division complete with men and equipment each hour, for a surprise attack on the South Korean capital. You can go down to the tunnel mouth if you like, it requires just a little agility. The entrance to the North Korean tunnel itself is cemented up, with the exception of a small area with a machine-gun post. There is a caged canary, like in the old mining days, to alert watchers to lethal gas.

To arrange the full-day tour, go to any Korea Travel Bureau (KTB) office or tour desk—they're located in most of the hotels. You need to book at least a day ahead—earlier is better as the tour is often fully booked— with your name and passport number. The tour departs from the Lotte Hotel at around 9:30 A.M. returning between 5 and 6 P.M. Cost is W31,000.

TO THE SOUTH

The Suwon Area

Suwon (Water Field) is the capital of Kyonggido Province, just 30 miles south of Seoul. The town is largely the creation of King Chongjo, who ruled from 1776 to 1800. To honor and to vindicate the memory of his father (who as crown prince had been unjustly and cruelly executed by his father the king, Chongjo's grandfather), Chongjo sought to turn the town near his father's resting place into a properly fortified city and move the capital there. He succeeded in fortifying it, as the gates and walls— many well restored—testify, but he could not move the capital.

Suwon has a South Gate, a North Gate, a towered West Gate, and a picturesque Water Gate where the city wall crosses a stream. A diverse collection of old Korean architecture is displayed in a smaller area here than in any other town, making it well worth a day's visit. While the town today has become an industrial center and a popular residential suburb of Seoul, it retains something of an old-world charm. On summer days, in an airy pavilion just above the Water Gate, you'll often see a group of elders gathering to catch the breeze, smoke a pipe, and chat to while away the heat of the day. Nearby are some ancient archery grounds, still maintained, which are the scene of periodic contests.

Suwon is also famous for its *kalbi* restaurants—kalbi is delicious grilled ribs—and its surrounding strawberry fields and grape orchards.

Just a few miles south of Suwon is Yongjusa (Dragon Jewel Temple). A spacious complex, the walls of its buildings are painted with Confucian scenes designed to reinforce the virtues of filial piety. One of them shows a whimsically drawn tiger smoking a long Korean pipe with the help of some improbable-looking bunnies. The paintings depicting filial piety are highly appropriate, even if this is a Buddhist temple, since King Chongjo was a frequent guest and often visited his father's grave nearby to pay his respects. Chongjo's grave is now next to his father's. The temple itself is the beneficiary of Chongjo's piety, since it was he who, after a dream about a dragon with a jewel in its mouth, had the temple reconstructed on the site of a much older one founded in A.D. 840. Yongjusa is also noted for keeping one of the two early Koryo bells that survive in the country. Buses for Yongjusa leave from Suwon's South Gate.

To get to Suwon from Seoul, take the No. 1 subway (which uses the Suwon line of the National Railway—make sure you get the right subway train as another one heads for Inchon), or take a bus from the Yongsan terminal.

The Korean Folk Village (Minsokchon)

What Virginia's restored colonial village of Williamsburg is to the United States, Minsokchon is to Korea. Urbanization was changing the countryside so rapidly that it was thought the country needed somewhere to preserve and reconstruct the life that is quickly vanishing. Open from 9 A.M. to 5 P.M. every day of the year, this open-air living museum covers a vast acreage on which farmhouses typical of every province in the peninsula have been built. There is also an example of the largest aristocrat's home formerly allowed and a provincial-government building that includes a jail. Displays include an operating blacksmith's shop, a pottery shop, and a brass forge. A large open-air market has an excellent collection of souvenir stores and cafes.

The houses and buildings are not empty shells, but are furnished with antique chests, pots and pans, and farm implements. People live and work here—a fortune teller, calligrapher, embroiderers and sewers of the glorious national costumes, basket weavers, and charcoal and paper makers. The fields are cultivated and harvested, the thatched roofs repaired when necessary by traditionally attired workmen, and the gourd vines trained to trail over the roofs as they should.

Every day has at least one celebration—either a wedding in the old style or a farmer's band raucously driving out evil spirits with drums and gongs. A spirited farmers' dance is often the highlight of the arena. Sometimes there are special events—a kite-flying contest in the spring, for instance.

Korean visitors often seem to get into the spirit of the village, too; on New Year's Day, whole families dressed in *hanbok,* the national costume, come out to spend the day blending in with the ambience. There is also a playground for children.

The Folk Village is wonderful for photography, so bring lots of film. And be happy when you get hungry and thirsty—the market sells what is perhaps the best rice wine in the country *(tongdong-ju)* and there are plenty of snack stalls and restaurants.

You can reach the village by direct bus through several tour agencies in Seoul (your hotel can advise), or more slowly by subway to Suwon and local bus from the Suwon railroad station. On weekends, be prepared for crowds.

Yongin Farmland

Some 20 miles southeast of Seoul, and just off the Seoul-Pusan Expressway is a spacious area of parkland combining zoo and amusement park. You can ride a roller coaster and bumper cars, see a variety of animal shows, eat at a Chinese or Korean restaurant, wander in a splendid formal garden, and take a bus ride through Lion and Tiger Country. This "safari park" is very spectacular, and a little scary. Full-grown tigers stand on platforms and peer through the bus windows while you gape at them, and they are much bigger than you might think.

The attractions at the Yongin Farmland have been considerably upgraded with the opening of the Hoam Museum. Housed in a beautiful Korean-style building is one of the premier art displays in the country, the private collection of the Korean magnate who controls the Samsung Group, Lee Byung-Chull. Among the over 6,000 items, 12 have been designated National Treasures or Treasures, and there are some very fine pieces of Koryo Dynasty celadon and Yi Dynasty blue-and-white porcelain. Aside from the art objects of historical interest, the collection also includes the works of some 200 modern artists, and some selected works by such Western artists as Henry Moore, Auguste Rodin, and Antoine Bourdelle. The combination of the outdoor pleasures of zoo and garden and a collection of masterpieces in ancient and modern art make an excellent day's outing. Buses from many tour agencies make regular runs to Yongin Farmland in the warm seasons, or you can easily take a taxi or shuttle bus from Suwon.

Yoju

The Yi King Sejong was much revered, as is evident in the grandeur of his tomb just outside Yoju, a town about 50 miles south of Seoul and most easily reached from a turnoff on the Yongdong Expressway. Intercity buses connect Seoul and Yoju on a frequent schedule. Once in Yoju, take a taxi to Sejong's tomb, as it's some distance outside the town. The tomb is properly called Yongnung.

Just beyond the entrance gate (there's a small fee to enter), you'll see an imposing monument. There, cut in marble, is the royal proclamation of Hangul, the Korean writing system. Sejong's 32-year reign (1418–1450) resulted in many advances for Korea: scientific inventions, the restoration of ancient musical instruments and music notation, and significant literary works. The era is considered a high point in Korea's cultural history; its achievements are recorded and displayed in a small museum here.

Every year, on May 15, the anniversary of Sejong's death, Confucian rituals are held at the tomb in his honor. The burial mound itself is in typical style—a high grassy mound with a granite altar, guarded by carved stone statues of scholars and zodiac animals.

On the other side of Yoju is Silluksa, a temple dating from A.D. 580. Situated on a high bluff, it offers a splendid view of the curving Han-gang

River. Silluksa is noteworthy for its brick pagoda, one of only five or so constructed, dating from the Shilla period, and for a number of other national and cultural treasures on its grounds. These include a nine-story pagoda, a marble lantern, important carved stone tablets, and a 370-year-old gingko tree inviting meditation under its cool shade. Bring a picnic lunch and eat it perched on the huge rock outcropping overlooking the river, or buy food and drink at the booths and small restaurants near the temple entrance. The wide sand beaches attract summer visitors to bask here in the sun.

Ichon

On your return journey from Yoju, stop at one of the pottery kilns situated along the Kwangju-Ichon highway (this is a different Kwangju from the city in Chollanamdo Province), and see the best reproductions of Koryo and Yi celadon and porcelain. It is often possible to see artisans working at the potter's wheel, applying the underglaze designs, painting, or carving and inlaying the pots in preparation for firing.

The soil around Ichon has two important elements necessary for the production of quality pottery—good clay and mineral-free water—and many of the country's most famous potters have set up shop here. Most of the studios have showrooms, and prices tend to be lower than in Seoul's hotels or shopping arcades. Do bear in mind that good reproductions, especially those signed by Korean masters, are always expensive.

Namhansan-song Fortress

South Mountain Fortress, a favorite picnic and hiking spot, is beautifully green in summer, and blazing with color in fall and spring. From its highest point, you can see Seoul in the distance, often bathed in a haze of smog. At Namhansan-song, you can breathe deeply the clear mountain air even though Songnam, a satellite of the capital, lies just beneath the city's western ramparts.

Drive a rental car or have a taxi drive you up the winding road from Songnam to the fort's highest entrance gate. You can also go by bus or taxi through the eastern entrance, which winds in from the highway to Kwangju past a rocky stream to a dusty terminal area.

Of the two routes, the way via Songnam is much quicker, but the way via the eastern gate is the more beautiful and exciting. From here, you'll have to hike up the rest of the way to see the battlements that were first built during the Paekche kingdom and later rebuilt by Yi kings to defend themselves against the Chinese and the Manchus during the seventeenth and eighteenth centuries.

Unfortunately, the fort did not prove to be impregnable—it fell to the Manchus after a long siege. The encircling wall has been rebuilt, and it's possible to hike all along its circumference, a distance of some five miles.

The major points of interest within the fortress walls are the Changgyongsa Temple, the sole survivor of nine Buddhist temples said to have existed within the fortress compound; the Chisudang Pavilion overlooking a lotus pond; Hyoncholsa Shrine, built by King Sukchong to commemorate the spirits of the officials who opposed King Injo's surrender to the Manchus (they were later executed under the terms of the surrender); the

Korean-style buildings of Yonmugwan and Chimgwajong; the Sungnyol-jon Shrine, with a signboard in the calligraphy of King Chongjo; and the Chongnyangdang Shrine, to commemorate the spirits of Yi Hoe, the "engineer" of the southern sector of the fortress wall who killed himself after being falsely accused of incompetence, and his wife who drowned herself on learning of his death. The best lookout point is Suojangdae, the West Command Lookout, a two-story pavilion which provides an excellent view of the area. The original building was erected in 1624 and was used by King Injo during the Manchu invasion. The second story was added in 1751, at which time the pavilion was called Mumangnu, the Hall of Not Forgetting, a reference to the shame of the defeat under the Manchus.

TO THE EAST

The Upper Han-gang River

In the river districts of eastern Seoul, in the area of the Sheraton Walker Hill on the north bank, and the Chamshil area on the south, are a number of recreational parks. These have been recently developed as part of the reclamation project of the Han-gang River.

In the same area of the river, on the south bank beyond the Kwangjin Bridge, is the Olympic Regatta Course, built for the Asian Games in 1986.

A major center for the new boating facilities is the Kwangnaru Resort, on the south bank, which offers speed boat rides for W3,000–W6,000 per hour, and small yachts for W10,000 to W20,000 per hour. Here it is also possible to rent equipment for water skiing for W10,000 per hour.

The North Han-gang River Valley

A number of dams for hydroelectric power plants have turned the Buk-han-gang River (the North Han River) into an area of small resorts, all within easy distance of Seoul.

The main city in the area is Chunchon, capital of Kangwondo Province, which is a rail terminus and highway junction.

Namisom, a small islet at Kapyong, roughly halfway between Seoul and Chunchon, has grown in popularity over recent years and now has a small hotel, cabins, and various recreational facilities.

Farther downriver, there is the long artificial lake of Chongpyong with many inlets, popular with Seoul's foreign residents. Here there are a number of hotels and bungalows, and a wide variety of opportunities for swimming, waterskiing, boating, windsurfing, and fishing.

Even closer to Seoul is the Paldang Reservoir, which is especially noted for sailing. Not far away is the Yongmun Mountain, excellent for short hikes in autumn, which has the Yongmunsa Temple, founded in the Silla Dynasty period. There is also a huge gingko tree, said to be over 1,000 years old, and a number of pretty waterfalls.

It is possible to visit any of the above attractions in a day trip from Seoul, but good, inexpensive accommodations are available if you decide to stay longer. Bear in mind, however, that during the most popular seasons for these resorts, finding a place to stay at the last minute may be difficult.

Royal Tombs at Kumkok

The last resting places of King Kojong, his son Sunjong—the last Yi king—and their queens are unique in Korea because each tomb is approached along an avenue of 18 stone animals. These animals are miniature copies of the great avenue of animals through which one approaches the Ming tombs in China. The decorations here are smaller but still interesting and imposing. King Sunjong's are the most elaborate; this tomb is, in fact, by far the grandest of all Yi Dynasty burials—the animals and statues of attendant civil and military officials were carved with great attention to detail by skilled Chinese craftsmen. At King Kojong's tomb, on the left of the entrance to the tomb grounds, the workmanship is quite different—indeed, the elephants and camels seem to have been carved by craftsmen who had never actually seen the live animals. Nevertheless, they have their own peculiar charm. Beyond the avenues of statues stand the usual shrine buildings, and behind them are the high-mounded tombs. Sunjong's tomb is properly called Yunung and Kojkong's, Hongnung.

Kumkok is inevitably a popular picnic and recreation area. No one—least of all the buried royalty—seems to mind that people play badminton or drink sodas between the tombs.

You can reach Kumkok by intercity bus from Chongnyangni train station (crowded), by taxi (expensive), or in leisurely fashion by slow train that leaves from Chongnyangni Station. It's an easy walk from the Kumkok train station to the tombs.

East Nine Tombs, Tonggunung

Instead of picnicking at Kumkok, you can catch a bus back to Seoul and get off at Tonggunung. It's a bit of a hike from the bus stop to the tomb area, but once you're there, you'll see that it's worth it—acres of green grass, low ridges, and an abundance of shady trees. It's such a huge area that you can easily find an isolated spot to have a quiet lunch, look at the scenery, and read about the turbulent history of the Yi Dynasty that took place here all around you.

Within this complex are nine royal tomb sites, each of them a variation on the standard pattern of royal tomb construction. They all have the following complement of structures: a *honsalmun,* or red arrow gate, to mark off the sacred enclosure; a *pigak,* or pavilion, to house the stele giving the biographical data of the royal figure interred; the *subokchong,* which houses the ritual implements used during the royal ancestral ceremonies; and the *chongjagak,* the building in which the ritual sacrifices were conducted.

The time span represented by the interred royalty at Tonggunung stretches from the first Yi monarch, Taejo (who founded the dynasty in 1392), to Honjong, who ruled from 1834 to 1849—more than 450 years. The Yi Dynasty lasted longer than any Chinese dynasty, and the stories and legends of the era and its rulers are truly fascinating.

Kwangnung, to the Northeast

Here you'll find more tombs. Again the setting is very pretty, with an avenue of tall, spreading trees leading to the tomb of King Sejo, who ruled from 1455 to 1468, and his queen consort, Chonghui. Although Sejo was an excellent administrator, he is more remembered as the king who deposed his nephew, the boy king Tanjong (who ruled only from 1452 to 1455) and had him murdered. This act became a major issue among Confucianists and brought into question the legitimacy of Sejo's line. Courtiers who attempted to restore the rightful king were executed. The tombs of six of these loyalists are located opposite the National Cemetery in Seoul, across the Seoul-Inchon Highway, marked by a tall stone monument on top of an evergreen hill overlooking the Han-gang River.

King Sejo is also remembered for his support of Buddhism, and the construction of the Wongaksa Temple on the site of today's Pagoda Park in Seoul. The temple pagoda remains, and represents the last flowering of Buddhist art in Korea.

In the neighborhood of the Kwangnung Tombs is the Botanical Experimental Station (turn right after leaving the Kwangnung parking lot), where you can wander through the grounds. There is also an interesting botanical museum.

TO THE WEST

Haengjusan-song Fortress

This is a mountain fortress commanding the north bank of the Han-gang River west of Seoul, site of a famous victory over the Japanese in 1593. Within the fortification are several worthwhile sights, particularly if you have developed an interest in sixteenth-century Korean warfare. There is a shrine to the spirit of General Kwon Yul, who led the Korean victory, although this was only built in 1973 to replace the original that was destroyed in the Korean War. From here you can look east, toward the mouth of the Han-gang River. Above the shrine, on the way up the mountain, is a small museum dedicated to the great battle, with three large paintings showing the course of the fighting, and many military relics. Among these are rocket launches used to fire multitudes of arrows, various old guns, several types of cannon, different arrows, and examples of cask and tube bombs. Near the mountaintop are two monuments to commemorate the battle, one erected in 1602 and the other larger and more modern. At the hill's summit is a refreshment stand (which you'll welcome after all this historical exploration), with spectacular views of the Han-gang River looking toward the west.

The Haengjusan-song Fortress is located near the north end of the Haengju Grand Bridge, easiest to reach by taxi.

Inchon

A small fishing village called Chemulpo during the 1880s, Inchon is today a thriving harbor and major industrial site. Historically, it has been an important port since the time of the Kingdom of Koguryo, which occupied the area in 475. It served central Korea during the Unified Silla period (670–935) and Koryo period (935–1392), and during the Yi Dynasty became even more important as the port which linked the capital with China. More recently, Inchon has had interest as the site of the earliest foreign communities in Korea, at the end of the nineteenth century. However, today Inchon is undoubtedly best known as the scene of General Douglas MacArthur's brilliantly successful Inchon landing, a military maneuver that led to the recapture of Seoul from the North Koreans only 12 days after the assault. The general is memorialized with a bronze statue (famous cap, sunglasses, and all) facing the Yellow Sea from a hill in Chayu Park (Freedom Park). He's accompanied by another memorial sculpture, set up in 1982, to commemorate 100 years of diplomatic ties and friendship between the United States and Korea. The sculpture includes two abstract forms, suggestive of a linked chain.

Below Freedom Park is a small museum which houses the city's collection of archeological and historical materials. Also below Freedom Park is Chinatown, containing some of the most interesting groupings of early twentieth-century Chinese architecture to be seen anywhere.

To appreciate the tidal rise and fall for which the Yellow Sea is famous, you need only wander down to the mud flats. When the tide is out, they stretch a long way in a gentle slope down to the water's edge. Where the coastline is rocky, the tide rises more than an inch per minute.

The Hotel Olympos, situated on a small hill (Inchon is an uphill-downhill city), commands a fine view of the harbor and operates a casino, one of the seven in Korea.

Near the hotel is the lively wharf area, also worth visiting to see the Protestant Centennial Monument, erected to commemorate the arrival in Korea of the first Protestant missionaries, on Easter Sunday, 1885. The monument is 55 feet high and consists of three arches from which is suspended a central cross. At the base are three statues, of the Reverend and Mrs. Henry Appenzeller (Methodist) and the Reverend Horace Underwood (Presbyterian). The grandson of Horace Underwood today runs one of the schools for foreign children in Seoul.

For the seafood that has made Inchon famous, venture out to Wolmido (Moon Tail Island) or Sowolmido (Small Moon Tail Island)—they're both land linked to the mainland—and enjoy platters of fresh fish, either raw or grilled. Korean raw fish is not given any fancy treatment—it's killed and served on the spot and is considered a very special delicacy.

You can pick out your own fish "on the fin" at Inchon's massive seafood market. Here you'll find almost any kind of edible sea life—fresh, frozen, or dried. Some people go even further, however, and catch their own. It's possible to hire a boat for the day—and some people even catch something.

In summer, many people head for Inchon to catch a ferry to one of the outer islands, to bask on white-sand beaches, swim in the gentle waves of the Yellow Sea, or relax under awnings. The Songdo Resort is about a 20-minute taxi ride south of Inchon city and is a good place to spend an afternoon picnicking and boating on a small lake. Monkeys are a popular attraction here.

Walking east of the Songdo Railway Station for about 15 minutes will bring you to the foreigners' cemetery, located on a small knoll south of the main road. This was the first burial ground for foreigners in the country and contains the remains of sailors, merchants, diplomats, and missionaries, mainly from the turn of the century.

Inchon is an hour's ride by subway from Seoul. Be sure you get the train marked Inchon, not Suwon; all the subways from the City Hall station of the No. 1 line go to one or the other. Once there, the easiest way to travel is by taxi. You could make the return journey more entertaining by taking the narrow-gauge railway from Songdo Station in Inchon to Suwon, and taking the subway from there back to Seoul. The Inchon-Suwon rail trip of 31 miles takes about an hour and a half.

Kanghwado Island

A large island in the Yellow Sea linked to the mainland by a bridge that spans the swiftly flowing Yomha Straits, Kanghwado is rich in history. The oldest artifact on the island is a prehistoric dolmen dating to Paleolithic times. Possibly an ancient tomb, the three slabs of stone are about two miles northwest of Kanghwa town in the midst of a farmer's vegetable garden.

Next oldest, at least in legend, is Tangun's altar on top of Manisan, a 1,500-foot peak on the opposite side of the island from Kanghwa town. Tangun, Korea's mythical founder, born of a heavenly god and a she-bear, is said to have erected the earth altar here in 2333 B.C. to worship his father. More likely, it was built during the seventeenth or eighteenth century as part of a cult of the legendary king. The climb to reach the altar rewards the hiker with a lovely view of the sea as well.

Chongdungsa (Temple of the Inherited Lamp) is on the southern end of the island, about 20 miles from Kanghwa town, and was built in A.D. 381. It still contains a few wooden blocks of the thirteenth-century version of the famed Tripitaka Koreana Buddhist scriptures that were carved here in a plea for divine help in driving off Mongol invaders. That act of faith was only partially successful: the Mongols did not invade Kanghwado, where the king had fled from Seoul, possibly because they were deterred by the swift flow of the straits. The palace that housed the exiled king for 39 years in Kanghwa town has been restored, as have several of the fortifications built to keep more recent invaders—the French and the Americans—out of Korea.

During the nineteenth century, an American naval force shelled the island's defenders in retribution for the sinking of an American ship, and the French burned the town in revenge for the execution of some French priests. They also tried to haul away the town bell but didn't succeed: It weighs 8,624 pounds and hangs in its pavilion in Kanghwa town today.

A beautiful, traditional Korean-style Anglican church is located up an alley north of the Kanghwa town main market. This was built in 1900, restored in 1984, and is the oldest church building in the Korean architectural style. It is a protected government cultural property.

At the northern end of the island is a military checkpoint, and if you can talk your way past the soldiers, you can gaze across the straits at North Korea. A sign made of large whitewashed stones proclaims the Korean language equivalent of "Yankee, go home."

Modern Kanghwa town is small and easygoing, and a good place to buy the white rush mats and baskets that local people are known for weaving.

From the west side of Kanghwado Island, you can take a ferry across to the islet of Songmodo to see the Pomunsa Temple, which claims to have been founded by a Silla monk in 635. The temple is noted for a grotto containing figures of the 16 disciples of the Buddha, and for a large statue of the Bodhisattva Kwanum created in 1928. The ferry crossing takes about 20 minutes and the temple is a 20-minute taxi ride from the ferry landing.

Buses for Kanghwado Island leave every 10 minutes from the Shinchon Bus Terminal in western Seoul; the trip takes one and a half hours. On Kanghwado itself, plan a leisurely day riding local buses or hire a taxi for the day. As you tour the island, notice the fields of ginseng, the plants lying sheltered under low straw roofs.

PRACTICAL INFORMATION FOR SEOUL

GETTING TO SEOUL. Most travelers enter Korea through Kimpo International Airport, about 11 miles west of downtown Seoul. In addition to Korean Air, the privately owned national airline, some 21 scheduled airlines fly into the Korean capital. More are likely to start services during the months to come.

Another airport terminal has opened on the south side of the Han-gang River in the Samsung district of Kangnam-ku. This new terminal became operational in about the middle of 1988, handling departure formalities for passengers and their baggage. Passengers entering the country will also be able to go through immigration procedures at the airport, and claim their baggage at the Kangnam terminal—similar to the system that now operates between Narita Airport and the downtown terminal in Tokyo.

A new international airport is scheduled to open in Taegu, located approximately 185 miles from Seoul in North Kyongsang Province, at the end of 1993. However, the project may be delayed for political reasons.

The new airport terminal in Kangnam was part of a massive extension to the present Korea Exhibition Center complex, which also involved the construction of a 54-story world trade center, a department store, and the 650-room deluxe Inter-Continental Hotel. The hotel opened in the middle of 1988.

Other ways to reach Seoul are by bus or train from Pusan, if you arrive in Korea through Kimhae International Airport in Pusan, or have taken a ferry from Shimonoseki or Osaka in Japan. An express bus (W7,770) or train (W21,000 for first-class or W16,400 economy class) Saemaul Super-Express, will bring you to Seoul from Pusan in four and one half hours. From Seoul Station or the Express Bus Terminal, you can then take a city bus, the subway, or a taxi to your hotel.

You can, of course, also fly from Pusan on domestic service—a shuttle flight leaves for Seoul every hour between 8 A.M. and 9 P.M. daily. The current fare is W31,500 one-way, flight time is 50 minutes, and you land at Kimpo Airport. For more details on getting to Seoul, refer to the *Facts at Your Fingertips* section of this guide.

GETTING AROUND. From the airport. You can get to the City Hall area in downtown Seoul by airport bus (No. 601, W580); by express city bus (No. 63 or 68, W470); by regular taxi (about W4,500); or by the larger 88 taxi (about W6,000), identified by an "88 Taxi" label on the side of the car. The ride will take around 30 minutes. If you take a taxi, make sure the meter is turned on—some drivers, especially of the 88 taxis, like to charge a flat fee. If you need to go to the south side of the Han-gang River, to the area of the Express Bus Terminal or farther to the Seoul Sports Complex, take the airport bus No. 600 (W580) or a taxi (W4,000–W6,000), and expect it to take between 30 and 50 minutes, depending on your destination. Some of the hotels run their own buses to the airport, so check with the airport information counter to see if your hotel has such a service.

Public Transportation around Town. Quite often the most practical way of getting around the city is on foot. Most places of interest lie within a relatively small area around City Hall and the old capitol building, now the National Museum. But for getting around the longer distances of the city, you have several choices of transportation that all run frequently.

The purple buses cost W210 if you use a token (purchased at little kiosks scattered along most city streets), or W220 if you pay in cash. You pay at the front as you enter and exit by a center door. These buses are often very crowded, especially at rush hours. Or you can take the **green "sit buses,"** where everyone gets a seat (the driver simply doesn't take on more passengers once the bus is full). The fare is W500. So far, it doesn't sound too difficult. Here's the problem: All buses are marked with numbers and signs indicating their routes and stops—but they're only in Korean. Many bus stops now have wonderful directories, where you push a button for your destination and little lights tell you the buses that serve it in both Korean and English; but bus maps are hard to find, routes change with astonishing frequency, and the distance between stops can be lengthy. The Koreans, however, seem to understand the system well and you can ask at your hotel for assistance.

The subways are better—wonderful in fact. The city's four-line network was completed in 1986—a total of over 72 miles, and it is being expanded. The system is new, modern, and efficient, connecting most of the major areas of the city. Line 1 runs through the center of the city under Chongno Street (connecting the main rail stations, Seoul Station and Chongnyangni Station). It emerges aboveground with branch lines to Suwon in the south, Inchon on the west coast, and Uijongbu in the north. Line 2 makes a circuit of the city, crossing the Han-gang River to the south. Called the "loop line," it serves the Seoul Sports Complex. Line 3 runs from the northwest to the southeast, linking both sides of the Han-gang River through the heart of downtown. Line 4 is its mirror opposite, running northeast to southwest. The city is divided into two zones, with fares of W250 in the inner zone, W350 to go farther. It costs a little more to link up by subway with the lines of the National Railroad—for example, W550 from the center of town to Inchon, W600 to Suwon.

Subway tickets can be purchased at automatic machines, or at ticket windows (you may find this easier than interpreting the machine's instructions). You use the ticket to go through the turnstile; the turnstile spits it out again. Keep the ticket—you'll need it to get out.

One of the pleasures of the subway system these days is that just about all the signs and maps are written in both Korean and English. Finding your way out of the stations to where you want to be aboveground can be confusing, though, as you often have to walk through a maze of arcades and exit passages. Remember that the subway, like all forms of public transport in Seoul, can be crowded at rush hours.

Taxis are plentiful, except when it's raining, or around 3:30 P.M., when it seems as if all taxis are rushing back to their depots to change shifts. Most drivers are friendly and willing to practice their English. Their language skills are improving all the time, not just through increasing contact with tourists, but because of special language training, provided to boost Seoul's services for the Olympics.

For regular taxis (the small cars in all colors), the fare is W750 for the flag drop (the first 1.25 miles), with an additional W50 every quarter mile.

A new system has introduced a time/distance addition: passengers must pay an extra W50 every 96 seconds in addition to the basic fare when the taxi runs at less than 10 miles per hour (in heavy city traffic, for example). From midnight to 4 A.M., there is a surcharge of 20 percent, which is added to the meter fare. It is not necessary to tip drivers unless they assist you with baggage. Covered taxi stands are found all over the city, and it is permissible to hail a taxi on the street. You do not give a taxi driver a street address; instead, you tell him the area of the city you want to go to, or even better, the name of a nearby prominent landmark. You direct him right or left from there. To avoid confusion, ask someone to write out your destination in Korean.

Today, however, only a few small taxis still operate; almost all taxis in Seoul these days are "88 taxis", which are different. They are always white, with an "88 Taxi" identification on the side. They are larger than the regular taxis, and usually air-conditioned. The fare is W800 for the first 1¼ miles, W100 for each additional ¼ mile. Again, you can hail these on the street or pick one up at a taxi stand. The hotel concierge can arrange an 88 call, or you can telephone any of several operators in the city (one company can be reached at 414–0150), but language can be a problem when ordering.

There is another kind of taxi, identified by a "Tourist Taxi" label on the side. These are a muddy shade of brown and usually don't have meters. Be careful, for they are expensive. They will charge a minimum of W10,000 for a short journey within the city center, and more as you get farther afield. Find out how much you'll be charged before you get in. At our press time, only a handful of hotels were operating tourist taxis, so do not expect to see an abundance of them.

You may decide to **hire a car,** but if you're not used to driving in traffic such as that in Seoul, do yourself a favor and hire a driver, too. There are many rental agencies, and most can arrange for English-speaking drivers. Your hotel will be able to help with the arrangements, or you can call Korea Car Rental Union (552–8772). The union has offices scattered around the city and a good range of cars, all Korean-made. Rates range from W29,150 to W101,200 per 10 hours, including insurance (but you'll need to pay extra for collision-damage coverage). A driver costs W39,500 for the 10-hour day, including his meals. There are special rates for weekly hire, and arrangements can be made for you to leave the car in another city. The drop-off charge to leave a Seoul car in Pusan, for example, would be W45,000.

More information on driving in Korea can be found in the *Facts at Your Fingertips* section of this guide.

ACCOMMODATIONS. Accommodations in Seoul are basically of two types—Western-style hotels and Korean inns (*yogwan*). On the whole, the hotels are more expensive than the inns, though some good-quality inns overlap in price range with modest hotels. The hosting of the 1988 Summer Olympics has brought many accommodation benefits for Seoul's tourist travelers. Most of the hotels have undergone major face-lifts and have upgraded and added facilities to cater to a wider variety of visitors.

Our list of hotels is divided by class into five groups: superior deluxe, deluxe, 1st class, 2d class, and 3d class. We have not always used the rankings of the Korea National Tourism Corporation, which is inclined to group hotels into broad price categories rather than in accordance with the scope and quality of facilities. One of our categories, superior deluxe, is in addition to the KNTC grading. You will see some price overlaps between the other categories—a room at a good first-class hotel, for example, could cost as much as a room at the lower end of the deluxe hotel scale. But you can expect a similar range of facilities and services.

Our categories are priced as follows, for a twin or double room: *Superior Deluxe,* W125,000 to W190,000; *Deluxe,* W90,000 to W125,000; *1st class,* W60,000 to W80,000; *2d class,* W40,000 to W60,000; and *3d class,* W30,000 to W40,000.

These prices do not include a standard 10 percent service charge, and 10 percent Value Added Tax (VAT). Most goods and services in Korea are subject to this 10 percent Value Added Tax, including spending at hotels. However, items billed to a foreign visitor's hotel room account are exempt from VAT. Everything that you sign for in the hotel, therefore, will be exempt from tax, but on your spending outside (when you use cash or a credit card)—even at the restaurants of other hotels—you'll be charged 10 percent VAT, in addition to the service charge. (See under "Taxes," in the *Facts at Your Fingertips* section of this guide.)

Occupancies can run high in Seoul, particularly at the top end of the accommodation scale. The capital is very much the center of business and trade, so the best seasons climatically are not just the peak times for tourist arrivals but also for international conferences and buying missions. The situation is being eased by the opening of lots more hotels, including several affiliated with international chains, but you would still be advised to have a confirmed reservation in Seoul before you arrive. Months to be especially careful are April–May and September–October. (See also the "Staying in Korea" section of *Facts at Your Fingertips* for details on accommodations.)

Here are some brief descriptions of hotels in Seoul, divided by area of the city. Credit card abbreviations are as follows: American Express, AE; Diner's Club, DC; MasterCard, MC; Visa, V.

Near City Hall Plaza

Superior Deluxe

Lotte. 1, Sogong-dong, Chung-ku, Seoul; Tel. 771–1000, Telex K2353315, Fax. (02) 752–3758. With 1,484 rooms, the Lotte is Seoul's largest hotel/department store complex. It has over 20 restaurants and cocktail lounges, and a nightclub with international shows. The lobby lounge is one of the city's most popular meeting places. The hotel connects underground with the Lotte Department Store and extensions of the Sogong Arcade. Credit cards: AE, DC, MC, V.

Seoul Plaza. 23, 2-ka, Taepyongno, Chung-ku, Seoul; Tel. 771–2200, Telex K26215, Fax. (02) 756–3610. 540 rooms, many overlooking the City Hall and Toksu-kung Palace area. The top-floor cocktail lounge is a great place from which to watch the traffic heading off in all directions from City Hall Plaza. It provides a number of good restaurants, and the lower floor has an arcade of shops linking up with the underground Sogong Arcade. Credit cards: AE, DC, MC, V.

Westin Chosun. 87, Sogong-dong, Chung-ku, Seoul; Tel. 771–500, Telex K24256, Fax. (02) 752–1443. About 480 rooms, many of them especially furnished for business visitors. Excellent restaurants include the Ninth Gate, one of the city's best French/Continental restaurants, a top-floor lunchtime buffet, and a Japanese Sushi room. O'Kim's Pub is lively. The lower level has a flower market, and access to underground arcades. Credit cards: AE, DC, MC, V.

1st class

President. 188-3, 1-ga, Ulchiro, Chung-ku, Seoul; Tel. 753–3131, Telex K27521, Fax. (02) 752–7417. Has 300 rooms, on the eastern edge of City Hall Plaza, between the Lotte and Westin Chosun. Guests are predominantly Japanese; restaurants are limited. Credit cards: AE, DC, MC, V.

Near Kwanghwamun Intersection

Deluxe

Koreana. 61-1, 1-ka Taepyongno, Chung-ku, Seoul; Tel. 730–9911, Telex K26241, Fax. (02) 734–0665. Has 280 rooms in a building that is also an office complex, within easy walking distance of City Hall, the National Museum, and major palaces. Mainly caters to Japanese guests; has a popular coffee shop overlooking the street. Credit cards: AE, DC, MC, V.

1st class

New Seoul. 29-1, 1-ka, Taepyongno, Chung-ku, Seoul; Tel. 735–9071, Telex K27220, Fax. (02) 735–6212. Located behind the Press Center, with just 141 rooms. Credit cards: AE, DC, MC, V.

Seoulin. 149, Sorin-dong, Chongno-ku, Seoul; Tel. 732–6000, Telex K28510, Fax. (02) 732–2774. Just over 200 rooms, in a location that is just five minutes from City Hall. Good value in western and Japanese restaurants. Credit cards: AE, DC, MC, V.

2d class

New Nai ja. 201–9, Nai ja-dong, Chongno-ku, Seoul; Tel. 737–9011, Fax. 730–6939. With 68 rooms, almost directly across the street from Kyongbok Palace and the National Museum. Caters mainly to Americans. Credit cards: AE, DC, MC, V.

Seoul Tourist Hotel. 92, Chongjin-dong, Chongno-ku, Seoul; Tel. 735–9001, Fax. (02) 733–0101. A small hotel (about 100 rooms), with Western and Japanese restaurants, and a cocktail lounge. Credit cards: AE, DC, MC, V.

3d class

YMCA. 9, 2-ka, Chongno-Chongno-ku, Seoul; Tel. 732–8291. Has less than 80 rooms, and in spite of its name accepts both male and female guests. On the fringes of the "near Kwanghwamun" area, but a most handy location for catching the subway or exploring the busy Chongno avenue. Has a small restaurant. Credit cards: AE, DC, MC, V.

In Myong-dong

1st class

Seoul Royal. 6, 1-ka, Myong-dong, Chung-ku, Seoul; Tel. 756–1112, Telex K27239, Fax. (02) 756–1119. Over 300 rooms in an excellent location for enjoying the fashionable days and lively nights of Myong-dong. It caters mainly to Japanese guests and has a good collection of facilities. Credit cards: AE, DC, MC, V.

2d class

Savoy. 23-1, 1-ka, Chungmuro, Chung-ku, Seoul; Tel. 776–2641, Telex K23222, Fax. (02) 755–7669. A small hotel, again in an excellent spot for the pleasures of Myong-dung. Credit cards: AE, DC, MC, V.

Along and Near Toegyero Street

Toegyero Street is a wide, busy boulevard that crosses the southern part of the central city, at the base of Namsan Mountain. Along its length are a number of small hotels, many of them in the 2d-class category, but all offer a good collection of facilities near to Myong-dong, the Namdaemun market, and the city center. Here are some examples:

Deluxe

Ambassador. 186-54, 2-ka, Changchung-dong, Chung-ku, Seoul; Tel. 275–1101, Telex K23269, Fax. (02) 272–0773. Over 400 rooms in a grand hill-top setting above Toegyero. A little farther away from the city center but a short stroll to Changchungdan Park. Credit cards: AE, DC, MC.

1st class

King Sejong. 61-3, 2-ka, Chungmuro, Chung-ku, Seoul; Tel. 776–1811, Telex K27265, Fax. (02) 755–4906. On the far south end of Myong-dong, on Toegyero facing Namsan Mountain. Owned and operated by Sejong University, 250 rooms. Well known for its Korean buffet. Credit cards: AE, DC, MC, V.

Pacific. 31-1, 2-ka, Namsan-dong, Chung-ku, Seoul; Tel. 777–7811, Telex K26249, Fax. (02) 755–5582. Off Toegyero, opposite the southern end of Myong-dong, with just over 100 rooms. A good range of facilities. Credit cards: AE, DC, MC, V.

2d class

Astoria. 13-2, Namhak-dong, Chung-ku, Seoul; Tel. 267–7111, Fax. (02) 274–3187. Near the Toegyero-Chungmuro intersection, handy to Korea House (a traditional restaurant, theater, and display of handicrafts worth visiting). Minimum facilities, 80 guest rooms. Credit cards: AE, DC, MC, V.

Seoul Prince. 1-1, 2-ka, Namsan-dong, Chung-ku, Seoul; Tel. 752–7111, Telex K25918, Fax. (02) 752–7119. Very basic facilities, but good value. Credit cards: AE, DC, MC, V.

On the Slopes of Namsan Mountain

Superior Deluxe

Hyatt Regency Seoul. 747-7, Hannam-dong, Yongsan-ku, Seoul; Tel. 797–1234, Telex K24136, Fax. (02) 798–6953). On the southern side of Namsan, with outstanding views of the Han-gang River and beyond. The location is also good for its proximity to Itaewon, the best shopping area for foreign visitors. The hotel was redecorated in 1987, and is highlighted by a fine selection of restaurants, including Hugo's—a renowned Hyatt name for Western/Continental dining. A health club, indoor pool, plus good outdoor facilities including a pool and tennis courts. 600 rooms. Credit cards: AE, DC, MC, V.

Seoul Hilton International. 395, 5-ka, Namdaemunno, Chung-ku, Seoul; Tel. 753–7788, Telex K26695, Fax. (02) 753–2361. On the eastern edge of Namsan, overlooking Seoul Station and the Namdaemun Gate, 714 guest rooms, and an impressive collection of restaurants for all tastes, including Italian, Chinese, and Japanese. Also noted for buffets and brunches. Has a health club, indoor pool. Part of the hotel complex is the city's largest private convention center, with sophisticated conference and exhibition facilities. Credit cards: AE, DC, MC, V.

Shilla. 202, 2-ka, Changchung-dong, Chung-ku, Seoul; Tel. 233–3131, Telex K24160, Fax. (02) 233–5073. On the northeastern slope of the mountain—640 rooms, and a full range of restaurants and facilities. Its grounds are enriched by the beautiful Korean architecture of the old government guest house, now a banquet annex of the hotel. La Continental, the top-floor French restaurant is the most expensive in the city, and excellent. Has a health club, swimming pool, and tennis courts. Credit cards: AE, DC, MC, V.

1st class

Tower. 5-5, 2-ka, Changchung-dong. Chung-ku, Seoul; Tel. 236–2121, Telex K28246, Fax. (02) 235–0276. East of Namsan, opposite the National Theater. A good collection of facilities, including tennis courts and one of the city's largest outdoor swimming pools. 205 rooms. Credit cards: AE, DC, MC, V.

Itaewon Area

Deluxe

Seoul Capital. 22–76, Itaewon-dong, Yongsan-ku, Seoul; Tel. 792–1122, Telex K23502, Fax. (02) 796–0918. This hotel opened in 1988, with 287 rooms. Offering a variety of restaurants, its chief attraction is its location in the popular entertainment and shopping district of Itaewon. Credit cards: AE, DC, MC, V.

1st class

Crown. 34-69, Itaewon-dong, Yongsan-ku, Seoul; Tel. 797–4111, Telex K25951, Fax. (02) 796–1010. With just over 150 rooms and basic facilities, this hotel owes most of its business to its proximity to Itaewon shopping and nightlife, and the nearby U.S. Army base. Credit cards: AE, DC, MC, V.

In Mapo District

This area in southeast Seoul, on the north side of the Han-gang River, is a new area of Seoul as far as hotels are concerned. Until recently, the only hotel of note was contracted out to the U.S. military, but the Seoul Garden (see below) has now been refurnished as a business and tourism hotel. Other hotels nearby were constructed recently. The new hotels are a different concept for Seoul—the "office-hotel"—which incorporates an office building with limited accommodation and restaurant facilities.

Deluxe

Seoul Garden. 169-1, Tohwa-dong, Mapo-ku, Seoul; Tel. 717–9441, Telex K24742, Fax. (02) 715–9441. With 390 rooms, refurnished in 1986. Facilities include a grill restaurant (featuring Middle Eastern specialties), coffee shop, and nightclub. Credit cards: AE, DC, MC, V.

1st class

Seokyo. 354-5, Sogyo-dong, Mapo-ku, Seoul; Tel. 333–7771, Telex K26780, Fax. (02) 333–3388. Just over 100 rooms, at the eastern edge of the Mapo district. Facilities include a health club with indoor and outdoor swimming pools. Credit cards: AE, DC, MC, V.

On Yoido Island

1st class

Manhattan. 13-3, Yoido-dong, Youngdungpo-ku, Seoul; Tel. 780–8001, Telex K24767, Fax. (02) 784–2332. Close to the airport; near the National Assembly Building. With 180 rooms and good basic facilities. Credit cards: AE, DC, V.

2d class

Yoido Tourist Hotel. 10-3, Yoido-dong, Youngdungpo-ku, Seoul; Tel. 782–0121, Fax. (02) 785–2510. Has 116 rooms, also close to the National Assembly Building and the Yoido Plaza. Credit cards: AE, DC, MC, V.

South of the Han-gang River

Superior Deluxe

Inter Continental Seoul. 159-8, Samsung-dong, Kangnam-ku, Seoul; Tel. 555–5656, Telex K34254, Fax. (02) 559–7990. With 602 rooms, and several restaurants, health club, indoor swimming pool and large conference facilities. Credit cards: AE, DC, MC, V.

Lotte World 40-1 Chamshil-dong, Songpa-ku, Seoul; Tel. 419–7000, Telex K33756128, Fax. (02) 417–3655. With 530 rooms, this hotel is actually a hotel/department store/theme park complex. Facilities include 11 restaurants, health club, folk village, trade show center, satellite studio, ice skating rink, bowling alley, and theater. Credit cards: AE, MC, DC, V.

Ramada Renaissance. 676, Yoksam-dong, Kangnam-ku, Seoul; Tel. 555–0501, Telex K34392, Fax. (02) 553–8118. With 500 rooms, the Ramada offers a variety of restaurants and a health club. Credit cards: AE, DC, MC, V.

Deluxe

Riverside. 6-1, Chamwon-dong, Kangnam-ku, Seoul; Tel. 543–1001, Telex K22063, Fax. (02) 543–5310. More than 180 rooms, just over the Hannam Grand Bridge. A full range of facilities, including a health club with indoor and outdoor swimming pools. Credit cards: AE, DC, MC, V.

Seoul Palace. 135, 63-1, Panpo-dong, Socho-ku, Seoul; Tel. 523–0101, Telex K22657, Fax. (02) 532–0399. 300 rooms, near the Express Bus Terminal. A good collection of facilities and restaurants, particularly popular with Japanese guests. Credit cards: AE, DC, MC, V.

1st class

Nam Seoul Washington. 602-4, Yoksam-dong, Kangnam-ku, Seoul; Tel. 552–7111, Telex K25019, Fax. (02) 556–8855. Facilities include a health club and a theater-restaurant. 205 rooms. Credit cards: AE, DC, MC, V.

Sam Jung. 604-11, Yoksam-dong, Kangnam-ku, Seoul; Tel. 557–1221, Telex K26680, Fax. (02) 556–1126. Has 160 rooms, in one of the busiest commercial districts south of the river. Good basic facilities. Credit cards: AE, DC, MC, V.

2d class

Young Dong. 6, Non-hyun-dong, Kangnam-ku, Seoul; Tel. 542–0112, Telex K29310, Fax. (02) 546–8409. 160 rooms, in one of the liveliest entertainment sections of the Shinsa-dong area. Good basic facilities, including a theater-restaurant. Credit cards: AE, DC, MC, V.

Farther Afield

Superior Deluxe

Sheraton Walker Hill. San 21, Kwangjang-dong, Songdong-ku, Seoul; Tel. 453–0121, Telex K28517, Fax. (02) 452–6867. This hotel complex has long been recognized as a major resort, and has the distinction of housing Seoul's only casino. It has a highly popular theater-restaurant that is featured on many Seoul night-tour itineraries. It also has several swimming pools with great slides and chutes, tennis courts, and a golf driving range. 629 rooms, to the city's southeast, overlooking the Kwangnaru Resort area of the Han-gang River. Credit cards: AE, DC, MC, V.

Swiss Grand. 201-1, Hongeun-dong, Soedaemun-ku, Seoul; Tel. 356–5656, Telex K34322, Fax (02) 356–7799. Located in a parklike area on the northwest fringes of the city. Swiss, Italian, Japanese, Chinese, and Korean restaurants, and plenty of recreation facilities including a health club, swimming pool, and tennis courts. Credit cards: AE, DC, MC, V.

Deluxe

Ramada Olympia. 108-2, Pyongchang-dong, Chongno-ku, Seoul; Tel. 353–5121, Telex K23171, Fax. (02) 353–8118. In a scenic valley north of the city, with excellent views of the northern mountains. A good range of restaurants, facilities, and services. 310 rooms. Credit cards: AE, DC, MC, V.

2d class

Bukak Park. 113-1, Pyongchang-dong, Chongno-ku, Seoul; Tel. 352–7101, Fax. (02) 356–5559. 120 rooms, located north of the city near the Ramada Olympia. A beautiful mountain setting, and very basic facilities. Credit cards: AE, DC, MC, V.

Green Park. San 14, Ui-dong, Tobong-ku, Seoul; Tel. 900–8181, Fax. (02) 902–0030. On the slopes of the Pukhansan Mountain in northeastern Seoul, 90 rooms. Very basic facilities, but features a large outdoor pool and tennis courts. Credit cards: AE, MC, V.

Hankang Tourist Hotel. 188-2, Kwangjang-dong, Songdong-ku, Seoul;
Tel. 453–5131, Fax. (02) 455–4921. With 120 rooms, near the Sheraton
Walker Hill Hotel, overlooking the Kwangnaru Resort. Basic facilities,
and an outdoor swimming pool. Credit cards: AE, MC, V.

Korean Inns (Yogwan).

There are many Korean-style inns in the city.
Finding them can be a problem, however, as they are often tucked away
in remote corners. Costs per night range from W12,000 to W30,000 per
room. Remember that the facilities will be basic—and you will undoubtedly have more of a language problem than at a hotel. Yogwan rarely have
any restaurant facilities but you can usually arrange in advance for a Korean breakfast or dinner. Almost all of the yogwan recommended here have
private baths and toilets. If you happen to stay in a yogwan that has public
baths, remember not to clean yourself in the tubs; these are for soaking
after you're clean. More general information on the Korean inns is in the
Facts at Your Fingertips section.

Here is a list of yogwan scattered around Seoul, most of which offer
a choice of Western- or Korean-style rooms. This is really just a random
sample; there are literally hundreds of the inns in all areas of the city.

North of the Han-gang River

Arirang. 103-1, Wonnam-dong, Chongno-ku (Tel. 745–4114). 14 Korean, 20 Western rooms.

Chahamun. 119, Kugi-dong, Chongno-ku (Tel. 354–7771). 9 Korean,
26 Western rooms.

Chonpung. 58, Toson-dong, Songdong-ku (Tel. 295–9365). 14 Korean,
32 Western rooms.

Chungsoojang. 829 Chungnung-dong, Songbuk-ku (Tel. 914–0731). 6
Korean, 6 Western rooms.

Dong Kwang. 416–1, Itaewon-dong, Yongsan-Ku (Tel. 795–8024).

Hanam. 16-1, Chong-dong, Chung-ku (Tel. 777–7181). 26 Korean, 12
Western rooms.

Junhuibin. 380–11, Hapchong-dong, Mapo-ku (Tel. 332–7771). 12 Korean, 20 Western rooms.

Kaya. 98-11, Karwol-dong, Yongsan-ku (Tel. 798–5101). 19 Korean,
32 Western rooms.

Paegunjang. 345-10, Changan-dong, Tongdaemun-ku (Tel. 212–9388).
17 Korean, 12 Western rooms.

Paekchon. 7-1, Pongik-dong, Chongno-ku (Tel. 742–6671). 16 Korean,
24 Western rooms.

Pagoda. 150-1, Nagwon-dong, Chongno-ku (Tel. 743–1411). 17 Korean, 17 Western rooms.

Palace. 92-6, Hoehyon-dong, Chung-ku (Tel. 777–7731). 7 Korean, 25
Western rooms.

Sehwajang. 36, Chongno 6-ga, Chongno-ku (Tel. 764-7431). 17 Korean,
20 Western rooms.

Jonggakjang. 38, Kongpyong-dong, Chung-ku (Tel. 735–4811). 10 Korean, 10 Western rooms.

Mirabo. 104-36, Taehyon-dong, Sodaemun-ku (Tel. 392–9511). 8 Korean, 30 Western rooms.

Taeyujang. 416-6, Changan-dong, Tongdaemun-ku (Tel. 247–4558). 17
Korean, 14 Western rooms.

West of the Kwanghwamun intersection, in the second alley north from
Sinmunno Street, are a couple of yogwan especially popular with young
travelers. These are the **Daiwon** and **Daeji** inns, costing around W8,000
per night.

South of the Han-gang River

Chamshiljang. 250-5, Chamshil-dong, Kangdong-ku (Tel. 415–3111).
12 Korean, 20 Western rooms.

Chongsanjang. 901-2, Pangbae-dong, Kangnam-ku (Tel. 582–0767). 10
Korean, 15 Western rooms.

Highland. 7-1, Nonhyun-dong, Kangnam-ku (Tel. 541–1250). 12 Korean, 43 Western rooms.

Highway. 444-1, Shinsa-dong, Kangnam-ku (Tel. 544–9394). 24 Korean, 59 Western rooms.

Myongwonjang. 99-11, Samsung-dong, Kangnam-ku (Tel. 546–7251).
11 Korean, 19 Western rooms.

Oska. 563-1, Panpo-dong, Kangnam-ku (Tel. 599–3155). 14 Korean,
16 Western rooms.

Silverstar. 182, Chamshil-dong, Kangdong-ku (Tel. 416–3131). 18 Korean, 24 Western rooms.

Sokchujang. 605-17, Yoksam-dong, Kangnam-ku (Tel. 562–2151). 16
Korean, 40 Western rooms.

Songnyu. 48-3, Chongdam-dong, Kangnam-ku (Tel. 543–5051). 17 Korean, 16 Western rooms.

Sunshine. 587-1, Shinsa-dong, Kangnam-ku (Tel. 541–1818). 16 Korean, 64 Western rooms.

Yewon. 603-5, Yoksam-dong, Kangnam-ku (Tel. 562–5101). 15 Korean, 32 Western rooms.

Youth Hostels. There are two youth hostels in Seoul, one on the north
side of the Han-gang River, the other on the south. Prices range from
around W6,500 per person for an eight-bunk room, to W38,000 for a twin
room. The Korea Youth Hostel Association has its headquarters in Seoul
at 27-1, Supyo-dong, Chung-ku (Tel. 266–2896), and will provide details
on membership and available facilities throughout the country.

Academy House. On the northern outskirts of Seoul at San 76, Suyoo-
dong, Tobong-ku, Seoul (Tel. 993–6181). Just 48 rooms including six-bunk
rooms and twins. Coffee shop, restaurant, and cocktail lounge. Credit
cards: AE, DC, MC, V.

Olympic Youth Hostel. 88, Pangi-dong, Songpa-ku (Tel. 421–2111).
Limited facilities. No credit cards.

S.E.C. Center. 202, Yangjae-dong, Socho-ku (Tel. 571–8100). A range
of bunk and private rooms. No credit cards.

RESTAURANTS. Seoul offers Chinese, Japanese, Italian, French, and,
of course, Korean cuisine in all its variations. Restaurants run the full
gamut, from the very luxurious and expensive to street stalls and alleyway
chicken eateries.

In the past, most of the good restaurants were in the major hotels, but
more and more independent places are opening, catering to both busi-
nessperson and tourist in all areas of the city. Prices vary widely. You can

pay as little as W4,500 for a simple rice or noodle dish at an inexpensive Korean or Chinese restaurant; W15,000 to W30,000 for lunch or dinner at a deluxe hotel restaurant; and up to W60,000 to W100,000 for an elaborate Korean dinner at the very high-class establishments.

Hotel restaurants are open seven days a week, with lunch usually from noon to 2:30 P.M. and dinner from 6 to 10 P.M. Independent restaurants are often closed twice a month. Most places don't require reservations, but at the better restaurants it is advisable. American Express, Diner's Club, MasterCard, and Visa are the most accepted credit cards. Price categories used are as follows for lunch or dinner for one person: *Deluxe,* W25,000–W40,000; *Expensive,* W15,000–W30,000; *Moderate,* W10,000–W20,000; *Inexpensive,* W8,000–W12,000. *Note:* These estimates do not include any taxes, service charges, or drinks. Bear in mind, too, that eating at a good Japanese restaurant, for example, would be on the high end of a category, a good meal at an Italian restaurant lower.

Following are some of the dining opportunities in Seoul.

Small Korean Restaurants

These are simply everywhere, always crowded at lunchtime, serving delicious noodles, rice dishes, the famous ginseng chicken, and beef soups. They are often specialty restaurants, serving just one or two of the traditional "fast foods." Unfortunately, language is a problem. It's easiest just to sit down and point to something served at a neighboring table. Prices are very reasonable—around W4,500 for *Pibimpap* (a rice dish with a fried egg and assorted vegetables); W4,500 for *Manduguk* (a soup with meatballs wrapped in dough); and W5,500 for *Samgyetang* (a small chicken stuffed with rice and ginseng in a tasty broth). Myong-dong is a good area for such small restaurants, as is the maze of small streets behind the Seoul Plaza Hotel. Just down the hill from the Hyatt Regency Hotel are a number of small places that are used to serving foreigners. These are larger than the average "fast-food" Korean restaurant, but prices are most reasonable.

Department Stores and Office Buildings

These provide some excellent, *inexpensive* opportunities to try a wide variety of different foods—Korean, Japanese, Chinese, and the ever-popular pizza.

DLI 63 (the Daehan Life Insurance Building on Yoido). The upper-floor restaurants are rather expensive (but the view is magnificent), while level B1 has buffet restaurants and fast-food corners that are good value.

Daewoo Building. Opposite Seoul Railway Station, the lower level of the building has small Korean, Chinese, and Japanese restaurants, and a pizzeria.

Dongbang Plaza. In the basement of the big, brown building to the northwest of the Namdaemun Gate are a dozen restaurants—again Korean, Japanese, Chinese, and Western (including a pizza place)—that are catered by the Shilla Hotel. Great value.

Kyobo Building. The brown building to the east of Admiral Yi's statue, just down from the Chongno and Sejong Street corner. The basement has a cafeteria-type restaurant. The mezzanine floor has a wonderful French restaurant overlooking the street. (See *L'Abri* under the Western/French/Continental heading below.) An excellent European-style bistro is located on the ground floor; prices are reasonable.

Lotte Shopping Center. Very near the Lotte Hotel. The ninth and tenth floors have 18 small Korean, Japanese, Chinese, and Western restaurants, plus tea shops, bakeries, and a curry house. Delightfully inexpensive. Closed on Tuesdays. Very crowded between noon and 1 P.M.

Korean

Bright Moon Hall (Sheraton Walker Hill Hotel). San 21, Kwangjang-dong, Songdong-ku, Seoul (Tel. 453–0121). *Deluxe–Expensive.* A charming name for a traditional-style restaurant, serving ribs and beef dishes.

Mu Gung Hwa (Hotel Lotte). 1, Sogong-dong, Chung-ku, Seoul (Tel. 771–1000). *Deluxe–Expensive.* A traditional setting, for a wide à la carte selection.

Daewongak. 323, Songbuk-dong, Songbuk-ku, Seoul (Tel. 762–0034). *Expensive.* Meals are served in small, thatch-roof pavilions scattered over a hillside in a premier residential area of the city. *Pulgogi* (barbecued beef) and *kalbi* (ribs) are served with a wide variety of side dishes. Very popular, so call for a reservation.

Eunhasoo (King Sejong Hotel). 61-3, 2-ka, Chungmuro, Chung-ku, Seoul (Tel. 776–1811). *Moderate.* Korean buffet, with traditional music.

Gardenia (Hotel Lotte). 1, Sogong-dong, Chung-ku, Seoul (Tel. 771–1000). *Moderate.* A daily buffet, good value.

Hanilgwan. 50-1, Myong-dong, Chung-ku, Seoul (Tel. 776–3388). *Moderate.* The largest of a chain of restaurants, with standard Korean fare.

Korea House. 80-2, Pildong, 2-ka, Chung-ku, Seoul (Tel. 266–9101). *Moderate.* An excellent buffet serving many dishes not normally found in other restaurants, all labeled in both Korean and English. There is also an à la carte menu. After dinner, you can watch a presentation of traditional Korean performing arts at a special theater. Closed Sundays and public holidays. Reservations recommended.

Koryo Samgyetang. 55-3, Sosomun-dong, Chung-ku, Seoul (Tel. 752–2734). *Moderate.* A specialty restaurant for Korea's famous ginseng chicken soup, *Samgyetang.*

Nak San Garden. 1-36, Tongsung-dong, Chongno-ku, Seoul (Tel. 742–7470). *Moderate.* Another popular *kalbi* house.

Nam Gang Garden. 140-3, Samsung-dong, Kangnam-ku, Seoul (Tel. 566–3819). *Moderate.* Another one specializing in *Kalbi.*

Pine Hill. 88-5, Cho-dong, 2-ka, Chung-ku, Seoul (Tel. 266–4486). *Moderate.* Chopped roast beef prepared on a Korean grill.

Sanchon. 2-2, Kwanhun-dong, Chongno-ku, Seoul (Tel. 735–1900). *Moderate.* Vegetarian Korean food.

Shin Jung. 21, 2-ka, Myong-dong, Chung-ku, Seoul (Tel. 776–1464). *Moderate.* Genghis Khan (hot pot of sliced beef and vegetables) and Korean roast beef.

Sukchonho. 28, Pangi-dong, Sonpa-ku, Seoul (Tel. 422–6050). *Moderate.* The specialty is broiled eel.

Vegetarian Korean

There are two branches of the one restaurant, the **Sanchon,** which is well known for its vegetarian cuisine prepared under the direction of a Buddhist priest. You must make reservations in advance, and you are given a choice of two different set menus, each costing W18,000. You'll be entertained by short presentations of Korean music and dance. The addresses are: 244-11, Huam-dong, Yongsan-ku (Tel. 777–9696), and 2-2, Kwanhun-dong, Chongno-ku (Tel. 735–1900). The latter is known as the Cafe Sarang and is in the area of Insa-dong, famous for its antique and art stores.

Chinese

Arisan. 258-6, Itaewon-dong, Yongsan-ku, Seoul (Tel. 794–0022). *Expensive.* Directly across from the entrance to the Hyatt Hotel.

Golden Dragon (Sheraton Walker Hill Hotel). San 21, Kwangjang-dong, Songdong-ku, Seoul (Tel. 453–0121). *Expensive.*

Hee Lae Deung. In Building B of the Namsan Village Apartments (near the Hyatt Hotel). San 10, Hannam-dong, Yongsan-ku, Seoul (Tel. 795–6633). *Expensive.* Szechuan cuisine.

The Phoenix (Seoul Hilton Hotel). 395, 5-ka, Namdaemunno, Chung-ku, Seoul (Tel. 753–7788). *Expensive.* Excellent buffet lunches.

San Su (Hyatt Regency Hotel). 747-7, Hannam-dong, Yongsan-ku, Seoul (Tel. 798–0061). *Expensive.* Peking and Szechuan cuisine.

Toh Lim Palace (Hotel Lotte). 1, Sogong-dong, Chung-ku, Seoul (Tel. 771–1000). *Expensive.* Good value buffet lunches.

Dongbosong. 50-8, Namsan-dong, 2-ka, Chung-ku, Seoul (Tel. 755–2727). *Moderate.* A huge, beautiful restaurant on the slope of Namsan Mountain.

The Mandarin. 640-2, Shinsa-dong, Kangnam-ku, Seoul (Tel. 542–3456). *Moderate.* An eye-catching interior.

Panda. 4–10, Chongdam-dong, Kangnam-ku, Seoul (Tel. 547–3333). *Moderate.* Near the Seoul Customs House. Good value.

Japanese

Akasaka (Hyatt Regency Hotel). 747-7, Hannam-dong, Yongsan-ku, Seoul (Tel. 798–0061). *Deluxe.*

Ariake (Hotel Shilla). 202, 2-ka, Changchung-dong, Chung-ku, Seoul (Tel. 233–3131). *Deluxe.*

Benkay (Hotel Lotte). 1, Sogong-dong, Chung-ku, Seoul (Tel. 771–1000). *Deluxe.*

Genji (Seoul Hilton Hotel). 395, 5-ka, Namdaemunno, Chung-ku, Seoul (Tel. 753–7788). *Deluxe.* Has an excellent Teppanyaki section.

Eryoudo. 99-18, Chongdam-dong, Kangnam-ku, Seoul (Tel. 543–9600). *Expensive.*

Misori. In the area behind the Seoul Plaza Hotel, on the street running from opposite the Chosun Hotel to Taepyongno. (Tel. 778–1131). *Moderate.* In the same general area is **Sungjin** (Tel. 754–4960), also *moderate.*

Sushi-cho (The Westin Chosun). 87, Sogong-dong, Chung-ku, Seoul (Tel. 771–0500). *Moderate.* A delightful little restaurant tucked away in the lower lobby of the hotel, good for fans of sushi and sashimi, and for those taking their first taste. The staff are helpful.

There are small Japanese-style snack bars in just about every district of the city, and prices are very reasonable. At some, you sit at a counter with plates of raw fish and other delicacies revolving in front of you. You take what you fancy, and the total bill is tallied from your number of empty plates.

Western/French/Continental

Hugo's (Hyatt Regency Hotel). 747-7, Hannam-dong, Yongsan-ku, Seoul (Tel. 798–0061). *Deluxe.* Recently redecorated; outstanding food and service.

La Continental (Shilla Hotel). 202, 2-ka, Changchung-dong, Chung-ku, Seoul (Tel. 233–3131). *Deluxe* (one of the most expensive restaurants in Seoul). On the top floor of the hotel; charming decor and views.

The Ninth Gate (The Westin Chosun). 87, Sogong-dong, Chung-ku, Seoul (Tel. 771–0500). *Deluxe.* One of Seoul's old favorites, recently redecorated. Has a popular bar with the same name. Overlooks a historical landmark, the Temple of Heaven.

The Seasons (Seoul Hilton Hotel). 395, 5-ka, Namdaemunno, Chung-ku, Seoul (Tel. 753–7788). *Deluxe.* The hotel's top restaurant; very pretty.

Bear House. San 5-1, Songbuk-dong, Songbuk-ku, Seoul (Tel. 762–1448). *Expensive.* At the east end of the Skyway Drive to the north of the city, with lovely views. A cocktail terrace is open in the summer. Limited menu, basically steaks and grills.

Banjul. 12-16, Kwanchol-dong, Chongno-ku, Seoul (Tel. 733–4432). *Moderate.* A fascinating layout of several floors comprising tearoom, bar, and restaurant. Decor is an interesting mixture of African and South American. Live entertainment. Generally good food.

Chalet Swiss. On the winding street between the Hyatt Hotel and the center of Itaewon (Tel. 795–1723). *Moderate.* European atmosphere and cuisine, sometimes a live yodeler.

El Toro (Seoul Plaza Hotel). 23, 2-ka, Taepyongno, Chung-ku, Seoul (Tel. 771–2200). *Moderate.* Good steaks and do-it-yourself salads.

L'Abri. In the Kyobo Building, 1, 1-ka, Chongno, Chongno-ku, Seoul (Tel. 739–8830). *Moderate.* A quality French restaurant with a bright and airy decor. Excellent value.

Italian

La Fontana (Shilla Hotel). 202, 2-ka, Changchung-dong, Chung-ku, Seoul (Tel. 233–3131). *Moderate.* A good selection; nice decor.

Il Ponte (Seoul Hilton Hotel). 395, 5-ka, Namdaemunno, Chung-ku, Seoul (Tel. 753–7788). *Moderate.* The menu is extensive, and pasta is made fresh daily. A happy atmosphere.

Sejong Restaurant. 81-3, Sejongno, Chongno-ku, Seoul (Tel. 737–7863). *Inexpensive.* In the Sejong Cultural Center; good selection.

American Fast Foods

These have caught on well in Seoul and many of the big names are represented—mainly in the area of Itaewon, but also in districts like Myongdong and the commercial center of Yongdong, south of the river. You'll find **Burger King, Kentucky Fried Chicken, Wendy's** (the latest Wendy's opened right outside the Chosun Hotel downtown), **Denny's, Baskin Robbins, Winchell's, Dunkin Donuts, Shakey's, Pizza Hut,** and a host of local imitations. **McDonald's** first put up its golden arches in Korea early in 1988, south of the Han-gang River in Kangnam-ku. You will pay around W5,000 for a full meal there.

For inexpensive Western food, Itaewon has the most variety, not only of the well-known fast foods, but also of specialty cuisines such as German and Mexican.

Pakistani

The **Mogul Restaurant** in Itaewon at the back of the Hamilton Shopping Center (Tel. 796–5501). *Moderate.* Open noon to midnight daily. It is one of a small number of restaurants in the city specializing in Pakistani and Indian cuisine.

TOURS. Around Town. Although most travel agencies conduct city tours, the two most accessible, in major hotel lobbies, are **Global Tours** and the **Korea Travel Bureau.** Head office telephone numbers are Global, 335–0011, and KTB, 585–1191. Both offer daily half-day tours of the city, morning and afternoon, taking in palaces and temples, markets, a lookout point like the Bukak Skyway or Seoul Tower, and shopping districts. Prices are around W15,000–W20,000, depending on the program.

Farther Afield. Both companies mentioned above also offer tours to the Korean Folk Village (see the Southern section of *Day Trips Out of Seoul*). The Global tour is an afternoon trip for W30,000, while the KTB program takes a full day and includes a visit to the Olympic Stadium and the town of Suwon. Lunch is included in the W44,000 price.

KTB operates the full-day tour to Panmunjom, in the Demilitarized Zone (see the "To the North" section of *Day Trips Out of Seoul*) for W37,000. You must book at least a day ahead, with your name, nationality, and passport number. Global operates a daily tour that visits the last military checkpoint, on the southern side of the Imjin River, overlooking the "Bridge of Freedom" and the end of the railway line that points towards the north. Tour cost, W18,000.

The **United Service Organization (USO),** which arranges tour programs for U.S. military personnel, operates a number of specialized tours that civilians can join. Trips include a regular tour to the DMZ, factory visits and handicraft tours, and overnight programs that explore some of Korea's historic and cultural sites. (Tel. 7914–7003).

The Korea Branch of the **Royal Asiatic Society** arranges Saturday and Sunday tours to similar sites—potters' shops, basket villages, silk factories, and temples—during the spring and fall seasons. It also organizes group day hikes in the countryside. Call 763–9483 for details on programs and space availability.

Water Tours. These are new to Seoul, a result of the major redevelopment of the Han-gang River. A number of boats operate between Yoido Island and Chamshil, with cruises taking between 60 and 90 minutes.

See also "Organized Tours" in the *Facts at Your Fingertips* section for tours out of Seoul.

WHAT TO SEE. Historical Sites. If you "subtract" from present-day

Seoul the buildings that have risen since the end of the Korean War in 1953, almost everything else qualifies—to a greater or lesser degree—as a "historical site." Since the old city dates from 1394, any surviving structure—royal palace, temple, institute of learning—of the final royal period (the Yi Dynasty), provides visitors with fascinating insights into Korean history, culture, and the ancient way of life.

Along the northern rim of the city are **Kyongbok-kung, Changdok-kung,** and **Changgyong-kung** palaces, surrounded by beautiful parklike settings. In the center is **Toksu-kung,** smaller in scale but no less important as a place of history.

Great South Gate (Namdaemun) and **Great East Gate** (Tongdaemun) are the two surviving gates into the old city, each a marvel of Oriental engineering and architecture. The **Kwanghwamun Gate,** in front of the old capitol building (now the National Museum), is guarded by two haetae, carved stone animals reputed to protect the city from fire.

Tongnimmun or Independence Arch is historic but not ancient. It was built in 1896 as a symbol of the Korean people's resistance to foreign dominance and their will to safeguard national independence. Designated Historical Site No. 32, the granite arch is located at a busy intersection northwest of City Hall.

Pigak is a small pavilion at the northeast corner of the Kwanghwamun intersection, next to the Kyobo Building. This was erected in 1902 to house a stele commemorating the 40th anniversary of King Kojong's accession to the throne.

The **Sajik Altar** is in Sajik Park, northwest of City Hall, at the site of one of the most sacred spots of the capital during the Yi Dynasty. Here, annual sacrifices to the spirits of grain and harvest were offered, on altars that are now two raised grass mounds with fitted stones on the sides. Behind the altars are two statues: to Yi Yul-Gok (1536–1584), one of the most important scholars of Korean Confucianism during the Yi period, and to his mother, Sin Sa-Im. She was instrumental in his early training and is revered as a model of Confucian womanhood.

The **Tangun Shrine** is located just above Sajik Park, accessible only by the entrance road to the Pukak Skyway, which runs alongside the west of the park. It is a modern shrine, built in 1967, but is interesting in that it commemorates the founders of the various Korean states and dynasties. It is open every day except Sunday.

Kwanchondae is a meteorological observatory, one of the three remaining observatories from premodern Korea. Built in 1434 for the use of the Office of Meteorology and Astronomy, it is now designated a historical site. Some 13 feet high and 7 ½ feet square, it was restored in 1984 when the Hyundai Group built its headquarters behind the observatory site, on Yulgokno Street.

The national Confucian Shrine, **Mun-Myo,** and the premier academy of the Yi Dynasty, **Sungkyunkwan,** are located on the grounds of the modern Sungkyunkwan University. The structures were originally built in 1398, burned in 1400, rebuilt in 1407, and destroyed again in the Japanese invasions of the 1590s. The present structures date to 1600, and are the site today of one of Seoul's major Confucian rituals. Sokchonje is held twice a year, in the second and eighth lunar months (in 1993 on February 25 and September 23), to honor Confucius, his disciples, and great Korean and Chinese sages. Sungkyunkwan University is in Hyehwa-dong, north of the Changgyong Palace.

Chogyesa Temple today is the head temple of the Chogye-jong, the principal sect of Buddhism in Korea. While the temple was founded at the turn of the twentieth century, it was given this name in 1954, when orthodox Korean Buddhism split up into two sects—the married-monks order and the celibate-monks order. Chogye-jong emphasizes the meditation tradition and maintains the purity of monastic celibacy while the other major order, the Taego-jong, permits its monks to marry. The temple is down an alley off the west side of Ujongkukno Street, northwest of the Poshingak Belfry.

Today there is a new Korean bell in the **Poshingak Belfry** at the Chonggak intersection. The original bell was hung by Taejo, the first king of the Yi Dynasty, in 1395, but it was destroyed by the Japanese invasions of the 1590s. Its replacement, which also dates to the early Yi era, developed a crack in the early 1980s and is now in the National Museum. The pavilion was built in the late 1970s, a copy of the type built in the 1400s. Like all Korean bells, this is not rung by a clapper from the inside but is struck on the outside, in this case by a log suspended on chains.

Near downtown Seoul are two of the city's most important shrines, the **Chongmyo** and **Tongmyo.** Located on the north side of Chongno Street, between Chongno 3-ka and 4-ka, Chongmyo is the Royal Ancestral Shrine, first built by the founding monarch of the Yi kingdom, Taejo, in 1396. The forested grounds are open every day, but the main shrine buildings are open only on the first Sunday in May, for the reenactment of an ancient Confucian ritual. Classified as Treasure No. 142, the Tongmyo shrine to the Chinese god of war, Kuan Yu, is located east of the Tongdaemun Gate. It was originally constructed in 1602, and most recently renovated in 1975.

To see a charming temple building that dates to 1897, when Korea declared herself an empire, head for the Westin Chosun Hotel, on the southeast side of City Hall Plaza. Commonly known as the **Temple of Heaven,** although it is properly called the "Temple of the Imperial Firmament," the structure that remains was used for ceremonial preparations and is located in the garden of the hotel. The original complex was created around an altar at which imperial-level rites could be celebrated and was used until Japan annexed Korea in 1910. The building makes a very pretty backdrop for the hotel's Ninth Gate Restaurant and bar.

The above historical sites are all in or near the central section of the city, and some have been outlined in more detail in the *Exploring Seoul* section of this guide. There are many more places of historical interest, however, and if you are a dedicated Oriental historian, get hold of a book published by the Royal Asiatic Society called *Discovering Seoul.* (It's on sale at the RAS office on Chongno 5-ka.) The book not only outlines all the historical sites by area, it also tells you how to find them by subway.

Outside the city, you can make interesting day trips to ancient fortresses, royal tombs, and a number of other sites of historical importance. See the section *Day Trips Out of Seoul* in this guide for more details.

Parks. There are a number of parks—large and small—both in and on the edges of Seoul. On the western side of the central city, from north to south, are **Sajik, Sosomun,** and **Hyochang** parks, all worth a visit if you're exploring the areas. Forming the inner city's southern fringe is **Namsan Park,** with several historical sites within it. The highlight here is Seoul Tower, which you can reach from the northern slope by cable car, offering sweeping views of the center and the outer suburbs.

Changchungdan Park is close to the Shilla Hotel and the National Theater on Namsan Mountain, and is also rich in historical monuments, particularly statues of patriotic warriors and Confucian scholars.

In addition, visitors will find all they expect from a park in the grounds of the city's palaces, in Chongno Street's **Pagoda Park,** and the Chongmyo Royal Shrine. These are all covered in the *Exploring Seoul* section of this guide.

What may surprise you is that one must pay to enter most of the city's shaded areas. This is because most parks are palaces, shrines, or places of other historical importance, and the fees (usually around W550 per person) go toward cultural preservation. Another surprise may be that the walkways are mostly sand, or gravel, and that grassy areas are rather rare. Visitors are usually required to stick to the paths, but there are plenty of stone or wooden benches—often in places that encourage quiet contemplation of a particularly pretty scene made up of water, pavilion, trees, and garden.

Zoos and Botanical Gardens. The main city zoo is in **Seoul Grand Park,** south of the Han-gang River (see *Exploring Seoul*). Here there is also a major botanical garden. Another garden is on **Namsan,** behind the public library, concentrating on ferns and cacti. Nearby is a small animal center, with ducks, deer, and monkeys.

Museums and Galleries. Korea's historic treasures and cultural legacies are on display at many places throughout the city. The most comprehensive collection is in the **National Museum,** the old capitol building at the northern end of Sejongno Street. It is closed Mondays (Tel. 738–3800). There are branches of this museum in five provincial cities—in Kyongju, Kongju, Puyo, Kwangju, and Chinju.

Near Seoul's National Museum is the **National Folklore Museum,** on the grounds of Kyongbok-kung Palace. Closed Tuesdays (Tel. 720–3138).

The **War Museum** is on Yoido, opposite the National Assembly Building, and is an open-air display of military airplanes and tanks. There are several Russian MIG fighters captured during the Korean war, along with the north Korean leader's Zil car (also captured during the Korean war), and a model of an infiltration tunnel. It is open every day (Tel. 782–2329).

Near the northeast corner of the Changgyong-kung Palace is the **Science Museum,** known as the Hall of Industry and Technology, which is fun if you're keen on electrical gadgets.

Two other museums of specialized interest are the **Postal Museum,** at Chungmuro 1-ka (Tel. 756–2858); and the **Embroidery Museum,** 89–4,

Nonhyon-dong, Kangnam-ku (Tel. 515–5114); prior appointment is required.

There are some 50 universities and colleges that house their own collections (viewings are only by appointment); and more and more private museums are opening their doors to the public. One of the latter is the **Hoam Museum,** at Yongin Farmland (south of Seoul), which is one of the premier art displays in the country (see *Day Trips Out of Seoul*).

The **National Museum of Modern Art** is in the suburb of Kwachon, on the south side of the Han-gang River near Seoul Grand Park. This has over 350 works by contemporary artists on permanent display and special exhibitions are held throughout the year. It is closed on Mondays (Tel. 503–7744).

There are a host of **art galleries** in Seoul, displaying contemporary paintings and sculpture or Oriental brush works. The Chongno Street area around Insa-dong, and Yulgokno Street toward Kyongbok-kung Palace are where several of the most well-known galleries are located. The Lotte and Shinsegae department stores also have galleries, and there is one in the shopping arcade of the Westin Chosun Hotel. Check the "What's On" columns of the *Korea Times* or *Korea Herald* for details of current exhibitions.

SPECIAL EVENTS. To find out what's happening in town during any particular week, check the page of cultural news and the events columns of the two English-language newspapers. They print lists of current plays, special films, art exhibitions, concerts, club meetings, special seminars open to the public, and social events. Two other publications that can be helpful, often available free at hotels, are *This Week in Seoul* and *Korea Tourist Guide.*

The national holidays and festivals are all celebrated in some way in Seoul. Watch out for the **Chongmyo Ritual** on the first Sunday in May, at the Chongmyo Shrine, and the **Sokchon rites** honoring the Great Sage Confucius. **Buddha's Birthday** is a very pretty event in Seoul, with the area around the Chogyesa Temple decorated with paper lanterns. The celebration really gets under way in the evening, with a lantern parade winding through city streets. Other Buddhist temples, mostly on the outskirts of the city, also stage rituals and processions on this occasion. (Dates and details of the main events are in the listings of "National Holidays and Festivals" in the *Facts at Your Fingertips* section of this guide.)

SPORTS. In addition to the traditional and modern sports enjoyed in Seoul, outlined in the *Facts at Your Fingertips* section of this guide, **golf** deserves special mention here as it is a sport that is gaining in popularity among business and tourist visitors. There are some 29 courses in the vicinity of Seoul, within an hour's drive or closer. Here are the names of the courses, their locations, and Seoul telephone numbers for information:

Ansugn (18 holes), Ansung (512–1925).
Anyang (18 holes), Kunpo (866–1414/5).
Cheil (27 holes), Ansan (233–6202).
Chungbu (18 holes), Yongin (745–8338).
Club 700 (18 holes), Yoju (554–5512).
Duckpyung (18 holes), Ichon (553–3838).

88 (36 holes), Yongin (745–1988).
Gold (36 holes), Yongin (744–8111).
Hanil (36 holes), Yoju (762–3744).
Hansung (27 holes), Yongin (236–4511/2).
Hanwon (18 holes), Yongin (Tel. (0339) 73–7111/4; no Seoul no.).
Hanyang (36 holes), Koyang (354–5000).
Inchon International (18 holes), Inchon (783–7091).
Kihung (36 holes), Hwasong (Tel. (0339) 72–4005; no Seoul no.).
Kwanak (36 holes), Hwasong (252–3171).
Nam Seoul (18 holes), Songnam (233–1301).
Nam Suwon (18 holes), Hwasong (Tel. (0331) 37–1201; no Seoul no.).
Namsongdae (18 holes), Songpa-ku, Seoul (403–0071).
New Korea (18 holes), Koyang (352–0071).
New Seoul (36 holes), Kwangju (745–5778).
Plaza (36 holes), Yongin (745–5311).
Royal (18 holes), Yongin (739–3937).
Suweon (27 holes), Yongin (233–5597).
Taegwang (18 holes), Yongin (764–7858).
Tong Seoul (18 holes), Kwangju (470–2141).
Yangji (27 holes), Yongin (744–2001).
Yanju (18 holes), Namyangjin (Tel. (0343) 592–0561; no Seoul no.).
Yeojoo (27 holes), Yoju (752–3489 or 752–6490).
Yuksa (18 holes), Tobong-ku, Seoul (972–2111).

It is usually not difficult for a visitor to get permission to play on these courses, particularly on weekdays. For further information, you can also call the **Korea Golf Course Business Association** in Seoul, 783–8271.

Health Clubs and Fitness Centers. A number of the major hotels have health and fitness centers with gymnasiums, saunas, indoor or outdoor pools (or both), and tennis courts.

Staff at hotel information desks will be able to advise you on how to find out about current programs of spectator sports (consult the sports pages of the local English-language newspapers, too).

SHOPPING. The paragraphs on shopping in the *Facts at Your Fingertips* section of this guide outline the wonders of Seoul as one of the best bargain centers of the Orient. There we give you general information on the range of products available, and where to find them. Here is some more specific information on the different types of shopping available.

Markets. The area of the **Tongdaemun Market** has the largest selection of textiles and fabrics, clothes in Korean sizes, bedding, household items, sports equipment, and electronic goods. It is closed on the first and third Sundays of each month. **Namdaemun** Market is much smaller than Tongdaemun and is close to the city center. It is closed on Sundays.

Insa-dong, or Mary's Alley, is an area off Chongno Street, famous for its cluster of art and antiques stores, galleries, and small restaurants.

Myong-dong, within easy walking distance of downtown hotels, is being promoted as the "chic" place to shop. It's full of boutiques, tailors, and shoe stores, and is a lively entertainment center at night.

Itaewon is the "foreigners' shopping center," for ready-made clothes and tailoring of all descriptions, sports shoes, eelskin products, brass beds, bedspreads and "mink" blankets, duty-free furs, and leather goods of every variety. Itaewon is lots of fun, for its stores by day and its bars and nightspots by night.

Changan-dong Market is on the eastern outskirts of Seoul, made up of some 150 stores of antiques and good and bad reproductions.

There are also a fish and farm market in **Karak-dong,** Kangdong-ku; a plant market in **Socho-dong,** Kangnam-ku; and a massive fish market in **Naryangjin-dong,** Tongjak-ku.

Department Stores. Dongbang Plaza, Taepyongno Street (Tel. 757–1234); closed on Sundays. **The Galleria,** Apkujong-dong, Kangnam-ku (Tel. 515–3131); closed first and third Monday of each month. **Hyundai Department Store,** Apkujong-dong, Kangnam-ku (Tel. 547–2233); closed on Mondays. **Lotte Shopping Center,** Sogong-dong (Tel. 771–2500); closed on Tuesdays. **Lotte World,** Chamsil-dong, Songpa-ku (Tel. 4111–2500); closed on Tuesdays. **Midopa Department Store,** near Lotte on Namdaemunno (Tel. 754–2222). **New Core Shopping Center,** Panpo-dong, Kangnam-ku (Tel. 532–3311); closed third Tuesdays. **Printemps Department Store,** downtown in Changgyo-dong (Tel. 774–0811); closed on second and fourth Wednesdays of each month. **Shinsegae Department Store,** downtown on Chungmuro (Tel. 754–1234); closed on Mondays. **Young Dong Department Store,** Nonhyun-dong, Kangnam-ku (Tel. 544–3000); closed on Thursdays.

These stores are generally open from 10:30 A.M. to 7:30 P.M.

Duty-free Shops. Kimpo Airport Duty-Free Shop, managed by the KNTC (Tel. 665–2133). **Donghwa,** Sejongno, Chongno-ku (Tel. 399–300). **Intercontinental,** at the hotel in Samsong-dong, Kangnam-ku (Tel. 559–7070). **Hanjin,** Pongnae-dong, Chung-ku (Tel. 778–7181). **Hotel Shilla,** Changchung-dong, Chung-ku (Tel. 230–3663). **Jindo Fur Salon,** Itaewon (Tel. 797–5601). **World Korea,** Hyundai Building, Mugyo-dong, Chung-ku (Tel. 775–8711). **Lotte,** Sogong-dong, Chung-ku (Tel. 776–3940); closed on Tuesdays. **Pagoda,** Insa-dong, Chongno-ku (Tel. 732–2511). **Paradise,** Changchung-dong, near Ambassador Hotel (Tel. 277–0181).

Whatever you buy in these stores—and the selection is great if a little expensive—will be delivered to you at the airport on your departure.

Tax-Refund Stores. Foreign visitors to Korea are eligible for refunds of Value Added Tax, Special Excise Tax, and Defense Tax when shopping at authorized tax-refund stores. You need to present your passport at the time of purchase and complete a tax-refund form. You will be given documents to show a customs officer as you leave the country, and you must also show him the articles purchased. If these have already been mailed out of the country, you need to produce a postal receipt. The purchase price of each item needs to be over W50,000, and the goods have to be taken out of the country within three months. The system is a little complicated, but it does work. See "Shopping" in the *Facts at Your Fingertips* section of this guide for more details.

The tax-refund stores are designated as follows: **Dongbang Plaza,** Taepyongno (Tel. 757–1234). **Hotel Shilla Arcade,** Changchung-dong

(Tel. 233–3131). **Lotte Department Store,** Sogong-dong (Tel. 771–2500). **Midopa Department Store,** Namdaemunno (Tel. 745–2222). **New Core Department Store,** Panpo-dong, Kangnam-ku (Tel. 532–3300). **Samick Musical Department Store,** Chungmuro Chung-ku (Tel. 778–5588). **Shinsegae Department Store,** Chungmuro (Tel. 676–1234 or 754–1234 for the Shinsegae branch in Yongdungpo). **Young Dong Department Store,** Nonhyun-dong, Kangnam-ku (Tel. 544–3000). **Kolon Sports,** Chungmuro, Chung-ku (Tel. 776–7475). **Esquire,** two stores, both in Myong-dong, Chung-ku (Tel. 778–3371). **Kumgang Shoes, Myong-dong, Chung-ku** (Tel. 753–9411).

Other Stores of Interest. Chonsu-gongbang: The full name of this fascinating place is the Korean Traditional Folk Arts Training and Education Association, which displays and sells an excellent collection of folk crafts and souvenir items. It is in Samsung-dong, Kangnam-ku, near the Korea Exhibition Center; Tel. 552–5445.

Tong-in Department Store. Downtown, along the main street in Insadong. Available here are reasonably priced reproductions of Korean chests and other furniture. Make sure you drop by the upper floors, which are stocked with a good variety of less expensive items.

Human Cultural Assets Handicraft Gallery. First floor, Ankuk Building, Ankuk-dong, Chongno-ku; Tel. 732–8178.

Korea Folk Handicraft Center. Near the Seoul Express Bus Terminal, at Chamwon-dong, Kangnam-ku; Tel. 532–9161.

Kanghwa Handicrafts Center. Farther out of the city, in Kanghwa, with a range of products native to the area; Tel. (0349) 2–6156.

Koryo-doyo. A pottery workshop and kiln of Chi Sun-Taek, in Ichon; Tel. 745–0063.

Haegang-doyo. The kiln and studio of Yoo Keun-Hyeong, also in Ichon; Tel. 745–0064.

Parka Crystal. A factory and showroom for the Korean crystal that has achieved recognition worldwide. It is in the area of the small town of Kwangju, about an hour's drive from Seoul; Tel. (0347) 2–4101.

NIGHTLIFE AND ENTERTAINMENT. Theater restaurants. Glossy stage shows predominate at these, offering comedy, pop singers, acrobats, jugglers, or snippets of Korean drum dances—chiefly for the drinking crowd. The food is usually Western fare, ranging between good and mediocre. The **Kayagum Theater** at the Sheraton Walker Hill, and the **Holiday In Seoul** at the Pacific Hotel sometimes import interesting performers, as do the top hotels for their nightclubs. There is also **Korea House,** which features a traditional Korean dinner followed by a program of Korean music and dance in its small theater, and the **Po Suk Jung** restaurant in the Lotte Hotel, which stages music and dance during dinner. For reservations, call the following: Sheraton Walker Hill, 453–0121; Pacific Hotel, 777–7811; Korea House (closed Sundays and public holidays), 266–9101; Lotte Hotel, 771–1000.

The **Global** and **KTB** tour agencies arrange night tours in Seoul. These usually include a night view of the city, such as from Namsan Tower, plus a theater-restaurant meal and performance. Prices range from around W57,000 per person for the Korea House tour to W65,000 per person for the Kayagum Theater trip (time is included to visit the Sheraton Walker

Hill casino). All the major hotels have a tour desk operated either by Global or KTB if you need details or reservations.

Movies. Motion pictures, both Korean and foreign, are extremely popular, so evening and weekend shows are apt to be crowded. Locally made films tend to be historical dramas or weepy family melodramas, but the Korean film industry has achieved international recognition for several recent art films. With the relaxation of import restrictions, first-run Hollywood films are being shown in Seoul not too long after their release abroad, although subject to rather strict censorship on sex or politics. Ticket cost is around W3,500. Foreign films are subtitled in Korean, so the original language remains on the soundtrack.

Following is a list of some of the better class theaters in Seoul:

North of the Han-gang River

Chungang. 48, 1-ka, Cho-dong, Chung-ku (Tel. 776–8866).
Dangsungsa. 56, Myo-dong, Chongno-ku (Tel. 764–3745).
Hollywood. 284-1, Nagwon-dong, Chongno-ku (Tel. 742–1481).
Korea. 50-14, 2-ga, Myong-dong, Chung-ku (Tel. 776–4273).
Kukdo. 310, 4-ka, Ulchiro, Chung-ku (Tel. 266–1444).
Myungbo. 18-5, Cho-dong, Chung-ku (Tel. 274–2121).
Myungbo Art Hall. 198-42, Kwanhyun-dong, Chongno-ku (Tel. 732–2131).
Scala. 41, Cho-dong, Chung-ku (Tel. 678–1014).
Seoul. 59-7, Kwansu-dong, Chongno-ku (Tel. 277–3011).
Taehan. 125, Chungmuro 4-ka, Chung-ku (Tel. 278–8171).

South of the Han-gang River

Damoa. 164-7, Nonhyun-dong, Kangnam-ku (Tel. 540–5134).
Yongdong. 97-26, Nonhyun-dong, Kangnam-ku (Tel. 544–4529).

Music, Dance, and Theater. As Koreans are extremely fond of Western classical music, many concerts with both local and foreign artists are scheduled during the fall and spring seasons. On the eastern slopes of Namsan Mountain (opposite the area of the Shilla and Tower hotels) is Korea's **National Theater,** with two auditoriums that are home to the National Ballet, National Opera Company, National Symphony Orchestra, Seoul Philharmonic Orchestra, and several theater companies. Right next door is the **National Classical Music Institute,** a combination school-and-research center committed to the preservation of, and instruction in, Korea's traditional classical music. At the **Sejong Cultural Center,** on the east side of Sejongno, there is an impressive dual theater for the performing arts, where both musical and dramatic performances are staged. Similar presentations are given at the **Munyye Theater,** a fairly new, modern building with both large and small theaters, at Chongno 5-ka; and the **Minye Theater,** across from the entrance to Changdok-kung Palace. "Little Theater" also flourishes, presenting works by Korean playwrights and translations of popular foreign writers. Dramatic events are in Korean language.

There are often **outdoor performances** of authentic Korean song, dance, and drama at "madang" arenas. One is located within the National Theater Complex; the other, Seoul Nori-Madang, is near the Sokchon Lake in Chamshil, on the south side of the Han-gang River. The Sokchon area, near the Olympic Main Stadium, was part of a major redevelopment project by the Lotte Corporation. The lake bed was cleaned and a complex of recreation and entertainment facilities known as "Lotte World" opened in mid-1988.

Another recent addition to the south side of the Han-gang River is a major art and culture complex of the **Korea Broadcast Advertising Corporation.** This complex, which opened just prior to the Olympics, has four auditoriums for the performing arts, and a collection of other cultural facilities.

Tearooms. These are favorite entertainment places for all of the city's populace, especially the young. Tearooms always provide music with their beverages (usually coffee and Korean-style teas), often using excellent stereo equipment. Each one specializes in a particular type of music, and therefore caters to a certain clientele. Some are for the serious aficionado of classical music, others for the rock-and-disco crowd. Shop around until you find one that suits your tastes. For a visitor from abroad, at least half the entertainment in a tearoom will result from watching the people: young courting couples, businessmen making deals, and housewives discussing the problems of home and family. Tearooms are everywhere—just about every major building has one in its basement.

Nightclubs and Discos. Just about every hotel has one or the other, in varying degrees of sophistication. The most popular Western-style discos are **J.J. Mahoney's,** at the Hyatt, and **Rain Forest,** at the Seoul Hilton. Another, **Rumours,** is next to the Crown Hotel, just around the corner from the Itaewon area. And now that we've mentioned Itaewon, this area is really the liveliest in town for all kinds of nightlife. It is true to say that you'll find whatever you're looking for—be it jazz, country and western, or rock and roll. This is the playground of the American soldiers in Korea, and it lives up to all its promises.

Information on What's On. The best sources of information on current entertainment events in Seoul are the English-language newspapers, the *Korea Times* and *Korea Herald,* and a give-away tabloid called *This Week in Seoul,* available at most hotels.

See the "Nightlife and Entertainment" section of *Facts at Your Fingertips,* earlier in this guide, for general details on the types of entertainment available.

USEFUL ADDRESSES AND TELEPHONE NUMBERS. Medical Attention. There are a number of hospitals in Seoul that maintain high standards of hygiene and medical care. Most hospitals, the larger ones certainly, have English-speaking doctors on their staff. However, the best source of assistance for any kind of medical attention during your stay is your hotel. The major hotels either have doctors actually on the staff or on call, and will also be able to recommend a dentist.

There is a new **international clinic** set up in the Hannam-dong area of Seoul, just past the entrance to the U.N. Village residential area which most taxi drivers know. The doctors have been trained in the United States, and they are available on a 24-hour basis for emergencies. They will also provide direct referral to consultants in various fields of medicine who are fluent in English. The telephone number is 796–1871.

Another international clinic is at **Severance Hospital,** in Shinchon-dong, Sodaemun-ku, which is staffed by foreign doctors. Tel. 392–3404.

The **Seoul Diagnostic Medical Clinic** also offers services to foreigners. It is located in the Hanaro Building, Insa-dong, Tel. 732–3030.

Any of the above clinics will help you avoid the confusions of the Korean medical system. The Korean custom is to go not to a doctor's office but to one of the hospitals, register for a small fee, then wait to be examined by one of the staff physicians. He may then refer you to a specialist, order tests or treatment, or prescribe medication. You pay at a counter and, if you have a prescription, present your receipt at the hospital's pharmacy counter and wait for your number to come up on a large signboard. It can take some time. For a foreigner, the system is even more complicated because while the doctors may speak English, other hospital staff do not.

Regarding **pharmacies,** there's just about one, or more, on every corner in Korea. While the pharmacist may, or may not, know a little English, he's likely to know the written name of the product you are looking for, or its local equivalent. Write the name down—the pharmacist's pronunciation is different from yours. Your hotel is likely to have a pharmacy counter in its lobby store, and here you'll undoubtedly find the standards like aspirin, cold remedies, antiseptics, and sanitary supplies.

Religious Services. The best sources of information on English-language services are the Saturday editions of the English-language newspapers, the *Korea Times* and the *Korea Herald,* which list all the services for foreigners, including the church locations and telephone numbers.

The following all hold English-language services, but you will need to check frequency and times:

Seoul Union Church (Protestant), with services at the Memorial Chapel of the Foreigners' Cemetery; service Sunday, 10:45 A.M. Tel. 333–7393.

International Lutheran Church, at Hannam-dong, just north of Hannam Supermarket; service Sunday, 8:30 and 10:45 A.M. Tel. 794–6274.

Christian Science Church, behind Korea House, in Pil-dong; service Sunday, 11 A.M. Tel. 263–9043.

Seoul Bible Church, Teheranno Street, Kangnam-ku; service Sunday, 11 A.M. Tel. 568–3932.

Youngnak Presbyterian Church, in Cho-dong, downtown Seoul; services Sunday, 10 A.M. and 11:30 A.M. are simultaneously translated into English. Tel. 273–6301.

Yoido Full Gospel Church, in Yoido, at its World Mission Center; several Sunday services. Tel. 782–4851.

Hallelujah Christian Church, in Kangnam-ku; service Sunday, 9 A.M. Tel. 571–3889.

The Church of Jesus Christ of the Latter Day Saints, at the chapel in Sindang-dong; service Sunday, 10:20 A.M. Tel. 745–6830.

Seoul International Baptist Church, on Yoido; service Sunday, 11 A.M. Tel. 338–2896.

Catholic International Parish, at the Franciscan Chapel in Hannam-dong, south of the Hannam Supermarket; service Sunday, 9 and 11 A.M. Tel. 793–2070.

Anglican Church, at the Anglican Cathedral on the small street running along the south side of Toksu-kung Palace; service Sunday, 9 A.M. Tel. 730–6611.

Tourist Information. Information is readily available at **KNTC's Tourist Information Center,** at information counters at the international airports, and at major tourist sites. Each center provides complimentary city maps, brochures, and useful information on tours, shopping, dining, and accommodations. The KNTC's information center at the head office in Ta-dong, is open every day from 9 A.M. to 6 P.M. Others are open from 9 A.M. to 6 P.M. Monday through Friday, and from 9 A.M. to 1 P.M. on Saturday. The telephone numbers are as follows:

The KNTC Tourist Information Center (the best), Tel. 757–0086; Kimpo Airport, Tel. 665–0088; Seoul City Tourist Information Center, behind City Hall, Tel. 731–6337; Seoul Express Bus Terminal, Tel. 537–9198; Chongno, Tel. 273–0348; Kwanghwamun, Tel. 735–0088; Myong-dong, Tel. 757–0088; Namdaemun, Tel. 779–3644; and Tongdaemun, Tel. 274–8588.

Lost and Found. Information regarding lost property can be obtained from the Citizens' Room of the Seoul Metropolitan Police Bureau at 201–11, Nai ja-dong, Chung-ku, Seoul, Tel. 755–4400.

Tourist Complaints. Any suggestions or grievances about your stay in Korea can be registered with the KNTC Tourist Complaint Center, Tel. 735–0101 (C.P.O. Box 903, Seoul, Korea).

EAST COASTAL AREA

With a gentleness befitting the region's Buddhist history, the wrinkled ridges and craggy stone faces of Mt. Soraksan and Mt. Odaesan blend into the white-sand beaches that line the coast of the Sea of Japan. This is Korea's spectacular East Coastal area. A cavalcade of sights, it is here that you will find granite cliffs, white water boiling its way through rugged gorges, sheer waterfalls, rivers rushing down into the sea, fascinating caves, hot springs, unusual rock formations, and mist-shrouded pines. If culture is your main interest, you will find more than a dozen historically significant temples, ornate gates that reveal the perfection of ancient Oriental architecture, a feudal castle many centuries old, pavilions dotting the coast in placid settings that reveal the Korean eye for natural beauty, and a number of hermitages built when Buddhist monks retreated from worldly affairs to embrace ascetic contemplation. You can visit a half dozen remote and charming coastal villages where fishing is still the major way of life, as well as one main port, Pohang, home of Korea's world-renowned steel mill.

The East Coastal area is Korea's four-season playground. Hiking is the thread that runs through every season. Some say that autumn is the region's finest hour. The mountains present visitors with a dazzling palate of flaming fall colors. The cool air takes a little of the effort out of hiking. Fall sunsets wax sentimental as the days get shorter. The crisp sunlight of late afternoon makes everything—the mountain peaks, the colorful temples, the docile sea—contrast sharply with the deep-blue skies that are so common here in autumn.

But even in winter you'll find hearty climbers trudging up the trails of Mt. Soraksan, accommodating the snow and ice with one or two cleats to guarantee their footing. Their extraordinary efforts are well spent. Snow enthusiasts argue that the mountains are at their best in winter. The air is clear and cold, and the snowcapped peaks glisten in the sun. It's a time for solitude in the mountains. Skiers can delight in world-class skiing, and finish the day with a little ice skating or tobogganing.

Spring is a different story. The snows give in to the season and melt their way into the sea. Azaleas and dogwood fill the senses with their freshness. On the coast, the chill that gave the wind its bite during the preceding season disappears to be replaced by a warmer relative. As the angriness of the sea in winter slips away, visitors are once again beckoned to the beaches for a stroll.

Summer brings green velvet to the East Coastal area. The mountains seem to thrive in the moist air. Clouds of mist roll through the hills and across the beaches. The water is inviting at the area's outstanding beaches, and everyone is out having a good time.

Opened up and developed relatively recently, the East Coastal area, because of its easy accessibility, has become the place where Koreans, especially Seoulites, go to escape the madding crowds of urban life. Although the area can become quite crowded, it is entirely possible that you will find solitude and peace even at the height of the tourist season. One weekend in late July, for example, the beaches around Kangnung were virtually empty. If crowds pose a special problem for you, by all means try to schedule a mid-week visit regardless of the season. Do remember that at peak times, available hotel accommodations can become scarce.

Geography

The East Coastal area seems to define its own limits, largely based on its accessibility from Seoul, which is the departure point for most visitors. Since it is "over the mountains" from the capital, the Taebaek Range establishes its western edge. The Sea of Japan, usually called the East Sea by Koreans, constitutes the area's eastern edge. From top to bottom, the East Coastal area stretches 250 miles, starting in the north from a point below the Demilitarized Zone and extending south to an east-west line running from the port of Pohang on the sea, inland to the city of Waegwan. In breadth, it ranges from 10 to 50 miles. From a political point of view, the area includes most of two provinces, Kangwon in the north and Kyongsanpuk in the south, as well as a small wedge of Chungchongpuk sticking into the center from the west.

Three Major Sections

To help you decide which part or parts of this elongated area might most be worth your attention, we have divided it into three sections: northern, central, and southern. Although these demarcation lines may seem somewhat arbitrary, they are based on available transportation into each section. First, here's a thumbnail sketch of each section to give you a quick overview. Following that is a detailed description of each. The practical information you will need, in detail, follows the descriptive sections.

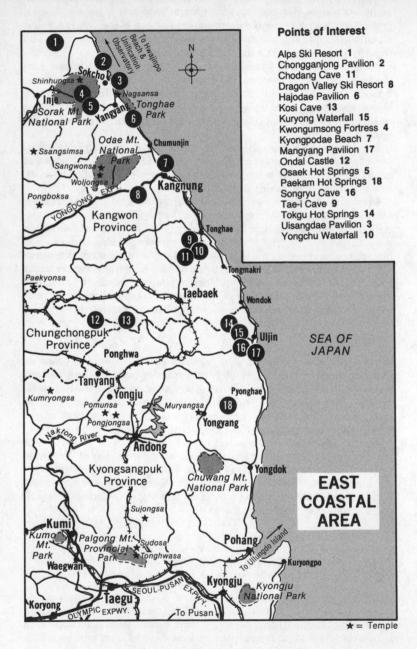

Points of Interest

Alps Ski Resort 1
Chongganjong Pavilion 2
Chodang Cave 11
Dragon Valley Ski Resort 8
Hajodae Pavilion 6
Kosi Cave 13
Kuryong Waterfall 15
Kwongumsong Fortress 4
Kyongpodae Beach 7
Mangyang Pavilion 17
Ondal Castle 12
Osaek Hot Springs 5
Paekam Hot Springs 18
Songryu Cave 16
Tae-i Cave 9
Tokgu Hot Springs 14
Uisangdae Pavilion 3
Yongchu Waterfall 10

EAST COASTAL AREA

★ = Temple

The Northern Section. Home to Mt. Soraksan National Park, this is easily the most popular of the East Coastal area's three areas because it offers the most to do and see in terms of recreation and culture. Consequently, it is here that you will probably find the most people, as well as the best and most varied modes of transport. From Seoul, you can reach the northern section by train, plane, or bus. In this section you'll find three major parks: two national and one provincial. Three major mountains ranging in altitude from 4,500 to 5,000 feet are located here, one in each park. The country's best ski resorts make this area a jewel for winter vacationers. This section also boasts five important temples and several hot springs, all surrounded by a variety of accommodations. Of the three sections, this is the quickest and easiest to reach.

In addition, this section also provides an opportunity to view what has been called "one of the most scenic spots in Korea"—Mt. Kumkang, in North Korea. An observation tower has been opened to the public in Myonghori, a coastal village near the boundary of the DMZ, and there is a daily tour departing from the entrance of Sorak Village.

The Central Section. This portion of the East Coastal area has somewhat less to offer in terms of variety, but that may be a plus for those who like to get off the tourist track and engage in a little unguided exploration. Those who make the effort are likely to get closer to the Korean people and view their lives from an untainted perspective. Since this area does not have an expressway leading directly into it, you must arrive via one of the many local buses that travel the coastal road. Worthy sights in this area include several caves, a feudal castle, hot springs, a number of waterfalls, plus excellent swimming and saltwater fishing on the coastal beaches.

The Southern Section. As in the northern section, you will find three major parks, four of the taller mountains, four temples, and excellent swimming and fishing in the waters around the port of Pohang. This section is reached via the Kyongbu Expressway by way of express-bus service from Seoul. Or you can arrive by local bus from nearby cities.

The Northern Section

In the Northern Section are two prominent national parks, which lie about 15 miles apart at their nearest points. Mt. Soraksan National Park, which covers about 140 square miles, is the more northern one. Sometimes called the Switzerland of Korea, its focal point is Mt. Soraksan with an elevation of about 5,200 feet. Soraksan means "Snow Peak Mountain," and the Sorak chain of mountains stretches into North Korea where it becomes the fabled Diamond Mountains.

The Taebaek Mountains, which form the Korean peninsula's backbone, divide Soraksan into two parks, Inner Sorak, which lies on the western side, and Outer Sorak on the eastern side. Both parts are in the park, but Outer Sorak is more remote. Here you will find waterfalls, astonishing rock formations, lonely hermitages, and the famous Shinhungsa Temple. Originally built in 653, the temple was destroyed by fire and rebuilt twice then finally rebuilt in its present location in 1645. A short hike to the north leads to Hundulbawi Rock or "Rocking Rock," which, although gargantuan, can be set into gentle motion by the push of an average person. Virtually in the same spot is the Kyejoam Hermitage, a cave shrine with a seated stone Buddha image. Here Korean monks of the Silla period once practiced ascetic ways. Close by is Ulsanbawi Rock, which although it appears to have six peaks is actually a single rock, reputed to be the largest rock in the Orient. Legend has it that a god was carrying the rock from Ulsan, a southern coastal city, north to the Diamond Mountains when he learned that those mountains already had 12,000 peaks. So, he simply dropped it.

Southeast of Shinhungsa Temple are several mountain peaks that combine in an imposing fashion. What appears to be a silvery ribbon suspended between these peaks are the Piryong and Towangsong Falls.

A favorite tourist activity is to take the cable car from Sorak-dong Tourist Village up to Kwongumsong Castle, located on the summit of a precipitous stone mountain. Although the exact date of construction is unknown, the castle is said to have been built some 1,500 years ago during the Silla period to defend against outside invasions or rebellions by local bandits.

Paektamsa, or "One Hundred Pools Temple," is the gateway to Inner Sorak. Founded in 643 as Pigumsa Temple, it was plagued with fires. Although it was moved and renamed, the temple continued to have fire problems until monks found the solution in a dream. They gave the temple its present name and there have been no fires in more than 350 years.

Tumbling 88 feet to form a rainbow at the bottom is Taesung Waterfall, South Korea's biggest. It is located in Inner Sorak, not too far from Paektamsa. Also in Inner Sorak is Pongjongam, or "Phoenix Peak" Hermitage, which, according to legend, was founded by the Silla monk Chajang in 643, but rebuilt in 1226 and again in 1518. An ancient five-story pagoda just below the hermitage supposedly enshrines some relics of Buddha, which Chajang is said to have brought with him when he returned from China. Today, a villa offers climbers a cozy shelter for the night.

If you are coming to the Northern Section from Seoul, you will most likely arrive in one of two coastal towns—Sokcho, if you fly, or Kangnung if you travel by road or rail. Until roads in the area were improved, Sokcho was just a little fishing village. Today it is booming with tourist expansion and has more than 71,000 residents. Kangnung is about 20 miles south of Sokcho.

A tourist village and three of the bigger hotels lie at the edge of Mt. Soraksan Park. These offer tennis, swimming pools, and golf right there, with plenty of shuttle buses to take you into the park itself.

Along this northern coast, are three famous pavilions—Chongganjong, Uisandae, and Hajodae. Naksansa Temple lies a few miles away on a site overlooking the sea. Here, early risers can treat themselves to a spectacular view, looking over pine forests to watch the sun rising for the start of a new day.

To visit the observation tower overlooking the spectacular Mt. Kumgang or Diamond Mountain and its 12,000 ridges, you should call (0392) 34–0388/9 at least two days in advance and provide your name, address, arrival date and time, as well as a credit card or passport number. The tour departs once a day from the entrance to the Sorak Village and takes about one hour. It includes a 15-minute educational talk, in English if there are enough passengers to warrant it.

The second big park in this northern section is Mt. Odaesan National Park, located about 15 miles south of Soraksan. Arriving by bus from Seoul, you will pass the Dragon Valley Ski Resort, a year-round holiday spot with a ski lodge, chair lifts, and snow-making machines for when winter is uncooperative.

Mt. Odaesan National Park, which is 190 square miles, is home to three majestic mountains: Odae at 4,800 feet, Kyebang at 4,700 feet, and Hwangbyong at 4,300 feet. The park has four Buddhist temples—Ssangsimsa, Sangwonsa, Pongboksa, and Woljongsa, the last one being the most famous. Located just four miles from the highway, Woljongsa Temple is a cluster of buildings set in a forest of pines and cedars. The outstanding structure in the compound is a nine-story octagonal pagoda made of granite, dating back to 645 when the Silla Kingdom ruled Korea. Its interior is famous for its carved "Dragon Pillars," regarded as being among the very best in the country.

The third park is Tonghae, right on the Sea of Japan, directly east of Mt. Soraksan Park and close to the village of Yangyang.

If you plan to spend several days in this area, you can easily remain at lodgings in the Mt. Soraksan area and cover Mt. Odaesan Park, the city of Kangnung, and the nearby temples on day trips from your "base camp." Kangnung, also a fishing village, offers excellent swimming at Kyongpodae Beach and first-rate fishing on the coast south of town.

At the lower end of this section lies the coastal town of Samchok, another fishing village and a good jumping-off point for side trips to Paekam Hot Springs or the 300-foot Songryu Cave.

The Central Section

To reach this middle section, you will have to go from Seoul to Sokcho or Kangnung and then rely on local buses, which make local stops, to penetrate and explore. Although this section is not teeming with the spectacular sights of the northern area, there is still plenty to see and do here. Camera buffs, in particular, will find the picture possibilities of the area to their liking. Golf and tennis are in short supply, but there is plenty of swimming and fishing on the coast. And the very fact that this area is less crowded will appeal to many visitors.

The area has two notable mountains: Mt. Paekamsan (3,020 feet), inland from the coastal town of Pyonghae, where you can take in the Paekam Hot Springs on the same trip; and Mt. Taebaeksan (4,700 feet), inland from the coastal town of Chukgyon, which provides you with the option of visiting Tokgu Hot Springs on your return trip to the coastal road.

Four major caves are located in the central section: Kosi, Songryu, Tae-i, and Chodang. Yongchu and Kuryong are the area's two impressive waterfalls. There is only one pavilion—Mangyang—but it's a beauty with its panoramic view of the Sea of Japan.

There are five temples—Muryangsa, Pongjonsa, Pomunsa, Kumryongsa, and Taekyonsa. But the most special sight in the central section is Ondal Castle, located 35 miles inland from the coastal town of Wondok. It's worth a visit if you enjoy ancient structures, as Ondal is the only castle in the entire area.

As for the coast, it offers swimming beaches north of Tongmakri and near Mangyangdae Pavilion, as well as good saltwater fishing at Uljin and just south of Pyonghae.

If the central section seems a bit spread out as you study your tourist map to make plans, it offers scenic and cultural variety—in experiences that are not found up north.

The Southern Section

The bottom third of the East Coastal area is reached via the Kyongbu Expressway from Seoul (the main highway between Seoul and Pusan, the southern port that is the country's second-largest city), which crosses the Taebak Mountains in a more southeasterly direction through Kumi, Taegu, and Kyongju. (These last two cities are covered in separate chapters of this guide.) You can also travel down the east coast by bus from any of the coastal cities mentioned in the previous two sections. From the steel center of Pohang, you can make day trips inland to the various attractions by bus, or, more conveniently, take taxis from your hotel.

Like the northern section, this area has three major parks: Mt. Chuwangsan National Park (2,200 feet), Mt. Palgongsan Provincial Park (3,500 feet), and Mt. Kumosan Provincial Park (1,750 feet).

Except for Mt. Chuwangsan Park, about 45 miles north of Pohang (inland from the coastal village of Pyonghae), most of the southern attractions seem to lie in a rather narrow belt running inland from Pohang, which is probably the best base. If you want to stay inland, try the town of Kumi, far to the west of Pohang. In this location, you will be right next door to Mt. Kumosan Park, and just a one-hour drive from Mt. Palgongsan Park. Or, you can cover the southern tier of this section from the city of Kyongju, which offers a much wider choice of hotels than Pohang. The ancient center of Kyongju has a wealth of history and culture to be explored, covered in detail in the separate section of this guide.

Besides the three parks mentioned, which offer trails and breathtaking scenery, three temples within this area are worth attention: Sudosa, Tonghwasa, and Sujongsa. But probably the prime attractions of the Pohang area are its excellent beaches and ocean fishing, both inside and outside the wide bay. An excursion to the offshore island of Ullungdo offers the adventurous something a little different to explore. Ullungdo Island, which lies about 100 miles off the East Coast, is easily one of the country's most remote tourist spots, particularly for foreign visitors. Unless you visit there at the height of the domestic vacation season (mid-July through August), you probably won't run into any crowds. Ullungdo Island is populated by fishermen, just as it has been for centuries. It was only a few years ago that the island was developed for tourism. It offers rugged scenery—its steep mountains were once volcanoes—fine beaches, succulent seafood, and isolation.

Swimming, boating, fishing, and snorkeling are the recreational activities here. As on Cheju Island, you can witness wet-suited women divers collecting your next meal of abalone, shellfish, and edible seaweed from the sea bottom. In the evenings, you can watch the fishing fleet set out, each boat festooned with huge, brilliant incandescent lights to attract the squid.

PRACTICAL INFORMATION FOR
EAST COASTAL AREA

WHEN TO GO. Korea's East Coast is a year-round resort area, especially in the north. Wildflowers paint the mountains with color and sweet smells in the spring, while summer offers swimming at some of the nation's best and most splendid beaches. If the sea is too chilly for you, you can take a dip in your hotel pool. Outdoor sports such as hiking, golf, and tennis are especially well suited to the East Coastal area. But autumn with its spectacular foliage is the most popular season, particularly for Mt. Sorak. Its fame brings people congestion, so, if possible, schedule a midweek stay. But don't let the crowds scare you away, because the colorful trees of fall make it worth mingling with the multitude. If skiing is your sport, you won't find better in Korea. Try Dragon Valley or the Alps—both have excellent facilities.

HOW TO GET THERE FROM SEOUL. Northern Section. To Sokcho, a coastal town: **By air** from Seoul's Kimpo Airport on Korean Air; 40 minutes flying time, flights departing once daily and twice on Tuesday, Thursday, Saturday, and Sunday. **By express bus** from Seoul's Kangnam bus terminal, 5 hours, 15 minutes driving time, buses departing every 40–60 minutes, 6:30 A.M. to 6:40 P.M. **By local bus** from Seoul's Sangbong-dong bus terminal, 5 hours driving time, buses departing every 40 minutes, 6 A.M. to 6:00 P.M.

To Kangnung, a coastal town. **By air,** from Seoul's Kimpo Airport on Korean Air; 45 minutes flying time, flights departing twice a day. **By express train** from Seoul's Chongnyangni Station, at 10 A.M., and a daily overnight sleeper (taking around seven hours) departing at 11 P.M.; on holidays and weekends, another express train departs at 10:40 P.M. **By express bus** from Seoul's Kangnam bus terminal, 3 hours, 40 minutes driving time, departing every 10 minutes, 6 A.M. to 7:40 P.M. **By local bus** from Seoul's Dong Seoul bus terminal, 4 hours, 20 minutes driving time, departing every 30 minutes, 6:30 A.M. to 6:55 P.M.

To Tonghae, down the coast from Kangnung, at 2 P.M. and 5 P.M. daily, from Seoul's Chongnyangni Station, is an air-conditioned **express train** which takes about 5 hours, 30 minutes. This journey offers some really spectacular mountain views, as well as a memorable ride through a tunnel that turns some 360 degrees.

To Yangyang, a coastal town: **By local bus** from Kangnung bus terminal, one hour driving time, departing every 10 minutes, 5:40 A.M. to 9:30 P.M.

To Woljongsa Temple, in Mt. Odaesan Park: **By local bus** from Kangnung bus terminal, two hours driving time; the bus leaves every 30 minutes, 5:50 A.M. to 7:30 P.M.

Central Section. To Samchok, a coastal town (at the lower edge of the northern section and a pretty good starting point for exploration of the central area): **By express bus** from Seoul's Kangnam bus terminal, five hours driving time; buses departing around every hour, 6:30 A.M. to 6:50 P.M.

Southern Section. To Pohang, the port city. By air from Seoul's Kimpo Airport, 50 minutes flying time, flights leaving three times daily. **By express bus** from Seoul's Kangnam bus terminal, five hours driving time, departing every 20 minutes, 6:30 A.M. to 6:30 P.M.

To Kuryongpo, a beach near Pohang. By local bus from Pohang bus terminal, 35 minutes travel time, buses leaving every 8 minutes, 5:30 A.M. to 11 P.M.

To Yongdok, a coastal town north of Pohang: By local bus from Pohang bus terminal, one hour, 10 minutes driving time, buses leaving every five minutes, 4:20 A.M. to 7:50 P.M.

To Mt. Chuwangsan National Park: By local bus from Pohang bus terminal, three hours driving time, buses leaving twice daily, at 8:12 A.M. and 9:36 A.M.

It is also possible to get **to Mt. Soraksan partway by water.** A shuttle shipping service travels from Soyang Dam to Inje three times daily at 11 A.M., 1 P.M., and 3 P.M., one hour, 10 minutes travel time. From Inje, you can take a taxi to Sorak. You can get to Lake Soyang easily by bus from Chunchon, which is reached from Seoul's Sangbong-dong bus terminal by local buses leaving every 10 minutes.

HOW TO GET AROUND. The East Coastal area is best explored by bus or car. The **Yongdong Expressway** connects Seoul to Kangnung in the north, while the **Kyongbu Expressway** and a connecting highway link the capital city to Pohang in the south. Numerous suburban bus lines travel to all East Coast towns, as well as to interior towns and tourist attractions. Your hotel will be able to assist with information. Taxis can be found at any of the major hotels. These can be hired for short trips, or by the day. But do be aware that English can be a problem. One taxi driver said that only about 10 of the area's some 700 taxi drivers know any English. Ask one of the hotel staff to help you with negotiations for a half-day or full-day hire, and get your destinations written down in Korean. Short journeys should not present difficulties, as most drivers will be familiar with the most popular tourist spots.

It is possible to hire a car in Sokcho, with a driver if you prefer. Call **Daehan** (0392) 33–0801, **Hankuk** (31–6688), or **Kangwon Rent-a-Car,** 33–0011. Again, the hotel can help if you have a problem with language.

ACCOMMODATIONS. Approximate price ranges for a double room in the East Coastal region are: *Deluxe,* W65,000 to W100,000; *1st class,* W40,000 to W60,000; *2d class* and *3d class,* W20,000 to W40,000. There are often seasonal variations in rates, and you should check on the availability of rooms before leaving Seoul. The larger hotels have Seoul reservation offices that you can call for information.

While the area has no hotels that really measure up to international deluxe standards, the range of facilities is good and your general comfort will be similar to that found in Seoul. Language will be more of a problem than in the capital, except at the top resort hotels (such as at the ski resorts), which are accustomed to catering to foreign guests.

We have divided the hotels by area, with an indication of each property's basic services. Credit card abbreviations are: American Express, AE; Diner's Club, DC; MasterCard, MC; and Visa, V.

NORTHERN SECTION

Sorak Mountain

New Sorak Hotel. At the National Park, 106-1, Sorak-dong, Sokcho, Kangwondo; Tel. (0392) 34–7131, Seoul office (02) 514–0211, Fax. (0392) 34–7150. *Deluxe.* 120 rooms; Western, Korean, Japanese, and Chinese food available; a cocktail lounge, nightclub, and a miniature golf course. Credit cards: AE, DC, MC, V.

Sorak Park Hotel. At Sorak Village, 74-3, Sorak-dong, Sokcho, Kangwondo; Tel. (0392) 34–7711, Seoul office (02) 753–2585, Telex K24142, Fax. (0392) 34–7732. *Deluxe.* 120 rooms; Western, Korean, and Japanese restaurants, nightclub, and the area's only casino. Credit cards: AE, DC, MC, V.

Mt. Sorak Tourist Hotel. At the entrance to the park, 170, Sorak-dong, Sokcho, Kangwondo; Tel. (0392) 34–7101, Seoul office (03) 989–7773, Fax. (0392) 34–7106. *2d class.* 54 rooms; Western and Korean dining facilities; cocktail lounge. Credit cards: AE, DC, MC, V.

Sorak Youth Hostel. 155, Tomun-dong, Sokcho, Kangwondo; Tel. (0392) 34–7540, Seoul information (02) 763–9871. Eight-bunk rooms and some twin rooms available; Western or Korean food facilities. No credit cards.

Naksan Temple Area

Naksan Tourist Hotel. 3-2, Chonjin-ri, Kanghyon-myon, Yangyang, Kangwondo; Tel. (0396) 672–4000, Seoul office (02) 742–9000. *1st class.* 137 rooms; Western, Korean, and Japanese restaurants; nightclub. Overlooking pretty Naksan Beach. Credit cards: AE, DC, MC, V.

Naksan Youth Hostel. 30-1, Chonjin-ri, Kanghyon-myon, Yangyang, Kangwondo; Tel. (0396) 672–3416, Seoul information (02) 752–0803. Dormitory accommodations are around W3,500 per bed, and there are also a number of Korean-style rooms from around W20,000. Western and Korean food served. The road leading to the hostel, located on a wooded hill near Naksan Temple, turns off from the main road connecting Yangyang and Sokcho. No credit cards.

Dragon Valley Ski Resort

Dragon Valley Tourist Hotel. 130, Yongsan-ri, Toam-myon, Pyongchang, Kangwondo; Tel. (0374) 32–5757, Seoul office (02) 548–2251. *Deluxe.* 190 rooms, including dormitory-style accommodations; Western, Korean, Chinese, and Japanese dining facilities; cocktail lounge, indoor swimming pool, tennis courts, and a popular disco. Ski facilities include six slopes with six chair lifts, four T-bars, and snow-making machines. Credit cards: AE, DC, MC, V.

Mt. Odae, Kangnung Area

Dong Hae Tourist Hotel. 274-1, Kangmun-dong, Kangnung, Kangwondo; Tel. (0391) 44–2181, Seoul office (02) 737–0037, Fax. (0391) 236–5012. *2d class.* 83 rooms; Western and Korean food; swimming pool and tennis courts. A charming beach-side location, and friendly staff who speak English. Credit cards: AE, DC, MC, V.

Hotel Kyongpo Beach. 303-4, 255, Kangmun-dong, Kangnung, Kangwondo; Tel. (0391) 44–2277, Fax. (0391) 44–2397. *3d class.* A good range of facilities for a small hotel (just 56 rooms), including a couple of restaurants, an outdoor swimming pool, and facilities for fishing and boating. Also has a theater-restaurant. Credit cards: AE, DC, V.

CENTRAL SECTION

Uljin Area

A good location for visiting the highlights of the East Coast's central section, including the beautiful Manyang Pavilion, the Songryu Cave, the Guryong Waterfall, and the Tokgu and Paekam Hot Springs.

Baekam Hot Spring Resort Hotel. 964, Onjong-ri, Onjong-myon, Uljin, Kyongsangbuk-do; Tel. (0565) 787–3500, Fax. (0565) 787–4233. *1st class.* Just over 100 rooms, two restaurants, a cocktail lounge and nightclub, plus a sauna and hot spring baths. Credit cards: AE, DC, MC, V.

Sungryu Park Hotel. 968-4, Onjong-ri, Onjong-myon, Uljin, Kyongsangbukdo; Tel. (0565) 787–3711, Fax. (0565) 787–3081. *3d class.* Over 150 rooms, with a couple of restaurants, a nightclub, and hot spring baths. Credit cards: DC, MC, V.

SOUTHERN SECTION

Pohang

Pohang Beach Hotel. 311-2, Songdo-dong, Pohang, Kyongsangbukdo; Tel. (0562) 41–1401, Telex K54507, Fax. (0562) 42–7534. *2d class.* 56 rooms; Western and Korean food, cocktail lounge and nightclub, and facilities for boating and fishing. Credit cards: AE, DC, MC, V.

Mt. Kumosan Provincial Park

Keumosan Tourist Hotel. San 24-6, Namtong-dong, Kumi, Kyongsanbukdo; Tel. (0546) 52–3151, Telex K54470, Fax. (0546) 52–2764. *2d class.* Just over 100 rooms; Western, Korean, and Japanese restaurants; cocktail lounge and nightclub. Credit cards: AE, DC, MC, V.

RESTAURANTS. Generally, the best dining in this area is at the resort hotels. This is particularly the case if you're searching for Western cuisine. There is little incentive for residents of these small towns to open Western-style restaurants as most foreign visitors stay and dine at the resorts, usually those at Mt. Sorak, Mt. Odae, and Dragon Valley. However, if you enjoy Korean cuisine, you'll find plenty of restaurants to chose from. If you don't feel confident enough to select a "native" dining spot on your own, ask your hotel manager for advice.

The area's specialty is raw fish, Korean-style, but it's definitely an acquired taste. If you're adventurous, give it a try. A cluster of restaurants serving such delights as spicy fish chowders is located along the shore at the entrance to the Sorak Park area. At some you'll be shown a tank of live fish from which to choose your dinner. Prices may be rather expensive.

The Sorak area is especially famous for its flavorful pine mushroom dishes. Definitely worth a try, as they really are delicious.

TOURS. Several tour operators in Seoul offer trips into the East Coastal area, the most common being a 1-night/2-day program to Mt. Sorak. Tour cost is around W156,000, inclusive of coach transportation, deluxe accommodations, and breakfast. Make contact with an office or tour counter (all major hotels have them) of **Global Tours** or **Korea Tourist Bureau.** Or you can telephone Global at (02) 335–0011, KTB at 585–1191.

The port of Pohang is the departure point for **Ullungdo,** the island lying about 100 miles offshore and a good off-the-beaten track excursion for foreign visitors. A hydrofoil departs from Pohang daily at 10 A.M. during the April 16 to October 15 period and five times per week October 16 to April 15. From July 26 to August 15, a second ship leaves Pohang at noon. The regular return trip from Ullungdo is at 10 A.M. daily, but actual departures vary frequently so be sure to check. The one-way hydrofoil trip takes 3 hours, 20 minutes and the fare is W26,230. Additional service is available by regular ship, but the journey takes more than 7 hours.

During the day, it is sometimes possible to rent one of the fishing boats for a short cruise around the entire island. The journey takes two or three hours, depending on how long and how often you stop to explore. If you'd rather stay on land, you may be able to rent a car to drive around the island. Songinbong Peak offers serious and casual hikers alike an opportunity to enjoy some solitude. The island has two ports—Todong, the larger one, where the hydrofoil lands, and Chodong, located on the opposite side of the island.

Plan on staying in a Korean inn, or *yogwan,* while you're on Ullungdo. You'll be able to find a place to stay once you get there, but if you like to know these things in advance, make contact with the Korean National Tourism Corporation for a recommendation. The information center is at the lower level of the KNTC Building, 10, Ta-dong, Chung-ku, Seoul (Tel. 757–0086).

For more information and hydrofoil reservations, you can call Seoul (02) 514–6766 or Pohang (0562) 42–5111. The number in Ullungdo is (0566) 791–4811.

HISTORIC SIGHTS. The East Coastal area serves up many outstanding sights in addition to its natural beauty. Some are worth special mention. In Outer Sorak, the most distinctive temple is **Shinhungsa,** said to be the oldest Zen temple in the world. In a two-and-one-half-hour walk from Sorak Village, you can visit not only Shinhungsa (which literally means "Temple of Divine Revelation"), but also the **Hundulbawi "Rocking Rock,"** a huge granite boulder that can be pushed back and forth by one person, **Ulsanbawi Rock,** a spectacular outcropping of granite, quartz, and mica that is said to be Asia's largest rock, and the **Kyejoam Hermitage,** a cave shrine at the base of Ulsanbawi.

If you head for Inner Sorak, you'll be able to visit **Paektamsa Temple,** the most famous temple in the park's remote regions. With a literal meaning of "The Temple of One Hundred Pools," Paektamsa has had a long and complex history since being founded in 643.

The road leading into Mt. Odaesan National Park is literally dotted with tiny hermitages and other remnants of Buddhism that date to the seventh century. Most notable of the four temples actually in the park is **Woljongsa,** the oldest temple of the Silla Kingdom. Located four miles off the highway, Woljongsa is home to a nine-story stone pagoda that was constructed during the Silla period by the monk Chajang. Midway to the mountain's summit is **Sangwonsa Temple,** noted for its bronze bell. Cast in 725, the bell is said to be the oldest and most beautiful in all of Korea.

The East Coast has a number of pavilions. Three of the most famous— **Chongganjong, Uisandae,** and **Hajodae**—are easily reached from Sokcho. Also in the vicinity is the impressive **Naksansa Temple,** one of the few Korean temples built with a view of the sea. The most spectacular sight at the temple is a statue of the Goddess of Mercy that stands more than 50 feet high. Visitors particularly enjoy Nakansa and the "Madonna of the Sea" at sunrise when sea mists rise among the ancient pine trees.

On the north shore of Kyongpodae Lake, near Kangnung, is the **Kyongpo Pavilion,** looking out over a busy sailing and boating resort. Noted as one of the "Eight Scenic Wonders" of the East Coast, the wooden structure was first built in 1326 during the Koryo Dynasty. It was moved to its present site in 1508.

BEACHES. This section of Korea's east coastline has plenty of beaches, so you'll have no trouble finding one that suits your fancy. Simply make your way to the coast and stop at the most inviting place. Summer facilities at the tourist beaches are good. The most developed have parking lots, toilet facilities, showers, umbrellas, inflated inner tubes for rent, and plenty of open-air snack bars. Prices tend to rise with the temperatures, however, and a cool drink under a parasol can be surprisingly expensive. Check the prices before you order.

Swim only in designated areas—they are clearly marked—as not all the sandy shores are free from pollution.

Northern Section. Hwajinpo Beach at Kansong lies about 20 miles up the coast from Sokcho, and is similar to its more famous neighbor, **Naksan Beach,** which is located in Tonghae Park near the town of Yangyang. **Kyongpodae Beach** is just north of the town of Kangnung, while **Pukpyong Beach** is at the town of Mukho, just south of Kangnung.

Central Section. Near the fishing village of Samchok are **Kunkok Beach** and **Hujin Beach,** both white-sand beaches that are apt to be less crowded than their more famous counterparts up the coast. Also in this area, near Uljin, are the **Paekam Hot Springs** and the **Songryu Limestone Cave,** which measures more than 500 yards in length. Also, there is a fine swimming beach just a few miles north of the coastal town of Tongmakri.

Southern Section. Near Pohang there are three excellent beaches. **Pohang Beach** is at the southern rim of the great bay that forms the port of Pohang; **Kuryongpo Beach** is on the outside off the great arm that forms this bay, facing the Sea of Japan; and not far from these two is **Chongha Beach.** All three are renowned for being clean and unpolluted.

SPORTS. Skiing. The East Coastal area boasts Korea's "real" ski areas. **Mt. Odaesan National Park** offers what is regarded as the peninsula's premier ski area at Yongpyong, or **"Dragon Valley" Ski Resort,** in the Taegwallyong Pass area, near Kangnung. At an altitude of around 2,120 feet, the resort meets international standards. Artificial snow-making machines have been installed, and chair lifts and T-bars carry skiers to slopes for different levels of ability. Skis and other equipment are available for rent. Lift tickets are W18,100 for a full day, and W17,050 for a half day. See "Accommodations" above for details of the resort's hotel facilities, and telephone numbers to call for more information.

North of Mt. Soraksan National Park in the Chinburyong Pass is a ski resort called **Alps.** While it does not yet rival Dragon Valley in size and scope of facilities, it is a charming area with eight ski slopes, four chair lifts and three T-bars. Accommodations are available in three small hotels, with a number of restaurants, bars, and snack bars. The resort also offers a discotheque, ski shop, indoor swimming pool, tennis courts, and an archery field. From Sokcho, it takes about 45 minutes by bus. For more information, call (0392) 4–2788, or the Seoul office (02) 756–5481.

Golf. There is one golf course in the area, the **Sorak Plaza,** with 18 holes. For details, call (0392) 32–7711, or Seoul (02) 729–3811.

Saltwater Fishing. The major surf-casting beaches, from north to south, are at **Kangson** (north of Sokcho), **Kangnung, Uljin, Pyonghae,** and **Pohang** (on the Sea of Japan side). Ask at your hotel about hiring boats if you would like to try your luck farther out.

Backpacking and Mountain Climbing. If hiking and camping in the midst of rugged mountains is your idea of fun, the East Coastal area is where you should go. Excellent backpacking trails traverse both the **Outer and Inner Sorak areas,** and guides are available for hire if you're into serious climbing in the area's more challenging mountains. But remember that these mountains must be respected, so you should be in top physical condition, and carry first-rate clothing and gear. A number of day hikes and overnight trips are available, using Sorak Village as a starting point. To backpack through the entire park would take at least four nights and five days.

For more specific information, contact the KNTC in Seoul (757–0086). They will provide you with the current telephone numbers for Korea's several hiking groups, all of which organize regular hikes in Soraksan Park.

SHOPPING. All the major hotels and many of the smaller ones have souvenir shops, but you will find it more interesting to browse through the marketplaces located in just about every small town. In the markets, you'll rub elbows with Koreans shopping for things that they will really use—to you such things may be ideal souvenirs. Don't worry about the language barrier. Storekeepers may not know English, but you will be able to communicate. At any rate, you'll find a fascinating range of goods, all for a fraction of the cost you'd pay in a hotel gift shop.

CULTURAL EVENTS. Kangnung Tano Festival. This is a ritual to pray for a good harvest which takes place on the fifth day of the fifth lunar month (June 24 in 1993). Held at a mountain shrine in Kangnung city, Tano is still observed as a primary rural holiday. The major event is a dance procession of shamans, followed by a presentation of mask dance and drama. The Tano festival ranks as Korea's Intangible Cultural Asset No. 13.

Sorak Festival. This celebration of Mt. Soraksan is held in the area of Sokcho. In 1993, the festival will take place at the end of September or the beginning of October, featuring candlelight processions, rituals to the mountain spirits, a fireworks display, and various cultural events.

The Arirang Festival. Held annually in the town of Chongson, this is Korea's most famous folk-song contest. It usually occurs early in October and includes a number of lively music and dance performances.

The national holidays and festivals are celebrated throughout the area also. Look under "National Holidays and Festivals" in *Facts at Your Fingertips* for details.

NIGHTLIFE. This part of the country has no cities like Seoul or Pusan, so don't plan on partying the night away. However, most hotels have a bar where you can enjoy a drink before dinner, and perhaps listen to music and other entertainment. In addition, several hotels have nightclubs, cocktail lounges, or both. The major nightclubs that cater to foreign visitors are at the Sorak Park, New Sorak, and Naksan Beach hotels. The ski resorts also feature a variety of evening entertainments. The Dragon Valley resort has a very popular disco, and the Sorak Park Hotel has the area's only casino.

USEFUL ADDRESSES AND TELEPHONE NUMBERS. Medical Care. There are two major hospitals in the area: the **Dong In Hospital** in Kangnung, Tel. (0391) 43–6161; and **Sokcho General Hospital,** Tel. (0392) 32–6821. The best thing to do if you need medical attention is to request the assistance of the hotel manager.

Tourist Complaint Center. The center for the East Coastal area is in Sokcho, Tel. (0392) 30–2544. You can also call this number for advice and information.

KYONGJU

In December 1979, at the UNESCO conference held in Thailand, Korea's Kyongju Valley was selected as one of 10 major ancient historic sites in the world. Located in the southeast of the country, around five hours' drive from Seoul, the Kyongju area has become Korea's most popular tourist destination outside the capital. Kyongju valley, the cradle of Silla culture, and the site of that dynasty's capital from 57 B.C. to A.D. 935, is in a geographically secluded basin between Taegu and Pusan, along the route of the Kyongbu Expressway that runs between Seoul and Pusan.

Temple sites with weathered stone pagodas, royal tombs, Buddhist bas-reliefs, and fortress ruins are scattered throughout the countryside surrounding this ancient city. The impact of these artistic achievements built in devotion to Buddha is still felt and recognized throughout Korea and the world.

The unified Silla period (668–935) carried Korean art and culture to unprecedented heights. As Tang was one of the most brilliant dynasties in Chinese history, Silla's close relationship with Tang was fruitful both politically and culturally. During the eighth century, this Silla capital had more than 1 million inhabitants and was the fourth-largest city of the ancient world, next to those of Constantinople, Baghdad, and Changan. That era is still referred to as Korea's "golden age."

A Little History

From 57 B.C. through the next millennium of Silla Dynasty rule, geographic isolation was an important factor in protecting the kingdom from China's predatory advances. Then, during the seventh century, in an alliance with Tang China, Silla defeated the other two Korean kingdoms on the peninsula, Paekche in 660 and Koguryo in 668. Following these victories, China tried but was unable to subjugate the Silla Dynasty, so all the territorial land south of the Taedong-gang River came under Silla rule.

The area effectively controlled by the Silla kingdom extended as far north as a line linking present-day Pyongyang with the east coast port of Wonsan, both now in North Korea. Being relatively free from external threat for the first time in its history, Silla was able to concentrate on internal progress.

In 424 Buddhism was informally introduced by a priest named Ado; however, not until a century later did Buddhism become the official state religion of the Silla nation. Then, in 503, Confucianism was introduced into Korea and was to affect the political, social, and cultural lives of the Korean people for nearly 5,000 years as secular Confucianism clashed with the ascetic and devout demands of Buddhism.

Yet Buddhism, with its arts, scholarship, and the magnificence of its temples and religious festivals, continued to spread and prosper. Today we still can admire some of Korea's outstanding treasured relics shaped by the creative genius and religious fervor of the artisans of that period. These achievements in temple architecture, sculpture, painting, metalwork, ceramics, and jewelry were matched by advances in mathematics, astronomy, and engineering. However, by the ninth century, Silla began to fall into a gradual decline, partly as a result of the contradictions arising from applying the Confucian Chinese system to an established aristocratic society that considered itself to be the protector of Buddhism.

Weak and immoral leaders were the cause of rebellions in the countryside, and in the year 918, one of the stronger rebels declared himself king of a new dynasty called Koryo, with the intention of restoring the glories of the once-powerful Korguryo. Eventually he forced the last Silla ruler to abdicate. The capital was moved to Kaesong, and Kyongju rapidly declined into a quiet country village, a shadow of its glorious past amidst the surviving historical monuments.

Thus this great dynasty, after a sequence of 56 kings peacefully ruling in turn, came to an end in 935, having lasted almost a millennium and leaving valuable relics for study by scholars in succeeding centuries.

Exploring the "Museum Without Walls"

You really need at least two days to see the highlights of Kyongju's marvelous Silla culture. A dedicated student of Korean history would not find this nearly enough time, but the most fascinating and visually dramatic sights are within easy distance of the city center, and over two days you could see them all. However, if you have time for further exploration, some important relics are still well off the beaten paths.

Unfortunately, there are few directional signs to guide you. A good publication for assistance is *Korea's Kyongju,* published in 1979 by the Seoul International Publishing House. It is the only complete and detailed historical guide of Kyongju in English and is available at most international hotel bookstores for about W10,000.

Other publications that go into less detail are also available in English and are most readily available in Kyongju at bookstores and souvenir shops.

If you only have one day for your Kyongju exploration, then the following sites are recommended (most have small admission charges): the Kyongju National Museum, Tumuli Park, Chomsongdae, Punhwangsa Pagoda, the Tomb of General Kim Yu-shin, the Tomb of King Muyol, Posokjong Bower, Sochulchi Pond, Pulguksa Temple, the Sokkuram Shrine, and the Kwaenung tomb.

National Museum

This museum should not be missed, as it displays some of Silla's most awesome relics. It is near the city center, to the southeast of City Hall, and is a long, low building with the upswept roof eaves of Korean traditional architecture. One of the main attractions is in a pavilion in the grounds—the 11-foot-high, 23-ton Emilleh Bell (pronounced Em-ee-leh), which was cast in the year 771 and is one of the largest and most resonant bells in all of Asia. The name comes from an ancient Silla term literally meaning "mommy." One legend says that the bell was named Emilleh because its sound resembles a small child calling for its mother; another tells of the sacrifice of a young girl for the successful casting of the bronze.

Inside the main building, displays begin with some of the prehistoric artifacts found around Kyongju and the more sophisticated implements of the Three Kingdoms era. You can see the strong native shamanist influence in relics from Korea's pre-Buddhist times, such as the golden crowns, and the glories of Buddhist inspiration in pottery and sculpture.

As you study the various displays in the museum, their effects are dazzling. The incredible skills that produced these beautiful works of art were fully developed by the eighth century, while Europe was still in the Dark Ages.

You must realize, too, that Korea has only scratched the surface of a vast wealth of archaeological discoveries. Many of the displays are outside the museum buildings, and the museum itself is open from 9 A.M. to 5 P.M. every day except Monday.

Tumuli Park

This is Kyongju's Tomb Park, just a short walk south of City Hall, an area that was first opened to the public in 1975. It holds 20 of the larger royal tombs—there are some 200, large and small, in the city and environs, and a hundred more scattered around the nearby countryside. None of the tombs appear to have been disturbed during a period of 1,000 years, although many have been found to contain objects of great value.

Two large tombs in Tumuli Park were excavated in 1973, and one of them has been converted into an underground museum. This is the famous "Heavenly Horse" tomb (Chonmachong), so named because of a rare painting of a horse on a birch bark saddleguard found during the archeological excavations. The interior of the tomb has been rebuilt to show how the tombs were constructed, and all the artifacts on display are replicas. In all, more than 10,000 items were excavated, and the precious originals are in the Kyongju National Museum.

Another tomb of interest here is that of Michu, the 13th Silla king, a seventh-generation descendant of Kim Al-Chi, the founder of the Kim Clan (see a later paragraph about the Kyerim Forest). A legend claims

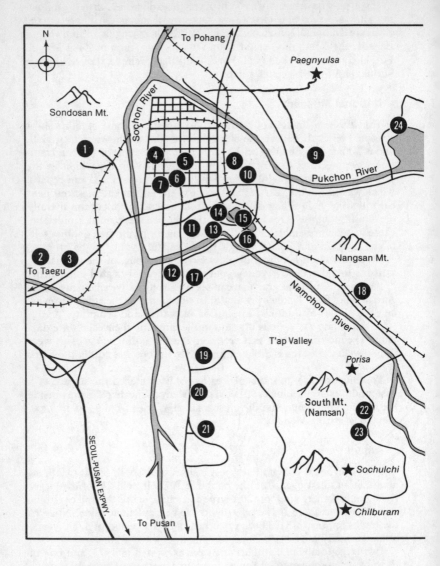

N

To Pohang

Paegnyulsa

Sochon River

Sondosan Mt.

1

4 5

8

10

7 6

9

Pukchon River

24

14

15

11 13

16

2 3

To Taegu

Nangsan Mt.

12 17

18

Namchon River

T'ap Valley

19

Porisa

20

South Mt. (Namsan)

22

21

23

SEOUL-PUSAN EXPWY.

Sochulchi

Chilburam

To Pusan

Points of Interest

Anapchi (Duck and Goose Pond) **15**
Buddhist Triad **20**
Bus Station **7**
Chomsongdae (Star Tower) **14**
City Hall **5**
Folk Craft Village **27**
Gyelim Youth Hostel **31**

Hwarang House **22**
Hyupsung Hotel **4**
Kolon Hotel **29**
Kuchongni (Square Tomb) **32**
Kwaenung Tomb **34**
Kyerim (Chicken Forest) **11**
Kyongju Chosun Hotel **25**
Kyongju Hilton Hotel **26**
Kyongju Train Station **8**

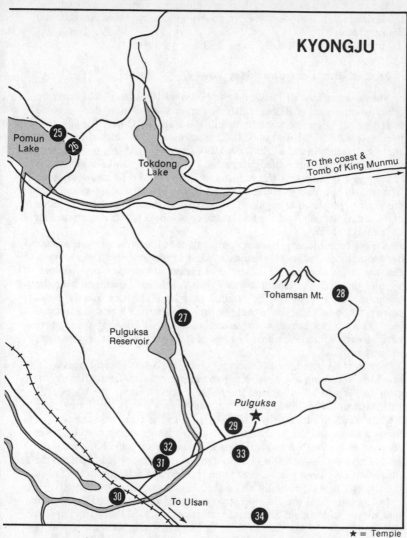

KYONGJU

Pomun Lake

Tokdong Lake

To the coast &
Tomb of King Munmu

Tohamsan Mt. **28**

Pulguksa Reservoir

Pulguksa ★

To Ulsan

★ = Temple

Najong Shrine **17**
National Museum of Kyongju
  (containing the Emilleh Bell) **16**
Onung (Five Tombs) **12**
Panwolsong Fortress **13**
Pomunho Hotel **24**
Posokjong Bower **19**
Pulguksa Hotel **33**
Pulguksa Train Station **30**
Punhwangsa Pagoda **10**

Queen Sondok Tomb **18**
Samnung Tombs **21**
Soak Sowon Confucian Hall **2**
Sokkuram Grotto Shrine **28**
Tomb of General Kim Yushin **1**
Tomb of King Muyol **3**
Tomb of King Talhae **9**
Tongilchon Hall **23**
Tumuli Park **6**

that after Michu's death, when the country was under attack, troops of soldiers with bamboo leaves in their ears appeared from his tomb to defeat the invaders. His tomb is therefore known as Chukyonnung, or Bamboo Soldier Tomb.

Tumuli Park is open daily from 8:30 A.M. to 6 P.M.

Around Chomsongdae "Star Tower"

Not far from Tumuli Park and the National Museum is what may be the most renowned of Korea's historic remains—Chomsongdae—a stone astronomical observatory built during the reign of Queen Sondok (the twenty-seventh Silla ruler) in 634. Chomsongdae is considered the oldest such observatory in the world. It is a 29-foot tower that was built according to complex mathematical principles. For example, the 12 stones of the base appear to represent the months of the year; the 30 layers of stone from top to bottom symbolize the days of the month; the 24 stones that are slightly projected at regular intervals show the seasonal subdivisions of the lunar calendar; and the total number of blocks is 366, corresponding to the days of the year.

A more recent theory, however, suggests that this structure was a Buddhist ritual altar rather than an astronomical observatory. The theory is that the actual observatory indicated in historical records was sited nearby, and that today's "Chomsongdae" was mistakenly identified over the centuries once all traces of the original were lost. The controversial viewpoint is based on suggestions that the present structure is not in a suitable location for astronomical observation, and that its bottle shape is more suggestive of a Buddhist altar. The age of the tower is not in dispute, only its purpose.

Nearby is Kyerim Forest (Chicken Forest), a glade of ancient trees within which, according to legend, Korea's ubiquitous Kim family has its origins. The legend is that during the reign of King Talhae, the fourth Silla ruler, a man found a golden box hanging from a tree in this forest, with a white cock crowing nearby. He reported it to the king, who came to the forest and opened the box, finding an infant inside. Later the child was adopted as the king's crown prince and given the surname Kim, meaning gold. The seventh-generation descendant of this Kim Al-Chi became the thirteenth Silla king, Michu, and from the seventeenth king to the fall of the dynasty in 935, virtually all of the kings were his descendants.

In the same area are the meager remains of Panwolsong Fortress, all that survive of the main Silla royal residence. It is said that in its heyday, this castle was so large that to walk through it would wear out a pair of straw sandals.

On the grounds of Panwolsong is Sokpinggo, a well-preserved ice house constructed of stone. You can peer through the doorway of this cavelike structure, which is covered with earth. Over a thousand stones were used in the construction.

Across the road from Panwolsong is Anapchi Pond (Duck and Goose Pond), in the garden where the last Silla ruler surrendered to Koryo forces. The garden was originally within the fortress walls, and featured an exotic collection of unusual trees, plants, and animals from all over the world. Lakes and hills were sculptured to represent the beautiful Musan region of China. The largest pavilion was Imhaejon, which could hold some thousand people. Today's replica is about a quarter of the original size. Excavations of the lake revealed a treasure of Silla artifacts, including a fully outfitted royal barge. These items are now on display at the National Museum.

Punhwangsa Pagoda

Listed as a national treasure, the stone pagoda on the grounds of Punhwangsa (Famous Emperor Temple) is considered one of the two oldest Silla structures (the other is Chomsongdae). Built to honor Queen Sondok in 634, the pagoda is unique for two reasons—its superlative carvings and statuettes, and the fact that although it appears to be constructed of brick, it is actually of cut stones, each shaped to the form of a brick. At its base are four rectangular openings, with fierce guardians carved in bold relief on each panel.

The temple site is a short distance east of City Hall.

The Tomb of General Kim Yu-Shin

Several Silla tombs contain zodiac animals carved in bas relief, and these along with the civilian figures clad in traditional costume on the tomb of General Kim are regarded as among the finest. Kim Yu-Shin served as Silla's greatest general under King Muyol and later under his son, Munmu, during the period of Silla unification. The tomb is about 10 minutes from town, to the west, in the Songhwasan district.

Tomb of King Muyol

King Muyol, the twenty-ninth Silla ruler, is considered to be one of the greatest kings of the dynasty. His tomb is south of General Kim's and is distinguished by a type of stone monument that was new at the time of unified Silla—a huge tortoise base from which rises a shaft topped by a capstone that carried the inscription. The tortoise tablet in front of King Muyol's tomb is difficult to match anywhere in terms of skill and elegance.

The grave of King Muyol's son, Munmu, who became king upon his father's death, is in a most interesting location—in the nearby shallow coastal waters of the East Sea (the Sea of Japan).

Lying about 220 yards offshore at the north end of Ponggil Beach is a series of granite knobs containing the king's underwater tomb. In the center of a cross-shaped waterway cutting through the rocks is a tortoise-shaped slab of granite, said by some historians to be the place where Munmu's ashes were scattered, and by others to be the cover of his remains. Whatever the truth about his burial, it is known that Munmu had one great wish—to rid the coastal region of Silla of Japanese pirates. Among his parting words was a promise to be reborn as a dragon of the East Sea.

You can reach the coast by bus from Kyongju, a distance of around 19 miles along highway No. 4 and then a local road. The information center at the bus terminal (Tel. 2–9289) will be able to give you departure details.

Near Muyol's tomb is Soak Sowon, the West Peak Confucian Hall, established during the sixteenth century to honor great scholars, and one of Silla's distinctive three-storied pagodas.

The Posokjong (Abalone) Stone Bower and Sites Nearby

On the western slopes of Namsan Mountain is the site that marks the final tragedy of the Silla Dynasty. Kyongae, the fifty-seventh ruler, and his queen were assassinated in 927 while in the midst of a festive celebration. All that remains of this site of an old royal detached palace are some stone channels that gave the course of a stream (now dry) the shape of an abalone shell. In ancient days, cups of wine were floated on the stream's waters during poetry contests held by the aristocracy.

Five minutes away, north toward the city, is Onung (Five Tombs), which is said to be the burial site of the very first Silla king, Pak Hyokkose, his queen, and three later kings. And between Onung and Posokjong is the shrine called Najong, which is said to be the spot where Pak Hyokkose was hatched from an egg laid by a heavenly horse.

Farther to the south, along the same road, is the Sungbang valley area where there stands a Buddhist triad in stone. This is considered to be the oldest of the Silla period, perhaps dating to the sixth century. The central image of the Buddha of the Western Paradise is over eight feet tall and is carved from a single block of granite. It is flanked by two, slightly smaller Bodhisattvas, and they are all characterized by round plump faces and conspicuous smiles. Nearby, also, are a number of other relief Buddha images and stone statues and the Samnung tombs of Atala (the eighth Silla king), Shintok (the fifty-third), and Kyongmyong (the fifty-fourth). A little farther south is the tomb of Kyongae (the fifty-fifth king). These rulers were all from the Pak (forerunners of today's "Park") clan, while the majority of Silla kings, as mentioned earlier, shared the family name of Kim. The other surname that appears in Silla royalty is Sok.

Eastern Namsan, the Porisa Temple, and Sochulchi Pond

On the eastern slope of Namsan Mountain are the remains of the Temple of Porisa (the Enlightening Awakening Temple), with several striking stone relief carvings. Farther to the south, near Namsan Village, is Sochulchi, a pond with a fine pavilion within easy walking distance of the entrance road. Nearby are a relief image of a seated Buddha and a rare example of two pagodas of different styles standing as a pair. One has its stories and "roofs" carved from a single piece of rock, with no ornamentation, and the other has a double-layered base and eight guardian demons sculptured in relief on each side.

If you have time, you can take a hike of an hour or so beyond Namsan Village to Chilburam (Seven Buddha Hermitage). The sculptures here are the finest in Kyongju after the Sokkuram Grotto, and it is one of the most worthwhile hikes on Namsan Mountain.

This whole area of Namsan Mountain, of which we've discussed only the sites on its fringes, was a "holy land" for the Silla people, and the center of Silla Buddhism. Over 100 temple sites are within the range that is only eight miles long and five miles wide, along with some 60 stone Buddha images and 40 stone pagodas.

Pulguksa Temple

The Pulguksa Temple, 10 miles out of Kyongju to the southeast, probably draws more tourists than any other temple in Korea. Dating to 535 and expanded in 751, many of the present buildings were reconstructed in the most recent renovation, in 1973. The temple holds six national treasures (pagodas, bridges, and Buddhas), and the balance and symmetry of its former glory are still seen in its walls, bridges, pillars, and stone pagodas. This temple remains one of the most remarkable achievements of the ancient world in the Far East.

During the popular holiday seasons of spring and fall, the temple grounds are packed with people on tours, so that Pulguksa loses the sense of serenity once found at most Korean temples. Nevertheless, to visit Kyongju and not visit this famed temple of Silla's golden age would be to miss one of the area's real treasures.

Sokkuram Shrine

Built at about the same time as Pulguksa Temple on a mountain peak just above, the stone-grotto shrine called Sokkuram holds a great granite Buddha and wonderful bas-reliefs of guardian figures. The domed roof is also a remarkable engineering feat that has withstood the test of time. Unfortunately, today many of the images cannot be seen. The humidity caused by too many visitors brought the threat of damage and the grotto itself can now only be viewed through glass. It is still well worth a visit, however, as the location is exquisite and what you can see of the carvings is spectacular.

The grotto is easy to reach by road, on a scenic drive through forest, or you can go in a more traditional manner by taking a hiking trail up from Pulguksa Temple.

The Kwaenung Tomb

This is the most elaborate of the Silla Tombs, with stone military and civilian officials as well as sculptured lions and the 12 signs of the zodiac still guarding the grassy mound. The zodiac figures are dressed in military attire.

Legend says that this is the grave of the thirty-eighth Silla king, Wonsong, who reigned at the end of the eighth century.

Kwaenung is in the same area as Pulguksa Temple.

Other Recommended Sites

If you have more time, a visit to the Paengnyulsa Temple, northeast of the city center, is interesting. There are no records to show when the temple was built, but it was already in existence at the beginning of the seventh century. Legend says that the head of Korea's first Buddhist martyr, Yi Cha-Don, landed on the site when he was beheaded.

Nearby are a group of Buddhist figures, in the ruins of a temple called Kulpulsa. A total of nine images have been sculpted on four sides of a huge rock, each using a different technique and assuming a different pose. All of them, however, have the plump and serene characteristics of the early Unified Silla Buddha images. According to legend, King Kyongtok was on his way to Paengnyulsa Temple when he heard an underground voice reciting Buddhist chants. He had the site excavated and found the huge rock. Accepting his discovery as a sign from heaven, he had the images carved and built the temple of Kulpulsa.

A little more to the south is the tomb of Sok Talhae, the fourth Silla king. He is another king who according to legend was hatched from an egg, and was given the surname "Sok," part of a Chinese ideogram meaning magpie, as these birds were seen hovering over the box in which he was found. He became a member of the royal family by marrying a princess and succeeded to the throne when he was 62 years old.

Sites around Nangsan Mountain (Wolf Mountain) are also recommended, including Queen Sondok's tomb, the ruins of various temples, and the remains of ancient kilns.

Modern Sites in Remembrance of History

On the eastern slopes of Namsan Mountain are two Korean-style complexes of recent construction to commemorate the importance of the Silla era in Korean history. Tongilchon, the "Palace of Reunification," is on the site of the original Hwarang, a Silla education center for the young elite. The buildings are grand, and the grounds are pretty, but the magnificence of Silla style simply cannot be captured in a modern structure. Farther south is the new Hwarang Education Center, established in 1977 for the purpose of educating today's young Koreans in the philosophies of ancient Silla.

PRACTICAL INFORMATION FOR KYONGJU

WHEN TO GO. Kyongju is in one of the mildest areas of the country, still hot in summer and cold in winter, and simply perfect in spring and fall with warm days and cool evenings. Like all areas of the country with hills, autumn brings the most stunning foliage, which makes all the temple settings particularly beautiful. No matter the season, Kyongju is an easy place to get around in, with few extremes of weather to keep you indoors.

HOW TO GET THERE. Kyongju is on the Kyongju Expressway, the main road link between Seoul and Pusan, and forms the corner where the road turns to directly head south. It lies 223 miles from Seoul, 42 miles from Pusan, and 34 miles from Taegu.

From Seoul. By **superexpress train** (Saemaul) from Seoul Station, departures twice daily at 9 A.M. and 5:30 P.M. The trip takes around four hours, and reservations are necessary (W18,000 first-class and W14,800 economy regardless of travel day). Call the Seoul Station foreigners' ticket counter for more details (Tel. (02) 392–7811). Most of Kyongju's tourist hotels offer a free **shuttle-bus** service from the train station. By **express bus,** from Seoul's Kangnam terminal, a 4-hour, 15-minute ride, departing every 35 minutes, 7 A.M. to 6:10 P.M. (W6,620). No planes go directly to Kyongju.

From Pusan. By **air-conditioned express train** (Mugunghwa) and **ordinary express train** (Tongil), and the slower Pigeon. Call (051) 463–7788 for details. You can also ask about the special **tourist steam train** that operates between Pusan and Kyongju in the summer peak holiday season, which gives you time to enjoy the scenery along the way. By **express bus,** from the Express Bus Terminal, a one-hour ride, departing every 30 minutes, 7 A.M. to 7:30 P.M. (W1,500). You can also take an **intercity bus** from Pusan's Tongbu terminal.

From Taegu. By **train,** superexpress, air-conditioned express, ordinary express, and Pigeon, with a wide choice of departures. Call the foreigners' counter (053–92–7788) at the Tongtaegu (East Taegu) train station for details. By **express bus,** from the Tongbu Express Bus Terminal, a 50-minute ride departing every 18 minutes, 4:30 A.M. to 10 P.M. (W1,260).

HOW TO GET AROUND. With limited time, your best travel solution is to hire a **taxi** for the day. The cost will be around W50,000, less if you're a good bargainer and it's not peak season. Plenty of **buses** run out to the Pulguksa Temple from the downtown bus terminal, and there are a number of **bus tours** around the major sights that also operate from here (see "Tours" below for more details). You can hire **bicycles** downtown or at the Pomun Lake Resort. This is a fun way to get around, but not particularly practical if you want to see a lot of Kyongju in a short time. Rental fees are around W15,000 per day.

Car Rental. This is another good way to get around, and even better if you also hire a driver. Cost will be in the range of W29,000 to W120,000 per 12 hours, plus another W15,000 or so for a driver. Your hotel can advise, or you can call Samjin Rent-a-Car (Tel. 0561-42-3311).

ACCOMMODATIONS. There are three main areas for tourist accommodations—downtown, the Pomun Lake Resort, and in the area of the Pulguksa Temple. For a twin or double room, rates are as follows: *Superior Deluxe/Deluxe*, W80,000 to W135,000; *2d class*, W35,000 to W65,000; and *3d class*, W25,000 to W35,000. There are no hotels classified as 1st class in the Kyongju area, and we should remind you that the deluxe category here is not as luxurious in facilities and services as it is in Seoul. Language will be more of a problem than in the capital, or even Pusan, but as more and more Western tourists are visiting the area, much effort has been going into the improvement of language skills for everyone connected with the travel industry. Note that seasonal rate variations often apply at the major hotels. Credit card abbreviations used are American Express, AE; Diner's Club, DC; MasterCard, MC; Visa, V.

At Pomun Lake Resort

Kyongju Hilton. *Superior Deluxe.* 370, Shinpyong-dong, Kyongju, Kyongsangbukdo; Tel. (0561) 745–7788, Seoul (02) 753–7788, Fax. (0561) 745–7799. With 325 rooms, this hotel, affiliated with the Hilton International chain, is the newest addition to Kyongju. It features banquet rooms, a health club, indoor/outdoor swimming pools, tennis courts, a sauna, and a nightclub. Credit cards: AE, DC, MC, V.

Kyongju Chosun. *Deluxe.* 410, Shinpyong-dong, Kyongju, Kyongsangbukdo; Tel. (0561) 745–7701, Seoul office (02) 753–0300, Telex K54467, Fax. (0561) 40–8349. Just over 300 rooms, and an impressive collection of facilities including Korean, Japanese, and Western restaurants, a cocktail lounge, a nightclub, and a theater-restaurant. There are also large outdoor and indoor swimming pools, tennis courts, and facilities for bowling, boating, and fishing. The hotel also operates the 36-hole golf course. Credit cards: AE, DC, MC, V. (This hotel is not affiliated with the Westin Chosun in Seoul.)

Kyongju Hot Spring. *2d class.* 145–1, Kujong-dong, Kyongju, Kyongsangbukdo; Tel. (0561) 746–6661, Fax. (0561) 46–6665. This 100-room hotel offers several restaurants, an indoor swimming pool, a night club, and a health club. Credit cards: AE, DC, MC, V.

Near Pulguksa Temple

Kolon. *Deluxe.* 111-1 Ma-dong, Kyongju, Kyongsangbukdo; Tel. (0561) 746–9001, Seoul office (02) 777–4393, Telex K54469, Fax. (0561) 746–6331. 240 rooms, Western, Korean, and Japanese restaurants, a coffee shop, cocktail lounge, and nightclub. The Kolon Hotel has Kyongju's only casino. There are also an indoor swimming pool, sauna, tennis courts, fishing pond, and a nine-hole golf course. Credit cards: AE, DC, MC, V.

Pulguksa Tourist. *3d class.* 648-1, Chinhyon-dong, Kyongju, Kyongsangbukdo; Tel. (0561) 746–1911. 81 rooms, with a choice of restaurants and a coffee shop, cocktail lounge, nightclub, and tennis courts. Credit cards: AE, DC, MC, V.

Downtown Area

Hyupsung Tourist. *3d class.* 130-6, Noso-dong, Kyongju, Kyongsang-bukdo; Tel. (0561) 41–3335. Just 30 rooms, conveniently located near the bus terminal. It has one restaurant, a coffee shop, cocktail lounge, and nightclub. No credit cards.

Korean Inns (Yogwan). These are excellent value in Kyongju if you're economy-minded. The two major locations for the inns are downtown, and out near the Pulguksa Temple. Facilities are very limited—you may have to share a bathroom, and there are no dining facilities (although you can arrange to have Korean meals brought in). However, you'll pay less than W18,000 per day. The following are used to catering to foreign visitors: **Sillajang,** near City Hall (Tel. 2–1004); **Wangnimjang,** also near City Hall (Tel. 2–6602); **Kwibinjang,** in downtown Sobu-dong (Tel. 749–4681); **Yongbinjang,** near the bus terminal (Tel. 2–6303); and **Pulguksa Pyoljang,** near the temple (Tel. 746–4748).

Youth Hostel. There is one good youth hostel in Kyongju, the **Gyelim Youth Hostel** at 700–1, Chinhyon-dong; Tel. (0561) 746–0601 or 743–9677 in Seoul. There are dormitory-style accommodations, plus a few double and twin rooms, and Korean-style rooms, as well as a restaurant and a coffee shop. No credit cards.

RESTAURANTS. The three major hotels—**Chosun** and **Hilton** at Pomun Lake, and the **Kolon** near Pulguksa—offer the best quality and variety in cuisine. Here are the choicest Japanese restaurants (where costs range from moderate to expensive), and the only Western restaurants of any caliber (outside these major hotels the Western food is, at best, mediocre). If you insist on Western food, you can keep costs down by eating in the coffee shops, where the selection is limited but prices inexpensive to moderate. The **Pomunho Hotel,** the annex of the hotel training school at Pomun Lake, serves good Western food but tends to be expensive. As is the case in any small Korean town, the best dining values are in Korean food, and there is an excellent assortment of small restaurants downtown, and in the areas around the Pulguksa Temple. Consult the *Food and Drink* chapter earlier in this guide for an idea of the dishes to order. Your hotel manager will be able to advise you about places that have some experience with Western visitors. For a more expensive (W15,000–W30,000) Korean meal, you can go to **Yosokkung,** in Kyo-dong to the south of the central city area (Tel. 2–3347), which is an old-style Korean home converted into a charming restaurant. This place caters well to foreign visitors. You can also try **Maeil Garden,** 120-7, Nodong-dong (Tel. 42–6500) where the pulgogi is reasonably priced, or **Suhojong Shiktang,** 235–1, Nodong-dong (Tel. 43–0953), which is popular with Westerners. A popular *kalbi* (beef ribs) house is **Kyongju Kalbi,** in Inwang-dong near the National Museum (Tel. 2–5262). An inexpensive (W6,000–W10,000) Korean restaurant that has become popular with Western tourists is **Ilshimok Shiktang,** in Nodong-dong (Tel. 2–3891).

At the Pomun Resort, one of the most pleasant settings for dinner is at **Hobanjang** (Tel. 40–6260), which is a Korean lakeside restaurant, run by the Concorde Hotel, featuring a nightly performance of traditional music and dance. At the Pomun Resort, also, there are a number of small restaurants within the "amenity" core of the resort. Here some 14 Korean buildings surround an outdoor theater, and you'll find a number of outdoor cafes and air-conditioned "diners" tucked in among the souvenir stores.

There is a well-known Chinese restaurant in Kyongju, called **Choongkukseong,** in Tonggu-dong (Tel. 2–3875). The exterior these days does not look welcoming, but the food is above average and moderately priced (W10,000–W15,000).

TOURS. Depending on the time of year, there are a number of **bus excursions** departing from the Kyongju train station or the bus terminal. These take two hours, 30 minutes, and are reasonably priced at W5,500, excluding any admission fees to enter temples and other historic sites. A typical full-day program would take in the Tomb of General Kim Yu-Shin, the Muyol and Onung Tomb sites, Posokjong, Tumuli Park, Chomsongdae, Panwolsong, the Anapchi Pond, Punhwangsa Pagoda, the Museum, Unification Hall, Pulguksa Temple, and the Sokkuram Grotto, with short stops at each. Half-day tours would visit just a couple of the major attractions, such as the Pulguksa Temple and Sokkuram Grotto, or the Museum and Tumuli Park. Current details on these tours are available from Kyongju's information centers—at the bus terminal (Tel. 2–9289); the railway station (Tel. 2–3843); Pulguksa Temple (Tel. 746–4747); and the Kyongju Tourist Association (Tel. 41–2277).

There are a number of **package tours,** requiring a minimum of just two people, operated out of Seoul by several travel and tour agencies. These either visit just Kyongju for two days or more, or include the "outdoor museum" as part of programs that also visit Pusan and other centers of the Southeast Area. The "Tours" section of the *Southeast* chapter of this guide has more details of operating companies, programs, and prices.

WHAT TO SEE. Just about everything in Kyongju that's worth exploring is a historic site. These have been highlighted earlier in this chapter. There are just a couple of other sites not as impressive but which could be of special interest to some.

On the way to Pulguksa Temple is the only square tomb of the Unified Silla period found in Kyongju. Known as **Kuchongni,** the tomb is 31 feet by 31 feet and six-and-a-half feet high, with the entrance to the stone chamber on the south side. Signs of the zodiac decorate the sides. The actual age of the tomb and the name of the person buried are not known.

If you are interested in ancient fortifications, the remains of the earliest known Silla fortress, **Myonghwalsansong,** can be glimpsed on the south side of the road that leads to the Pomun Lake Resort. One historical record states that the fortress was built in the year 405 and repaired in 554 and 593. It is over half a mile in length.

The Museum. A visit to the National Museum, in a very convenient downtown location, will show you the artistic triumphs of the Silla era of Korean history. Historically important artifacts and treasured art objects have been collected from tombs, temples, and cultural sites all over

You've Let Your Imagination Go, Now Get Up And Follow Your Dreams.

For The Vacation You're Dreaming Of, Call American Express® Travel Agency At 1-800-YES-AMEX*

American Express will send more than your imagination soaring. We'll fly you, sail you, drive you to any Fodor's destination and beyond. Because American Express believes the best vacations happen from Europe to the Orient, Walt Disney® World to Hawaii and everywhere in between.

For dependable service, expert advice, and value wherever your dreams take you, call on American Express. After all, the best traveling companion is a trustworthy friend.

AMERICAN EXPRESS **Travel Agency**

It's easy to recognize
a good place
when you see one.

American Express Cardmembers have been doing it for years.

The secret? Instead of just relying on what they see in the window,

they look at the door. If there's an American Express Blue Box on it, they

know they've found an establishment that cares about high standards.

Whether it's a place to eat, to sleep, to shop, or simply meet, they

know they will be warmly welcomed.

So much so, they're rarely taken in by anything else.

Always a good sign.

Kyongju and brought here for permanent display. The museum is open daily except Mondays and Korean public holidays (Tel. 0561-2-5193).

SPORTS. Hiking. The most popular outdoor activity in Kyongju is hiking as the entire area is a parkland of cultural treasures. **Namsan Mountain** is the most rewarding area, less than four miles from the city center. Most of the trails can be hiked in two hours or less, and you're not likely to get lost, although there are few directional signs. One of the most popular routes is from Namsan Village up to Chilburam, the Seven Buddha Hermitage, which takes about an hour. The hike is well worth the effort, as the statues and carvings here are the finest in Kyongju after the Sokkuram Grotto.

Golf. There is one outstanding course of 36 holes, at the **Kyongju Country Club** overlooking Pomun Lake. Your hotel can help you arrange play, or call (0561) 40-8412 for details. There is a Seoul office (Tel. 02-753-1974). The **Kolon Hotel** has its own nine-hole course, and the **Tokyu Hotel** has some indoor practice facilities.

Cycling. This is a fun way of getting around Kyongju, combining recreation and sightseeing. Talk to the hotel information staff (or the tourist offices) about places to hire bicycles, possible both in the city and out at the Pomun Lake Resort, for rates of around W15,000 per day.

Dotoruk World, at Pomun Lake. This combines an amusement park with sports facilities. There are carnival-type rides, several swimming pools, tennis courts, a camping ground, and sports grounds for soccer and baseball. Crowds are common.

THE POMUN LAKE RESORT. This is about five miles to the east of downtown Kyongju, and involves the full-scale tourism development of the east side of the Pomun Lake. Here are Kyongju's top hotels (apart from the Kolon which is near Pulguksa Temple); a 36-hole golf course at a membership country club plus a six-hole public course; an amusement park and sports facilities; a vast complex of shops and snack bars; a small zoo and aquarium; an outdoor theater; ornithology and anthropology pavilion; facilities for horseback riding; lake-side restaurants with all manner of foods and entertainment; and a full array of watersports including paddle-boating, cruising by unusual "Swan" launches, fishing, and swimming. The hotels also offer their own resort facilities, including tennis courts, bowling alleys, and outdoor and indoor pools.

SHOPPING. Kyongju's specialties are, of course, the pottery and folkcrafts reminiscent of the Silla Dynasty. Antiques are plentiful but are inclined to be more expensive than in Seoul. Most of the stores are located in the downtown area, within walking distance of the station. The tourist information centers can guide you to reputable dealers. (Remember, you need a permit to take any genuine antique out of the country—ask the dealer for help with this.) There is a good local market in Chungang-dong downtown, plus a host of small stores along the main street and side alleys that are worth exploring. For souvenirs and curios, one of the best areas is the giant arcade at the **Pomun Lake Resort** (Tel. 40-7332). Other recommended gift shops are as follows: **Kyongdo Gift Shop** in downtown In-wang-dong (Tel. 42–6429); the **Silla Store** near City Hall (Tel. 2–0307); the **Dalwoo Sangsa,** in Hwangnam-dong (Tel. 41–0683); and **Minsoggwan,** in the Chinhyon Arcade, near Pulguksa Temple (Tel. 746–4976). This last store is also an authorized tax-refund store. See the "Shopping" section of *Facts at Your Fingertips* for details on how to obtain refunds.

The **Kyongju Folk Arts Village** is worth a visit, and you can include it on your trip to the Pulguksa Temple area. The complex includes a main display and sales hall, plus pavilions where you can watch various artisans produce ceramics, metalwork, baskets, bamboo and lacquerware, embroidered items, jewelry of cloisonné and precious stones, wood carvings, and stone statuettes. The telephone number is 746–7270.

CULTURAL EVENTS. Apart from the countrywide holidays and festivals, there are a number of special events that are celebrated exclusively in Kyongju. Most of them are cultural celebrations of ancient Silla, Confucian rites, or ceremonies to honor Silla rulers, and they follow the lunar calendar. Remember, also, that **Buddha's Birthday** (May 28 in 1993) is a particularly beautiful celebration in Kyongju, as all the temples are traditionally decorated with lanterns and there are candlelight processions in the evening.

The KNTC will be able to advise you on the exact dates for the following events:

Confucian Memorial Ceremony, usually February 5 and August 5. A traditional ritual at Soak Sowon to honor Confucius and other famous scholars of the Silla period.

Samjon, at the spring equinox. Ceremonies are held at Kyongju's three major shrines to commemorate the founders of the three Silla clans of Pak, Sok, and Kim. The rituals take place at Onung, and near the tomb of Michu in Tumuli Park.

Kumsan, usually March 25 and September 25. This is another traditional Confucian rite, especially to honor Kim Yu-Shin, Silla's greatest general who served under the kings Muyol and Munmu during the period of unification. The rites are held near the general's tomb.

Priest Wonhyo Ceremony, March. Held at the Punhwangsa Temple, this ceremony is to honor one of Korea's greatest Buddhist priests. His portrait is enshrined at the temple.

Ceremony to Yi Cha-Don, September. This is a Buddhist ceremony held at Hungnyunsa Temple, the site of Silla's earliest temple (near the Onung tombs), to honor this sixth-century martyr.

Six Village Elders Ceremony, September. This is held at the Najong Shrine, to honor the six village chiefs who witnessed the legendary appearance of Pak Hyokkose who was hatched from an egg laid by a heavenly horse. He founded the Pak clan and became the first Silla king.

Samnung Ceremony, at the fall equinox. Rites take place at the Samnung tombs, on the western slope of Namsan Mountain, to honor the Silla kings of the Pak clan.

Paegyol Memorial Ceremony, October. This is held at Hyanggyo, the Confucian institute near Panwolsong Fortress, to honor a poor Confucian scholar and master of the traditional Komungoo musical instrument.

The above ceremonies are small but fascinating, whereas the highlight of the Kyongju year is the **Silla Cultural Festival** (usually held at the beginning of September), which involves the whole area in a pageant of culture and entertainment. Amid the countless historic sites of royal tombs, stone pagodas, and ancient temple sites, you can watch a wealth of processions, performances, and demonstrations of dance, drama, and martial arts. It's a wonderful time to be in Kyongju, but make sure you have reservations for your hotel and transportation there and back.

NIGHTLIFE. For the Western styles of evening entertainment, you should head for the major hotels—the **Kolon, Kyongju Chosun, Hilton,** and **Pulguksa Tourist Hotel**—which offer nightclubs, cocktail lounges, discotheques, and theater-restaurants. There are a couple of downtown nightclubs worth a visit—**Taebon** (Tel. 42–8225), and the **Hyopsong** (Tel. 41–3335) in Nosodong. The **Kolon Hotel** has the only casino (Tel. 746–9001).

With its small-town atmosphere, Kyongju is an excellent place to experience the local evening entertainments. You can explore the beer halls, wine houses, and tearooms in the area of the railway station, or along the side streets of Nodong-dong and Hwango-dong.

USEFUL ADDRESSES AND TELEPHONE NUMBERS. Medical Attention. For any medical emergency, ask your hotel manager for assistance, or you can go to the **Keimyung University Kyongju Dongsan Hospital,** at Seobu-dong (Tel. 42–8515–9).

Tourist Information. There are four tourist information centers in Kyongju. The staff are helpful, but sometimes their printed materials are in short supply. The KNTC (especially the information center in Seoul), Tel. (02) 757–0086, has some pictorial brochures on Kyongju that you will find useful, but, surprisingly, it is not easy to find a good map.

These telephone numbers (the prefix for out-of-town calls is 0561) could be useful:

Kyongju Express Bus Terminal Tourist Information Center, Tel. 2–9289
Kyongju Railway Station Tourist Information Center, Tel. 2–3843
Kyongju Railway Station Foreigners' Counter, Tel. 43–8053
Kyongju Tourist Association, Tel. 41–2277
Pulguksa Temple Tourist Information Center, Tel. 746–4747
Tourist Complaints and Advice, Tel. 749–0101

TAEGU

Taegu is in the heart of Kyongsangpukdo Province and, with a population of over 2 million, is the third-largest city in Korea. Like Pusan, because of its size and importance as a commercial hub, Taegu has the status of a province, under the direct control of the central government.

Surrounded on all sides by mountains rising to more than 3,500 feet, the city has peculiar variations in weather that give it the distinction of being both the hottest and coldest city in the country.

Taegu is the only Korean metropolis completely removed from the coast—thus it regards itself as a true interior city. Situated in a large basin, the city slopes northward toward the Kumho-gang River, which meanders and then joins the Naktong-gang River west of Taegu. Over recent years, city planners have broadened the streets, established parks, and built another railway station. This is called Tongtaegu and is on the east side of the city, the direction in which the city has been rapidly expanding. It is now the station for all express-train services.

Taegu is known as Korea's college town. The educational traditions of the city began late in the nineteenth century when foreign Presbyterian missionaries arrived and founded Western schools. James Adams and his wife Nellie were the first Western missionaries to settle permanently in Taegu, in 1897. Soon afterward, Adams started Keisung Boys' Academy. Today, Taegu has several colleges and five respected universities: Kyongbuk National University, Yongnam University, Kyemyong Christian University, Hyosong Women's University, and Taegu University.

Taegu is probably best known for its crunchy apples. James Adams discovered that a native crabapple grew well in the Taegu basin but that the fruit was never eaten except by young children. So he imported cuttings from America, which he grafted onto the local crab apple trees. Adams's intent was that members of his growing Christian community could raise apples to produce a side income. Now, more than 80 years later, Taegu has become the center of Korea's thriving apple industry and is famous throughout the Orient.

A Little History

Taegu is an ancient city with evidence of early settlements that go as far back as the Neolithic period, attested by the discovery of polished stone axes and pottery. A high level of cultural sophistication in the Bronze Age was indicated by a large number of dolmens (prehistoric burial sites), although these unfortunately disappeared during the last part of the Japanese colonial rule. In the Iron Age, Taegu emerged as a tribal state of some importance, known as Talgu-bol, and the mud-walled fortress that is today's Talsong Park dates from that era. Clustered in the vicinity of this site were numerous tombs, with stone chambers from which important relics were excavated. The styles of art and culture were found to be similar to those of nearby Kyongju, suggesting that by the fourth or fifth century, the area of present-day Taegu had attained a rather high level of barbaric civilization.

With the spread of the great Silla state, Talgu-bol was absorbed into the kingdom, and remained in a position of relative unimportance during the following Koryo period. During the thirteenth century, the Taegu area was devastated, like so many others in Korea, by the invasions of the Mongols, and this was when the original version of the Tripitaka Koreana—a special revision of the first Chinese translation of the Buddhist canon—was destroyed. The first set of these 80,000 wooden printing blocks was housed in Puinsa Temple on Mt. Palgonsan, north of Taegu, which is now largely in ruins. It is the second set, commissioned by King Kojong in 1236 while in exile on Kanghwa Island, that is now treasured in the Haeinsa Temple, on Mt. Kaya to the west of the city. It is ironic that the first set was created as an act of Buddhist piety in the hopes of averting a Khitan invasion; the second was to enlist the aid of Buddhist gods in ridding Korea of the Mongols.

It was during the Yi Dynasty that Taegu grew in commercial importance. Goods and gifts sent from Japan to Seoul were brought upriver from Pusan, and inspected by officials from Taegu. What was not considered suitable for the royal court and the higher aristocracy ended up in the local markets. The city was walled shortly before the Japanese invasions of the 1590s, when the imposing street pattern still evident today in the city center was developed.

During the seventeenth and eighteenth centuries, three cities in Korea were noted for their herbal medicine markets—Pyongyang and Kaesong, now in north Korea, and Taegu, which was the largest of the three. The semiannual market was held outside the south gate of the city, and this is why today's street of Namsongno is lined with fascinating herbal medicine shops.

When the first Westerners arrived during the 1880s, they found the residents of this walled city extremely conservative in their social attitudes and resistant to new ideas. The Westerners were permitted to build homes only outside the city wall in a potter's field. This poor man's cemetery eventually became the site of the present-day Presbyterian Mission compound and hospital.

Before the Korean War, Taegu's population was just over 200,000. Because it lies south of the Naktong-gang River, where the north Korean advance was halted, the city was spared the ravages of the war. However, the population swelled dramatically with the influx of people from the captured areas farther north.

Taegu Today

Although Taegu's surrounding area possesses a natural mountainous beauty, the city itself is somewhat drab. This is because it is among the most industrial of Korean cities, although it cannot rival cities like Ulsan and Yosu (both also in the southeast), which have grown up around such heavy industries as shipbuilding, steel, and petrochemicals. Taegu's original emphasis was on textiles, and considerable modernization of textile manufacturing has taken place, based on Korea's national plan for economic development. While most of the industries are still on a small scale, Taegu continues to expand production for international trade, with more diversification and increasingly advanced technology. One advantage of the city is its highly skilled labor force, which is attributed to its excellent educational facilities. Lately, however, there has been concern about the drain of manpower from Taegu to Seoul and other growing industrial areas of the region.

In addition to its industries, Taegu also serves as an agricultural market center. The Somun Market (West Gate Market) is one of the oldest and largest traditional Korean markets in the country. It is well worth a visit, as you will be amazed by the diversity of items displayed.

Taegu and its surroundings may not be one of the major destinations for visitors to Korea, but it does have sights not found elsewhere. It is a large city with just a few historical and scenic highlights, unlike Kyongju, which is a small town with many, and you do have to put a little more effort into your sightseeing. But there are rewards in Taegu, not the least of which are the two major temples in the area—both historically important and scenically magnificent.

Haeinsa and Tonghwasa

Haeinsa Temple, one of the most famous in Korea, is in the Kaya Mountains and is usually reached by passing through Taegu. From the city, it is about a one-hour drive along the '88 Olympic Highway. On the way, sheer mountain cliffs with cascading streams provide some of the most spectacular woodland beauty to be found anywhere in the country.

Terraced on different levels, the temple is large and expansive. Although the word *temple* usually brings to mind a single building, throughout Korea it means a cluster of buildings that grew up over the centuries. In the case of Haeinsa Temple, the complex holds no fewer than 93 structures within a four-mile radius—shrines, hermitages, and satellite temples surrounding the main structure.

Haeinsa not only has a rich and important history, but remains a vital monastic center and one of the greatest places of Buddhist scholarship in the Orient. There are usually some 250 monks and nuns in residence at Haeinsa, either studying the ancient scriptures stored there or meditating in the hermitages.

First built in the year 802, the temple is the repository for a number of extremely valuable historic treasures. Principal among them is the Tripitaka Koreana, mentioned earlier, a collection of 81,258 hand-carved wooden printing blocks. As a basic medium for printing on paper, these blocks represent the most complete compilation of Buddhist religious teachings in all Asia. Although they were carved in the year 1236, they are still in such perfect condition—stored in a cleverly ventilated building to prevent rot, and guarded over the centuries by Buddhist monks—that they can still be used for printing today.

Besides the Haeinsa main temple complex, Kayasan National Park itself is enjoyable, especially for those who like mountain hikes. You can stay in the area overnight if you wish. The bus from Taegu lets you off near a small village resort, which has a dozen inns and numerous restaurants famous for mountain mushrooms and fresh vegetables.

Another important monastery in the Taegu area is Tonghwasa Temple, on the slopes of Palgongsan Mountain, around 30 miles north of the city. This well-known Silla temple is situated in a quiet forested glen, with boulder-strewn streams flowing past it down the mountainside. Like Haeinsa Temple, it has many small trails leading out from the main compound to small hermitages farther away. A large stone Buddha statue sits near the peak of this mountain, along with a three-story stone pagoda—both national treasures. At the top is the hermitage Yomburam, offering a truly breathtaking view and two fine sculptures carved on the bare rockface of a cliff. These sights can be reached only after a vigorous two-hour climb, but it's worthwhile for those who are equal to the hike.

According to historical records, Tonghwasa Temple was founded by the monk Kukdal in the year 495 and has a number of sculptures, shrines, gates, and pavilions that date to the various periods of Korean Buddhist history.

It is also possible to stay overnight comfortably in the Tonghwasa area. The bus from Taegu will leave you at the temple parking lot, which is surrounded by a cluster of inns, souvenir stores, and small restaurants.

PRACTICAL INFORMATION FOR TAEGU

HOW TO GET THERE. Taegu is on the Kyongbu Expressway between Seoul and Pusan, about 185 miles from Seoul and 75 miles northwest of Pusan.

From Seoul. By air, Korean Air has three flights daily to Taegu, while Asiana has two (W23,500 one-way). **By train,** superexpress (Saemaul), air-conditioned express (Mugunghwa), or ordinary express (Tongil) from Seoul Station; departures are frequent. The Saemaul takes about three and a half hours, and fares are W15,300 first-class and W12,000 economy, regardless of travel day. Call the foreigners' counter at Seoul Station for details; Tel. (02) 392–7811. **By express bus,** from Seoul's Kangnam terminal, a three-hour, 50-minute ride, departing every five to 10 minutes, 6 A.M. to 8 P.M. (W5,100).

From Pusan. By all types of **train,** with frequent departures from Pusan Station. Saemaul superexpress fares are W6,800 first-class and W4,500 economy. Call the foreigners' counter at Pusan Station for details, Tel. (051) 44–7788. **By express bus,** from the Express Bus Terminal, a one-hour, 50-minute ride, departing every 15 minutes, 5:40 A.M. to 9 P.M. (W2,570).

HOW TO GET AROUND. The best way to get around the city is by **taxi.** They're plentiful, with the same fare structure as in Seoul and Pusan.

You can take **local buses** to the two major temples. To visit Haeinsa Temple, you depart from the Sobu bus terminal, for a one-and-a-half-hour drive (W1,480). The first departure is at 6:30 A.M. the last is at 7 P.M., and the buses leave every 20 minutes. You can also visit the Haeinsa Temple directly from Pusan. The drive takes around three hours, and buses depart from the Sobu terminal once a day. You can call the terminal for details, (051) 322–8301.

To reach Tonghwasa Temple from Taegu, you take the No. 76 bus from outside the Fatima Hospital, or, to be sure of a seat (especially on weekends), get on at Kyemyong University, toward the southwest part of the city. The buses are very frequent, and the drive takes around 40 minutes.

Details of how to reach other sights are given in the "What to See" section below.

Car Rental. There are several car-rental agencies in Taegu, all offering a range of vehicles from around W29,000 to W120,000 per day. Do yourself a favor and pay around W50,000 more for a driver. Contact Yongil Rent-a-Car in Puk-ku (Tel. 952–1001), or Korean Rent-a-Car (Tel. 955–0801).

ACCOMMODATIONS. There are two hotels in Taegu rated by the KNTC as *Deluxe* (around W60,000 for a double or twin room); five that are *1st class* (W35,000 to W50,000); and several that are ranked as *2d* or *3d class* (W24,000 to W35,000). The hotels on our list are all recommended by the KNTC, but since Taegu is a major industrial and market center, there are many more hotels that are equally as comfortable. The area just to the west of City Hall has many good 2d- and 3d-class hotels, and is also the major commercial district with the greatest concentration of banks, department stores, and restaurants.

The telephone area code for Taegu is 053.

Credit card abbreviations are American Express, AE; Diner's Club, DC; MasterCard, MC; and Visa, V.

Kumho. *Deluxe.* Downtown, at 28, Haso-dong, Chung-ku, Taegu (Tel. 252–6001, Seoul office (02) 544–6585, Telex K54545). 128 rooms. As one of only two hotels in the city rated as deluxe, the Kumho has good facilities, including a choice of Western and Oriental restaurants, a coffee shop, a cocktail lounge, a nightclub, and a theater-restaurant. There is also a health club with a sauna and an indoor pool. Credit cards: AE, DC, MC, V.

Crystal. *1st class.* Located at 1196–11, Turyu 1-dong, Talso-ku, Taegu (Tel. 252–7799, Fax. 253–0323), 20 minutes by car from Tong-Taegu Railway Station. With 70 rooms, this hotel features banquet facilities, a lounge, a nightclub, and a restaurant. Credit cards: AE, DC, MC, V.

Dongin. *1st class.* Downtown, at 5-2, 1-ka, Samdok-dong, Chung-ku, Taegu (Tel. 426–4211, Seoul office (02) 735–3626, Telex K54325). 92 rooms; Western, Korean, and Japanese restaurants; a coffee shop and a nightclub. Credit cards: AE, DC, MC, V.

Taegu Susong. *1st class.* Near the small lakeside resort of Susong, to the south of the city. 888-2, Tusan-dong, Susong-ku, Taegu (Tel. 763–7311, Fax. 764–0620). Just 66 rooms, with Western and Korean restaurants, coffee shop, and a nightclub. There is a sauna and an indoor pool, and limited facilities for golf. Credit cards: AE, DC, MC, V.

Tongtaegu. *1st class.* Near Dongtaegu Station, at 326-1, Shinchon-dong, Tong-ku, Taegu (Tel. 756–6601). 60 rooms, with a choice of restaurants, coffee shop, cocktail lounge, and nightclub. Also sauna facilities. Credit cards: AE, DC, MC, V.

New Jongro. *2d class.* Downtown, at 23, 2-ka, Chongno, Chung-ku, Taegu (Tel. 23–7111). Just 48 rooms, with Korean and Japanese restaurants, coffee shop, cocktail lounge, and nightclub. Credit cards: AE.

New Yongnam. *2d class.* A little east of the downtown area, at the Pomon Rotary. 177-7, Pomo-dong, Susong-ku, Taegu (Tel. 752–1001). 73 rooms, with Korean, Japanese, and Western dining facilities. Also a sauna. Credit cards: AE, V.

Dongsan. *3d class.* At the west side of downtown, at 360, Tongsan-dong, Chung-ku, Taegu (Tel. 253–7711). 22 Western double rooms, and 32 Korean-style, with a good range of facilities including Korean, Japanese, and Western dining, and a nightclub, a health club, and sauna. Credit cards: AE, DC, V.

Royal. *3d class.* Downtown, at 24-4, Namil-dong, Chung-ku, Taegu (Tel. 253–5546). A total of 50 rooms, with Korean and Western restaurants, a cocktail lounge, and a nightclub. Credit cards: AE, DC, MC, V.

RESTAURANTS. While you can find good Western, Japanese, and Chinese restaurants in Taegu (there's even an Italian restaurant downtown, called Italiano), the best selection in all classes is Korean.

Prices vary greatly among the different styles of food, but as a general rule, a meal for one person, excluding drinks, service charges, and taxes, would cost the following: *Expensive,* W15,000–W40,000; *Moderate,*

W10,000–W15,000; *Inexpensive,* W8,000–W12,000. You should note that eating in the smaller "noodle and rice" shops and the small market restaurants is much cheaper—you can pay as little as W3,500 for a full meal. The following areas and specific places have been recommended by foreigners who live in Taegu, and will provide you with lots of local "color" as well as the true flavors of the Taegu area.

Korean

In Tongin-dong, near the Tongin Rotary, is an alleyway lined with small restaurants specializing in steamed beef ribs, Kalbi-chim. The food is not only good, it is inexpensive. Also great for inexpensive dining is a row of places specializing in barbecued beef and beef ribs (*bulgogi* and *bulgalbi*) running down an alley from the northeast side of the Talsongno and Soshinno intersection. For an amazing assortment of regional Korean cuisines, head for the basement of the Somun (West Gate) Market. There are some 30-odd tiny restaurants, none of them fancy. And for excellent Samgyetang, a whole small chicken cooked in a ginseng broth, try the **Seoul Samgyetang** (Tel. 425–9122), in the alley running east alongside the Kaya Department Store. Other Korean restaurants recommended are the **Kugil Shiktang,** Namil 2-dong (Tel. 23–7623), or the **Sudo Hoekwan,** near Daegu Department Store (Tel. 425–4355), both with a general selection (*moderate*); **Wharan Dongsan,** on Tongsongno (Tel. 422–3137), and **Nulbomgongwan,** at the Susong Resort (Tel. 762–6600), with a general selection and excellent noodles; **Gyongbuk Bulkalbi,** 1651-2, Bisan-dong (Tel. 32–2526), for charcoal-broiled beef ribs (*moderate*); and **Garam,** 39-2, Jangkan-dong (Tel. 255–4359), for a full range of Korean food (also *moderate*). These last two restaurants are near the Daegu Department Store. Others in this same area that are recommended are the **Wonsanmyonok** (Tel. 423–0151), **Chungjubusot Shiktang** (Tel. 425–5668), and **Cheju Garden** (Tel. 72–1780), all with prices ranging from *inexpensive* to *moderate*.

Western

Best selections are at the major hotels, but prices are high in relation to the quality of the food. The biggest Western restaurant in Taegu is the **Renaissance** (Tel. 628–3337), just in front of Apsan Park. This place smokes its own meats, but it is *expensive.* Western food at *moderate* prices can be found at the **Duksan Restaurant,** at 96 Duksan-dong (Tel. 425–0077), Chung-ku, near the Dong-A Department Store.

Chinese

The **Kirinwon** is a two-story Chinese restaurant down the street from the Kumho Hotel, at 24, Suchangdong (Tel. 255–1888), which serves Peking-style food at *moderate* prices. The Kaya Department Store, on Tongsongno, has a Chinese restaurant, the **Arisan,** popular with both Koreans and foreigners. The menu has English translations, and the food is *moderately* priced (Tel. 44–7285). A place that is *expensive,* but said to be the finest in Taegu, is **Mallijangsong,** at 55-39, Taebongdong (Tel. 46–0100), across the road from the Chonggu Apartments, with a very extensive menu. At the other extreme, a most *inexpensive* general Chinese restaurant is the **Asowon,** on Dongsongno (Tel. 253–9392).

Japanese

One of the best Japanese restaurants, **Unsong Shiktang,** has *moderate* prices, specializes in sukiyaki, and is located at 41 Sangsodong, in a small street near the Kumho Hotel (Tel. 252–6001). There is a main restaurant area and a number of private rooms. The Kumho Hotel itself also has a noted Japanese restaurant, the **Hirak,** which tends to be *expensive* (Tel. 252–6001). A Japanese restaurant near the Taegu Hotel, the **Daehwa** (Tel. 253–0828), is highly recommended, but it is *expensive.* Prices at the **Samdado Shiktang** are *moderate.* It is at 594-3, Bomo-dong (Tel. 756–3553) and serves a variety of foods. The specialty is sukiyaki. Another Japanese restaurant worth trying is the **Wolsungchobap,** at Pojung-dong (Tel. 253–6633). Prices are *moderate.*

Kisaeng Restaurants

This is the traditional style of sophisticated Korean dining, with very elegant surroundings, hostesses, and most attentive service. There are three that are especially popular with foreigners in Taegu—the **Chunhaenggak,** at 20-2, Sangso-dong (Tel. 23–2320); **Baeknon,** at 140-5, Namildong (Tel. 252–3312); and **Seokbin,** 76, 1-ka, Chung-ku (Tel. 23–0066). Prices will run about W120,000 per person plus a tip of W50,000 per hostess. These places offer a complete range of Korean food; the staff are familiar with serving foreigners.

TOURS. Like most Korean towns outside of Seoul, there are inadequate tour facilities for foreign visitors. There are many travel agencies around town that organize domestic tour programs, often single-day excursions to important historic sites, but all communication would be in Korean. However, as mentioned earlier, getting around Taegu by yourself is not difficult by taxi, and there are good bus services to the nearby attractions. Your hotel information desk will be able to provide assistance.

WHAT TO SEE AND DO. As mentioned earlier, Taegu is a large commercial city with just a few historic and cultural highlights. It's main attractions for visitors are the temples of Haeinsa and Tonghwasa—easily reached by public transport from the city—described earlier in this chapter. However, for those with more time to spend in Taegu, the city itself offers a number of other sightseeing opportunities.

Talsong Park. This is a spacious and charming park at the west of the downtown area, where you can see the remaining walls of the ancient fortification and get a sweeping view of the entire Taegu Valley. There are also monuments to the Suh Clan, who took over the fortress from the twelfth to the fifteenth centuries, and a pleasant zoo.

Medicine Alley. Known in Korean as Yakchon Kolmok, this is an area along the downtown Namsongno Street which has the largest concentration of herbal medicine stores in Korea, a distinction which dates to the early seventeenth century. The smells, not at all nasty, are incredible, and you'll see all kinds of herbs, roots, and dried reptiles. Most unusual, and fascinating.

Chungang Park. This is in the center of town, noted for its lotus pond and two wooden pavilions—the province governor's headquarters and residence during the Yi Dynasty. The buildings, unfortunately, are replicas; the originals were destroyed by fire in the early part of the last century. The park also contains a small aviary, a modern Buddhist bell, and numerous spots to sit and relax.

Chilsong Pawi. These are a curiosity rather than a sightseeing attraction, but the seven rocks to the right of the car park of Citizens' Hall are explained by legend. The Chilsong Pawi, or Seven Star Rocks, were seen by a late eighteenth-century governor of this region in a dream. He dreamed that he saw the stars of the Big Dipper falling from the sky outside Taegu's north gate, and he went and found them there in the morning. Taking this as a good omen, he prayed for sons—and later his wish was fulfilled. People wanting sons pray here today.

Temple of the Tenrikyo Sect, and the Taean Catholic Church. In Taeandong, behind the Chungang Park, is Taegu's principal temple of the Tenrikyo sect (called Cholligyo in Korean). This is a mixture of Japanese Shinto and Buddhism, which has had some success in Korea, and the temple occupies the site of part of a Japanese Zen temple built during the Japanese colonial period. Nearby is another templelike structure, the Taean Roman Catholic Church, which is unquestionably one of the finest church structures in Korea.

Taegu Confucian Shrine. Hyanggyo, to the south of the central city area, between Chungangno and Talguro streets, is still an active Confucian school, and has a typical Confucian shrine, quiet gardens, ceremonial buildings, and monuments to scholars and magistrates. Ceremonies to honor Confucius are held here twice yearly, on the fifteenth day of the fifth and tenth lunar months.

Pohyonsa Temple. This is also in the south of the central city area, a little south of the major intersection of Chungangno and Taesoro streets. This small but very beautiful temple was built some 65 years ago by a nun to honor the compassionate heart of the Buddha. It is used as a study center of Buddhism.

Apsan Park. From the Nambu Market (the Great South Market), you can take a bus, No. 101 or 111, to Taedoksan Mountain, more commonly known as Apsan Park. Here there are various sports facilities, an amusement park, and a cable car to the top of one of the peaks. It is a most pleasant spot for short hikes (or you can hire horses), and there are a number of small Buddhist temples in the area. Unjoksa Temple was first built in the year 1036, during the Koryo Dynasty. There is a historic Buddha image enshrined in the main hall, along with a series of pictures portraying the important events in the Buddha's life. Another temple in the area is Taedoksa, the "Temple of Great Virtue," which has three Buddhist figures on its central altar, and a small shrine dedicated to the god of mountains behind the main hall.

Susong Resort. This is a small but very popular resort which has grown up around the Susong Reservoir. There are a number of tourist hotels and inns, many small restaurants and shops and a happy atmosphere year-round. The major pleasures here are boating in the summer and ice skating in the winter.

Naengchon and **Mangu parks.** These have been created over recent years in response to the need to offset Taegu's commercial growth with leisure facilities. Naengchon is noted mainly as a great outdoor zoo, and is a private park in the south of the city near the Susong Reservoir. You can reach it by taking bus No. 33 from the center of the city. Mangu Park is on the high cliffs of the Kumho River, near the Taegu entrance of the Kyongbu Expressway. Here are a reconstruction of the city's south gate, and a statue of General Pwak Chae-Gyom, who defended Taegu during the Japanese invasions of the 1590s. It is easiest to reach Mangu by car or taxi.

There are several more excursion opportunities out of Taegu, the most popular to more temples in the surrounding hills and parks. In **Palgongsan Park,** in the same area as Tonghwasa, you can visit the temple of Pagyesa, dating to the year 804 and rebuilt last in 1695. Also in Palgongsan Park is the temple of Puinsa, which requires a hike of an hour and a half to see the site where the original printing blocks of the Tripitaka Koreana were stored, and destroyed by fire. However, the walk through an area of thatch-roofed houses and mountain scenery is well worth the day's outing from Taegu.

Museums. Three museums in the Taegu area provide a very good cross section of the cultural and historical treasures that have been preserved. These are all attached to universities and have flexible opening times. You should call to check current schedules: **Kyemyong University Museum** (Tel. 626–1321); **Kyongbuk National University Museum** (Tel. 955–5001 or the direct line 952–2996); and **Yongnam University Museum,** considered Taegu's best with over 10,500 articles on display (Tel. 82–5111, or the direct line 82–7809).

SPORTS. There are a number of sports grounds in Taegu and you should check with your hotel information staff regarding current matches. There are also numerous tennis courts, bowling alleys, and other sports facilities and, again, the hotel staff can assist you with information and arrangements. Taegu has one major **golf course,** an 18-hole course to the east of the city; Tel. (053) 955–8080, Seoul office (02) 554–0622. You will need a reservation to play, especially on weekends. The Taegu area offers many opportunities for hiking, especially in the Kayasan and Palgongsan parks.

SHOPPING. Shopping in Taegu is delightful, especially if you like exploring local markets. There are some 60 of these in and around the city, of which six are especially recommended as being of interest to foreign visitors. The biggest is the **Somun** or **West Gate Market,** across the street from Tonggsan Presbyterian Hospital. The market itself has several multistory buildings and many outlying shops and stalls, selling just about everything you can imagine, but particularly noted for fabrics, brass, and fish. The **Chilsong Market** is the second largest, near Taegu Station, and specializes in farm products from the surrounding rural areas. (The pig heads are said to be especially good here.) **Kyodong** is the "Yankee" market, which got its name from a thriving black market that grew here after the Korean war. **Nammun** is the South Gate general market; **Pongdok,** farther south, offers large quantities of fresh fruits and vegetables; and **Chonggwamul Market,** across and more to the east from Kyodong, is devoted solely to fruit. Make a point of trying the famous Taegu apples. They're a tasty experience.

Department Stores

There are some 10 department stores in the city, with the **Daegu Store** the best known among foreigners. It is located behind the Hanil Hotel on Tongsongno Street (Tel. 423–1234). Others are the **Dong-A,** in the area of the Kojong market (Tel. 422–2111); the **Dong-A Shopping Center** in Toksan-dong (Tel. 252–2111); the **Daebo** (Tel. 23–5111) and **Mugunghwa** (Tel. 253–5338), both east of Chungang Park; and the **Mido** (Tel. 46–1811), across the street from the Royal Hotel. Like their Western counterparts, the department stores are always having sales of one kind or another, and they're always fun for browsing.

Pottery

There are kilns near Taegu that produce reproductions of traditional Korean pottery, and the city sales outlet is the **Chongbaekwon Pottery Store** on Chungangtong, between the Mido Department Store and the Hanil Hotel (Tel. 253–1121). It is also possible to visit the kiln, which makes an interesting day's outing. Ask for details at the store.

Handicrafts

The best collection is at the **Taegu Handicrafts Cooperative,** 53-1, 1-ka, Puksongno, Chung-ku, Taegu (Tel. 351–9982).

Tax-Refund Stores

These are stores where, if you spend over W50,000 per item, you are entitled to a refund of various taxes. Details of how to arrange for refunds are given in the "Taxes" section of *Facts at Your Fingertips.* The stores in Taegu which offer this privilege are the **Taegu** and **Dong-A** department stores and the **Dong-A Shopping Center** (addresses are given above).

CULTURAL EVENTS. There are no major festivals unique to the Taegu area, but most of the national events are celebrated in some form or other. Any Buddhist temple is particularly lovely, with its decorations and procession for **Buddha's birthday,** but in Taegu the temple of Wonhyosa is especially popular with foreign residents. This is on a hill south of the downtown area, and is a nunnery of recent origin, dedicated to the great Silla monk Won-hyo. The Buddha's birthday evening procession leaves from the Buddhist high school next door (May 28 in 1993).

Ceremonies to honor Confucius are held at the Taegu Confucian Shrine (*see* "What to See and Do," above) on the first of February and the fifth of August on the lunar calendar. In 1993, these days fall on February 25 and September 23.

NIGHTLIFE. Most of the tourist hotels have bars and nightclubs, some have theater-restaurants, and there are a few Western-style clubs outside the hotels. For a look at the local styles of evening entertainment, go to the area of Dongsungno Street, near the Dong-In Hotel in Samdok-dong.

There are a number of alleys filled with eating and drinking establishments—wine shops, beer halls, small restaurants, tearooms and clubs. There is no casino in Taegu.

USEFUL ADDRESSES AND TELEPHONE NUMBERS. Medical Attention. Ask your hotel manager for advice about any medical situation, since the hotel probably already has a system for handling medical emergencies. However, you can also make contact with good hospitals in Taegu, such as the **Kyongbuk University Medical Center,** in Samdok-dong (Tel. 422–1141).

Tourist Information. For information on current events or general advice, the best place to call is the **Taegu Tourist Association** (Tel. 558–5893). It has a downtown location at 1092–7, Pyongri-dong, Seo-ku. Other numbers that could be helpful are as follows:

Railway Station (Tongtaegu), Tel. 92–7788
Information on Express Buses, Tel. 72–0111
Intercity Bus Terminals: Tongbu (East), Tel. 756–0017
Sobu (West), Tel. 66–2825
Pukbu (North), Tel. 32–1851
Nambu (South), Tel. 72–4464
Tourist Complaints and Advice, Tel. 422–5611

PUSAN

An increasing number of Korea's visitors are arriving by air and sea at the southern port city of Pusan rather than at Seoul, where people arrive from abroad exclusively by air. Ferries arrive at Pusan's downtown piers either from Shimonoseki or Osaka in Japan, and two airlines—Korean Air and Japan Air Lines—serve the city's international airport from Tokyo, Osaka, or Fukuoka.

Over recent years, several ocean cruises have included Pusan as a port of call, with passengers using their ship as a base for touring not just the city and surrounding sights, but the historic temples and vast outdoor museum of Kyongju.

Archeologists have determined that Pusan's first inhabitants settled during the Neolithic period, some 5,000 years ago. A tribal group around the first century established a nation called Kochilsanguk; later it became Tongnae, then Kimhae ("metal sea") when the area became a prime source of precious iron ore for the peoples of northeast Asia.

The name Pusan, "Cauldron Mountain," was first used during the fifteenth century, referring to the ring of peaks, rising to over 2,500 feet behind the city, that were thought to resemble the rim of a cauldron. It was during the Yi Dynasty that Pusan played key roles not only in trade with Japan, but in repelling its invasions. It was off the coast of the Southeast Area in 1592 that Admiral Yi Sun-Shin defeated the Japanese armada with his ironclad "turtle ships."

Pusan was formally opened for trade with the outside world in 1876, when the Yi Dynasty was forced to abandon its isolationist policy and sign a treaty imposed by Japan.

During the Korean War of 1950–1953, Pusan served as the country's temporary capital. At the bleakest point of the war it was the only major city not in enemy hands, and the number of inhabitants swelled to over 4 million with the influx of refugees.

Today the city of Pusan covers an area of 166 square miles and has the administrative status of a province under the direct control of the central government. It has a population of around 3.6 million, making it Korea's second-largest city; it is still the largest port for imports and exports; and it has established and maintained essential links with commercial interests around the world. The Pusan area has a great diversity of commercial and industrial activities—the major heavy industry complexes of Pohang and Ulsan are nearby—but it is also known for its recreational resorts, parks, and ancient temples tucked away in forested hills.

Climatically, the city lies in Korea's southeast region, which is the country's warmest area except for Cheju Island. Pusan's summer heat is intensified by the surrounding hills. It can really get hot on a windless midsummer day—you'll want to head out of the sheltered port area to the seaside nearby with its cooling breezes. On the other hand, Pusan has a milder winter than other parts of Korea, rarely seeing snow.

Geographically, Pusan lies entirely in Kyongsangnamdo Province. As Korea's principal port, it has excellent road and rail links in all directions. By air you can leave from the Pusan International Airport for Seoul, any one of three cities in Japan, or Cheju Island. Going anywhere from Pusan, there is frequency of all modes of transportation.

An increasing number of visitors are finding success in a plan that brings them into Pusan to begin a leisurely exploration of the cultural and scenic attractions on the way north to Seoul. You would really need at least two weeks, including time in Seoul and for some side trips from there. The program would work equally as well in the reverse, beginning in Seoul and ending with departure for Japan from Pusan. The section on travel arrangements in *Facts at Your Fingertips* gives an outline of how this "cross country" tour would work.

The Shores of Pusan

It is worth noting that Pusan is not just a port city surrounding a single harbor. Rather, the city's configuration is like a set of irregularly shaped, pudgy fingers jutting out into the Sea of Japan. This creates an enormously long shoreline. The main port is in the center, where you can watch the usual hurly-burly of great ships unloading container cargoes and smaller vessels of the local fishing fleet unloading their catches.

But you're still just a stone's throw from sandy beaches and cool water. All you have to do is cross the inner end of one of those fingers and you'll find yourself in an entirely different scene—long sweeping bays with sandy beaches and first-rate ocean swimming in clean salt water. It must be mentioned, however, that others have discovered these escape spots from Pusan's sultry heat, so you will not be alone. In fact, it is estimated that over 8 million people visit the beaches of Haeundae and Songdo during the summer season. It would be wise to make hotel reservations well in advance if you're planning a visit in July or August. Also, Korea is pushing forward the development of many of these areas around Pusan as resorts,

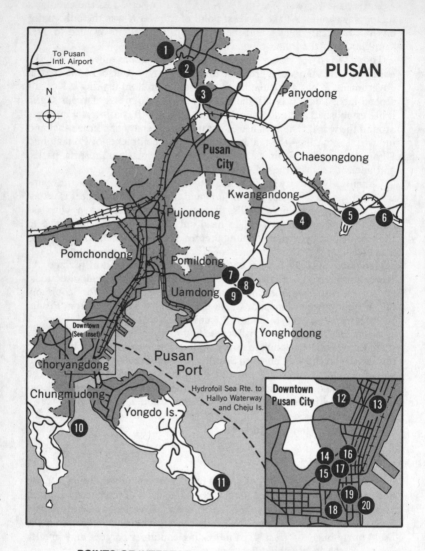

PUSAN

To Pusan Intl. Airport

N

Panyodong

Pusan City

Chaesongdong

Kwangandong

Pujondong

Pomchondong

Pomildong

Uamdong

Yonghodong

Downtown (See Inset)

Choryangdong

Pusan Port

Chungmudong

Hydrofoil Sea Rte. to Hallyo Waterway and Cheju Is.

Yongdo Is.

Downtown Pusan City

POINTS OF INTEREST

Chosun Beach Hotel 5
Chungyolsa Shrine 3
City Hall 17
Commodore Dynasty Hotel 12
Fish Market 20
Hotel Sorabol 16
Kumgang Park 1
Paradise Beach Hotel 6
Pusan Museum 7

Pusan port area 19
Songdo Beach 10
Taechon Park 15
Taejongdae Resort 11
Taeshin Park 14
Tongmyung Temple 8
Tongnae Resort 2
Train Station 13
UN Memorial Cemetery 9
Yachting Center 4
Yongdusan Park 18

so don't expect splendid isolation here as you might on Cheju Island or in some parts of the East Coastal area.

Haeundae

For Koreans, the Haeundae area of Pusan is best known for its beach, which has record crowds of up to a half million a day at the peak of the summer. For Pusan's foreign community and many visiting businessmen, however, the resort has also been the center of social activities. Until mid-1987, the Westin Chosun Beach Hotel, overlooking Haeundae, was Pusan's only international chain hotel, offering good accommodations and restaurants, and a range of business services along with its attractive location.

Now Haeundae has the new deluxe Paradise Beach Hotel (the old hotel has been torn down), and the nearby Pusan Hyatt opened just before the 1988 Summer Olympic Games. These hotels give a very international flavor to a resort that is just a 30-minute drive from the heart of the city.

In addition to the hotel facilities, there are also a number of good restaurants in the area, including a charming Korean restaurant with a name that translates as Moon Viewing House. The Paradise Beach Hotel has Pusan's only casino.

Haeundae is where you will find the best collection of water sports. Many of them are organized by the hotels, like the wind surfing and parasailing facilities at the Paradise Beach, so you can be confident of good safety standards. You can hire fishing boats from the pier at the east end of the beach (safety standards are questionable), and there is a regular launch cruise out to the Oryukdo Islands. These lie at the approach to Pusan's commercial harbor and have become a symbol of the city. At high tide there are six islands in the group, but two are linked together when the tide is low. (Other resorts in the Pusan area are covered in the "Practical Information" section at the end of this chapter.)

A New Yachting Center

Near the Haeundae Resort, where the Suyong-gang River reaches Suyong-man Bay, is the Pusan Yachting Center. This was the site of all the yachting events in the 1988 Olympic Games. The heart of the development is a huge marine center with an advanced mooring system for up to 1,300 yachts, and four racing courses. The yachting contests for the Asian Games in 1986 were held here, and the Olympic plans included the addition of an athletes' village, a press center, and a large tourist complex with a water park, marine museum, and shopping arcade.

The New Subway System

There's a great new way to get around Pusan, and that's by subway. The first line runs from the downtown station of Chungangdong, near the ferry terminals, all the way out to the area of the Pomosa Temple and the Pusan Country Club. In mid-1988, it was extended in a loop that continues from Chungangdong down around the central city and wharf area, ending near the Kudok Stadium at Sodaeshindong Station. Fares are just W220 for a single sector, W250 for two sectors, and W300 for three sectors.

The line is very convenient in that it connects such tourist spots as the ferry terminals, train station, express-bus terminal, the Tongnae resort area, Kumgang Park, and beautiful Pomosa—all places and facilities that are likely to appear on your Pusan schedule.

Highlights of the Central City

Now let's start aboveground in downtown Pusan and work our way outward to the surrounding areas. Right near the center of the city is the attractive railroad-depot plaza. Clustered around it are a number of international-class hotels. If first-rate accommodations are your preference and you want to stay in the city rather than out at the Haeundae resort, you'll find a good collection of hotels here. You are also centrally situated for any kind of transportation (bus, subway, train), are surrounded by department stores, can enjoy the widest choice of restaurants, and can take in the major sights on day trips from your hotel. Also nearby is "Texas Town," an area of bars and nightclubs ranging from pleasant to raunchy, with all manner of music and entertainment.

If you enjoy waterfront activity, head down to the main fish market in Nambumin-dong, where the fleet comes in. The southern part of Pusan's port is dedicated to the fishing industry, separated from the eastern commercial section by the Yongdo and Pusan bridges. Go to Nambumin-dong early if you want to see the whole show—say around 6 A.M.—when the massive fish catches are auctioned. Some 60 percent of the catch is eaten in Pusan, the remainder destined for other cities in Korea. The Chagalchi Market in Nampo-dong, closer to the bridges, is also a major marketplace for fish, but you can come any time of day to see not just fish and other marine edibles on sale, but all manner of household goods. It's a good place to see household commerce at its liveliest.

While you're at the waterfront, check the schedules for the hydrofoils that ply the Hallyo Waterway. It's an all-day trip to go and return (the other end is the town of Yosu in the Southeast area), but you won't want to miss it. This really is a wonderful way to capture the whole sweep of this southern coast. Next to the coastal ferry terminal are the international ferry piers, where the boats from Shimonoseki and Osaka in Japan arrive.

In this waterfront area, spreading out from City Hall, you'll find another collection of hotels, a tourist information center (another is near the train station), and Pusan's best shopping districts. In Kwangbok-dong and the nearby Nampo-dong area there is a fascinating collection of small stores jammed cheek-by-jowl, each specializing in a single kind of merchandise in gloriously cluttered displays. Also in this part of town is the Nampo-dong Amusement Street, with a bright collection of beer halls, soju bars, tearooms, and other local entertainment. For a different approach to shopping, you can try the department stores (there are several in the area), or the Kukje underground market.

Ranging outward from the city center, you have a number of sights to choose from. Start with Yongdusan Park, the core of the downtown area, as you'll already have walked its fringes on your strolls. The name means "Dragon Head Mountain," symbolized by a large bronze dragon that stands in the park grounds. The main feature of the park is Pusan Tower, 540 feet high, which commands a magnificent view of the city below, the distant hills, and the entire sweep of the vast harbor and sea beyond. The observatory is served by two elevators (insufficient on Sundays!). Unfortunately, security considerations forbid photography. Below the tower is an octagonal pavilion, where you can pause for refreshments. Nearby is a bronze statue of Admiral Yi, the much-honored, much-memorialized naval hero.

For a place to just sit and relax for a while, head northwest of the central city to Taechong Park. Some 620 feet above sea level, it offers excellent views of the harbor areas and the city. Its centerpiece is the Tower of the Royal Dead, another symbol of the city, which contains over 7,000 memorial tablets to heroes of the Korean war.

To the North

Take the subway and head north to Tongnae, about nine miles from the city center. Since the seventeenth century, the area of Tongnae has been famous for its medicinal hot springs. Countless bathers continue to visit them today in all seasons. You can stay out here, if you like—the Tongnae Tourist Hotel was recently extensively refurbished to first-class standards and costs around W50,000 for a twin room. The hotel mineral water is piped directly into the bathrooms of the hotel.

The area also has Kumgang Park, which draws thousands of visitors in the spring when the cherry blossoms are in bloom. The park has many scenic spots—wooded slopes, rushing streams, and many convoluted rock formations that can be seen from the winding paths. It also houses a zoo, botanical gardens, aquarium, folklore museum, and amusement park offering carnival rides.

Within the park are several historic sites, including a lofty fortress reached by Korea's longest cable-car ride, several temples, and a pretty pagoda.

Carry on farther to the north, still by subway, and visit the Pomosa Temple, one of the oldest in the country. The earliest buildings in the compound date to 678, but most of them are from a massive reconstruction carried out in 1717. The temple complex is on a wooded slope, with the approach an easy walk on a paved path. The surrounding woods are filled with small shrines and hermitages, each showing how religion has stimulated creativity.

The approach to the main temple is across a stone bridge that arches over a mountain brook, and through a four-pillared gate that marks the entrance to the temple grounds. This gate is Korea's Tangible Provincial Property No. 2 and is interesting in that the four central pillars support all the weight of the upper structure.

Another local treasure at Pomosa is a three-story pagoda, believed to have been built during the ninth century, toward the end of the Silla Dynasty. The main section was cut from a single block of granite, and its foundation stones have intricate engravings of lotus flowers.

Like all Korean temples in mountain locations, Pomosa is at its most enchanting in the early morning when the setting is tranquil and the monks are chanting their morning prayers.

The United Nations Memorial Cemetery and Surroundings

There is a worthwhile excursion area east of the main city—about midway between City Hall and Haeundae. Here in the suburban hills overlooking the Sea of Japan (to Koreans the East Sea) is the United Nations Cemetery, where the war dead of the non-American allied troops in the Korean War are buried. (The American dead were brought back to the United States when the truce ended the war in 1953.) There is an impressive central plaza where the flags of the 16 nations that fought with the U.N. forces are flown. Memorial services are held there on special occasions, and there is an interfaith chapel nearby.

Just along the road from the cemetery is the Pusan Municipal Museum, housing a variety of historic and cultural treasures from prehistoric to modern times. It is closed on Mondays and Korean public holidays.

About one and a quarter miles from the cemetery is the Tongmyung Temple, donated to the city by a local businessman. The bell here is said to be the largest in the Orient, and the sanctuary the largest in Korea.

A Day Trip to the Tongdosa Temple

Northward toward Kyongju, but closer to Pusan, is the Tongdosa Temple, which has its own exit from the highway. The road is lined with carved-stone lanterns of great antiquity, which once lighted the way for visiting pilgrims and worshipers. Beside this path is a swift-flowing mountain stream twisting through pine woods.

This Zen Buddhist temple dates from the year 646, when it was built to hold religious artifacts related to Buddha that had been brought back from China by Korean monks. The temple layout is unique among the many hundreds in Korea—the main building is T-shaped and entered through a side wall, and the altar is at the head of the T. The roof has four gables, and the walls are unadorned, unusual in a Korean temple. Ceiling panels, however, are masterpieces of Korean art, depicting a distinctly native version of the Shamanism that marked the early form of Korean religious belief.

Excursions from Pusan

As this chapter of the guide is limited to Pusan and its immediate vicinity, we have not described the many attractions of the Southeast area that surrounds it. They include more parks, royal tombs, several ancient temples and hermitages, more hot springs, a few special annual festivals, and other places of cultural and historical interest. So, if your time in Pusan permits more excursions, check the chapter on the *Southeast* for additional places to visit that lie only a half day's ride from the center of Pusan. And do not forget the Hallyo Waterway, as this is certainly one of the best experiences the Southeast has to offer.

PRACTICAL INFORMATION FOR PUSAN

WHEN TO GO. As we've discussed, Pusan can be very hot in summer, particularly in the confined streets of downtown at midday. This is because the city lies in a bowl-like hollow, surrounded by hills that trap the muggy heat. In fact, Koreans claim that the word *cauldron* was originally coined to describe the heat of Pusan in the summer, rather than the historic version that the city was named for its shape. However, sea breezes do provide some relief along the shore, and the many boat rides available are fun ways to beat the heat. All this summer heat means that early spring and late fall are milder than in other parts of Korea, and the winters are less severe. But remember, near the sea in winter the cold is usually raw and damp, not nearly as crisp and clear as in the mountains. Also, there are no opportunities for winter sports in the south.

HOW TO GET THERE. By Air. Pusan is the second-most-likely arrival point in Korea, after Seoul. Korean Air and Japan Air Lines both fly into Pusan's Kimhae International Airport. Korean Air and Asiana fly from Seoul and Cheju Island; JAL flies from Tokyo, Osaka, and Fukuoka in Japan. From Seoul, the flight takes 50 minutes and costs W31,500 one-way. The service from Seoul is an hourly shuttle, with the first flight leaving at 7:30 A.M., the last at 8:30 P.M. From Pusan, the first flight to Seoul each day leaves at 8 A.M., the last at 9 P.M. If you want to arrive in Pusan by air after visiting Cheju, consult either Asiana or Korean Air for schedule details. The availability of flights depends on the season, but there are at least five each day, for W25,000 each way. Call Korean Air, (02) 756–2000, Asiana (02) 774–4000, or Japan Air Lines, (02) 757–1711 in Seoul; and in Pusan, Korean Air (051) 463–2000, Asiana (051) 465–4000, or Japan Air Lines (051) 44–1121.

By Ship. You can reach Pusan from Shimonoseki, on Honshu Island in Japan, by the Pukwan Ferry, a 15-hour cruise. This sails from Shimonoseki daily, with capacity for some 900 passengers. Departure time is 6 P.M., arriving in Pusan at 9:30 A.M. the following morning. The reverse journey, Pusan to Shimonoseki, is from 5 P.M. to 8:30 A.M. Fares per person: "A" first-class, one-way (two-person cabin), $90; "B" first-class, one-way (four-person cabin), $80; second-class, six to 10 persons with tatami sleeping facilities, $65; and economy class, nonsleeping, open cabin, $55. The charge for a car is $160, one-way. It is only possible to arrange for car transportation for Shimonoseki–Pusan–Shimonoseki, not the reverse. For bookings and information, call (02) 738–0055 in Seoul, (051) 463–3161 in Pusan, (0832) 24–3000 in Shimonoseki, (03) 3567–0971 in Tokyo, and (06) 345–2245 in Osaka.

Another ferry service, by the *Kuk Jae*, links Osaka, Japan, with Pusan. It leaves Osaka every Wednesday and Saturday at noon and arrives in Pusan the following day at 9 A.M. From Pusan, departures are at 5 P.M. every Monday and Thursday, arriving in Osaka at 2 P.M. the next day. Fares are from $100 to $250, depending on the class of travel. For information, call (02) 754–7788 in Seoul, (051) 463–7000 in Pusan, and (06) 266–1111 in Osaka.

There is also a daily ferry service between Cheju Island and Pusan, with different companies operating a variety of schedules. Call for current information: Dong Yang, Seoul (02) 730–7788, Pusan (051) 463–0605; *Car Ferry Queen,* Seoul (02) 312–2583, Pusan (051) 464–6601; *New Cheju Express Car Ferry,* Pusan (051) 465–6131.

An increasing number of cruise ships are stopping in Pusan, with passengers using the ship as a base for excursions into the city and surroundings.

By Rail. The superexpress train, *Saemaul,* operates out of Seoul to Pusan (with stops in Taejon and Taegu), taking four hours, 10 minutes. The Saemaul departs Seoul 14 times daily. Fares are: W21,000 first-class and W16,400 economy regardless of travel day. Apart from the superexpress, there are air-conditioned express (mugunghwa), and ordinary express (Tongil) trains making the same run. Ticket reservations and advance purchases are available from travel agencies and the rail stations. You can also travel between cities along the line. For information, call the Foreign Ticket Counters at the stations—Seoul (02) 392–7811, Pusan (051) 463–7551.

By Express Bus. The trip takes five hours, 20 minutes from Seoul to Pusan, with departures every five to 10 minutes from the Kangnam Express Bus Terminal. The first departure is at 6 A.M., the last at 6:40 P.M. The fare is W7,770, one-way.

From Taejon to Pusan, the traveling time is 3 hours, 30 minutes by bus, with departures every two hours from 6 A.M. to 6:30 P.M.; fare, W5,250. From Taegu to Pusan, the traveling time is one hour, 50 minutes, with departures every 15 minutes from 5:40 A.M. to 9 P.M.; fare, W2,570. From Kyongju, the bus to Pusan takes one hour and buses depart every 30 minutes between 7 A.M. and 7:30 P.M.; fare, W1,500. From Kwangju (West Plain and Coastal Area) to Pusan, the bus trip takes four hours, 10 minutes, with departures every 20 minutes between 6 A.M. and 6:20 P.M.; fare, W5,020.

HOW TO GET AROUND. From the Airport. You can get to the Pusan Station and City Hall area from Pusan International Airport by Airport Bus No. 201; fare, W500. It takes around one hour, with departures every seven minutes. Another bus, No. 307, departs less frequently and runs from the airport to Haeundae via the Tongnae hot springs area. Travel by taxi is a little faster and more convenient. Travel time is around 50 minutes to downtown, costing around W5,000. To Haeundae, the fare would be around W6,000.

Around Town. The **subway** is excellent. The first line runs from the downtown Chungangdong Station north to Pomosa Station, near the famous Pomosa Temple and in the same general area as the Pusan Country Club. In the middle of 1988, this single line was extended in a loop parallel with the waterfront, and encircling the main downtown area. Fares are W220 for a single sector, W270 for two, and W300 for three sectors. (*Note:* fare increases are due.)

Taxis are readily available, but unlike Seoul there is only one kind. The first 1 ¼ mile is W800, and each additional quarter mile is W100. From midnight to 4 A.M., you need to add a 20% surcharge (this is not shown on the meter). Few taxi drivers speak English, so it helps to have your destinations written out in Korean. Pusan taxi drivers seem to expect to be the exception to Korea's no-tipping policy.

Although **city buses** run frequently around all areas of the city and sub-urbs, again there is a language difficulty as signs are only in Korean. Your hotel staff will be able to advise about the correct buses to catch. The fare is W210 if you buy a token in advance, W220 if you pay in cash on the bus. One of the most popular routes with visitors to Pusan is by Bus No. 302, which travels from Chungmu-dong, via City Hall and the Pusan Station to the Yachting Center and Haeundae. You can take this, also, when you visit the U.N. Cemetery. Another route, Bus No. 301, runs from Kudok Stadium around the curve of the downtown south wharf area, north to the Pusan Sports Complex and the Express Bus Terminal, again via City Hall and the Pusan Station.

Car Hire. There are several car-rental agencies in Pusan that offer both limousines and microbuses. The cost begins at around W29,000 per day (10 hours) for a small car, and goes up to W101,000 for a sedan. The charge for a driver is W20,000 per 10 hours or 125 kilometers. Again, we warn you that standards of driving skill in Korea are probably not as high as you're used to, and that pedestrians, especially children, need watching carefully. You can call Pusan Rent-a-car at 469–2222, Youngnam at 44–5000, or Hankuk at 205–3240. The cost includes the charge for insurance and value-added tax.

Intercity Buses. There are two terminals. Sobu, to the west of the city is for departures to Masan, Chinhae, Chungmu, Chinju, Namwon, Nam-hae, Hadong, Taegu, Hapchon, and other cities and towns to the west and northwest of Pusan. Tongbu terminal, to the north near the Tongnae sub-way station, is for departures to Ulsan, Kyongju, Pohang, Kangnung and other centers to the northeast. The Express Bus Terminal is a little to the west of the Tongbu Intercity Terminal, and is for all the major routes through the center of the country to the northwest, and north to Seoul.

Departures for all destinations are very frequent, with the first departures at around 6 A.M., and the last at 8 P.M. The hotel staff can help you check the current schedules.

ACCOMMODATIONS. Except for Seoul, you will not find a city in Korea with a greater number of hotels to choose from. Because of the volume of business traffic, the growing tourist trade, and the fact that the city is the air, rail, and shipping hub of the entire southeast, the need for hotel rooms has brought the number of hotels to over 40. These are located mainly within the central city area or at the Haeundae resort.

Approximate price ranges for a double or twin room are: *Deluxe,* W80,000 to W120,000; *1st class,* W50,000 to W80,000; *2d class,* W30,000 to W50,000; *3d class,* W20,000 to W30,000.

Credit card abbreviations used are: American Express, AE; Diner's Club, DC; MasterCard, MC; Visa, V.

The area code if you're calling from outside Pusan is 051.

Note that we have not followed the KNTC rating system in grading these hotels, and have tried to be consistent in judging the scope and quality of facilities. All offer the basic facilities of laundry, dry cleaning, and room service; they usually have lobby stores for souvenirs and sundries; and often have additional facilities like a barber shop or game room. Some have health clubs and indoor pools. All have facilities for banquets and seminars.

Near the Railroad Plaza

Commodore Dynasty. *Deluxe.* 743-80, Yongju-dong, Chung-ku, Pusan; Tel. 466–9101, Seoul office (02) 735–8931, Telex K53717, Fax. (051) 462–9101). The architecture is distinctively Korean, and there is a model of a Turtle Ship at the front entrance. 325 rooms; Western, Chinese, Japanese, and Korean restaurants, a coffee shop, two cocktail lounges, and a nightclub. Also has a health club with an indoor swimming pool. Credit cards: AE, DC, MC, V.

Arirang. *2d class.* 1204-1, Choryang-dong, Tong-ku, Pusan; Tel. 463–5001, Seoul office (02) 753–0016, Fax. 463–2800. 121 rooms; Western, Korean, and Japanese restaurants, a coffee shop, snack bar, cocktail lounge, and nightclub. Credit cards: AE, DC, MC, V.

Ferry. *2d class.* 37-16, 4-ka, Chungang-dong, Chung-ku, Pusan; Tel. 463–0881, Fax. (051) 463–7832. 122 rooms; grill room, steak house, coffee shop, sky lounge, and nightclub. Also a sauna. Credit cards: AE, DC, V.

Plaza. *3d class.* 1213-14, Choryang-dong, Tong-ku, Pusan; Tel. 463–5011–9. 69 rooms; Western restaurant, Japanese noodle shop, and a coffee shop. Credit cards: MC, V.

The City Hall Area

Sorabol. *Deluxe.* 37, 1-ka, Taechong-dong, Chung-ku, Pusan; Tel. 463–3511, Seoul office (02) 267–7174, Telex K53827, Fax. (051) 463–3510. 162 rooms; Chinese, Japanese, and Continental restaurants, a buffet restaurant, coffee shop, cocktail lounge, and nightclub. Also a business center and a sauna. Credit cards: AE, DC, MC, V.

Pusan Tourist. *1st class.* 12, 2-ka, Tonggwang-dong, Chung-ku, Pusan; Tel. 241–4301, Telex K53657, Fax. (051) 244–1153. 270 guest rooms; a grill, Chinese restaurant, coffee shop, and bakery, two cocktail lounges, a nightclub, and a disco. Also a sauna and health club. Credit cards: AE, DC, MC, V.

Phoenix. *2d class.* 8-1, 5-ka, Nampo-dong, Chung-ku, Pusan; Tel. 245–8061, Fax. 241–1523. 107 rooms; one restaurant, a coffee shop, cocktail lounge, and nightclub. Also a sauna. Credit cards: AE, DC, MC, V.

Royal. *2d class.* 2-72, 2-ka, Kwangbok-dong, Chung-ku, Pusan; Tel. 241–1051, Telex K53824. 108 guest rooms; Western grill room, coffee shop, buffet restaurant, and a nightclub. Credit cards: AE, DC, MC, V.

Tong Yang. *3d class.* 27, 1-ka, Kwangbok-dong, Chung-ku, Pusan; Tel. 245–1205, Telex K53824. 108 rooms; one restaurant and a coffee shop; cocktail lounge. Credit cards: AE, DC, MC, V.

Tower. *3d class.* 20, 3-ka, Tonggwang-dong, Chung-ku, Pusan; Tel. 241–5151. 114 rooms; grill room, Korean restaurant, coffee shop, and nightclub. Credit cards: AE, V.

To the City's Northeast

Kukje. *1st class.* 830-62, Pomil 2-dong, Tong-ku, Pusan; Tel. 642–1330, Fax. (051) 642–6595. 140 rooms; Western buffet restaurant, Chinese and

Japanese restaurants, and a coffee shop; a top-floor sky lounge and a night-club. Also a sauna and hot tubs. Major credit cards.

Crown. *2d class.* 830-30, Pomil-dong, Tong-ku, Pusan; Tel. 642–1626, Telex K53422. 130 rooms; Western, Chinese, and Japanese restaurants, cocktail lounge, and nightclub. Also a sauna. Credit cards: AE, DC, MC, V.

Taeyang. *3d class.* 1-62, Sujong-dong, Tong-ku, Pusan; Tel. 465–7311. 80 rooms; Korean and Japanese restaurants, lobby coffee lounge, and a cocktail bar. Also a sauna. Credit cards: AE, DC, V.

Tongnae Hot Springs

Tongnae Tourist. *1st class.* 212, Onchon-dong, Tongnae-ku, Pusan; Tel. 555–1121. Recently enlarged and redecorated, the hotel now has 76 rooms, a French restaurant, a grill room, and a coffee shop. Water from the nearby hot springs is piped directly into the hotel bathrooms. Credit cards: AE, DC, MC, V.

Haeundae Resort

Hyatt Regency Pusan. *Deluxe.* 1405–16, Chung-dong, Haeundae-ku, Pusan; Tel. 743–1234, Telex K52688, Fax. (051) 743–1250. This is the newest deluxe hotel to be built on the beach. 363 rooms; Western, Korean, and Japanese restaurants, plus a pub, lobby lounge, and a night club. Leisure facilities include a health club and an indoor swimming pool. Credit cards: AE, DC, MC, V.

Paradise Beach. *Deluxe.* 1408-5, Chung-dong, Haeundae-ku, Pusan; Tel. 742–2121, Seoul office (02) 277–2121, Telex K52145, Fax 742–2100. The old 2d-class hotel has been torn down and its replacement has more facilities than any other hotel in Pusan. 250 rooms; Western, Korean, Chinese, and Japanese restaurants, coffee shop, pub and lobby lounge, and a Western-style disco. Sports and leisure facilities include a health club, an outdoor pool that's heated by a hot spring in the winter, and the hotel's own equipment for various water sports. The hotel also has Pusan's only casino, open 24 hours. Credit cards: AE, DC, MC, V.

Westin Chosun Beach. *Deluxe.* 737, U-ildong, Haeundae-ku, Pusan; Tel. 742–7411, Seoul office (02) 777–8433, Telex K53718, Fax. (051) 742–1313. The most popular hotel in Pusan for Western businesspeople and tourists; also well established as a social center for the city's foreign community. 331 guest rooms; French and Japanese restaurants, coffee shop, pub, and a lobby cocktail area. Also a health club, an outside swimming pool and terrace, and a Western-style disco. Credit cards: AE, DC, MC, V.

New Beach. *2d class.* 1412-7 Chung-dong, Haeundae-ku, Pusan; Tel. 742–8877, Fax. 742–8881. With just 30 rooms, this hotel offers banquet facilities, an outdoor swimming pool, and a nightclub. Credit cards: MC, V.

Green Beach. *3d class.* 1130, Chung-dong, Haeundae-ku, Pusan; Tel. 742–3211. 65 rooms; a general restaurant and a coffee shop. Major credit cards.

Youth Hostels. There are two youth hotels in Pusan, the Kumgang near the Tongnae Hot Springs and Kumgang Park, and the Aerin, to the west of the city center, near Taechong Park. Both offer good value.

The **Kumgang** is at 1-4, Onchon-dong, Tongnae-ku, Pusan; Tel. 554–3235. It offers four-, eight-, 10-, and 12-bunk rooms, and a number of Korean-style private rooms. There is a general restaurant and a coffee shop, and hot-spring baths. No credit cards.

The **Aerin** is at 41, 1-ka, Posu-dong, Chung-ku, Pusan; Tel. 257–2222. It offers six-bunk rooms and a number of twin and Korean-style rooms. There is a general restaurant and a coffee shop. Credit cards: AE, DC, V.

RESTAURANTS. Pusan is Korea's second-largest city after Seoul, and is also the second-best city after Seoul, for its range of Oriental and Western cuisines. The most variety is found in the hotels, which offer good Western, Korean, Chinese, and Japanese restaurants. Prices in general tend to be a little cheaper than in Seoul, and categories/costs are as follows: *Expensive,* W15,000 to W30,000; *Moderate,* W10,000 to W15,000; *Inexpensive,* W8,000 to W12,000. These costs are based on lunch or dinner for one person, excluding drinks, service charge, and taxes. There are, of course, extremes. At the very best Korean restaurants, if you order lavishly you'll be spending at the top end of the scale. You can also eat in the small rice-and-noodle shops, and spend less than W3,500 per person.

Fine Continental fare is a little rare, but if you're really in need of a good French meal, head for the **Ninth Gate** at the Westin Chosun Hotel, at Haeundae Resort. It's *expensive* and said to be Pusan's best; Tel. 742–7411. The **Paradise Beach Hotel,** also at Haeundae, probably offers the most extensive menu of Western foods, with restaurants in all price categories; Tel. 742–2121. Haeundae also has a new pizza-and-beer restaurant called **Park Place.** It's at the east end of the bay, *inexpensively* priced, and presents the rare pleasure in Pusan of foreign music videos. The address is 948-7, Chung-dong (1st floor of the Rose Motel), Tel. 742–2439.

Some downtown restaurants are recommended for Western food. There are the **Chung Tap Grill** in Nampo-dong (*expensive*), Tel. 246–0071; the **Hoban Grill** at the Crown Hotel (*moderate*), Tel. 646–1626; and the various restaurants at the Sorabol Hotel. The latter place is known locally for excellent buffets in its **Chungmaru** restaurant (*moderate*), Tel. 463–3511.

Excellent Korean restaurants abound in Pusan, and many of the larger ones are used to catering to foreigners. One of the most delightful is **Dalmaji,** or Moon Viewing House, again at Haeundae, but well worth the trip out there if you're staying downtown. The address is 1489-1, Chung 2-dong, Tel. 742–3386. Other Korean restaurants worth trying are **Ever Spring Park,** in Onchon-dong, Tongnae-ku (*expensive*), Tel. 54–1800; **Kaya,** Chungang-dong 4-ka (*moderate*), Tel. 463–3277; and **Green House** in Taeyon 3-dong, Nam-ku (*moderate*), Tel. 622–5551.

For Chinese food, the **New World Chinese Restaurant,** on the 13th floor of the downtown Heung-kuk Insurance Building, is recommended and *moderately* priced.

One of the best Japanese restaurants is at the Westin Chosun Beach Hotel, the **Kuromatsu,** which also offers Teppanyaki grills (*expensive*); another is the **Sakae** at the Paradise Beach Hotel (*expensive*). Closer to town is the **Suck Tap,** at Kwangan 2-dong, Nam-ku (*moderate*), Tel. 753–0010.

Local Specialties. Pusan is noted for six native dishes and one local wine, and the Pusan Tourist Association has drawn up a list of where foreign visitors can enjoy these delights. They are not to everyone's taste but are true flavors of the area.

Tongnae fried blue onions, a recipe imported from China during the Koryo Dynasty—**Cheil Restaurant,** Pokchon-dong in Tongnae-ku (Tel. 552–0792).

Abalone gruel, said to "refresh the health"—**Urijang,** in Amnam-dong, So-gu (Tel. 256–3565).

Sliced raw flounder, spread with hot pepper paste, garlic, ginger, sesame oil, vinegar, and sugar—**Kumo,** in Chung 2-dong, Haeundae (Tel. 742–0011).

Broiled eels, from the Naktong River—**Unhaengnamujip,** in Kumgok-dong, Puk-ku (Tel. 332–2909).

Wandang noodles, popular for breakfast—**Sipalbon Wandang,** in Nampo-dong, Chung-ku (Tel. 22–0018).

Amso-Kalbi, broiled beef ribs with a special Pusan sauce—**Haeundae Amso Kalbi,** in Chung-dong, Haeundae-ku (Tel. 72–0033).

It is said that the Pusan rice wine Sansong dates to the late sixteenth century—try it at the **Sanjang-jip,** in Kumsong-dong, Tongnae-ku (Tel. 57–0194).

TOURS. Pusan is the terminus of two rather long cruises; one to carry you elsewhere, the other an excellent sightseeing cruise that covers some of the prettiest areas of the Hallyo Waterway.

The first is the **Pusan–Cheju Island cruise** by ferry, which takes around 11½ hours, departing Pusan daily in the evening. Fares range from W12,340 to W88,060, depending on the class of travel. You can take a car on the ferry, also, for rates beginning at around W50,000. There are two companies operating the cruises. Call in Pusan: *Car Ferry Queen* (Tel. 464–6601) or Dong Yang (Tel. 463–0605).

The **Hallyo Waterway cruise** is by the *Angel* hydrofoil, which departs Pusan six times a day on a 90-minute run to Chungmu, with a brief stop at Songpo. It then leaves Chungmu three times a day on the one-hour, 40-minute cruise to Yosu, with stops at Saryangdo, Samchonpo, and Namhae. The one-way fare all the way from Pusan to Yosu is W16,310. You can call for details at Pusan (Tel. 469–3851), Chungmu, Tel. (0557) 2–2359, Yosu, Tel. (0662) 63–0116, and Seoul, Tel. 734–5636.

Local tour operators unfortunately do not handle tours on a "join tour" basis, but cater exclusively to groups. There are therefore no regular tour programs offered with English-speaking guides, making Pusan very much a "do-it-yourself" sightseeing city. There are, however, a couple of regular **bus trips** from the Pusan Station. These are the "no frills" way of sightseeing—the bus drives you to a site, leaves you for a set period of time, then carries on to the next stop. The most popular visits are to the Chungyolsa Shrine and the Pomosa Temple—all in three and a half hours, departing Pusan Station frequently. The fare is only W3,000. Another heads out of town in the morning on a 1-hour, 20-minute drive to the Bugok Hot Springs, leaves you there for five hours or so, and brings you back. The fare is W6,000. These programs change constantly, so ask your hotel to check the latest schedules for you. (Or you can try telephoning 246–7311 or 469–0101.) At peak holiday seasons, there are likely to be more programs available.

While the tour operators do not arrange regular sightseeing tours, they can provide you with an English-speaking guide, along with a **car and driver** if you would like to look around in style. The cost would be in the area of W80,000 per day. The Pusan office of Global Tours, one of the most well-known agencies in Korea, is at 83-1, 4-ka, Chungang-dong, Chung-ku, Pusan (Tel. 469–4561).

WHAT TO SEE. Historic Sites. Because of the bustling commercial aspect of Pusan's downtown area and ports, there are few historic sites of major interest right in the city. However, the trip by cable car up **Mt. Kumchong** from the Kumgang Park is enjoyable. The east and west gates of the Kumchong Fortress, designated as Historic Site No. 215, are about a 10-minute walk from the mountain's summit. The fortress was built around 1703, and was last reconstructed in 1825.

Closer to the city, a little east of the Tongnae subway station, is the **Chungyolsa Shrine,** a recently renovated area commemorating the patriotic deaths of Song Sang-Hyun, the municipal governor, and Admiral Jung Ball, the military commander, who fought against the invading Japanese forces in 1592. The shrine area contains some pretty pavilions and a display of paintings depicting the valiant defense of the city.

The **U.N. Memorial Cemetery** lies east of the city center, reached by the No. 302 bus, which runs between downtown and Haeundae. The cemetery was described earlier in this chapter, and it has a central plaza where the flags of the 16 nations that made up the U.N. forces during the Korean War are flown.

Temples. The most important temple in the Pusan area is **Pomosa,** easily reached by taxi from the last northern stop on the subway line. Even farther north, toward Kyongju, is the **Tongdosa Temple,** which you can visit on a day trip from Pusan. Both of these important temples were described earlier in this chapter. Other temples are the **Taegaksa** downtown, which is pretty but historically insignificant, and the **Tongmyung Temple,** near the U.N. Memorial Cemetery, which was donated to the city by a local businessman. A huge bell and sanctuary make the temple worth visiting if you're in the area.

Parks. Here Pusan excels. The parks near the city are all large and green, offering pleasant areas in which to walk and relax, and from which to admire the views over the city, port, and mountains. Forming the core of the downtown area is **Yongdusan,** with the Pusan Tower for really panoramic views. Farther northwest is **Taechong Park,** with its striking Tower of the Royal Dead, and **Taeshin Park,** which is densely forested with huge trees. Pusan also has a **Children's Park,** with a zoo and recreational facilities surrounded by forests of cedar, pine, and firs. Fun for children also is the **Kumgang Park,** beyond the Tongnae Hot Springs. Here you'll find an amusement park, a folk-art hall, the city zoo and botanical gardens, and numerous historical relics. Again, there are some pleasant walks.

Finally, ask your hotel to pack a box lunch (many of them will provide this service), and head out to **Taejongdae Park.** This is on top of a craggy point at the end of Yongdo Island, a 20-minute taxi ride from the downtown area. Here you can relax under shady trees and enjoy superb sea views.

Zoos and Botanical Gardens. There is a small zoo in Children's park but the main city zoo is at the southeast end of **Kumgang Park,** alongside the Botanical Gardens. The Pusan Marine Palace is also here, with an oceanarium. It is a three-storied aquarium displaying some 12,000 fish of 250 species.

On the city's far western fringe, south of the Pusan International Airport, the delta of the Naktong-gang River, and Ulsukdo Island with its shallow surrounding waters, provide food and shelter for many migratory birds, including Korea's beautiful cranes. Much of the area has been set aside as a sanctuary, and it is possible to visit. The bird visits are seasonal, so you will need to check whether it's worthwhile to go at the time you're in Pusan. Your hotel can help, or you can contact the Pusan Tourist Association (Tel. 246–7311).

Museums and Cultural Centers. The **Pusan Municipal Museum,** at Taeyon-dong, very near the U.N. Memorial Cemetery, houses a collection of over 2,000 historical and cultural treasures. It is open from 9 A.M. to 6 P.M. daily except Mondays and Korean public holidays (Tel. 624–6341). Nearby is the **Pusan Cultural Center.**

There is also a museum at the **Pusan National University,** with over 10,000 exhibits. It is at San 30, Changjon-dong, Tongnae-ku (Tel. 56–0171). The opening hours are flexible, so you should check before you go.

The **Pusan Citizens' Hall** has a large auditorium with performances ranging from ballets and symphonies to Korean traditional music and dance. The city has a symphony orchestra, a traditional music troupe, and a traditional dance group which give periodic performances in Pusan and provincial centers. Citizens' Hall is located across from the Crown Hotel, northeast of City Hall. Telephone 645–4951 for details of current performances.

BEACHES. There are five beaches designated as suitable for swimming, starting at the far southeast with **Tadaepo,** some 10 miles from the city center. Here the beach is quietly sheltered, and there are few facilities. It is still crowded in summer.

Closer to the city center is **Songdo,** Pusan's first swimming beach to be officially opened to the public. Some of the surrounding scenery here is lovely, a combination of pines and solid rock, and there are plenty of facilities for sailing, boating, and other water sports. There are many small hotels, Korean inns, and Korean restaurants. Again, it's very crowded during the summer.

Kwangali Beach is between the city and Haeundae, and is noted for its fine-grain sand and collection of fresh (raw) seafood restaurants.

We have already mentioned **Haeundae** as the most developed resort in the area, and for Western visitors it is the one with the most familiar flavor. Here are Pusan's best hotels, an excellent range of restaurants, and all manner of water sports. From here you can take a boat cruise out to the **Oryukdo Islands,** a symbol of the city. The cruise departs every two hours and takes about 1 hour, 20 minutes. The cost is W2,000.

The last beach for swimming is on the eastern outskirts of the Pusan shore. **Songjong Beach** is one and a quarter miles long, fringed by a dense forest of pines. Very pretty and very popular.

All the above beaches are well-equipped for visitors during the summer season. From early July to the end of August, such facilities as cafes and snack bars spring up along the shores. They are inclined to charge rather high prices, so check before you order. You will also find toilet facilities and showers, umbrellas and rubber tires for rent, and stalls selling beach-wear, play equipment, and shell souvenirs.

HOT SPRINGS. The most notable in the area is **Tongnae,** which has been renowned for centuries for the curative powers of the alkaline, chlorous waters. There is one first-class hotel here and a cluster of smaller hotels and Korean inns, all of which offer the services of hot-spring baths for visitors.

Haeundae is also a hot-spring area, with the water somewhat hotter than at other spas in the country. Natural water temperature here is 62° Fahrenheit, compared with 50° at Tongnae. Some of the hotels offer hot-spring baths, and the Paradise Beach uses the spring water to heat its outdoor swimming pool during the winter.

SPORTS. Pusan has two major sports stadiums—**Kudok Stadium,** just to the east of the downtown area, and the newer **Pusan Sports Complex,** near the Express Bus Terminal in the northern district, which has a modern gymnasium and a huge stadium designed for baseball games. Your hotel can help you find out about sporting events at these stadiums during your stay.

Pusan's **Yachting Center**—site of all the yachting events of the 1988 Olympics—is in Suyong Bay, near Haeundae, and can be reached by bus No. 302 from downtown.

Tennis. There are a number of good courts, but most of them are for tennis-club members. However, the top hotels often arrange play for their guests, and you should consult the hotel's health club or information desk. These days many Koreans are very keen on tennis, so you should have no trouble finding a partner.

Golf. Just outside the city in the northern suburbs, near the far end of the subway line, are two country clubs with excellent golf courses. The **Tongnae** 18-hole course is near the famous hot springs (Tel. 513–0101, Seoul office (02) 757–8877), and the **Pusan Country Club's** course is also 18 holes (Tel. 508–0707).

About an hour's drive east of Pusan is **Changwon,** which also has an 18-hole golf course, Tel. (0551) 83–4112; and to the north is the magnificent new 36-hole course at **Tongdo,** near the famous temple mentioned earlier in this chapter (Tel. 464–7751).

The courses are for the use of club members, but visitors are granted playing privileges. Equipment and caddies are available.

Fishing. There is good fishing along the coast of the entire Southeast Area—both surf casting from the beaches and breakwaters, and offshore from boats. Your hotel can help you make arrangements.

SOME OF THE BEST KNOWN SIGHTS IN ASIA.

Forty-five years of flying to Asia has made Northwest a familiar face. Especially when you consider we've been flying there longer than any other airline.

And now the leading airline to Asia can get you there faster. With new schedules that reduce travel time by as much as three hours.

We've even enhanced our fleet of 747s. So you'll find spacious surroundings, elegant meals and state-of-the-art audio and video programming.

Northwest flies to more cities in Asia from the U.S. than any other airline. And when you fly to Asia on Northwest, you'll be able to earn free travel with Northwest WorldPerks® after only 20,000 miles.

Be sure to ask your travel agent about the great savings on our Northwest WorldVacations℠ customized vacation packages to Asia, too.

To put yourself in the picture, call your travel agent or Northwest at 1-800-447-4747.

NORTHWEST AIRLINES
Some People Just Know How To Fly.

CALL YOUR TRAVEL AGENT OR NORTHWEST
1-800-447-4747

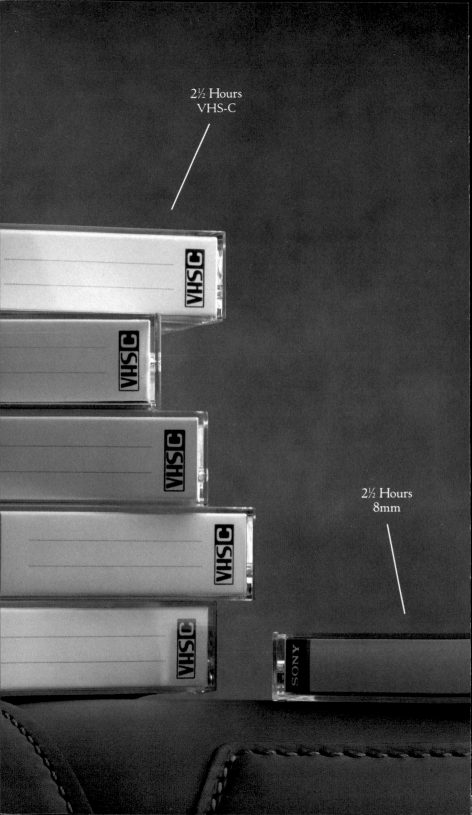

2½ Hours
VHS-C

2½ Hours
8mm

SONY

PACK WISELY.

Given a choice, the seasoned traveler always carries less.
Case in point: Sony Handycam® camcorders, America's most
popular. They record up to 2½ hours on a single tape.
VHS-C tapes record only 30 minutes.* And why carry five tapes
when you can record everything on one? Which brings us
to the first rule of traveling: pack a Sony Handycam camcorder.

American Express offers Travelers Cheques built for two.

American Express® Travelers Cheques *for Two*. The first Travelers Cheques that allow either of you to use them because both of you have signed them. And only one of you needs to be present to purchase them.

Cheques *for Two* are accepted anywhere regular American Express Travelers Cheques are, which is just about everywhere. So stop by before your next trip and ask for Cheques *for Two*.

 **Travelers Cheques**

Hiking. Pusan's larger parks have some wonderful walks. There are lots of trees, magnificent sea views, and it's not too difficult to find a little splendid isolation. The **Taejongdae Recreation area,** at the tip of Yongdo Island, is particularly recommended for hikers, and there is a popular walk north from the **Kumjong Fortress** (reached by cable car in Kumgang Park) to the **Pomosa Temple.**

Bowling. There are several bowling alleys in Pusan, very crowded in the evenings. Play during the day, or make reservations at **Pusan Bowling Center** (22 lanes), Pujon-dong, Pusanjin-ku (Tel. 819–9400); **Haeundae Bowling Center** (18 lanes), at U 1-dong, Haeundae Beach (Tel. 72–2345); and **Hyondae Bowling Center** (14 lanes), Pujon-dong, Pusanjin-ku (Tel. 802–2370).

Windsurfing. The Suyong Bay area, including Haeundae Beach, provides ideal conditions for windsurfing. The **Paradise Beach Hotel** provides equipment, or you can call the **Pusan Wind Surfing Federation** for advice and assistance (Tel. 742–2121).

SHOPPING. Except for Seoul, you probably won't find better opportunities for bargains than in Pusan. There are several department stores that take a very orderly approach to product displays, and duty-free shops and souvenir stores. These all have a wide choice of items, quality, and price. When you add to these the special treat of the Kwangbok-dong-Nampodong shopping district and the Kukje market area downtown, shopping in Pusan is lots of fun, and a real taste of Korean everyday life.

If you're looking for souvenirs or native artwork (especially ceramics), and you don't have much time to look around, you will find stores near the Pusan Tower in Yongdusan Park and in several of the hotels. A couple of stores in Kwangbok-dong are **Silla Native Arts** (Tel. 245–2828) and **Ilsung Native Arts** (Tel. 245–4994).

Department Stores and Shopping Centers

Pusan Department Store, 1412-1, Onchon 3-dong, Tongnae-ku (Tel. 553–5511).

Mihwadang Department Store, 7, 2-ka, Kwangbok-dong, Chung-ku (Tel. 246–7711).

Yuna Department Store, 5, 1-ka, Shinchang-dong, Chung-ku (Tel. 246–6231).

Taehwa Shopping, 193-1, Pujoon-dong, Pusanjin-ku (Tel. 805–1234).

Pusan Tower Shopping Center, 1-2, 2-ka, Kwangbok-dong, Chung-ku (Tel. 245–2966).

Duty-Free Shops

Airport Duty-Free Shop, managed by the KNTC (Tel. 98–1101).

Pukwan Ferry Terminal Duty-Free Shop, managed by the KNTC (Tel. 462–2501).

Jindo Fur Salon, 69, 6-ka, Chungang-dong, Chung-ku (Tel. 463–1444).

Nam Moon Duty-Free Shop, 168-1, Kamjon-dong, Puk-ku (Tel. 92–8926).

Paradise Beach Duty-Free Shop, at the hotel in Haeundae (Tel. 742–2121).

CULTURAL EVENTS. For a complete list of national holidays and the major national festivals, refer to the "Staying in Korea" section of *Facts at Your Fingertips*. Many of the festivals are celebrated in Pusan, some with a particularly local flair. At Haeundae Beach, for example, the **lunar new year** (called Folklore Day in Korea) is celebrated with the burning of a wood and straw "Moon House" in the middle of a giant circle. Other rituals and dances are to bring good luck for the coming year.

Buddha's birthday, on the eighth day of the fourth lunar month (May 28 in 1993), is also celebrated at the temples of Pusan. It's a lovely time to visit Pomosa or Tongdosa, the most spectacular temples of the Pusan area.

The only strictly local festival in Pusan is **Citizen's Day,** October 5, celebrated with sports events, traditional music, dance on a grand scale, and fireworks. The main center of festivities is the Kudok Stadium.

NIGHTLIFE. All the deluxe hotels and just about all the Western-style hotels of all classes in Pusan offer nightclubs or bars, or both. These, of course, have the advantage of being more likely to cater to foreigners and have English-speaking waiters, but they by no means exhaust the nightclubs in the city. Your hotel can advise you on the most interesting.

The **Western-style discos** are out at Haeundae Beach, at the Westin Chosun and Paradise Beach hotels. The latter hotel also has Pusan's only **casino,** open 24 hours a day with all the international games of chance (Tel. 742–2121).

For the city's liveliest spread of bars and hot little nightspots, head into **Texas Street,** near the Pusan Station. With bars like Susie's, Tiger, Lion, London, Hollywood, Miami, and New York, the range of music and entertainments is wide. The majority of customers are seamen (remember, Pusan is a large port city) and American soldiers, so you won't find many language difficulties.

Downtown you will find dozens of traditional Korean night spots— *suljip* (wine houses), *tabang* (tearooms), and noisy little beer halls.

USEFUL ADDRESSES AND TELEPHONE NUMBERS. Medical Attention. As in all Korean cities, your best source of information and assistance regarding medical attention is your hotel manager. Away from the hotel, however, there are a number of hospitals with good facilities— **Paik Hospital** (Tel. 895–3031), **Baptist Hospital** (Tel. 466–9331), **Maryknoll Hospital** (Tel. 465–8801), and **Pusan University Hospital** (Tel. 254–0171).

Diplomatic Missions. The **United States Consulate** is at 24, 2-ka, Taechung-dong, Chung-ku (Tel. 264–7791). The **Honorary British Consulate** is at Yoochang Building, 12th floor, 25-2, 4-ka, Chungang-dong, Chung-ku (Tel. 463–0041).

Tourist Information. The best place to obtain information on Pusan and its tourist attractions is the **KNTC office** at the Pusan Airport. The counter is in the international terminal, and there are a number of brochures and leaflets on local things to see and do (Tel. 98–1100). Get hold of a tourist map published by the **Pusan Tourist Association** (you may have to buy it at a bookstore if you cannot find one free). This is very useful as it gives a clear guide to the city and surroundings, and marks most of the hotels, police stations, postal and district offices, subway lines, bus terminals, and places of scenic interest.

Here are some phone numbers you may need:

International ferry terminal, 463–3161
Hydrofoil information, 469–0117
Information Center, Pusan Station, 463–4938
Foreigners' Counter, Pusan Station, 463–7551
Tourism Section, City government, 469–0101
Pusan Tourist Association, 246–7311
Lost and Found, Pusan Police Bureau, 413–9997
Tourist Complaints, 469–0101

THE SOUTHEAST

The Southeast area of Korea boasts the second- and third-largest cities in the country, after the capital city of Seoul. The second-largest is the port city of Pusan, which is covered along with its surrounding attractions earlier in this guide. Taegu, the third-largest city, and the only major city completely removed from the coast, is also covered in its own chapter.

Korea's Southeast is an excellent area for those who like seaside activity. It has a charming maze of islands scattered just off the mainland, vast bird sanctuaries preserved in their natural state, flora not matched anywhere in Korea, and a small but respectable collection of temples, historical sites, and monuments commemorating Korean naval history. Coupled with the major cultural attractions of Kyongju, and the international flavor of Pusan, the Southeast is an area unique in Korea. With its balmy climate and ease of getting around, it is an ideal region to explore.

Stretching for 94 miles both east to west and north to south, the Southeast area contains most of Kyongsangnamdo Province. Geographically, the Southeast runs from 34° to 36° north latitude, and lovers of sunshine will not find a warmer place in Korea. It can be hot in the summer, but on the shore fringes the climate is moderated by sea breezes. In the northeast corner of the region is Korea's most important cultural area, Kyongju—also covered in a separate part of this guide.

One natural boundary of Korea's Southeast is the Naktong-gang River, which flows down through central Korea, passes near Taegu, and then, about 30 miles from the South Coast, abruptly turns east toward Pusan. Just short of Pusan, the Naktong-gang turns south again and empties into the Korean Strait. For men who fought in the early days of the Korean

War, the Naktong-gang will bring back vivid memories, for this water barrier formed the western edge of the Pusan perimeter, the line where the unprovoked assault of the North Korean army was finally stopped by combined South Korean and United States forces.

To the west of Pusan lies Masan, a major industrial city, and midway between Pusan and Masan, but right on the coast is Chinhae. The city's magnificent natural harbor makes it an ideal spot for the headquarters of the South Korean Navy.

For the first two weeks of April, Chinhae has another distinction: It becomes the site of a splendid cherry-blossom festival that draws more than a million people from all over the country. All sorts of events are celebrated, such as the anniversary of the Navy's founding, and, of course, the heroic deeds of the national hero Admiral Yi Sun-Shin and his famous turtle ships. There are parades, beauty contests, sports events, exhibitions, and the re-creation of famous battles. And the cherry trees are always at their most spectacular for the festival.

The entire area is well served by all kinds of transportation, both to reach it and to move around once you're there—air, rail, bus, international or domestic ferry, and hydrofoil. The international ferries are the ones that connect Pusan with the Japanese ports of Shimonoseki and Osaka, so that anyone with an extended Far East vacation could visit Japan from Korea, or Korea from Japan without traveling between the two countries by air.

Taegu and Its Surroundings

Although Taegu is described in a separate section of this guide, for convenience we are including a brief overview here.

This major Korean city is a natural stopover point for anyone moving up or down the peninsula between Pusan and Seoul, by either rail or highway. It forms the gateway to the Kyongju district to the east, and to several worthwhile tourist destinations to the west and south. It is a traditional market city, serving as a commercial center and distribution point for all the small towns around it, and is the centerpoint of Korea's famous apple orchards. Because it is such a major hub of road and rail, Taegu's location makes it ideal as the logistical base for United States Forces in Korea. In addition, it is the home of several noted colleges and hospitals.

An expressway completed in 1985, the '88 Olympic Highway, links Taegu with Kwangju in the southwest, offering easy access to many cultural, scenic, and historic attractions. Taegu, with its good selection of hotels and transportation, provides an excellent base for visiting these areas.

To the west of Taegu, Talsong Park has several historical structures connected with the Suh Clan, a family of ancient lineage that has had its roots in this area for many centuries. South of the city is the popular little resort of the Susong Reservoir, with several tourist hotels and recreational facilities that often give it a carnival atmosphere. It is popular for ice skating in the winter, boating in the summer.

The most famous temple near Taegu is Haeinsa, in a secluded mountain setting within the Kayasan National Park. With the opening of the '88 Expressway, this is now less than an hour's drive from Taegu. There are no tourist hotels open yet in the park-temple area, but there are lots of Korean inns that provide comfortable accommodations.

The park itself is renowned for the 4,300-foot Mt. Kayasan, with its many hiking trails and towering trees, striking in any season but stunning in the autumn. This peak and all the adjacent ones are part of the Sobaek Range, which runs off in a southwesterly direction and is noted for its many cliffs, unusual rock formations, and wide variety of trees.

The other temple in the area, Tonghwasa, is about 14 miles north of Taegu, in the Palgongsan Park. This is an easy trip over good paved roads, and a worthwhile one. The temple is one of the most important religious sites near the city, with a Buddha image carved into the cliff face near the temple entrance. It is said to date to the ninth century. The temple gate was built in 1634 and is now a monument to the durability of superb wood construction and to the creativity of Korean architecture of the time.

The Coastal Attractions

For visitors who love railroads, there is an interesting trip along the coastal part of this area. It is a meandering train ride from Pusan that winds first northwest, then southwest for nearly 100 miles. There are a couple of options—one takes you to Chinju, from which you can head farther south to the coastal city of Samchonpo, via Sachon. You should stop at Chinju for a while, however. It is one of the country's most enchanting and least-visited small cities. The Nam-gang River runs through the center of the town, which has a maze of narrow streets, several small temples, and Chinju Castle, site of fierce fighting during the first battles of the Japanese invasions during the late sixteenth century. The walls of the castle and an inner pavilion, Choksongnu, have been extensively reconstructed, and several shrines, temples, and other pavilions have been preserved. Within the compound there is also a small village, which gives this castle a lively atmosphere, unlike other static historical structures.

If you head to Samchonpo, you'll find a vast seaside park, and a wonderful swimming area at Namilhae Beach. Alternatively, you can stay on the train through Chinju, still heading west, and pass through Hadong on the Somjin-gang River, Kwangyang, and end your ride at Sunchon, a large city.

It's a toss-up whether Sunchon should be included in the Southeast area we are discussing or in the West Plain Coastal Area. We've included details of this optional train trip here because Sunchon lies close to one of the area's beautiful parks. Also, although it is rather remote from Pusan, it's even more remote from any stopover point in the West Plain Coastal Area. Although most travelers heading from Pusan to Seoul by road will choose the direct route north and then northwest, some may like to strike out on their own to explore the more remote places of this Southeast Area. The option of heading west to Sunchon and then north to Seoul, stopping at cultural and scenic spots on the way, may turn out to be attractive. Although you will be able to count on finding only a few tourist hotels in the lower part of the country, you will always find a Korean inn when you need one.

If you go to Sunchon by train or bus, you will be just a short ride from Mt. Chogyesan Park. At 2,700 feet the mountain is not as tall as most lying along the eastern coast. That's because Sunchon is away from the mountainous spine that bisects Korea and is in the area leading to the lower elevations of the west. Right in the park is Songgwangsa Temple, a sprawling complex of buildings and courtyards that make up one of the three largest temples in the country. It is the center of Son Buddhism, the Korean version of Zen, and is the only temple in Korea with Western monks and nuns in permanent residence.

Instead of returning to Seoul from Sunchon, you could carry on by train or bus to Yosu and take the Angel hydrofoil cruise back to Pusan, stopping on the way to explore "Admiral Yi country," the Chungmu area.

Now let's talk about the seaside part of the Southeast, and something very special in Korea—the Hallyo Waterway.

The Hallyo Waterway

For those who enjoy islands, seascapes, beaches, and boating, this area is for you. The waterway is formed by a stretch of islands surrounded by the waters of the Korean Strait.

Following the route from Pusan west to the industrial port of Yosu, you'll pass to the north of several major islands that provide a buffer against heavy weather from the open sea. This waterway, 100 miles long from east to west and about 50 miles wide from top to bottom, contains 115 inhabited and 253 uninhabited islands. These create dozens of wide sounds, protected bays, tiny coves, seascapes of magnificent variety, and beaches superb for saltwater swimming.

The entire waterway area was officially declared a national maritime park in the late 1960s. However, owing to the cost of administering this vast area—more than 5,000 square miles of land and probably 5,000 miles of coastline—the government has up to now been able to put only six areas under strict preservation. These six areas are really individual parks.

One of the best ways to get a sweeping sample of the entire area is to take one of the hydrofoil cruises that operate out of Pusan, going to Chungmu or all the way to Yosu and back. Chungmu is the area that has received the most attention in tourism development and there are now good facilities for accommodations, shopping, and seaside recreation. There is also a marina and an exhibition hall for local handicrafts.

The cruise swings to the north of Kojedo, Hansando, Namhaedo, and Odongdo islands, stopping at the small ports along the route. For details of the cruise departure times and costs, see the "Tours" information in the *Pusan* section.

Here are the highlights of the area:

Kojedo Island. This is the second-largest island in Korean waters, after Cheju. On the south shore is an area, called Haekumgang, of sheer cliffs rising out of a cobalt-blue sea. The cliffs here are covered with great stands of pine and camelia trees, and are the roosting places for millions of sea birds. Kojedo has several monuments commemorating the sea victories of Admiral Yi against the Japanese in 1592–1593. Offshore, ocean waves break heavily on long stretches of rocky reefs. There is an excellent swimming beach, called Kujora, on the east side of the island.

Hansando Island. This is the next major protected area, just to the west of Kojedo. Hansando is equally famous as the site of more battles against the Japanese, in which the great Admiral Yi's iron-clad ships were victorious. On the island are the admiral's headquarters, a military training hall called Sebyongkwan, and the Chungyolsa shrine, where the admiral is reputed to have prayed for heavenly assistance before the climactic battle.

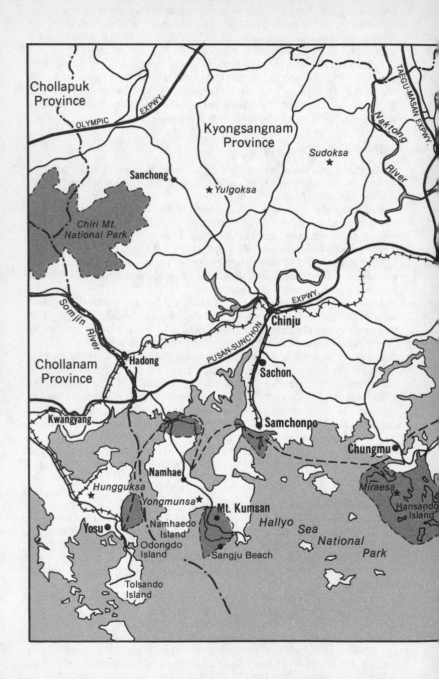

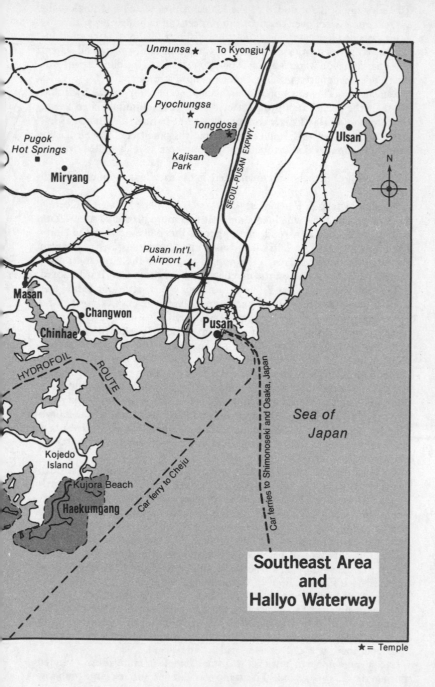

Unmunsa ★   To Kyongju

Pyochungsa ★

Tongdosa ★

Pugok Hot Springs ■

Kajisan Park

Ulsan ●

Miryang ●

N

SEOUL-PUSAN EXPWY.

Pusan Int'l. Airport ✈

Masan ●

Changwon ●

Chinhae ●

Pusan ●

HYDROFOIL

ROUTE

Sea of Japan

Car ferries to Shimonoseki and Osaka, Japan

Kojedo Island

Kujora Beach

Haekumgang

Car ferry to Cheju

Southeast Area and Hallyo Waterway

★ = Temple

To honor the brilliant design of the Korean ships, which had turtleshell-shaped iron covers over the decks to protect the fighting crews, there is a turtle-shaped lighthouse on a rock some distance offshore. To reach Hansando, you go by boat from the port of Chungmu on the mainland. Upon disembarking, you wander along cobblestone walks to the buildings of Admiral Yi's headquarters, Suryu, which is now a museum.

Samchonpo. This town on the mainland, another stop on the hydrofoil cruise, is the site of the third protected area. A small uninhabited island offshore, named Hakdo, is a sanctuary for white herons (designated as living national treasures), which roost high in the pine trees. The birds stay here in the summer. Unfortunately, their numbers have dwindled over recent years.

Just south of Samchonpo town, there is the excellent swimming beach of Namilhae.

Namhaedo Island. Farther west, we reach Namhaedo Island, Korea's third largest in area, which encompasses two more protected areas. You can reach this island by road, crossing from the mainland over the Namhae Grand Bridge. At 2,165 feet, this is the longest suspension span in the Orient. Just as you reach this island, you enter the Noryangri area, a small park that is half on the mainland, half on the island. It is honored as the spot where Admiral Yi, in the last hour of his victorious battle, was mortally wounded by a single shot from a Japanese sniper's musket. So Korea has its own Nelson, its own Trafalgar.

The island is visually interesting, being a series of peaks with low-lying areas between them. In the center of the island, near Namhae town, is Yongmunsa Temple, about halfway across the island toward the south shore. At this southern shore, there is a fine swimming beach called Sangju, as yet relatively undiscovered and thus uncrowded. Just inland from Sangju is Kumsan Mountain, rising 2,200 feet. This is famous as the place where King Taejo spent 100 days in prayer before overthrowing the Koryo kingdom to establish the Yi Dynasty. The mountain is a popular vantage point for viewing the off-lying islands in three directions, and for watching extraordinary sunrises.

Odongdo Island. This is the last protected area on our route westward. It is known locally as "Paulownia Tree Island," although it is acknowledged that the island holds few, if any, of these exotic Oriental trees. Indigenous to Odongdo, however, is the camelia, which grows in great profusion, and vast stands of a rare variety of bamboo, which grows both hard and straight. Legend has it that Admiral Yi had thousands of arrows made from this type of bamboo for his shipboard archers. The original archery range used by Yi's troops can still be seen and has recently been refurbished to its condition of centuries ago.

The island is reached by a 200-foot-long rock breakwater that connects it to the mainland. This causeway provides such excellent fishing that it is annually visited by thousands of anglers from all over Korea. If you arrive by hydrofoil, the western end of this waterway cruise is at Yosu, and from there it is only a short ride to the island.

A few miles north of Yosu is the historic temple of Hungguksa, founded during the Koryo period. The temple is famous for its large rainbow bridge, and the main hall is a designated treasure.

Pusan to Seoul Tour

If the idea of touring Korea from Pusan northward to Seoul is appealing, you might want to consider doing your sightseeing around Pusan, Taegu, and Kyongju first, then departing Pusan by hydrofoil for Yosu. From here you can get a suburban bus northward to Sunchon, on the edge of this Southeast area. Then, at Sunchon you have a choice of either bus or train transportation to Seoul. If time is limited, another bus will take you the 50 miles to Kwangju, another major cultural stop (see *West Plain and Coastal Area* chapter), and you can take a plane from there to Seoul.

PRACTICAL INFORMATION FOR
THE SOUTHEAST

WHEN TO GO. Except for the island of Cheju, off the southwest corner of Korea, the Southeast Area has the mildest climate of the entire country. This means more months of swimming and enjoyable days on the water, if these are your principal interests, and balmier days generally for every other activity from spring through fall. Fall beautifully offers the same brilliant foliage as other parts of the country, but winter has fewer sporting opportunities because of the lower latitudes and elevations that do not permit skiing. As for the Hallyo Waterway, this is the ideal shore area for any water activity: swimming, boat cruises, beach picnics, fishing, and puttering about in boats. The Southeast simply ranks high for summer fun.

HOW TO GET THERE. For details of how to get to the area's major centers of Pusan, Taegu, and Kyongju, consult the separate chapters on these areas. You can reach other destinations in the following ways:

To Chinju from Seoul. By air, from Kimpo Airport, a daily 70-minute flight (W33,400).
From Pusan. By train from the Pusan Station; both the air-conditioned express (Mugunghwa) and ordinary express trains (Tongil), have frequent departures. Call the foreigners' ticket counter at Pusan Station for current details; Tel. (051) 463–7551. **By express bus,** from the Express Bus Terminal, a two-hour, 10-minute journey, buses departing every 15 minutes, 6 A.M. to 9 P.M. (W2,180). **By intercity bus** from the Sobu Terminal, a direct one-hour, 20-minute ride, departing every 10 minutes, 5:30 A.M. to 9:30 P.M. Other intercity buses travel to Chinju via Kimhae, Kilsung, and Masan.

To Sunchon from Seoul. By superexpress train (Saemaul) from Seoul Station, on the Yosu line. Departures are twice daily (W19,700 first class, W15,100 economy). Call the foreigners' ticket counter at the station for details; Tel. (02) 392–7811.
From Pusan. By train, air-conditioned express (Mugunghwa) and ordinary express (Tongil) from Pusan Station. For details, call (051) 463–7788. **By express bus,** from the Express Bus Terminal, a three-hour, 30-minute ride, departing every 40 minutes, 7 A.M. to 7 P.M. (W3,690).

To Yosu from Seoul. By air, from Kimpo Airport, a four times daily 60-minute flight (W31,900). **By superexpress train** (Saemaul), twice daily (W21,200 first class, W16,600 economy). Call (02) 392–7811 for departure details. **By express bus,** from the Kangnam terminal, a five-hour, 50-minute ride, departing every 55 minutes, 6:40 A.M. to 5:40 P.M. (W7,950).
From Pusan. By express bus, from the Express Bus Terminal, a four-hour ride, departing every 50 minutes, 6 A.M. to 6:10 P.M. (W4,260). **By intercity bus,** from the Sobu Terminal, a three-hour, 50-minute ride, departing once daily at 1:50 P.M. (W5,270). **By Angel Hydrofoil,** three times

daily (five times daily from Pusan to Chungmu, but only two on to Yosu). The total trip takes around three and a half hours (W16,310).

To Chungmu from Pusan. By intercity bus from the Sobu Terminal, a direct two-hour ride, departing every 30 minutes, 6 A.M. to 7:40 P.M.. Buses also leave every eight minutes for Chungmu via Masan and Kosung (W3,300). **By Angel Hydrofoil,** five times daily, a trip of one hour, 35 minutes (W8,220).

To Kojedo Island from Pusan. By intercity bus from the Sobu Terminal, a three-hour, 50-minute ride, departing every 30 minutes, 6 A.M. to 7 P.M. (W4,590). **By Angel Hydrofoil,** 10 times daily to Changsungpo (W4,970).

To Samchonpo from Pusan. By intercity bus from the Sobu Terminal, a two-hour ride, departing every 25 minutes, 6 A.M. to 8:30 P.M. (W3,140). **By Angel Hydrofoil,** twice daily (11,850).

To Ulsan from Seoul. By air, from Kimpo Airport, a 50-minute flight departing five times daily (W28,300). **By express bus,** from the Kangnam terminal, a five-hour ride departing every 15 minutes, 6:30 A.M. to 6 P.M. (W6,850).
From Pusan. By air-conditioned express or **ordinary express train;** service continuing on to Kyongju. **By intercity bus** from the Tongbu Terminal, a one-hour, 15-minute ride, departing every 10 minutes, 5 A.M. to 9 P.M. (W1,570).

To Masan from Seoul. By express bus, from the Kangnam terminal, a five-hour ride, departing every 10 minutes, 6 A.M. to 6:30 P.M. (W6,430).
From Pusan. By intercity bus, from the Sobu terminal, with frequent departures.

HOW TO GET AROUND. Express bus or **intercity bus** services will enable you to move around within the Southeast area quite easily. From Pusan, you can move northward toward Kyongju or Taegu, and westward toward Masan, Chinju, and Sunchon. There is a **railroad service** in the same directions, but with less frequent departures. Finally, the **Angel Hydrofoil** can be used as principal transportation rather than just as a recreational excursion.
By Car. If you are using one of the main centers as a base, hiring a car is a good way to see the sights. All the conditions about driving in Korea outlined in the *Facts at Your Fingertips* section of this guide apply. The following companies will be able to provide a car for between W29,000 and W100,000 per day, depending on the class; special rates can apply: in Chinju, Wooju Rent-a-Car, Tel. (0591) 52–7500; in Masan, New Yongnam, Tel. (0551) 3–4131; in Ulsan, Kumgang, Tel. (0522) 87–9000, or Koryo Rent-a-Car, Tel. (0522) 75–3000.
Details of hiring cars in Pusan, Taegu, and Kyongju are provided in the practical information sections of those chapters.

ACCOMMODATIONS. Throughout the whole Southeast area, there is a good range of hotels from which to choose. However, with the exception of Pusan and Kyongju, you will not find many that reach international deluxe standards, but you can be sure of being comfortable. As a general idea of costs per night for a twin or double room, you can expect to pay W60,000 to W100,000 for *Deluxe;* W40,000 to W60,000 for *1st class;* W30,000 to W40,000 for *2d class;* and W20,000 to W30,000 for *3d class.* Credit card abbreviations are as follows: American Express, AE; Diner's Club, DC; MasterCard, MC; Visa, V.

Hotels in Pusan, Taegu, and Kyongju are covered in those chapters.

Ulsan

This city on the coast, about midway between Pusan and Pohang (in the East Coastal area), is the heart of one of the country's major industrial areas. Although it has little of tourist interest, it has good hotels and transport facilities and is a comfortable base for exploring the surrounding areas.

Ulsan Koreana. *Deluxe.* 255-3, Songnam-dong, Ulsan, Kyongsangnamdo; Tel. (0522) 44–9911, Telex K52550, Fax. (0522) 44–1665. 150 rooms, and a good collection of restaurants and facilities, including a cocktail lounge, nightclub, sauna and health club, and a theater-restaurant. Credit cards: AE, DC, MC, V.

Diamond. *1st class–Deluxe.* 283, Chonha-dong, Ulsan, Kyongsangnamdo; Tel. (0522) 32–7171, Fax. (0522) 32–7170. 290 rooms, a choice of restaurants, a coffee shop, and a nightclub. Also a health club, sauna, and indoor swimming pool. Credit cards: AE, DC, MC, V.

Tae Hwa. *2d class.* 1406-6, Shinjong-dong, Nam-ku, Ulsan, Kyongsangnamdo; Tel. (0522) 73–3301. 103 rooms; Western and Japanese restaurants, a coffee shop, cocktail bar, and nightclub. Credit cards: DC, V.

Ulsan Tourist Hotel. *2d class.* 570-1, Yuam-myon, Ulsan, Kyongsangnamdo; Tel. (0522) 71–7001, Fax. (0522) 71–7010. Near the Ulsan industrial complexes. Just 50 rooms, a restaurant, coffee shop, cocktail lounge, and nightclub. Credit cards: AE, DC, MC, V.

Masan Area

Both the Bugok Royal and Bu Gok Hawaii hotels, listed below, are between Taegu and Masan, in an area well known for its sulphurous hot springs.

Bugok Royal. *Deluxe.* 215-1, Komunri, Pugok-myon, Changnyon-gun, Kyongsangnamdo; Tel. (0559) 36–6661, Seoul office (02) 701–4209. A choice of restaurants, a coffee shop, cocktail lounge, and nightclub; health club, sauna, and hot-spring facilities. Credit cards: AE, DC, MC, V.

Bu Gok Hawaii. *1st class.* 197-5, Komunri, Pugok-myon, Changnyon-gun, Kyongsangnamdo; Tel. (0559) 36–6331, Seoul office (02) 265–0508. Limited restaurant facilities, but outdoor and indoor swimming pools, and a theater-restaurant for evening entertainment. No credit cards.

Chang Won. *1st class.* 99-4, Chungang-dong, Changwon, Kyongsangnamdo; Tel. (0559) 83–5551, Seoul office (02) 542–0112, Telex K52356. 166 rooms, and a good range of facilities, near one of the Southeast area's golf courses. A choice of restaurants, a coffee shop, cocktail lounge, nightclub, a health club, sauna, and outdoor swimming pool. Credit cards: AE, DC, MC, V.

Lotte Crystal. *2d class.* 3-6, 4-ka, Changgun-dong, Masan, Kyongsang-namdo; Tel. (0551) 45–1112, Telex K53822, Fax. (0551) 45–2111. In downtown Masan, with 120 rooms. Limited number of restaurants and facilities, but has a nightclub. No credit cards.

Hallyo Waterway Area

Chung Mu. *1st class.* 1, Tonam-dong, Chungmu, Kyongsangnamdo; Tel. (0557) 645–2091, Seoul office (02) 561–3811, Fax. (0557) 42–8877. On Hansando Island, overlooking the sea. Just 50 rooms. Korean, Japanese, and limited Western food available, and facilities for swimming and all kinds of seaside recreation. Credit cards: AE, V.

Okpo Tourist Hotel. *1st class.* 330-4, Okpori, Changsungpo-up, Koje-gun, Kyongsangnamdo; Tel. (0558) 687–3761, Telex K52482, Fax. (0558) 687–3934. 128 rooms, on Koje Island. A choice of restaurants, a cocktail lounge, and a nightclub. Credit cards: AE, DC.

Samchonpo Beach Tourist Hotel. *2d class.* 598, Taebang-dong, Samchonpo, Kyongsangnamdo; Tel. (0593) 32–9801. 36 rooms, with basic restaurant facilities, plus a night club and cocktail lounge. No credit cards.

Yosu

Yosu Beach. *1st class.* 346, Chungmu-dong, Yosu, Chollanamdo; Tel. (0662) 63–2011, Seoul office (02) 928–0411. 73 rooms, with limited restaurant facilities, a cocktail lounge, and nightclub. Credit cards: AE, DC, MC, V.

Yeosu Tourist. *3d class.* 766, Konghwadong, Yosu, Chollanamdo; Tel. (0662) 62–3131. Just 36 rooms, in a downtown Yosu location. A general restaurant and a coffee shop, a cocktail lounge, and a nightclub. No credit cards.

Sunchon

Keum Kang Tourist. *2d class.* 22-20, Namnae-dong, Sunchon, Chollanamdo; Tel. (0661) 52–8301. 52 rooms, with basic restaurant facilities, a cocktail lounge, and a nightclub. Credit cards: AE, MC, V.

YOUTH HOSTELS. There are two youth hostels in the Pusan area, and another in Kyongju (see those chapters for details).

RESTAURANTS. The culinary attractions of the Southeast area are considerable, but the best restaurants are in the area's three main cities—Taegu, Kyongju, and Pusan, each of which is covered in a separate chapter of this guide. In the smaller areas, you will find Western food only in hotels catering to foreigners, and the selection will usually be poor, the quality mediocre. You'll be better off in general eating Korean food (you'll probably by now have decided what you like and what you can live without), and, of course, around the southern coastal areas is an excellent selection of seafood.

TOURS. The only organized tours available of the Southeast area originate in Seoul and involve standard programs such as a two-day visit to Kyongju, or a three-day trip visiting Kyongju and Pusan, with transportation by bus and train. (Talk to people at any **Global** or **KTB** tour counter at major hotels in Seoul about these.) Variations on the standard theme are available, however. Here are some examples: three nights/four days Yosu, Pusan, and Kyongju, including travel by train, the Hallyo Waterway cruise, and the major sights of Pusan and Kyongju, for around W275,000 (minimum two persons); call **Aju Tourist Service** Seoul office (Tel. 753–5051) for details. This company also offers a three-night/four-day "industrial tour" to the area of the Southeast, covering Pohang (iron and steel) and Ulsan (shipbuilding and motorcars) on the coast, with visits for sightseeing to Kyongju and Pusan. The cost is around W300,000 per person, minimum two.

While you're actually in the area, touring is very much "do-it-yourself." Talk to the hotel managers or representatives of any tourist office about any special programs available. Local tour agents often put together day trips for local people to visit temples or beaches, and you may be able to join in. Language will undoubtedly be a problem, but travel is really all about meeting people and you could have lots of fun. (See the "Tours" section of the *Pusan* chapter for more information, especially about the major "tour" of the Southeast Area—the Hallyo Waterway cruise.)

WHAT TO SEE. Historic Sites. Apart from the places covered in the Pusan, Kyongju, and Taegu chapters, the Southeast area has a number of other historic sites worth seeing. The **Chinju Castle,** in the charming town of Chinju, is a lively example of how the present can blend harmoniously with the past. A small village within the reconstructed castle walls creates a happy atmosphere of brisk activity, quite unexpected in a structure of such historical importance.

The Hallyo Waterway is historically most famous for the mighty battles of **Admiral Yi,** who commanded the iron-clad "turtle ships" against the invading Japanese in 1592. On Kojedo Island there are monuments to the sea victories; on Hansando you'll see the admiral's headquarters and the shrine where he prayed for heavenly assistance; and on Namhaedo Island you'll find the small park area of Noryangri, the spot where Yi was mortally wounded during the last hour of his victorious battle. Namhaedo also has **Kumsan Mountain,** where legend says King Taejo spent 100 days in prayer before overthrowing the Koryo kingdom to begin the Yi Dynasty.

Temples. The region's major temples are covered in the specific area chapters— **Haeinsa** and **Tonghwasa** in the *Taegu* section; **Pomosa** and **Tongdosa** in the section on *Pusan;* and the **Pulguksa Temple** in the chapter on *Kyongju.* The area has other temples worth visiting, also, if your time allows. Each has something different to show. West of Ulsan, in the **Kajisan Park,** site of the Tongdosa Temple mentioned earlier, are several more temples, hidden away in the hills of Mt. Kajisan and Mt. Chwisosan. **Pyochungsa** and **Songnamsa** temples, for example, do not have the historic importance of Tongdosa, but they do have the most exquisite settings and the air of cool tranquillity for which even the humblest little Buddhist temple is noted. From Sunchon, in the far west of the Southeast area, you can make an interesting trip to **Songgwangsa Temple,** one of the largest in Korea. This is the center of Son Buddhism, the Korean version of Zen, and is the only temple in the country which permits residence by Western monks and nuns. The town of Chinju has a wonderful collection of temples, shrines, pavilions, and hermitages in the hills around the outskirts of the city. The Hallyo Waterway has just two temples of importance—**Yongmunsa Temple** on Namhae Island, and **Hungguksa Temple,** a few miles north of Yosu, which was founded in the Koryo period.

Zoos and Bird Sanctuaries. There are two zoos in the Pusan area (see separate chapter), plus a major bird sanctuary at the mouth of the Naktong-gang River. Kyongju has a small zoo, mainly displaying deer and birds, at the Pomun Resort, and Taegu also has its own zoo. There are a number of bird sanctuaries along the Hallyo Waterway. These include the southern shores of Kojedo Island, the roosting place for a variety of sea birds; and an uninhabited island called Hakdo, offshore from Samchonpo, which is a sanctuary for Korea's Living National Treasures, white herons. While you're in the Southeast area, your hotel manager or front-desk staff are the best people to help you visit these sites. You'll need to check on the seasonal population of the birds, whether the area is open to the public at that time, and the current best way to get there. In the past, the Royal Asiatic Society in Seoul has organized tours to the bird sanctuaries of the Southeast. Call (02) 763–9483 in Seoul for current information.

Museums. The whole area of Kyongju is called an outdoor museum, but apart from visiting the historic sites you should make a visit to the **National Museum,** in Inwah-dong near the center of town. This houses over 8,000 exhibits from the Silla era, including items excavated from the royal tombs and the Anapchi Pond. It is open from 9 A.M. to 5 P.M., every day except Mondays; Tel. (0561) 2–5193. Pusan has a **municipal museum,** east of the city center in Taeyoung-dong, which is open every day except Mondays and public holidays; Tel. (051) 624–6341. There is also a museum at the **Pusan University,** which has flexible opening hours; Tel. (051) 56–0171. The **Chinju National Museum** is within the reconstructed fortress walls, surrounded by the pavilions and shrines that make the area so attractive. The exhibits concentrate on the Kaya period of Korean history (A.D. 42–562). It is closed on Mondays; Tel. (0591) 42–5950. In Taegu, it is often possible to visit the **Kyungpook National University Museum,** to the city's northeast, which has over 5,500 exhibits on permanent display. Call (053) 952–2996 for details of opening hours.

BEACHES. There are a number of great places for swimming along the extensive shoreline, but among the very best are the following: the spread of beaches down the coast south of Ulsan; several resorts in the Pusan area (see separate chapter); Kujora Beach on the southern shore of Kojedo Island; and Namildae Beach south of Samchonpo town. There are many other secluded bays and coves, but be guided by the Koreans and do not swim outside the designated places. Owing to industrial pollution, not all sandy shores are safe for swimming.

The summer facilities along the shoreline are extensive. The major resorts have public toilets and showers, and just about every sandy cove that is designated an area safe for swimming will have beach umbrellas, deck chairs, and rubber tubes for rent. There are snack bars and refreshment stands. Check prices before you order; the extra you pay for a convenient location can be surprising. There are also shops and stalls selling beachwear, toys, and souvenirs.

HOT SPRINGS. In Pusan, you have the famous **Tongnae Springs** (alkaline, chlorous, temperature 50° Fahrenheit) and the **Haeundae Springs** (also alkaline and chlorous, but Korea's hottest at 62°), both with plenty of resort facilities to enjoy (see *Pusan* chapter). Elsewhere in the Southeast area, the most popular spa is at **Pugok,** just off the Taegu-Masan Expressway, about midway between the two cities. These springs are sulphurous (temperature 60°), and the area is well developed with hotels and resort facilities. Farther south in the same area are the **Magumsan Springs,** sulphurous and chlorous (temperature 48°) which are less well known, much less developed. In the Kyongsan district, a little southeast of Taegu, are the **Sangnae Hot Springs,** which are alkaline and just 29°. Facilities here are limited.

SPORTS. Golf. There are six excellent golf courses in the Southeast area: In Kyongju, a 36-hole course at the **Kyongju Chosun Country Club,** near the Pomun Lake Resort, Tel. (0561) 40–8412 or in Seoul, (02) 752–1974; **near Taegu,** an 18-hole course to the east of the city, just off the Seoul-Pusan Expressway, Tel. (053) 353–0003 or in Seoul, (02) 774–9847; at **Chang Won,** to the east of Masan and about an hour's drive from Pusan, an 18-hole course, Tel. (0551) 83–4112; at **Tongdo,** north of Pusan and near the Tongdosa Temple, 36 holes, Tel. (051) 464–7751; and two in the Pusan area, **Dongnae** with 18 holes, Tel. (051) 513–0101, or in Seoul, (02) 757–8877, and at the **Pusan Country Club,** 18 holes, Tel. (051) 508–0707. These are all membership clubs, but it is usually easy to arrange play for a foreign visitor. Hotels often have special arrangements with certain clubs, and it is likely you will need to make reservations, especially on weekends and public holidays. Check with your hotel information desk.

Hunting. Hunting areas and facilities are very limited in Korea, but from November to February hunting is permitted on Kojedo Island. Game includes wild boar, rabbit, pheasant, duck, and snipe. For information, contact the **Korea Safety Engineering Association of Explosives & Guns,** 541–11, Shinsa-dong, Kangnam-ku, Seoul, Tel. (02) 515–2343. While you're in the Southeast area, talk to your hotel manager about the current hunting possibilities.

Fishing. Anglers keen on surf casting and deep-water fishing will find the entire coastal area filled with possibilities—from Ulsan south to Pusan, and then westward across the stretch of the Hallyo Waterway. This area is especially noted for its half-dozen good fishing grounds lying in and around the small offshore islands. One especially popular surf-casting spot is the long breakwater that connects Odongdo Island with the mainland. It is possible to arrange boat rental in all the main coastal towns; you should talk to the staff at the hotel information desks about arrangements.

SHOPPING. The chapters on Pusan, Taegu, and Kyongju will give you details of the major shopping opportunities in these areas. Outside the main centers, you'll have the most fun exploring the local markets where food, household products, clothing, and hardware will invariably be displayed in glorious disarray. Generally, the hotels have souvenir shops, and the tourist centers will have displays of any local specialties. If you're in Chungmu, visit the **Kyongsangnamdo Handicrafts Cooperative,** at 2-6, Hangnam-dong, Tel. (0557) 645–4056, for a good selection.

CULTURAL EVENTS. Many of the national festivals are celebrated in the Southeast area, such as **Buddha's Birthday** (May 28 in 1993), when all the Buddhist temples are decorated with lanterns and candlelight processions are held for the faithful.

However, there are a number of festivals which are unique to individual towns and areas, including the following:

April, Cherry-Blossom Festival, Chinhae. In the first two weeks of April the town celebrates the inauguration of the Korean Navy (Chinhae is its home port), and the victories of Admiral Yi Sun-Shin. Thousands of cherry trees are beautifully in blossom, providing a magnificent setting for parades, contests, and traditional music and dance performances. (There are no major hotels in Chinhae, and all the small hotels and yogwans are full to bursting at festival time. It is easier to stay somewhere else in the Southeast area and commute to Chinhae by bus.)

May, Chinnam Festival, Yosu. Held in honor of Admiral Yi, there are parades, folklore exhibitions, and various cultural contests and demonstrations.

May, Arangje Festival, Miryang. Held around mid-May each year, in the small town of Miryang about halfway between Taegu and Masan. The ceremonies to honor Arang, a Silla lady who was distinguished for her marital fidelity, include a beauty contest and a ritual at the heroine's shrine.

September, Silla Cultural Festival. This is one of the largest and most impressive in the whole country, and the population of the Kyongju area almost doubles. The festivities are to celebrate the spirit and cultural achievements of the Silla kingdom, the "golden era" of Korean history.

October 5, Citizens' Day, Pusan. A day of sports events, parades, and performances of traditional music and dance.

October, Hansan Victory Festival, Chungmu. This commemorates the great naval victory of Admiral Yi Sun-Shin over the invading Japanese fleet in 1592. The festival begins with a ceremonial lighting of the sacred fire, a cannon salute, followed by a military parade. Local dances, such as the Chungmu victory dance and a sword dance are presented by highly skilled performers.

November, Kaechon Art Festival, Chinju. This usually occurs on the third day of the 10th lunar month, but for 1993, the final date has not been confirmed. The festival celebrates local cultural activity, with competitions in Chinese poetry, calligraphy, music composition, art, and drama.

Another annual event is held in Chinju, a small but charming ritual to honor Chu Non-Gae, a patriotic kisaeng hostess, who lured a Japanese general to his death, killing herself in the process, during the late sixteenth century. A special ritual is held at her shrine, located between the Choksongnu pavilion and the Nam-gang River, on the last day of the sixth lunar month.

A number of special events occur in and around Kyongju, associated with the Silla kings and culture. These are outlined in the Kyongju chapter.

At press time, the dates for most festivals in 1993 had not been confirmed. If you plan to be in any of these areas during the general months listed above, by all means contact the KNTC for more specific dates and information. Attending any of Korea's special festivals will give you a feeling for the Korean people and memories that you will always cherish.

NIGHTLIFE. Away from the major cities, nightlife in the Southeast area is limited to a few hotel nightclubs and the local beer halls, wine houses, and tearooms. The chapters on Pusan, Taegu, and Kyongju outline the special nightlife attractions of those areas, including details on the two casinos, in Pusan and Kyongju.

USEFUL ADDRESSES AND TELEPHONE NUMBERS. Medical Attention. Once again, for any medical assistance you may need, the best source of information and assistance is your hotel manager. Names of hospitals in Pusan, Taegu, and Kyongju are given in the area chapters.

Tourist Information. Generally, you will enter the Southeast area at Pusan (by ferry, plane, or bus), or, going there from the north, by train or bus into the major cities of Taegu or Kyongju, lying along the northern edge of the area. For maps and city information, ask at the information desks and bookstands at the train stations, or the local tourist offices.

Here are some telephone numbers that could be useful:

Pusan (Area code 051)

Pusan Airport Information Center (KNTC), Tel. 98–1100
Pusan Tourist Association, Tel. 23–7311
Korean Air, Tel. 463–2000
Asiana Airlines, Tel. 465–4000
Information Center, Pusan Station, Tel. 463–4938
Foreigners' Counter, Pusan Station, Tel. 463–7551
Sobu Intercity Bus Terminal, Tel. 322–8301
Tongbu Intercity Bus Terminal, Tel. 554–7811
International Ferry Terminal, Tel. 463–3161
Angel Hydrofoil Information, Tel. 469–3851
Tourist Complaints and Advice, Tel. 44–0101

Taegu (Area code 053)

Taegu Tourist Information, Tel. 558–5893
Taegu Express Bus Information, Tel. 72–2828
Korean Air, Tel. 423–2000
Asiana Airlines, Tel. 421–4000
Tongtaegu (East Taegu) Station, Foreigners' Counter, Tel. 92–7788
Tourist Complaints and Advice, Tel. 422–5611

Kyongju (Area code 0561)

Railway Station Tourist Information Center, Tel. 42–7788

Railway Station, Foreigners' Counter, Tel. 2–3843
Pulguksa Temple Tourist Information Center, Tel. 746–4747
Kyongju Express Bus Terminal, Tourist Information Center, Tel. 2–9289
Tourist Complaints and Advice, Tel. 749–0101

CHEJU ISLAND

Cheju, the largest of Korea's over 3,000 islands, was dubbed by *Newsweek* magazine in 1975 one of the 10 not-yet-discovered tourist attractions of the world. Eighteen years later, the island remains relatively untouched by international tourism, and this "Isle of the Gods" sometimes seems just too good to be true. Here is the holiday world of picture postcards—lush forests and tropical flowers, lava monuments sculpted by nature and man, tumbling clear waterfalls, a snowcapped mountain, glorious ancient pavilions and temples, and a sparkling shoreline with sandy beaches that invite you to explore. And it's all wrapped up in a balmy semitropical climate—at least during the few months of summer. While Cheju has been called "the Hawaii of the Orient," visitors should also remember that its temperate location provides a chilly winter; temperatures drop to 45–50° Fahrenheit from mid-November through March.

Cheju Island, or Chejudo, lies 60 miles off the southwest corner of the Korean peninsula and 35 miles from its nearest island neighbor. It is Korea's only island province, the smallest of the country's nine provinces, and has a population of just over 500,000 in an area of 700 square miles. The island is so remote that for centuries, mainland Koreans did not call it Cheju, but used a now obsolete Korean word that translates to "the place way over there." A long period of obscurity has left the island an uncrowded sanctuary that is only now becoming modernized.

To Koreans, Chejudo has a reputation for three things: rocks, women, and wind. Hence, occasionally you hear the locals call it *samdado* (the "three abundances island"), or, jokingly, *sammudo,* which means the "island lacking three things"—thieves, beggars, and gates.

Dominating the island's center is Mt. Hallasan, Korea's tallest mountain (5,850 feet), a volcanic cone that last erupted in A.D. 1007. At least 15 separate lava flows have been identified from previous eruptions, which left behind mazes of lava tunnels (some among the world's longest), pillars, and convoluted basalt sculptures. The volcanic past has created a landscape of dramatic contrasts with vivid greens of field and forest, the brilliant yellow of oil-seed rape flowers, the deep reddish brown of basalt boulders, and the multihues of sand and gravel derived from pulverized lava.

A Little History

Like the rest of Korea, Chejudo has had a turbulent and fascinating past. But it is unique in that its culture has developed in ways far different from that of the mainland peninsula.

According to Chejudo legend, the three ancient ancestors of the island people were called Ko, Yang, and Pu—demigods who appeared from three holes in the ground at a site called Samsong-hyol (today's Cheju City). They lived by hunting and fishing, and had the good fortune to marry princesses who introduced them to agriculture and the keeping of livestock. This myth of the three spirits is completely at variance with that of Korea's traditional mainland founder, Tangun. The actual cave where Ko, Yang, and Pu first appeared has long since eroded away, and only a slight depression remains to mark its location. There are special feast days in April, October, and December to celebrate the births and meetings of these original Cheju inhabitants.

The island first came under Korean control during the Koryo era, around A.D. 938, and was given its name, "the place way over there," by King Kojong, who ruled Korea from 1214 to 1260. When the Mongols swept down the Korean peninsula during the thirteenth century, Chejudo became a stopping-off point for the invasions of Japan by Kubla and Ghenghis Khan. The Cheju dialect, unlike those of the mainland, was permanently influenced by the Mongol conquerors. The Mongols also brought Buddhism to Chejudo and a flair for raising horses.

The first Westerners to visit and bring the outside world to Chejudo were Dutch sailors on the ship *Sparrow Hawk*, which was wrecked in a typhoon at Mosulpo on the island's southern shore in 1653. At that time, Korea was known to the world as the Hermit Kingdom and had absolutely no contact with the Western world. The Dutch sailors were taken to Seoul as curiosities, then conscripted into the Korean army as low-ranking soldiers. Some 13 years later, a few of them escaped by open boat to Japan and made their way back to Europe. One of the men, Henrik Hamel, later wrote the story of his Far Eastern adventure, and his book was eventually translated into English and published as *The Dutch Come to Korea*. As a result of the landing by the Dutch, the island was first called Quelpaert by the Europeans, a Dutch word for the type of sailing vessel used on trading voyages to the Far East. The Hamel Monument on the southern shore, near the hill called Sanbangsan, commemorates the arrival of Chejudo's first foreign visitors.

During the Yi Dynasty, Chejudo became a place of exile for political undesirables; today it is a highly desirable holiday spot, especially for hon-

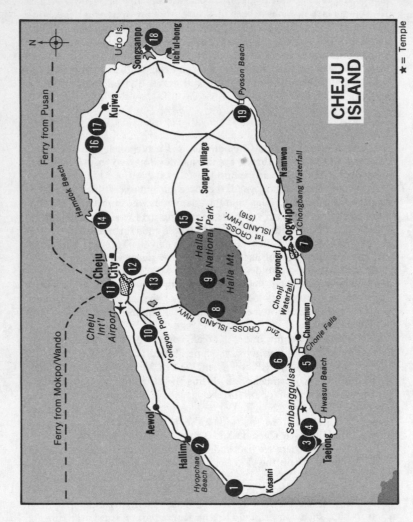

CHEJU ISLAND

N

Ferry from Pusan

Ferry from Mokpo/Wando

Udo Is.

Songsanpo

Ilch'ul-bong 18

Pyoson Beach

Kujwa

16 17

19

Hamdok Beach

Namwon

Songup Village

Chongbang Waterfall

Cheju City 11

14

Cheju Int'l Airport

12

13

15

Halla Mt. National Park

Halla Mt.

9

Halla Mt.

8

2nd CROSS-ISLAND HWY

1st CROSS-ISLAND HWY (516)

Sogwipo 7

Chonji Topyongri Waterfall

Chungmun

Chonje Falls 5

10

Yongyon pond

6

Sanbanggulsa

Hwasun Beach

Aewol

3 4

Taejong

Hallim 2

Hyopchae Beach

Kosanri

1

★ = Temple

Points of Interest

Chedong Ranch Area 15
Cheju Art Park 3
Cheju Folk Village 19
Cholbuam Rock 1
Chungmun Resort 5
Daeyu Hunting Grounds 6
Hangpaduri 10
Hyopchaegul Cave 2
Ilchulbong Peak 18
Manjanggul Cave 17
Moksogwon Park 13
Paekrokdam Lake 9
Sagul Cave 16
Samsonghyol 12
Sanbanggulsa 4
Waetolkwae Rock 7
Yongbukjong Pavilion 14
Yongduam Rock 11
Yongshil 8

eymooners, and has built up a thriving agricultural industry around cattle, semitropical fruits, and fishing.

Chejudo Today

The largest city, and the provincial capital, is Cheju City (population around 200,000), on the northern side of the island. The city has two main centers: Cheju City itself and a satellite center just to the southwest called Shinjeju, or New Cheju. Both areas are within ten minutes of the Cheju International Airport.

Paved roads encircle the island, and cross it from north to south on both sides of Hallasan Mountain. The roads connect the capital with the second-largest city, Sogwipo, on the south coast, and with Chungmun, site of a major tourism development by the Korea National Tourism Corporation, the Cheju tourism authorities, and private enterprise.

The future of Chejudo is laid out on a blueprint labeled "Tourism." The government has launched a building program to develop the island into a recreational haven for both Korean and foreign visitors. Consequently, the emphasis of the program rests on the expansion of hotels and other tourist facilities according to international standards. Happily, the developments so far have added to Chejudo's appeal—the Hyatt Regency Hotel at the Chungmun Resort, for example, is a wonderful base for exploration of the island—due to the fact that the number and type of resort-style establishments have been controlled.

It is also easy to get to Chejudo. Flying time from Seoul to the Cheju International Airport is less than an hour, and you can also fly from Taegu, Pusan, Yosu, or Chinju (all in Korea's Southeast area), or Kwangju (in the southern sector of the West Plain and Coastal Area). The biggest percentage of foreign visitors to Chejudo are Japanese, and it is possible to fly into Cheju from either Tokyo or Osaka. There are flights three times a week from each city, via Pusan, and there is also a weekly flight from Taipei in Taiwan. In addition to Korean Air, Asiana flies to Cheju. Each airline offers just about the same frequency of service. To get to Chejudo by sea, you can take a ferry from the Korean mainland at Pusan, Wando, or Mokpo.

Two of the traditional symbols of Chejudo that remain today are the *tolharubang,* "rock grandfathers," and *haenyo,* the women divers.

Tolharubang are primitive, dwarflike, lava carvings of human figures with bulging eyes, huge noses, and elongated ears. "Tol" means stone in Korean and "harubang" translates as grandfather from the Cheju dialect. These unique cultural artifacts are now treated as whimsical mascots and have become the symbol for Cheju's tourist promotion. Some scholars believe the figures originated as symbols of fertility, but there is general agreement that they were regarded as protective guardians for island villages during the Koryo Dynasty period (935–1392). Only about fifty authentic tolharubang survive on the island but the place is teeming with souvenir replicas.

The haenyo, women divers, range in age from 15 to over 50, and they must be among the hardiest people in the world. As has been the practice for centuries, particularly along the island's southern coast, they dive for edible seaweed, shellfish, sea cucumbers, and octopus. Traditionally, Chejudo has had a matriarchal society, with a long custom of men staying at home and women going out to work at the sea beds. Today, a rough estimate indicates that there are still some 20,000 haenyo in business, more than anywhere else in Asia. In the past, they wore one-piece cotton suits, but in recent years they have switched to more practical rubber wet suits. Even so, their apparent indifference to winter's icy blasts and the cold water is nothing short of astonishing. Often they dive to 60 feet and remain underwater for up to four minutes. While the women provide the island with one of its unique attractions, the young "diving beauties" of the tourist brochures are rarely seen in the flesh. A typical haenyo is more robust in physique, and more interested in collecting seaweed than in posing for a snapshot. Do be a little careful about photography—some of the divers may resent it, and others will expect to be paid.

For convenience in describing the island, we have divided it into a number of specific areas, discussing the special attractions of each.

Cheju City and Surroundings

Over 200,000 people live in this provincial capital, located at about the midpoint of the island's northern shore. One of the most popular tourist sites is the unusual rock formation called Yongduam or "Dragon Head Rock." This lies on the coast just west of the city and is a basalt rock, about 30 feet high, shaped like a dragon with an open mouth. The legend of Yongduam relates how a servant of the Sea Dragon King climbed Hallasan Mountain in search of Pullocho, a mythical fungus that if eaten, guarantees eternal life. The servant was killed by an arrow loosed by a *sinson,* a mountain spirit, from atop the mountain. The body of the servant was buried here on the coast and became a petrified dragon, with only the head protruding from the surface. If you have acquired a taste for raw fish, the diving women at this tourist area can provide it, and their price is the cheapest anywhere on the island. You can sit on the rocks and enjoy the view of Yongduam while feasting on soft-shelled mollusk, sea cucumber, abalone, or a small octopus, washed down with rice wine. The fish is served with a hot red-pepper sauce, and you can spend as little as W4,000 or W5,000 in one of Chejudo's prettiest open-air dining rooms.

Also west of the city, near Yongduam, is Yongyon (Dragon Pond), a pretty area of gentle forest. Long ago scholars gathered here on moonlit nights to sip wine and compose thoughtful poems. Today it remains an area for tranquil contemplation.

Moksogwon, the "Wood and Rock Park," features the private collection of its creator, Pak Un-Chol. It is an exhibit of naturally sculpted bits of stone and wood, which were found along the coast and in the mountains, and arranged in imaginative combinations. The park is at the entrance to Cheju National University, a short drive south on the First Cross-Island Highway.

A significant collection of tools and equipment used in Chejudo's folk crafts, along with over 9,000 preserved animals, birds, and fish, are housed in the Cheju Folkcraft and Natural History Museum, well worth a visit. East of the city is the Cheju Folklore Museum, founded by Chin Song-Gi to display his private collection of folk crafts and costumes. Nearby is a fifteenth century Confucian school with traditional buildings, situated in a pine and elm grove on the coast. Ceremonies are conducted here annually to honor early Confucian scholars.

Remains of the ancient city wall can still be seen in certain areas of Cheju City. In the center of the town is Kwandokjong, a pavilion built in 1448 and now designated by the Korean government as a cultural treasure. It is the oldest standing building on Chejudo, and has one of the island's finest tolharubang at its entrance. The painted wooden beams of the pavilion represent typical decorations of the Yi Dynasty era.

Near the city's South Gate is Samsonghyol, the "Cave of Three Spirits," declared a sacred place in 1526 in honor of the ancestors of the Cheju Islanders—the Ko, Yang, and Pu families. Local inhabitants will tell you that it rarely snows on Cheju, and what does fall will melt first at Samsonghyol because the ground is warmer here. This may be a sign of lingering volcanic activity under the island, for there is little doubt that hot springs and warm spots are encountered on the slopes of Hallasan Mountain.

The Northern Shore

Some seven miles east of Cheju City, along the northeast coastal road, lies Chochon, a small town with a pavilion called Yonbukjong. The original structure was built in 1374 during the late Koryo period. Like Kwandokjong in Cheju City, this pavilion has been declared a national cultural treasure, and was renovated in 1973. It marks the place on the coast where officials in disgrace for crimes not serious enough to warrant death were landed to begin their terms of exile.

Near the village of Kimnyong, about 20 miles east of Cheju City, is Manjanggul, the world's longest lava cave. It was discovered by a schoolteacher in 1958 and was not completely explored until 1981. It is certainly the most popular of the many lava caves on the island, and it is possible to explore just over half a mile of the more than four-mile length. Touring the caves is an eerie experience. There are resident bats and spiders, in addition to all the strange lava formations. A turtle-shaped rock is a popular spot where honeymooners pause and pray that their first child will be a son. The air inside is very fresh, and the dripping water has no minerals and is believed to have medicinal value. You should wear warm clothes as the interior temperature drops to around 50° Fahrenheit.

Nearby is Sagul, the Snake Cave, which has a total length of less than half a mile. This cave is associated with the legend of a sixteenth century governor who killed a demon serpent that lived in the cave. Each year, a young virgin was sacrificed to the snake to ward off disasters, and with the death of the snake the practice happily ended. Thereafter, the gods were honored with the traditional Buddhist gifts of food and wine. There is a memorial to the governor at the entrance to the cave.

The northern shore has some of Chejudo's prettiest beaches, the most notable being Samyang Beach, about a 10-minute drive from Cheju City, and Hamdok Beach, another 15 minutes farther east. Both of these areas have a number of good Korean inns and plenty of small restaurants. The specialty, of course, is seafood.

Highlights of the East

One of Chejudo's most exhilarating scenic experiences is the view from the castlelike Ilchulbong Peak, near Songsanpo at the extreme east of the island. It is particularly unforgettable at sunrise. The volcanic crater, Cheju's largest rock cone, is surrounded on three sides by the sea. The hike up the narrow, steep trail to the western edge of the crater and back takes about an hour, and it is quite a strenuous climb. It is often possible to hire ponies. The crater itself is almost a square mile in area, and is a perfect bowl shape. There is a small hotel at the foot of the hill in Songsanpo, appropriately called the Sunrise Hotel, which is a good place to spend the night if you want to tackle the climb at dawn. At the base of the northern side of the cone is a small basalt-sand beach, which is popular with foreign visitors.

You can reach the small island of Udo, or Cow Island, to the north of Ilchul Peak, by ferry from Songsanpo (the name of the town means "Fortress Mountain"). The trip is fun, but you'll need to allot a big part of a day to do it.

The Songsanpo area is one that has been designated for tourism development, part of the grand plan to "make the island more attractive to Korean and foreign tourists." However, many lifelong residents of Chejudo oppose any developments that will alter their unique lifestyle; some developments have been stalled.

Farther south around the coast, the small town of Namwon is also slated for developments, including another tourist "village," along with hotels and another casino. (There are two casinos on Chejudo already—one at the KAL Hotel in Cheju City and one at the Hyatt in Chungmun.)

The Central Mountain Area

Regarded as one of the three sacred peaks of Korea (the others are Chirisan in the West Plain and Coastal Area, and Odaesan on the East Coast), Hallasan was designated a national park in 1970. Although it is not considered a steep climb, one difficulty most hikers experience is the weather. The peak is often smothered with clouds. The yearly average for clear visibility is only 33 days. The rock formations and flora along the trails are lovely at any time during the year. The slopes in spring are covered in azaleas, and the autumn and winter scenery is also spectacular.

On Hallasan's southwestern slope, accessible by the second Cross-Island Highway, is an area called Yongshil, less than two miles from the summit. Here one finds the most magnificent collection of giant boulders and rugged crags all jumbled together in weird formations. This road, skirting the western slopes of Hallasan, is often steep and winding and not as well traveled as the other cross-highland highways. Tour operators are more inclined to use the more scenic eastern first Cross-Island Highway (commonly known as "516" or the Chungmun Highway).

There is a beautiful and peaceful drive across the top of Chejudo by taking the first Cross-Island Highway (the one leading to Sogwipo), and turning left to the area of the Chedong Ranch. Here is Korea's major cattle-raising operation, and you can also see the famous Cheju horses, descendents of the swift and sturdy Mongol ponies. This road will take you all the way to the eastern port of Pyoson, and on the way you can pause at the Sangumburi Crater. This is the island's second-largest crater, more than 450 feet deep and covered with over 420 species of plants and flowers. The crater is just a 10-minute walk from a parking area.

This road also takes you to the Songup Village, which has been designated a folklore-preservation zone. Founded during the fifteenth century, this village was once the island's capital, and the people still live in thatched-roof and rock homes, each with a high lava-stone wall surrounding its courtyard. Here you will also see some of the island's finest "rock grandfathers," and a couple of trees that are over 1,000 years old. Songup is also renowned for several small village restaurants that serve barbecued pork or beef, a specialty of the island. Not only is it delicious, but meals can cost less than W5,000.

There is a newly created "cultural village" near the Pyoson Beach. It opened in February of 1987, and was established by private enterprise to show visitors what life on Chejudo was like in the nineteenth century. Like the Korean Folk Village near Seoul, this Cheju Folk Village is not intended to be a formal exhibit, but shows artisans at work in the traditional ways. The village sets out to re-create the three island habitats—mountains, plains, and coastal areas—and some of the cottages on display are more than 200 years old, moved here from their original sites. There is a lively marketplace (with plenty of souvenirs), charcoal kilns, a blacksmith's shop, a millstone worked by a horse, and an outdoor arena with performances three times a day of folk plays and Shaman rituals. The Cheju Folk Village has become a major attraction for busloads of visitors, but it's worth a visit as it provides insight into Cheju's cultural past.

Sogwipo and the Chungmun Resort

Sogwipo is a small city on the south coast of the island, accessible from Cheju City either by the first or the slightly longer second Cross-Island Highway, which skirt the base of Hallasan Mountain. Another scenic approach is by the round-the-island road. Sogwipo is a town that's both pretty and pleasantly convenient. It is big enough to have good accommodations, restaurants, and a lively shopping district, yet small enough to be a pleasure to walk around. Sogwipo is Chejudo's principal fishing port, and it has a mild subtropical climate throughout the year that accounts for a thriving industry in tangerines and pineapples. For those who like waterfront scenes, a stroll along the docks with seagulls wheeling overhead will provide a charming contrast to the interior attractions.

A short walk east of the city leads to the Chongbang Waterfall, said to be the only one in Asia that empties directly into the sea. The falls drop some 75 feet to the beach below, an area surrounded by many small seafood restaurants. One of the best views of Chongbang Falls is from the ocean, and there are small rental boats available on the beach.

To the west of Sogwipo are the Chonji Falls, a cascade that tumbles from the heights of the cliff and then runs through a narrow gorge surrounded by tropical greenery. The area has been planted with cherry trees and is particularly attractive when the blossoms appear in early spring.

Just offshore, to the west of Sogwipo, is a strange "needle" rock formation called Waetolkwae. An old legend tells of a fisherman lost at sea whose wife came to the cliff every day until her death to await his return. After she died, a cluster of rocks appeared in the sea just off the needle rock, with the appearance of a floating man. The islanders believe that these rocks are the spirit of the lost husband returned to his wife.

The town of Chungmun is just a 30-minute drive west of Sogwipo. It can also be reached directly from Cheju City by the second Cross-Island Highway, over the western slopes of Mt. Hallasan, or the Chungmun Highway. Chungmun is the heart of Chejudo's recent tourism development, and it has become one of the most "international" centers because of the Hyatt Regency and Cheju Shilla hotels. The resort is probably now at its most charming: Although the facilities are limited, the development that's planned for the future is certain to detract from the hotels' current "unspoiled" flavor. Over the next 10 years, some 16 hotels and inns, three shopping centers, a Korean folk village, and umpteen restaurants and bars will be added, along with a host of new seaside facilities. A Marine Park has already opened, with lots of fishes on display and a dolphin and otter show. Completed prior to the 1988 Olympics were extensive botanical gardens and an 18-hole golf course.

A pretty focal point now is the area of the Chonje Falls, where fairies apparently frolic. A legend says that these heavenly divas once descended to bathe in a mythical lake that lay above the three distinctive cascades of water. There is now a "heavenly" pavilion, and a bridge decorated with fairies, both popular spots for Cheju's honeymoon couples.

Just west of Chungmun is the popular bathing beach of Hwasum, and west of this, on the coastal road, is the Sanbanggulsa Temple Cave. This is an ancient hermitage with a handsome seated Buddha, reached by a short climb from the roadside parking area. The Buddhist shrine has a pool of medicinal water formed by drops falling from the ceiling. A legend says that a *sonnyo* (heavenly female spirit) was born here and later fell in love with a humble priest. However, a local government official was obsessed by her beauty and wanted to marry her. He fabricated charges against the priest and had him exiled. The girl refused to marry the official, and as she wept for her lost love she slowly turned to stone. It is said that her tears now run down the wall and form the pool in the cave. An impression of the sonnyo appears on the rock wall behind the image of the Buddha. Below the parking area, a trail leads to the edge of the ocean, where there are views of spectacular rock formations along this stretch of rugged coastline. Occasionally, you'll see the women divers working in the sea close to the shore.

Sanbangsan Mountain now has a new cultural attraction—the Cheju Art Park, Korea's first open-air sculpture garden, at the foot of the hill. The first section of the park opened in October 1987, and it features some 150 sculptures by leading Korean artists. The complex, which was completed around 1991, features two large open-air exhibition areas, a museum, a research center, and an outdoor theater.

To complete our brief study of this southwestern part of Cheju, the Daeyu Hunting Grounds should be mentioned. Here, to the northwest of Chungmun, year-round hunting is permitted, and the area is stocked with wild pigeons and pheasant. Rifles and dogs can be rented by the hour.

The West Coast

Swinging around the beautiful craggy hump of Sanbangsan Mountain, you'll reach Chejudo's western coast where the beaches are smooth, the fishing is fine, and there are green pastures for cattle and sheep.

The highlight of the area is Hallim, a coastal village that has achieved fame for its homespun woolens. During the early 1960s, Father Patrick McGlinchey imported equipment and 500 sheep from New Zealand and Japan. The flock now totals some 2,500, and the products include some of the best Irish-style woolens produced outside Ireland. The handmade sweaters, scarves, caps, mittens, and woven blankets and fabrics are in traditional Irish patterns and rank among Korea's most unlikely souvenirs. They can be bought in Cheju City, the Hallim Handweavers' Complex, and in the Hallim Village itself. (There is also an outlet in Seoul, in the lower lobby of the Westin Chosun Hotel.)

On the southern outskirts of Hallim are two well-known tourist sites, the beautiful beach of Hyopchae and the Hyopchaegul Cave. This is one of the typical Cheju lava tubes, and it has some impressive stalactites and stalagmites formed from the leaching action of rains trickling down through the extremely porous rock.

About a 20-minute drive south of Hallim is another of Chejudo's unusual rock formations—the Cholbuam Rock. Another legend of lost fishermen and grieving wives is woven around this rock cluster, and it is said that here an eternal vigil is kept by the spirits of women who lost their husbands at sea.

About halfway between Hallim and Cheju City is Hangpaduri, one of the most significant of all the historical monuments on Chejudo. It is the remains of a fortress with an "anti-Mongol" monument, dedicated to those who fought against the Mongols who occupied the island during the late thirteenth century. After the Koryo kingdom surrendered, patriotic troops called *sambyolch* held on to this bastion for years before they were finally overwhelmed.

Cheju Exploration: Two Itineraries

Although two days is really the minimum stay for a reasonably good exploration of Chejudo, some visitors may have to hit the high spots in a single day. To follow the programs below, we suggest hiring a car, or arranging to hire a taxi for a full day. It is certainly possible to move around by bus, but with limited time available, your own transportation is more convenient and reliable.

One-Day Tour. Starting in Cheju City, take the second Cross-Island Highway (stopping just outside the city at the Dragon Head Rock, Yongduam, on the way) to Yongshil. Then visit the Chungmun Resort and Chonje Falls, and the Chonji Falls, Waetolkwae Rock, Sogwipo town and Chongbang Falls. Return via the Songup Village and Sangumburi Crater, linking up with the first Cross-Island Highway, to Moksogwon Park, and finally, Cheju City. You can enjoy lunch at the Hyatt Regency Hotel at the Chungmun Resort, or at Sogwipo. Be sure to allow at least an hour to explore the Songup Village, which has some of the best examples of traditional life on Chejudo.

Two-Day Tour. If you have two days to explore the island, you should visit the eastern half on the first day, stay overnight in Sogwipo or Chungmun on the south coast, and spend the second day touring the western half of the island. You could arrive back at the international airport in time to take an evening flight out. It works out this way: First day, to the east—begin by taking the coastal highway east, stop at the Cheju Folk

Museum, and the Yonbukjong Pavilion in Chochon, continue along the coast to the Samyang and Hamdok beaches, swing inland to the Manjang-gul and Sagul caves, return to the coast road to visit Ilchulbong Peak at Songsanpo, head inland again to the Songup Village, and then back to the scenic coast road for the drive to Sogwipo, stopping at the Chongbang Falls.

Second day, the western trip—take the coast highway to the Chonji Falls, and on to the Chungmun Resort, see Chonje Falls, Hwasum Beach, Sanbanggulsa Temple grotto and Cheju Art Park, Cholbuam Rock, Hyop-chae Beach and the Hyopchaegul Cave, Hallim and the Handweavers' Complex, Hangpaduri, Yongyon Pond, Yongduam Rock, and return to Cheju City (or the international airport).

PRACTICAL INFORMATION FOR CHEJU ISLAND

WHEN TO GO. Although Chejudo is called the "Hawaii of the Orient," you should bear in mind that such a comparison can only really be drawn in the summer. Although it is warm and sunny for much of the year (the average temperature is a balmy 75° Fahrenheit), during winter months temperatures of 43 to 45° are common. This is not to say that Chejudo is not a pleasant place to be between November and March. There's never much snow—except on the peak of Hallasan Mountain—and the craggy wind-swept shorelines are often at their most magnificent in winter. Cheju's mountain landscapes are always spectacular, no matter what the season. There are almost 2,000 different plants on the island, ranging from those that flourish in semitropical conditions to others of the frosty zones. In brief, Chejudo is fine any time of year, but you should plan your wardrobe according to the season—looking at a hot summer, warm and sunny spring and autumn (when the nights are cool), and a chilly winter. Remember, also, that Chejudo is famous for its winds, which often put an extra bite in the air.

HOW TO GET THERE. By air. Korea's domestic airlines, Korean Air and Asiana, offer more than 300 flights a week from six cities on the mainland: Seoul (which has flights every hour), Pusan (also every hour), Yosu (twice daily), Chinju (once daily), Taegu (twice daily), and Kwangju (three times daily). The basic schedules are increased during peak holiday seasons (especially in summer), and on holiday weekends. Flight time from Kimpo Airport in Seoul is just one hour, and the fare is W40,300 one-way. On the shortest air link, from Kwangju, flight time is just 40 minutes, and the fare is W15,500. For current details on flights, you can call Korean Air in Seoul, Tel. (02) 756–2000; Pusan, Tel. (051) 463–2000; Yosu, Tel (0662) 41–2000; Chinju, Tel. (0591) 57–2000; Taegu, Tel. (053) 423–2000; Kwangju, Tel. (062) 222–2000; and Cheju, Tel. (064) 52–2000. You can also call Asiana, in Seoul, Tel. (02) 774–4000; Pusan, Tel. (051) 465–8000; Cheju, Tel. (064) 43–4000; Kwangju, Tel. (062) 226–4000; and Taegu, Tel. (053) 421–4000.

It is also possible to fly to Cheju from Tokyo or Osaka in Japan. Flights are three times weekly from each city, with all flights via Pusan. There is also a weekly flight from Taipei, Taiwan, on Tuesdays. Service to Cheju is expected to increase.

By sea. Car ferries serve Cheju on regular routes from Pusan, Mokpo, and Wando (the last two ports being in the southern sector of the West Plain and Coastal Area). Services are daily, with fares depending on the class of travel. Top price between Pusan and Cheju, for example, is W88,060 for a deluxe berth, one-way; the lowest price is W12,340 for third class. Departures are at 7 and 7:30 P.M. from Pusan, with the voyage taking up to 12 hours. From Mokpo, ferries are usually daily, and the cruise takes up to seven hours. A first-class berth costs up to W22,950; third-class as low as W5,810. From Wando, services are irregular, depending on the ferry and the season, and the trip takes up to three hours for a first-class fare of up to W17,310; second-class, W7,780. The ferries land at a terminal in Cheju City, with the exception of one service, which makes a round-trip every three days, between Pusan and Sogwipo. This trip takes 16½ hours, and also makes a stop at the Cheju port of Songsanpo.

For information on current ferry schedules to Cheju City, you can call in Seoul, *Dong Yang*, Tel. 730–7788; *Hanil Express*, Tel. 535–2101; in Pusan, *Dong Yang*, Tel. 463–0605; *Car Ferry Queen*, Tel. 464–6601; in Mokpo, *Dong Yang*, Tel. (0631) 43–2111; *Car Ferry Queen*, Tel. (0631) 43–1927; and in Cheju, *Dong Yang*, Tel. (064) 43–4511; *Hanil Express*, Tel. (064) 22–4170. For the service from Pusan to Sogwipo, call 465–6131 in Pusan, 62–4757 in Sogwipo.

HOW TO GET AROUND. From the airport. Downtown Cheju is just a 10-minute drive away from the Cheju International Airport, and the satellite center of Shinjeju is even closer. There is a regular airport bus service, and many taxis are available. The major hotels also operate their own shuttle services.

The drive from the airport to the Chungmun Resort, on the southern side of the island, takes about 40 minutes by taxi or the bus operated by the Hyatt Regency Hotel for its guests.

By helicopter. A small sister company of Korean Air, called Air Korea, operates a helicopter service between the Cheju International Airport and the southern coastal town of Sogwipo six times daily. The flight takes 25 minutes and is one of the most entertaining forms of sightseeing on the island. The fare is W27,500, one-way. The Korean Air offices will provide full details, Tel. in Cheju (064) 52–2000.

By bus. Local bus services are excellent, in all directions. From Cheju City, you can cross the island to Sogwipo via Chungmun for less than W1,000. The trip takes around one and one-half hours, with departures every 15 minutes. You can also take a bus from Cheju City to Sogwipo around the coastal roads, either east or west, for about W1,500. Departures are every 10 minutes, and the trip takes about one hour, 45 minutes. Often the easiest way to reach Cheju's scenic highlights is by bus operated by one of the travel services, especially if you're short on time. There are several agencies, many clustered around the major hotels in Shinjeju, and all offer the same basic range of programs.

Car hire. For do-it-yourself touring, hiring a car certainly gives you flexibility. The roads are generally good—particularly the cross-island and coastal highways—and you won't find the traffic jams encountered in other major Korean cities. The standard of driving is still not impressive, however, so paying the extra W15,000 or so per day for a driver can be a happy investment. There are a number of car-hire companies, for example *Cheju Rent-a-Car* in Shinjeju, Tel. (064) 42–3301; and *Halla Rent-a-Car* in Sogwipo, Tel. (064) 42–7807. The information or tour personnel at the international hotels will also be able to assist you with car-hire arrangements. The cost per day is between W32,000 and W55,000, depending on the type of car.

It is also possible to hire a taxi for the day. The price will depend on the season, the weather, and your skill at bargaining. Generally, you'll pay about W50,000. Make sure the hours of hire and the price are clear before you start out. Language can be a problem, but the hotel staff will help by writing out your destinations in Korean.

ACCOMMODATIONS. There are several hotels with international standards on Chejudo, the best being the Hyatt Regency and Cheju Shilla, at Chungmun Resort, and the Cheju Grand, in Shinjeju. You should make reservations in advance for visits during the high summer season, July through mid-August. Conveniently, most of the major hotels have reservation offices in Seoul. Approximate price ranges for a double or twin room at a *Deluxe* hotel are W75,000 to W120,000; *1st class,* W60,000 to W75,000; and *2d class,* W40,000 to W60,000.

There are no international-style, third-class hotels on Chejudo. This category is taken up by the many excellent yogwan, Korean inns, which are found in the main centers and in the smaller coastal towns. As elsewhere in Korea, staying at a yogwan not only gives good value for little money, but also provides an opportunity for a very "local" accommodation experience. You don't have to make advance reservations at yogwan, and information on recommended, available rooms can be obtained from the tourist-information counter at the airport, and at local travel offices.

As Chejudo is a resort island, hotel rates do tend to be seasonal, and you'll pay top rate at the peak of the summer, the lowest rates in the cool of the winter. You will also find that double rooms are more common than twin, as Chejudo is Korea's most popular honeymoon spot.

Here is a list of the hotels recommended by the Korea National Tourism Corporation, arranged according to their location. Credit card abbreviations are American Express, AE; Diner's Club, DC; MasterCard, MC; Visa, V.

Cheju City

Cheju KAL Hotel. *Deluxe.* 1691–9, Ido 1-dong, Cheju, Chejudo; Tel. (064) 53–6151, Seoul office (02) 454–7981, Telex K66744, Fax. (064) 52–4187. 310 rooms. Korean, Japanese, and Western restaurants, coffee shop, cocktail lounge, theater-restaurant, and nightclub. This hotel has one of the two casinos on Cheju, open 24 hours. Resort-style amenities include an outdoor swimming pool, sauna, and indoor golf practice facility. Credit cards: AE, DC, V.

Paradise Cheju. *2d class.* 1315, Ido 1-dong, Cheju, Chejudo; Tel. (064) 22–3111, Telex K66728, Fax. (064) 52–8002. Just 57 rooms, and limited facilities. Restaurants serve Korean, Japanese, and Western meals. Credit cards: AE, V.

There are a number of other small hotels and Korean inns in Cheju City that are familiar with catering to Western visitors, particularly in the Samdo 2-dong/Ildo 1-dong area at the northern edge of the city. These include the Beach Hotel, the Haesang, the Namgyong, and the Kyongrim, with both Western- and Korean-style rooms. All are convenient to the waterfront, with its excellent collection of seafood restaurants, and the ferry terminal.

Shinjeju

Cheju Grand. *Deluxe.* 263, Yon-dong, Shinjeju, Chejudo; Tel. (064) 47–5000, Seoul office (02) 278–2100, Telex K66712, Fax. (064) 42–3150. 522 rooms and the city's best collection of facilities, including Korean, Western, and Japanese restaurants, a coffee shop, cocktail lounge, and night-club. A top-floor French restaurant offers a splendid view of Hallasan Mountain. Recreation facilities include a health club, sauna, and an out-door swimming pool. There is also a lava rock garden. The hotel operates the Ora Country Club, about a 15-minute drive to the south of the city by shuttle bus, which has a 27-hole, four-season golf course. Credit cards: AE, DC, MC, V.

Cheju Nam Seoul. *1st class.* 291–30, Yon-dong, Shinjeju, Chejudo; Tel. (064) 42–4111, Seoul office (02) 733–4111, Fax. (064) 46–4111. 171 rooms. Korean, Japanese and Western dining facilities, sauna, a coffee shop, cock-tail lounge, and nightclub. Credit cards: AE, DC, MC, V.

Cheju Royal. *1st class.* 272–34, Yon-dong, Shinjeju, Chejudo; Tel. (064) 43–2222, Seoul office (02) 733–4567, Fax. (064) 42–0424. 115 rooms. Ko-rean, Japanese, and Western dining facilities, a coffee shop, sauna, theater-restaurant, cocktail lounge, and nightclub. The hotel operates a cruise by glass-bottom boat, off the coast of Cheju City, and provides a shuttle-bus service to the landing. Credit cards: AE, DC, MC, V.

Cheju Marina. *2d class.* 300–8, Yon-dong, Shinjeju, Chejudo; Tel. (064) 46–6161, Seoul office (02) 764–1134. Just 80 rooms, with limited facilities. Korean, Japanese, and Western meals available. Credit cards: MC, V.

There are many other, smaller hotels/inns in Shinjeju, where prices are around W25,000 per night. Near the Cheju Grand Hotel are the Sejong and Island hotels, and in the same area as the Cheju Nam Seoul are the Hyondae, Sowon, and Kyongun hotels.

Sogwipo

Staying in the town of Sogwipo, on the south side of the island, is a pleas-ant alternative to Cheju City. While it is as convenient as the provincial capital for traveling to the major sights of the island, it is quieter and closer to some of the more splendid scenic highlights. Apart from the deluxe and 2d-class tourist hotels, there is a good choice of yogwan, some with excel-lent views of the seashore.

Cheju Prince. *Deluxe.* 731–3, Sohong-dong, Sogwipo, Chejudo; Tel. (064) 32–9911, Seoul office (02) 757–2491, Telex K66739, Fax. (064) 32–9990. 170 rooms, in a shoreside location to the southwest, west of the city. Korean, Japanese, and Western restaurants, a coffee shop, cocktail lounge, and nightclub. Resort-style facilities include an outdoor swimming pool, sauna, and arrangements for hunting, boating, and fishing. Credit cards: AE, DC, MC, V.

Seogwipo KAL Hotel. *Deluxe.* 486–3, Topyong-dong, Sogwipo, Cheju-do; Tel. (064) 32–9851, Seoul office (02) 454–2981, Telex K66717, Fax. (064) 32–3190. On the eastern outskirts of the city. 225 rooms. Korean, Japanese, and Western restaurants, a coffee shop, cocktail lounge, and nightclub. Also a health club, indoor and outdoor swimming pools, and facilities for golf and tennis. Credit cards: AE, DC, MC, V.

Seogwipo Lions. *2d class.* 803, Sogwi-dong, Sogwipo, Chejudo; Tel. (064) 62–4141, Seoul office (02) 776–2232. 60 rooms. Korean and Western restaurants, a cocktail lounge, and nightclub. Credit cards: MC, V.

Chungmun Resort

Cheju Shilla. *Deluxe.* Located at Chungmun Resort; Tel. (064) 33–4466, Seoul (02) 230–3684, Fax. (064) 33–2823. This hotel opened in mid-1990. It is owned and operated by Seoul's Hotel Shilla and offers Korean and Japanese restaurants, a café, a supper club, lounge/bar, tennis courts, heated swimming pool, and a health club.

Hyatt Regency Cheju. *Deluxe.* 3039–1, Saektal-dong, Sogwipo, Cheju-do; Tel. (064) 33–1234, Seoul office (02) 797–7819, Telex K66749, Fax. (064) 32–2039. The 224 rooms surround a splendid atrium lobby, each room with a balcony overlooking the ocean or spacious gardens. Continental, Japanese, and Korean restaurants, cocktail lounge, and nightclub. A 24-hour casino. This hotel forms the heart of the Chungmun scenic resort, the site of major tourism developments with many hotels and a collection of recreation and entertainment facilities. The hotel has indoor and outdoor swimming pools, tennis courts, a health club and gymnasium, and an 18-hole golf course. A shuttle-bus service is provided from the Cheju International Airport. Credit cards: AE, DC, MC, V.

RESTAURANTS AND NIGHTLIFE. For Western food, you'll need to eat in the top hotels (where the food will be good but expensive). Japanese food is more common (remember that the majority of Chejudo's foreign visitors are from Japan), but again the best selection is found in the hotels. Meal prices at the hotels tend to be in the same range as those in Seoul—at the *expensive* end of the scale, cost per person is between W15,000 and W30,000 for lunch or dinner; *moderate,* W10,000–W20,000; and *inexpensive,* W8,000–W12,000. Looking at the costs of different types of food, the Continental and Japanese restaurants will be the most expensive; best values will be found in the coffee shops. Buffet-style lunches are quite common at the better hotels, and these are also good value at around W20,000 per person.

There are no "high class" independent restaurants on Chejudo, but you will find the most delicious array of seafood. The shores of both Cheju City and Sogwipo, and all the little coastal villages, are noted for their spread of tiny restaurants and open-air dining rooms. The usual form is to point out your dinner in a large sea tank display, and watch the chef prepare it. Specialties are *hoe,* sliced raw fish, which is not to everyone's taste; and an abalone-rice stew called *chonbokchuk.* A plate of hoe costs between W10,000 and W15,000 in a restaurant, much less if you're sitting near Yongduam Rock in the open air, or at a seaside stall. A bowl of piping hot chonbokchuk served in a restaurant costs between W3,000 and W5,000. While the restaurants in the main areas, such as Tapdong near the ferry terminal in Cheju City, are now used to serving foreign visitors, you'll find little spoken English. However, the proprietors are usually friendly and accommodating, and other diners will also be willing to help you make a menu selection.

Just about all the hotels have nightclubs, and some have theater-restaurants. Often there is a cover charge, and the cost of drinks is high. You'll probably be happier pursuing a very Korean form of entertainment—visiting a local tearoom or wine or beer house. Certainly it will be less expensive. The hotel staff can guide you to the most suitable places near your hotel.

For those who like the excitement of gambling, you have a choice of two 24-hour casinos: at the Cheju KAL Hotel in Cheju City, Tel. (064) 53–6151; and in the Hyatt Regency Hotel at the Chungmun Resort, Tel. (064) 33–1234.

TOURS. Many travel agencies operate tours out of Seoul, either offering Chejudo by itself or in combination with visits to other Korean cities. For example, a six-night/seven-day program that travels to Kyongju by rail, then Pusan by road, Cheju by air, and back to Seoul by air—including hotel accommodations, some meals, and tours to the highlights of the three areas—costs around W570,000 per person (minimum two). *Aju Travel Service* in Seoul, Tel. (02) 753–5051, can provide details. A Cheju program from Seoul, covering two nights and three days, traveling to and from Cheju by air, costs in the area of W380,000 (minimum two people). This cost includes top hotel accommodations, breakfasts, and two tours of the island's major attractions. For details, contact a tour representative at your Seoul hotel, or call the agencies—*Global Tours* (335–0011), *Hanjin Travel Service* (777–0041), *Samhee Travel* (755–9251), or *Seoul Travel Service* (754–6831).

Once you're on the island, it is possible to join full-day tours planned by the Cheju Tourist Association. The tour routes change quite frequently, but basically there are three to choose from—covering the east of the island, the west, and the central sector. Each tour departs at 9 A.M., returns about 6:30 P.M., and is available either from Cheju City or from Sogwipo. Lunch is included. On the East Coast tour, stops are made at the Folkcraft and Natural History Museum, Manjanggul Cave, Ilchulbong Peak, Cheju Cultural Village at Pyoson, and the Chonji Falls. The cross-island drive is by the first Cross-Island Highway, "Route 516." Cost is W25,000 per person. The West Coast tour stops at Samsonghyol, Hallim, Hyopchaegul Cave, Cheju Art Park, Chongbang Waterfall, Sangumburi Crater (via Route 516), and the Moksogwon Park. Cost per person is W22,000. The Central tour visits Yongduam Rock, the Hangpaduri "anti-Mongol" monument, Sanbanggulsa Temple Cave, and the Marine Park and Chonje Falls in the area of Chungmun. One way is by the Chungmun Highway, the other by Route 516. The cost is also about W22,000. You can ask about these tours at any travel office, or your hotel information desk. Departures depend on demand, so if there is no tour operating on the day you want, the tour staff will assist you with other arrangements.

Remember that "do-it-yourself" touring is easy on Chejudo—buses are frequent, in all directions, and it's hard to get stranded even in the tiniest hamlet.

For tours with a difference, there is the helicopter trip between Cheju International Airport and Sogwipo (*see* "How to Get Around" above), and the ferry cruise from Songsanpo to Udo Island (see the introduction section about the east coast). Another seaside cruise is by glass-bottom boat off the shore of Cheju City. Operated by the *Cheju Royal Hotel*, Tel. 43–222, the trip takes an hour and costs W12,000.

WHAT TO SEE. Temples, Shrines, and Pavilions. In Cheju City, among the most notable sights are **Samsonghyol,** the sacred place from where the ancestors of the Cheju islanders emerged; and the **Kwandokjong Pavilion,** the oldest standing structure on Chejudo, which dates to 1448. Eastward along the coast is the small town of Chochon, with its **Yonbukjong Pavilion** marking the spot where disgraced officials from the Korean mainland arrived to begin their island exile. In Chejudo's southwest corner is the craggy lump of Sanbangsan hill, noted for the cave and shrine of Sanbanggulsa, an ancient hermitage with a graceful seated Buddha.

Lava Art and Legend. There are three famous lava rock formations on Cheju, each with a legend to color its origin— **Yongduam** (Dragon Head Rock), on the outskirts of Cheju City; the needle rock called **Waetolkwae** at Sogwipo; and the **Cholbuam Rock,** off the west coast. One of the island's most spectacular clusters of rock formations is at an area called **Yongshil,** a couple of miles from the summit of Hallasan Mountain, just off the second Cross-Island Highway. To the south of Cheju City is the park called **Moksogwon,** where the creative Pak Un-Cho has gathered and combined a clever collection of rock and wood. And, as a final note on lava, Chejudo's famous "rock grandfathers," tolharubang, confront the visitor all over the island, either in their impressive original state (at Song-up Village in the east, for example, and outside the Kwandokjong Pavilion in Cheju City), or as souvenir replicas.

Caves. Three are worth a visit. **Manjanggul,** to the east, near the village of Kimnyong, is the world's longest lava cave, and a half mile of it can be explored. Nearby is the **Snake Cave,** Sagul, which has a memorial to the sixteenth-century island governor who killed the resident demon serpent. Near the western shore, inland from Hyopchae Beach, is the **Hyopchaegul Cave,** noted for its impressive stalagmites and stalactites.

Waterfalls. Again, there are three, all on the southern coast around Sogwipo. One is where fairies play—the **Chonje Falls** near Chungmun, one of Cheju's most romantic spots, popular with honeymooners. The **Chonji Waterfall,** west of Sogwipo, is an impressive cascade that falls from a cliff and tumbles through a narrow gorge. The **Chongbang Waterfall,** to Sogwipo's east, plunges some 75 feet to a beach below. It is said to be Asia's only waterfall that falls directly into the sea.

Monuments. The most significant is the "anti-Mongol" memorial called **Hangpaduri,** about halfway between Cheju City and the western town of Hallim. Here are the remains of a fortress where patriotic troops of the Koryo kingdom resisted the Mongol conquerors of the thirteenth century, although the mainland rulers had already surrendered.

Near the Sanbangsan hill, on the southwestern shore, is the **Hamel Monument,** commemorating the arrival of Cheju's first Western visitors— the Dutch survivors of the shipwrecked *Sparrow Hawk* in 1653. One of the men, Henrik Hamel, eventually made his way to Japan and back to Europe, and wrote a book translated into English as *The Dutch Come to Korea.* (Copies are available from the Royal Asiatic Society in Seoul.)

Museums and Cultural Centers. The most notable museum is the **Cheju Folkcraft and Natural History Museum** (in Ildo 2-dong, Cheju City; Tel. 22–2465). It has an excellent collection of folk tools and examples of the island's plant and animal life. It is closed on Thursdays and major public holidays. To the east of the city in Samyang-dong is a private display of local crafts and customs at the **Cheju Folklore Museum,** Tel. 22–1976. The admission charge to either museum is W500; hours are 9 A.M. to 5 P.M.

Local creativity is dramatically displayed by Pak Un-Chol at his **Moksogwon "Wood and Rock" Park,** to the south of Cheju City, mentioned above under "Lava Art." This is a popular stop for tour groups, so some of the tranquillity has been lost, but the combinations of natural wood and stone are certainly impressive.

A little more peace and quiet can be found at the **Yongyon Pond,** west of Cheju City, near the Yongduam Rock. Here it is said one will be inspired with poetic thoughts—long ago scholars gathered here to sip wine and enjoy gentle contemplation.

Chejudo has Korea's first sculpture garden, the **Cheju Art Park** at the foot of the Sanbangsan hill, on the island's far southern coast. At present there are some 150 works by Korean sculptors on display, but there are plans for major extensions to the park and its facilities.

You can step back into Chejudo's past at **Songup Village,** north of the town of Pyoson on the southeast coast. Founded during the fifteenth century, Songup has been designated as a folklore-preservation zone to retain many of the island's traditional ways. The people still live in rock homes with thatched roofs, and each house has a high lava-stone wall around its courtyard. A couple of trees in the village center are over 1,000 years old, and the place generally has an atmosphere of gracious charm.

If you really want to feel like a tourist, visit the **Cheju Folk Village** at Pyoson. This was opened early in 1987, modeled on the theme of the Folk Village at Yongin near Seoul, and re-creates Chejudo's typical habitats—mountains, plains, and the coast—of the nineteenth century. The place is a neat and tidy replica of the way things were, and brightly polished for the tourist, and a couple of hours here can be fun. The village market place is lively, snacks and meals are reasonably priced, and you can watch a happy performance of local folk drama. The Shaman rituals presented are also interesting. Entrance fee to the Cheju Folk Village is W2,500.

Animal Entertainment. There is a Marine Park at the Chungmun Resort that displays lots of fishes, and puts on a dolphin and otter show. The entrance fee to the park is W3,000, and show times are 11 A.M. and 1:30, 2:40, and 4:30 P.M. daily.

SPORTS. So far, our concentration has been on things to see, but for people seeking active pursuits there is plenty to do on Chejudo.

Hiking. There are five established trails up Hallasan Mountain, all to the Paekrokdam crater lake. From the west side, along the Yongshil Trail, you should allow about two and one half hours to reach the top, less to go down. From the east, the trails are longer, and you should allow at least ten hours for the round-trip. The hiking is not particularly strenuous (nor is it for rank beginners), but the weather can be disappointing. You will need no special equipment except good hiking shoes and a warm jacket even in summer because it gets chilly at the peak. There is a small admission fee to hike on any of the trails, and free maps are available. Be sure to follow the trail, as it is easy to get lost on this mountain, especially since the weather is so changeable. The trails are often closed in winter after heavy snowfalls.

Another good walk is up the Ilchulbong Peak, at the port of Songsanpo on the east side of the island. The view from the top is stunning, as the almost perfect crater bowl is surrounded on three sides by the sea. It is quite a strenuous hike up to the top, taking about an hour, and is highly recommended at dawn, to watch the sunrise.

Hunting. Cheju is the best area in Korea for hunting, with the season beginning in November and ending in February. Game includes pheasant and duck. There is also a year-round hunting ground on Cheju, called the Daeyu Hunting Club, just north of the Chungmun Resort. The fee for each person is W110,000 daily, and it is possible to hire equipment and dogs. The area is regularly stocked with wild pigeon and pheasant. For information, you can call the *Daeyu Hunting Club* in Seoul, Tel. (02) 544–0432, or on Cheju, Tel. (064) 32–0500.

Fishing. Seashore or deep-sea fishing can be enjoyed at many locations around the coast of Chejudo. Travel agents organize trips for groups and also handle special arrangements for individuals. All equipment can be rented. Ask at your hotel information or tour desk. There is a good tackle shop in the Cheju Grand Hotel, Tel. 47–5000.

Golf. The Ora Country Club is operated by the Cheju Grand Hotel, which provides frequent shuttle-bus service to the 27-hole course. This is just a 15-minute drive to the south of Shinjeju, on the slopes of Hallasan Mountain. Equipment can be rented from the pro shop at the club. Telephone in Seoul (02) 278–2105, or on Cheju (064) 42–3211, for details.

Another golf course, with 18 holes, is the Cheju Country Club, which is reached via the first Cross-Island Highway (Route 516). The major hotels will advise on fees and arrange transportation. For details, call in Seoul (02) 739–3327, or on Cheju (064) 56–0451. An excellent 18-hole golf course opened in the Chungmun resort in 1988. Call the Hyatt Regency Cheju Hotel, Tel. 32–1202 for details.

Scuba Diving. The clear waters of Chejudo are attracting a growing number of Korean and foreign diving enthusiasts. For advice on sites, local conditions, and rental of equipment, you can make contact with the Cheju Leisure Center, (064) 42–1270, or the Won Dive Resort, (064) 43–7233.

BEACHES. There are several good swimming beaches around the island, including Samyang and Hamdok beaches, just east of Cheju City; Shinyang, south of Songsanpo; the shores of the Chungmun Resort area and Hwasun, a little farther west; and Hyopchae and Kwakchi beaches on the northwestern coast. All these beaches are really decked out for the summer—facilities generally include showers and toilets, deck-chair and umbrella rentals, and lots and lots of shoreside snack bars and refreshment stands. The beaches also have their own nearby villages or towns, so if you want to stay overnight there is always a handy Korean inn.

SHOPPING. The best shopping areas are in Cheju City and nearby Shinjeju, especially the areas around the main hotels. Bargaining is part of the game, and you'll rarely have to pay the first price quoted. Have a look around the local markets—every town has at least one, like the Somun (to the west) and Tongmun (to the east) in downtown Cheju, and the central Shinjeju market. You won't find many souvenirs, but you'll see the best of the island's fruits and all the necessities of daily living.

Talking about shopping, we have to mention once again the island's specialty—the rock grandfathers—available everywhere in up-to-awesome sizes. Most of the smaller, cheaper ones are no longer carved, but are made from molds. Some of the most "realistic" are actually candles.

Chejudo offers lots of shells and coral in jewelry and ornaments. Although pretty, they are not cheap when compared with what is available in other Asian cities. Korean tourists from the mainland often buy Cheju honey and mushrooms, and a popular gift for those back home is a pineapple.

Of special interest to foreigners is the wool clothing produced by **Cheju's Irish Catholic Mission,** at Hallim on the west coast. Here you can buy hand-knitted sweaters, caps, mittens, and woven blankets and fabrics—mostly in cream color, and all in distinctly Irish patterns. An adult's sweater costs in the area of W130,000. The telephone number in Hallim is (064) 22–7221.

There are a fair number of antiques shops on Chejudo, with prices usually lower than in Seoul. However, you should be wary of the authenticity of the pieces, and remember, you need a permit to take genuine antiques out of the country. Many folk items seen in the antiques stores are found only on the island. It's a good idea to first visit the Cheju Folk Museum, to get an idea of what is distinctive and what may be a good buy.

There are two duty-free shops on the island: the **Cheju Airport Duty-Free Shop,** operated by the Korea National Tourism Corporation, Tel. (064) 42–0030; and the **Hanjin Duty-Free Shop** in 2-do, 1-dong, downtown Cheju, Tel. (064) 58–0713.

Other stores offering souvenirs are the **Hanseong Moolsan,** in downtown Cheju City, Tel. 46–2356; and the **Hambang Souvenir Shop,** Tel. 46–3343, and **Sambo Souvenir Shop,** Tel. 42–4176, both in Yon-dong, downtown Shinjeju. The international hotels also have souvenir and gift stores.

CULTURAL EVENTS. Korea's national holidays and festivals are celebrated on Chejudo just as they are in other parts of the country. There are a number of special events, however, that are only celebrated here, with dates usually following the lunar calendar.

Halla Cultural Festival. This is the biggest cultural celebration of the year, to be held in early October in 1993. The center of the festivities is the Cheju Stadium, at the southwestern edge of Cheju City, with parades, folk music and dances, exhibitions, and concerts.

Chilmori Shaman Ceremony. Held on the 14th day of the second lunar month (March 6 in 1993), this is an ancient ritual to pray for the safety of fishermen and women divers, and for abundant harvests from the sea.

Samsonghyol Rituals. These are held on April 10, October 10, and December 10 every year, at the Samsonghyol Shrine in Cheju City. The ceremonies are to honor the Ko, Yang, and Pu demigods who emerged from the ground, married princesses, and were the original inhabitants of Cheju Island.

Yuchaekkot Celebrations. These take place in the spring, to celebrate the full bloom of the yellow, oil-seed rape flowers that dominate the island's scenic landscape.

Kamgyul Festival. This is an autumn celebration to honor the bountiful harvest of Chejudo's tangerines.

USEFUL ADDRESSES AND TELEPHONE NUMBERS. Medical Attention.

As elsewhere in Korea, in a medical emergency you should call the hotel manager for assistance. In Cheju City, the **Cheju Medical Center,** in Samdo 1-dong, is recommended, Tel. (064) 56–1191.

Tourist Information. The **Korea National Tourism Corporation** operates an information center at the Cheju International Airport, and has free maps and brochures, and staff to advise on hotels and transportation. The telephone number is (064) 42–0032. The **Cheju Tourist Association** also has an airport counter, with a number of representatives of local travel agencies. The downtown office of this association is in the center of Shinjeju, Tel. (064) 42–8861.

Cheju also has a tourist complaint center that you can call for information and advice, Tel. 46–0101.

WEST PLAIN
AND COASTAL AREA

This dual description of "West Plain" and "Coastal Area" arises from the region's two markedly different kinds of country—seashore and flatlands spotted with sharply upthrusting heights. Until now the scenery in the sections of Korea we have described has been filled with mountains in all directions. The north-to-south ranges that are the spine of the peninsula effectively split the country into east and west sections, as is dramatically demonstrated when you travel the express highways that cut across these mountains.

But as you reach the southern shore of Korea and begin to move west, you notice that the peaks are considerably lower. West of Sunchon, you begin to encounter genuine flatlands—often great stretches of rice paddies—punctuated by rugged granite extrusions.

Geographically, we are now discussing the western part of three provinces: Chollanamdo (southern Cholla, the farthest south), Chollabukdo (northern Cholla), and Chungchongnamdo, the province just below Seoul. This area is as long as the East Coastal area—about 250 miles. Climatically, it has the hot summers of Pusan and the Hallyo Waterway area, but in the northern reaches it has the very cold winters of the capital. It is not that the south is that much warmer in the winter, but the proximity to the Strait of Korea to the south and the Yellow Sea to the west does have a moderating effect.

Only recently has this remote corner been opened up to tourism. Emphasis has been placed on the reconstruction of the historic and religious

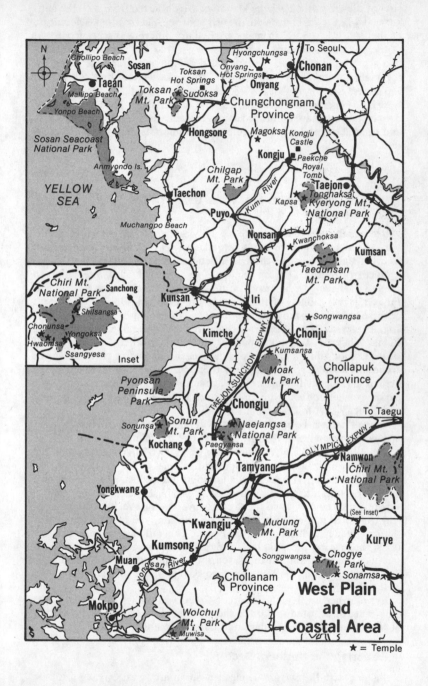

N

Chollipo Beach

Sosan

To Seoul

Hyongchungsa

Onyang Hot Springs

Chonan

Taean

Toksan Hot Springs

Mallipo Beach

Toksan Mt. Park

Sudoksa

Onyang

Yonpo Beach

Chungchongnam Province

Hongsong

Magoksa

Kongju Castle

Sosan Seacoast National Park

Kongju

Paekche Royal Tomb

Anmyondo Is.

YELLOW SEA

Chilgap Mt. Park

Taejon

Tonghaksa

Taechon

Kum River

Kapsa

Kyeryong Mt. National Park

Puyo

Nonsan

Kwanchoksa

Kumsan

Taedunsan Mt. Park

Chiri Mt. National Park

Sanchong

Kunsan

Iri

Shilsangsa

Songwangsa

Chonunsa

Yongoksa

Kimche

Chonju

Hwaomsa

Ssangyesa

Inset

Kumsansa

Pyonsan Peninsula Park

Moak Mt. Park

Chollapuk Province

TAEJON-SUNCHON EXPWY

To Taegu

Sonunsa

Sonun Mt. Park

Chongju

Naejangsa National Park

OLYMPIC EXPWY.

Kochang

Paegyansa

Namwon

Chiri Mt. National Park

Tamyang

(See Inset)

Yongkwang

Mudung Mt. Park

Kurye

Kwangju

Kumsong

Songgwangsa

Chogye Mt. Park

Muan

Yongsan River

Sonamsa

Chollanam Province

West Plain and Coastal Area

Mokpo

Wolchul Mt. Park

Muwisa

★ = Temple

sites of the era of the Paekche kingdom, which lasted from A.D. 250 until
A.D. 660, when it was united with the neighboring Silla kingdom. The culture
of the area was unique, in many particulars differing sharply from that
of the rest of the country. It is now known that the Paekche influences
had a profound effect on the cultural development of ancient Japan. In
fact, some of the early restorations in this area were at first called "too
Japanese," until it was discovered that the so-called Japanese elements
were based upon much earlier Korean Paekche designs. The Paekche kingdom is shown to have influenced Japan in such areas as ceramic technique
and decoration, architecture, sculpture, handicrafts, and tomb construction.

Three Sectors to Explore

Because the area is so long, we have divided it into three sectors: northern, central, and southern. Let's first take a brief look at each one, enough
to catch the essence, and then do a detailed exploration of each.

Northern Sector. This top section of the area is loaded with things to
see and do, having within it two culturally important centers, Kongju and
Puyo, the two capitals of the Paekche kingdom. In addition, just north
of these two centers are three more towns lying in an east-west arc, Onyang, Hongsong, and Sosan, which encompass several more interesting
sights. What may be most important about this northern sector is that if
your vacation time is limited, you can reach one end of this three-town
arc in just an hour from Seoul. It is therefore possible to make a day trip
here from the capital. Other notable attractions in this area are some major
parks, excellent ocean swimming at several places, a famous arboretum,
and Korea's best folk museum.

Central Sector. To get to this part will take three to five hours by train
or bus from Seoul, and requires at least one overnight stay at a hotel or
Korean inn. Here there are four major parks, two inland and two on the
Yellow Sea, and a number of important temples.

Southern Sector. To reach this far-south sector from Seoul, you face
a five- or six-hour trip by train or bus. The train service is by comfortable
superexpress, however, and the expressway, if you travel by road, is excellent. As noted in the Southeast Area description, you may decide to visit
this area while heading north from Pusan. You will find two major attractions, the provincial capital of Kwangju and its surroundings, and Chirisan National Park, and, far to the southwest, the port city of Mokpo. This
lies at the mouth of the Yongsan-gang River, where the river enters the
Yellow Sea.

Even farther south is the island of Chindo, noted for a dog that is the
only indigenous breed in Korea, and an annual "miracle" in the parting
of the waters between a village and its islet neighbor.

Exploring the Northern Sector

Starting with the Onyang-Hongsong-Sosan arc (with Onyang just over
an hour's drive from Seoul), we have the Onyang Hot Springs Resort, one

of the country's most popular spas. Legend has it that more than 600 years ago a local farmer wondered why one plot of his land never froze in winter. He dug down to find the answer, and a hot spring gushed forth. Today this spa is famous for the medicinal benefits of its carburetted, alkaline waters, which are at a natural temperature of around 52° Fahrenheit. Onyang is a favorite honeymoon site, and is the hometown of the famous Admiral Yi Sun-Shin (whom you keep meeting in your travels all over the country). There is a shrine, Hyonchungsa, in his honor in Onyang. On the outskirts of the city is one of Korea's finest folklore museums. From a cultural viewpoint, this is one of the major attractions of this northern sector, and we recommend you allow several hours for a visit. Some 14,000 folk crafts and paintings, a private collection, are on display, and effort has been made to provide written explanations in English.

East of Onyang is Chonan, the departure point for visiting the nearby Independence Hall (see the *Central Area* chapter). In Chonan, also, is the "Great Buddha of Mt. Taejosan," a 46-foot-high statue said to be the largest sitting Buddha of its kind in the Orient. It was created in 1977 as a symbol of hope for the reunification of the two Koreas.

Just a short drive to Onyang's west is another spa, the hot springs of Toksan. This is the site of a bizarre adventure during a reign of terror against Korean Catholics and their missionary priests in the 1860s. In a bold plot to end the religious persecution, three adventurers from China, led by a German, gathered a force of exiled Korean Christians, chartered a ship, and sailed into Asan Bay on the coast of this northern sector. From here, they headed inland, planning to open the tomb of the young king's grandfather, steal the body, and hold it for ransom until the regent ended the persecution. Unfortunately, when they reached the tomb, they found they did not have the right tools to open the crypt. So they made a hasty and embarrassed retreat to the coast, and escaped back to China.

On the southern slopes of nearby Mt. Toksan is Sudoksa Temple, which has some striking wooden structures surviving from the Koryo era (A.D. 935–1392). High above the temple is a Maitreya Buddha (Buddha of the Future), carved into the stone of the mountain. It is a worthwhile sight if you can face the arduous climb.

Further west is Sosan, gateway to the Taean Peninsula; west of Sosan is the town of Taean, the last major bus terminus for arrivals from Seoul and other inland cities. At Taean, you catch a bus to enter the vast area of the Sosan Sea National Park. The park offers some of the best swimming in all Korea, at Mallipo and Chollipo beaches, and at Yonpo Beach, which also has good facilities for sailing. From Taean, you can also visit Anmyondo Island, noted for its distinctive flora, including spectacular camellias in their spring season.

Sosan Park has another botanical attraction—one of the most remarkable collections of Oriental flora in the Far East, at the Chollipo Arboretum, near Chollipo Beach. This is a 200-acre sanctuary, owned by a resident foreigner (from Wilkesberry, Pennsylvania), who has put years of dedication into nurturing over 6,000 domestic and imported species of flowers, shrubs, and rare types of trees. People with a particular interest in Oriental flora will be delighted.

On the coast below Anmyondo Island is Taechon Beach, one of the favorite escapes for people living in Seoul. The northern end of the beach is more Korean in flavor, with lots of little inns, restaurants, and night spots, and a lively atmosphere throughout the summer. To the south is where Protestant missionaries set up a summer colony, and the tone is quiet. It is often possible to rent one of the bungalows. There are tennis courts nearby.

Well inland is Kongju, the first of the two principal stops in the northern sector and, in fact, a major cultural center for all of Korea. Here, as in nearby Puyo, there are rare links with the Paekche past, which were only recently discovered and are still being researched. In 1971, the digging of a simple drainage ditch revealed the tomb of a Paekche king. It was discovered to hold the remains of King Muryong, and his queen, who ruled the Paekche Dynasty from 501 to 523. Some 2,500 relics were unearthed, including plaques inscribed with information about the tomb and its occupants, gold floral ornaments, porcelain lamps, and weapons. Some of these artifacts are now on display in the Kongju Museum; others are at the National Museum in Seoul. The Konju Museum is in the middle of town, and is an essential stop for those intrigued by classical antiquities. The most notable items in the collection are the golden royal diadems. The tomb itself is about a 15-minute walk northeast of the town center, but it had to be sealed to prevent further damage from humidity. A replica is displayed nearby.

Kongju also has a wooded hilly park, on Kongsang Mountain, which crowds down into the northeast part of town. Here there are a number of pretty old buildings, pavilions, a pond, and the remains of an ancient fortress wall.

Hidden in the hills about 15 miles north of Kongju is the ancient temple of Magoksa, established by the Silla priest who also founded Tongdosa, north of Pusan. This temple has been left virtually untouched by modern civilization, and is a splendid example of traditional temple architecture. It is the Buddhist headquarters for Chungchongnamdo Province, and the head priest has administrative control over 70 other temples.

About 30 miles southwest of Kongju is Puyo, the other major stop of this northern sector, a former Paekche capital. In the middle of the city is a steep hill, with many meandering trails that offer panoramic views of the Kumgang River below. At the peak are the remains of the castle where the last Paekche king made his final stand against the combined forces of the Silla Dynasty and Tang China. It was this battle, in the year 660, that led to the unifying of Korea under the Silla kingdom. A wide, easy path leads to the top of the hill and the castle compound. On one side stands a pavilion, above a sheer cliff that drops straight down to a bend in the Kumgang River, called Paekma (White Horse). According to legend, this name originates from when General Su, the Chinese commander who was attacking with the Silla forces, believed that he could not cross the river because of a dragon living in its depths. He used the head of a white horse as bait, and managed to capture and kill the dragon.

It was from the dizzying height above the Paekma stretch of river that 3,000 ladies of the Paekche court leaped to their deaths, rather than surrender to the Silla warriors when the fortifications were breached and defeat seemed certain. The cliff today has the melancholy name of Nakhwaam, "Rock of the Falling Flowers," and is one of the most photographed sites in Puyo. Another pavilion, facing west in the castle compound, is called Songwoldae, or Moon-gazing Pavilion, where the king kept vigil on the night before his final battle. He watched his last sunrise from Yongilru, the Sun-greeting Pavilion, which faces east.

Below the Nakhwaam bluff is a small temple called Koransa, named for a medicinal herb that grows near a spring behind the temple. The water is said to be so pure it was the favorite drink of a Paekche king. From the banks of the Kumgang River nearby, you can take a ferry ride along the scenic route of the battles that ended the Paekche kingdom.

Also on the Puyo hill is the Samchungsa Shrine, built in honor of three loyal supporters of the last Paekche king. It is the site of a colorful pageant during the annual Paekche Culture Festival, usually held in October.

In town, at the base of the Puyo hill is the Puyo National Museum, a striking example of modern Korean architecture. It is filled with many examples of the Paekche art and artifacts—especially ceramics—and also has replicas of Paekche tombs on its grounds. Near the center of Puyo is a small park that houses two national treasures that were removed from the site of the ancient Paekche temple of Chongrimsa. One is an 11-foot-high Buddha on a stone pedestal; the other is a five-story pagoda, one of the oldest in Korea and typical of the Paekche style.

Between Kongju and Puyo, to the east, is the Kyeryongsan National Park (see "Taejon" in the *Central Area* chapter). Here there are excellent hiking trails and some beautiful old temples, well worth exploring if you have the time. Between the Kapsa Temple (noted for its splendid maple trees) at one park entrance, and Tonghaksa Temple at another, there is an exhilarating walk following the course of a cool mountain stream.

In the south of this northern section of the West Coast area is Nonsan, which has little tourist importance except as a convenient departure point for the temple of Kwanchoksa (the "Candlelight Temple"), a few miles to the south of the town. The temple itself is rather nondescript, but is famous for having the largest stone Buddha in the country. The Unjin Miruk is 1,000 years old, carved in the Koryo period, and is quite different from any other you'll have seen. The head and hands are disproportionately large in relation to the body—it was apparently created by a relatively unskilled local craftsman—and the figure is topped by an enormous, two-tiered headdress. The temple also has a five-story stone pagoda, lantern, and altar that are as old as the Unjin Miruk statue.

Exploring the Central Sector

This area is a fair distance south of Seoul and it is not practical to plan on any one-day jaunts from the capital. You are best off basing yourself at Chonju, the capital of Chollabukdo Province, which is the seventh-largest city in Korea and has a number of major hotels. To the west is the vast rice-growing district called Honam. To the east and south rise the Sobaek and Noryong mountain ranges.

Chonju is the ancestral home of the founder of the Yi Dynasty, Yi Song Gye, and the city has a shrine, Kyonggijon, which houses his portrait. Although the shrine itself is normally closed to the public, there is a museum on the grounds that houses a good collection of historical items and is open daily.

A well-preserved example of Yi design and engineering can be seen in the Chonju city gate, Pungnammun, in the downtown area.

About 20 miles southwest of Chonju is Kumsansa Temple, built in the year 766, burned by the Japanese in the invasions of 1597, and rebuilt in the middle of the seventeenth century. Kumsansa, meaning "Gold Mountain Temple," is nestled in a flat hollow surrounded by the wooded slopes of Mt. Moaksan. It is one of the most significant Buddhist shrines in the province, housing altogether more than 10 cultural treasures. The three-storied Mirukchon Hall makes the temple the tallest in Korea, and contains a 39-foot gilded statue of the Maitreya Buddha. Outside is a six-tiered Paekche pagoda, and in the nearby Nahanjon Hall there is a large stone Buddha surrounded by the figures of 500 disciples.

East of Chonju (about a one-hour ride) are the twin peaks of Maisan, or Horse Ears Mountain, and you can understand the name when you look from the small town of Chinan to the north. There is a good hike through the 132-step Chonghwang Pass (between the horse ears) up to a cave called Hwaom, and on to a unique temple compound called Tapsa, or Pagoda Temple. This is not a Buddhist shrine, but where an eccentric hermit spent a lifetime heaping stone upon stone, without mortar, to form pagodas. They range from just a few inches high to over 30 feet and have stood since the early part of this century.

On the way to Maisan, you can stop at the temple of Songwangsa, which has some of Korea's finest color murals on its walls and ceiling. These fascinating artworks are relatively recent in origin, about 150 years old, and feature flying fairies and sorceresses. There are also some splendid wood carvings. (There is a temple with a very similar name, Songgwangsa, to the south of Kwangju, in the southern sector of this West Plain and Coastal Area.) To the northeast of the Maisan park is the national park of Togyusan, which is noted for its two especially scenic areas of Muju and Kuchon-dong. These are about an hour's walk apart, an easy stroll along a paved road. Along the way, you'll see a gate leading through a ridge of rock that marked the fortified frontier between the Silla and Paekche kingdoms more than 1,300 years ago. There are several first-class Korean inns at Togyusan, and an unusual fish hatchery that raises rainbow trout.

To the southwest of this central section, near the town of Chongju (don't confuse this Chongju with the town of the same name north of Taejon in the Central Area of the country) is the Naejangsan Mountain. At 2,500 feet, this is one of the highest in the Honam area. It is designated as a national park, with excellent trails offering varying degrees of climbing or just easy walking. This is one of the best places in the country to see the magnificent foliage of autumn, and it is not as crowded as other famous areas (such as Soraksan in the northeast) during the traditional fall sight-seeing months. There are two important temples in the park—Naejangsa (the "Inner Sanctum Temple"), which has a good tourist hotel nearby; and Paegyangsa ("White Sheep Temple"), to the south. This latter Son, or Zen, temple was originally built in the year 632, and in spite of its secluded site, was destroyed by invaders four times. It was last rebuilt in 1917.

Exploring the More Remote Southern Sector

One of the two major highlights of this area is Kwangju, capital of Chollanamdo, the province that extends throughout most of the southern sector of the West Plain and Coast. Although the sector has many parks and half a dozen beautiful temples, the peninsulas that reach into the Yellow Sea and comprise nearly one-third of the land area make it rather spread out and difficult to explore. It is also rather thinly populated. Three expressways—Honam (from the north), Olympic (from the northeast), and Namhae (from across the southeast)—meet at Kwanju, however, and the province has a good internal network of roads, most of them now paved. There is also good access by train, by two lines of the Saemaul superexpress from Seoul, and by express and local trains from other areas. There is air service out of Seoul to Kwangju, and it is also possible to enter the southern sector by sea by taking the ferry from Cheju Island to Mokpo, in the southwest, or Wando in the far south.

Kwangju, like Chonju in the central sector, is famous for food and traditional Korean drinks. Whereas Chonju is known in particular for the rice dish *pibimpap* (rice with vegetables and egg), Kwangju is reputed to produce the best *chungchong* (barley and rice wine) and the more basic rice liquor, *makkoli.* Kwangju tea is also savored nationwide.

But there is more to Kwangju than Korean gourmet food and wine. The Mudungsan Mountain Park nudges right up against the city and is now a small scenic resort. There are two temples in the area, Wonhyosa, where excavations have yielded numerous artifacts from the Koryo and Silla periods, and Chungsimsa ("Pure Mind Temple"), which is next to one of Kwangju's more famous tea plantations, cared for by Buddhist monks.

The city's national museum houses a collection of Chinese ceramics from the Yuan Dynasty, discovered in a submerged 600-year-old trade ship at Shinan in 1975. This is now the largest collection of such celadon ceramics outside China. The museum also displays treasures from the south Cholla Province, including neolithic relics, eleventh- to fourteenth-century bronze Buddhist bells, scroll paintings, and exquisite white porcelain.

To the north of Kwangju, easily reached by the Olympic Expressway, is Tamyang, a small town that is the center of Korea's growing and crafting of bamboo. It is not only a great place to buy the distinctive baskets and mats, but there is also a bamboo museum displaying hand-crafted items from tiny pins to furniture.

To Kwangju's southeast is Chogyesan Park, site of the Songgwangsa Temple. This center of Son, or Zen, Buddhism is the third-largest temple complex in the country, and the only one that has Western monks and nuns in permanent residence. It is possible to stay overnight at this temple, and vegetarian meals are served. (We have also mentioned Songgwangsa Temple in the *Southeast* chapter, as an excursion out of the town of Sunchon.)

There are two more provincial parks in this southern sector, Wolchulsan and Turyunsan, both in the far southwest. Both are scenic spots of some renown, with old temples and spectacular landscapes. The parks are especially beautiful, and popular in the fall.

Apart from Kwangju, the other major tourism center in this area is the Chirisan National Park, in the extreme east. The park is known for its namesake mountain and two temples of particular importance. The main entry point for the park is Namwon, a small town 31 miles northeast of Kwangju, which has blossomed with the opening of the Olympic Expressway. There are now many resort facilities here, including small hotels, restaurants, and outdoor arenas for the staging of traditional music and dance performances. Namwon is also known as the hometown of Chunhyang, a Yi maiden with such fidelity that her story is often compared to that of Juliet. Chunhyang was the daughter of a kisaeng hostess who secretly married Myong-nyong, the son of a magistrate. The lovers were forced to separate when Myong-nyong's father was posted to Seoul, and the corrupt governor of Namwon tried to add Chunhyang to his list of conquests. She resisted and was beaten and imprisoned. Myong-nyong, who had been appointed Royal Inspector for Cholla Province, heard the story and rushed to her rescue. They, of course, lived happily ever after. The Kwanghallu Pavilion, located in a pretty park in the center of Namwon, is said to be the place where Chunhyang and Myong-nyong first met. A nearby shrine contains Chunhyang's portrait, and each spring there is a festival (on the same day as Buddha's Birthday) in her honor.

Within the Chirisan Park, the two temples of particular interest are Hwaomsa and Ssangyesa, both in southern areas of the park, and easy to reach from the small town of Kurye. Hwaomsa, founded in the year 544, is one of the oldest temples in Korea and houses several historical treasures. One is a 15-foot stone lantern, National Treasure No. 12, which is the largest of its kind in the country. Dominating the temple compound is the Kahwangjon (Awakening the Emperor) Judgment Hall, a massive two-story structure with 160-foot-high columns, considered to be one of the finest examples of early Yi Dynasty temple architecture. There are also several pagodas, one supported by four Silla stone lions representing the prime emotions of love, anger, happiness, and sorrow.

Ssangyesa Temple was established in 723, during the Silla Dynasty, by the priest Sambop who bribed a priest at the Kaiyum Temple in China into giving him the revered skull of the Zen master Hui-Neng. The shrine he built to house the relic gradually grew into Ssangyesa.

Hidden in a valley on the eastern slope of Chirisan Park is the village of Chunghak-dong, which has avoided the sweeping modernization of Korea's Saemaul (New Community) Movement. It is difficult to reach—you take a two-hour bus ride from the southeastern town of Hadong to the village of Muke, and from there it's another couple of hours of hard hiking. However, if you have a dedicated interest in traditional Korea, you won't find a better example. The dress, the architecture, and the atmosphere have all changed little with the times. The Confucian classics are still taught in Yi Dynasty style, and unmarried men still wear their hair in a single long plait. There are few comforts in Chunghak-dong, but there is a small inn and it is also possible to arrange an overnight stay with a resident.

In the far southwest of this southern sector of the West Plain and Coast is the port of Mokpo, a rather drab city in itself but important as a departure point for island-hopping throughout the area. From here you can head by ferry for Chejudo Island (it takes around seven hours), or to Hongdo Island, to the west. This involves an eight-hour trip to splendid isolation, as the island's only attractions are its camellia forests and strange rock formations. There are no accommodations here, but food and shelter can be found on other islands nearby.

South of Mokpo is Chindo Island, linked to the mainland by a fairly new bridge. The island used to be known especially for its characteristic breed of dog, and as a center of shamanism, but it is now famous for an annual "parting of the waters." There are fabulous legends woven around this annual phenomenon, which allows people to walk between the village of Hoedong and the small islet of Ado. It is actually caused by the moon's gravitational force on the tide, sometime in March or April, and the event has turned into a very colorful, and crowded, folk festival.

Wando, in the far south, is another departure point for Chejudo, with the trip taking from one and a half to three hours, depending on the type of ferry.

In this south-southwestern sweep, there are a number of opportunities for visiting other islands to swim, fish, or enjoy the quiet side of Korea. However, you should bear in mind that tourism is not well developed here, and the experience is only recommended for those adventurous enough to cope with language difficulties and sparse comforts. Accommodations and transportation are not problems—there is a wealth of small inns and local bus services—but standards will not match what you have seen in other, more tourism-oriented parts of the country.

So that is the West Plain and Coastal Area—a long stretch along the Yellow Sea Coast. The northern sector offers an even balance of culture and recreation while being fairly close to Seoul's hotels; the central and south still cling to much of Korea's tradition, with the cultural sights less developed, and, therefore, less crowded.

PRACTICAL INFORMATION FOR
WEST PLAIN AND COASTAL AREA

WHEN TO GO. Any time of year is possible, but winter is rather bleak. It's not that it's so cold, but it is raw and damp and there are few winter sports. On the other hand, many people love to walk on the beaches and shoreline in winter. The southern areas can be very hot in summer, but offer a milder spring and fall than farther north. In the fall, as all over Korea, greater crowds will be found at major attractions since this is a popular time to visit the temples and shrines.

HOW TO GET THERE. Following are the main ways to get to the tourist centers of the three sectors of the West Plain and Coastal Area. We have basically outlined the ways of traveling out of Seoul, but it is also easy to travel into the area from cities all over the country. Most of the train stations and express bus terminals have English-speaking staff to provide details, or you can ask your hotel staff for help. In Seoul, you can call the Information Center at the Express Bus Terminal in Kangnam, Tel. 591–3402, and at Seoul Station, you can call the special counter for foreigners, 392–7811.

To the Northern Sector. To Onyang. From Seoul. **By train,** the Changhang line from Sobu Station (near Seoul Station), a ride of around one hour, 30 minutes, with departures every hour, 7:35 A.M. to 7:35 P.M., W2,300. **By express bus** from the Kangnam Terminal, one hour, 30 minutes driving time, buses departing every 20 minutes, 6:30 A.M. to 9 P.M. (W1,900).

To Hyonchungsa Shrine (just outside Onyang). **By suburban bus** from Onyang; or from the bus terminal at Chonan, a 40-minute ride, buses departing every hour, 6:50 A.M. to 5:45 P.M.

To Sudoksa Temple (Mt. Toksan Park). From Seoul. **By local bus** from the Nambu Bus Terminal, a three-hour ride, departing twice daily, the first at 7:20 A.M., the last at 1:45 P.M. (W4,340). It is also possible to take the Changhang **train** line from Seoul, changing to a suburban bus at Sapgyo.

To Sosan. From Seoul. **By local bus** from the Nambu Bus Terminal, a three-hour ride, departing every 20 minutes, 6:40 A.M. to 7 P.M. (W4,080).

To Nonsan (to visit the Kwanchoksa Temple). From Seoul. **By train** on the Cholla or Honam lines from Seoul Station, around 25 departures daily, the first at 7:20 A.M. and the last at 8:20 P.M. Convenient buses are also available from Nonsan to the two major centers of Kongju and Puyo.

To Puyo. From Seoul. **By local bus** from the Nambu Terminal, a three-hour ride, departing every 20 minutes, 6:30 A.M. to 7 P.M. (W4,020).

To Kongju. From Seoul. **By express bus** from the Kangnam Terminal, a two-hour, 20-minute ride, departing every 40 minutes, 7 A.M. to 7 P.M. (W2,910). Also **by local bus,** departing from the Nambu Terminal every 10 minutes, 6:30 A.M. to 7:30 P.M. (W2,910).

To Taechon, on the coast. From Seoul. **By train,** the Changhang line from Sobu Station, a ride of around three hours, departing every hour, 7:35 A.M. to 7:35 P.M. **By local bus** from the Nambu Terminal, a three-hour, 20-minute ride, departing every 20 minutes, 7 A.M. to 6:54 P.M. (W4,650).

To the Central Sector. To Chonju. From Seoul. **By train,** the Cholla line from Seoul Station, a ride of around three hours, 11 departures daily, the first at 8:05 A.M. and the last at 11:50 P.M. (Two of the services are by Saemaul **superexpress** at 9:35 A.M. and 6:05 P.M.) **By express bus** from the Kangnam Terminal, a ride of around two hours, 50 minutes, departing every five to 10 minutes, 6 A.M. to 8:30 P.M. (W4,360).

To Chongju. From Seoul. **By train,** on the Honam line from Seoul Station, 17 departures daily, the first at 7:20 A.M. and the last at 11:30 P.M. (Three of the services are by Saemaul **superexpress,** departing at 9:05 A.M., 10:05 A.M., and 4:05 P.M.) **By express bus,** from the Kangnam Terminal, a ride of around three hours, 20 minutes, departing every 20 minutes, 6 A.M. to 8 P.M. (W4,920).

To Naejangsa Temple. From Chongju. **By suburban bus,** a 25-minute ride, departing every 20 minutes, 6 A.M. to 9 P.M.

To Kumsansa Temple. From Chonju. **By suburban bus,** a 40-minute ride, departing every 20 minutes, 6:40 A.M. to 8:20 P.M.

To the Southern Sector. To Kwangju. From Seoul. **By air** from Kimpo Airport, departures three times daily for a flight of 50 minutes (W24,600). **By train,** the Honam line from Seoul Station, a ride of around four hours, 15 minutes, departing 15 times daily with the first at 7:20 A.M. and the last at 11:30 P.M. (Three of the services are by Saemaul **superexpress,** the 9:05 A.M., 10:05 A.M., and the 4:05 P.M.) **By express bus** from the Kangnam Terminal, a four-hour ride, departing every five minutes, 5:30 A.M. to 8 P.M. (W5,880).

To Namwon (entrance to Chirisan Park). From Seoul. **By train,** the Cholla line from Seoul Station, a four-hour ride, departing 11 times daily. **By express bus** from the Kangnam Terminal, a four-hour, 10-minute ride, departing every 50 minutes, 6:30 A.M. to 6 P.M. (W5,420).

To Songgwangsa Temple. From Kwangju. **By suburban bus,** a one-hour, 30-minute ride, departing every hour, 8:45 A.M. to 8:50 P.M.

To Kurye (Hwaomsa Temple, Chirisan Park). From Kwangju. **By suburban bus,** a one-and-a-half-hour ride, departing every 20 minutes, 6:30 A.M. to 8:10 P.M.

To Mokpo. From Seoul. **By train,** from Seoul Station, a five-hour ride, with departures 10 times a day. (There are two Saemaul superexpress train departures). **By express bus** from the Kangnam Terminal, a four-hour, 40-minute ride, departing every 35 minutes, 6 A.M. to 6:30 P.M. From Cheju-do. **By ferry,** with daily departures, except Mondays, at 7 A.M. and every other day also at 9 A.M. The early morning trip takes five hours, 30 minutes, and the 9 A.M. trip takes seven hours as it stops at two islands on the way. Fares range from the lowest third class of W8,140 to the top first-class berth at W22,950. There is also a regular **ferry** service from Chejudo to Wando, in the far south of the southern sector, with daily departures depending on the season. You can call the following numbers for information on the ferry services, or ask your hotel manager for assistance: Seoul, (02) 535–2101; Mokpo, (0631) 43–2111; Chejudo, (064) 43–4511.

HOW TO GET AROUND. Schedules of local trains and buses throughout all three sectors of the West Plain and Coastal Area are excellent. By train between major cities, you often have a choice of **air-conditioned express, ordinary express,** and the slow-but-scenic **local trains.** When heading from the towns toward popular attractions, there are usually enough buses that you can ride out to a park, temple, or beach and return to your hotel the same day.

In the major cities, **car hire** is possible. There are **Hankuk Rent-A-Car** in Chonju, Tel. (0652) 74–1288, and **Sangmu Rent-a-Car** in Kwangju, Tel. (062) 941–6552. In other centers, your hotel manager will be able to advise if hired cars are available.

You can always hire **taxis** for the day—as in other parts of Korea the rate will depend on your bargaining power and the season. You can figure on at least W50,000 for a day. Language is likely to be a problem, so you should ask one of the hotel staff to write out your destinations in Korean.

ACCOMMODATIONS. International-style hotels are few and far between in this area. However, there are excellent *yogwan,* the traditional Korean inns, at just about all the scenic centers. Hotel costs range from around W50,000 to W60,000 for *1st class;* W25,000 to W50,000 for *2d* and *3d class.* For convenience, we are listing the hotels according to each sector of the area. The credit card abbreviations used are American Express, AE; Diner's Club, DC; MasterCard, MC; and Visa, V.

In the Northern Sector

Hotels listed here are in Onyang and the nearby Togo (or Dogo) resort (a short drive from Onyang by suburban bus), along with youth hostels in Onyang and Puyo. Don't be misled by the "hostel" label—along with the bunk rooms are a number of very comfortable private rooms. The one in Puyo is especially recommended. The location, between the Kumgang River and the Puyo Hill, is most attractive. Another way to explore this northern sector is to stay in nearby Taejon, in the Central Area. You don't need to stay in the town, there are a number of hotels in the area of the Yusong Hot Springs, on the slopes of the Kyeryongsan Park. (See "Accommodations" in the *Central Area* chapter for details on the Taejon vicinity hotels.)

Jeil. *1st class.* 228–6, Onchon-dong, Onyang, Chungchongnamdo; Tel. (0418) 44–6111, Seoul office (02) 775–6645, Fax. (0418) 42–6100. 93 rooms, many of them Korean-style. Western and Korean restaurants, a coffee shop, cocktail lounge, and nightclub. Resort facilities include an outdoor swimming pool, golf practice range, sauna and mineral-spring baths, and tennis courts. Credit cards: AE, MC, V.

Paradise Dogo. *2d class.* 180–1, Kigok-ri, Togo-myon, Asan-gun, Chungchongnamdo, at the Togo Springs area, near Onyang; Tel. (0418) 42–6031, Seoul office (02) 267–0767, Fax. (0418) 42–6040. 130 rooms, Western and Korean restaurants, and a coffee shop. There are also an indoor pool, hot mineral baths, a sauna, and an 18-hole golf course. Credit card: AE.

Western. *2d class.* 230–6, Onchon-dong, Onyang, Chungchongnamdo; Tel. (0418) 42–8151, Seoul office (02) 774–2420, Fax. (0418) 42–8156. With 65 rooms, this small hotel is near the Onyang Hot Spring Station.

It features banquet facilities, a lounge, and a nightclub. Credit cards: MC, V.

Onyang Admiral. *3d class.* 242–10, Onchong-dong, Onyang, Chung-chongnamdo; Tel. (0418) 2–2141, Seoul office (02) 797–9336 or 794–3491. Just 54 rooms, Western and Korean dining facilities, a cocktail lounge, and an outdoor swimming pool and mineral baths. Credit cards: AE, DC, V.

Youth Hostels. Sam Jung Buyeo Youth Hostel. 105–1, Kugyo-ri, Puyo-up, Puyo-gun, Chungchongnamdo; Tel. (0463) 2–3101, Seoul office (02) 557–1221. There are four-bunk and six-bunk rooms, plus double and Korean-style rooms (a double costs around W30,000 per night). The facilities are good—Western and Korean dining, a theater-restaurant, coffee shop, cocktail lounge, and facilities for boating, fishing, and outdoor swimming. Credit cards: AE, MC, V.

In the Central Sector

Hotels listed here are in Chonju, the capital of Chollabukdo Province; the area of Chongju, a town to the southwest; and Kunsan, on the northwest coast of this central sector. Kunsan itself has little of tourist interest—it is a growing commercial and industrial center—but with a couple of reasonable hotels (nothing 1st class) makes a convenient sightseeing base. Here you are also near some lovely coastal scenery. It is easy to confuse the names Chonju and Chongju. Chonju is one of the best bases for heading to the Kumsansa Temple, and the Maisan and Togyu mountain parks. Chongju is the access point to the Naejangsa Park, and the hotel we list here is conveniently located near the park's best attractions. It is a good base for mountain hikes.

Hotel Core. *1st class.* 627–3, Sonosong-dong, Chonju, Chollabukdo; Tel. (0652) 85–1100, Telex K66613, Fax. (0652) 85–5707. 110 rooms, Western and Korean restaurants, coffee shop, cocktail lounge, and nightclub. Also a sauna. Credit cards: AE, DC, MC, V.

Naejangsan Tourist. *1st class.* 71–14, Naejang-dong, Chongju, Chollabukdo; Tel. (0681) 535–4131, Seoul office (02) 777–3611, Telex K23216. Over 100 rooms, and good facilities including Western, Korean, and Japanese restaurants, a cocktail lounge, and nightclub. Also a sauna. Credit cards: AE, DC, MC, V.

Chonju Tourist. *2d class.* 28, 3-ka, Taga-dong, Chonju, Chollabukdo; Tel. (0652) 83–2811, Fax. (0681) 83–4478. Just 42 rooms, with limited restaurant facilities. Coffee shop, cocktail lounge, and a nightclub. Credit cards: AE, DC, MC, V.

Kunsan Tourist. *2d class.* 462–1, Kyongjang-dong, Kunsan, Chollabukdo; Tel. (0654) 43–0811. 113 rooms, with Western and East Asian restaurants, a coffee shop, cocktail lounge, and nightclub. No credit cards.

Victory. *3d class.* 21–1, Shinchang-dong, Kunsan, Chollabukdo; Tel. (0654) 445–6161. 63 rooms, limited restaurant facilities, a cocktail lounge, and nightclub. Credit cards: AE, MC, V.

In the Southern Sector

The international-style hotels in this area are limited to Kwangju, the provincial capital of Chollanamdo, but this is an excellent center for visit-

ing the "bamboo village" of Tamyang, the Chogyesan Park and Songgwangsa Temple, Namwon, and the hiking and cultural attractions of
Chirisan National Park. To stay in the other tourist centers of the more
remote areas, you will need to use *yogwan,* Korean inns. These are a good
value, and most comfortable.

Kukje Tourist Hotel. *1st class.* 1281-2, Chuwol-dong, So-ku, Kwangju;
Tel. (062) 673-0700, Fax. (062) 673-4300. With 57 rooms, this hotel features a restaurant, night club, and sauna. Credit cards: AE, DC, MC, V.

Shin Yang Park. *1st class.* San 40, Chisan-dong, Tong-ku, Kwangju;
Tel. (062) 228-8000, Fax. (062) 232-3731. 88 rooms; Western, Korean,
Japanese, and Chinese dining facilities, coffee shop, cocktail lounge, and
nightclub. Also a sauna and indoor golf facilities. Credit cards: AE, DC,
MC, V.

RESTAURANTS AND NIGHTLIFE. The central and southern sectors
of the West Plain and Coastal Area are reputed to have the best food in
the country. That is Korean food, of course, and Chonju (central sector)
and Kwangju (southern sector) both claim to be the traditional centers
of gourmet fare. Chonju is best known for its *pibimpap* (in fact this rice
dish to said to have originated here), and you will find it at just about any
Korean restaurant. If you have acquired a taste for *kimchi,* your pibimpap
in Chonju will be accompanied by at least five different kinds. The restaurant **Chungang Hoekwan** (78-1, 3-ka, Chungang-dong, Tel. 84-6166) is
especially recommended (every taxi driver knows it, or the hotel manager
can guide you). Here your pibimpap will cost you W4,000. Kwangju's
gourmet tradition is not just for food—the city is perhaps best known for
its *chungchong* (barley and rice wine) and a particularly potent *makkoli.*
Since nightlife here is limited to the Korean styles of entertainment, you
may want to sample Kwangju's specialty liquor while exploring the local
wine bars.

If you insist on Western food, you will have to limit yourself, in general,
to the hotels. Do not expect gourmet standards here—even at the better
hotels and resorts, which are more experienced with serving foreign guests,
the menus will be simple and the food mediocre.

Remember, also, that the farther south you head in this area, the less
developed are the tourist resources for Westerners. There is a truly local
flavor to food and entertainment, and the overall experience can be highly
rewarding. As in most parts of Korea, your hotel manager is the best
source of information about eating out in the area.

There is no casino in the West Plain and Coastal Area.

TOURS. The tour opportunities into this area are limited to packages
put together by travel agents for a minimum of 15 persons, and there are
no regular "join tour" programs. The **Royal Asiatic Society,** however,
docs cover the area extensively, (but unfortunately infrequently), primarily for the important Paekche relics and the unusual scenery. Tours are
arranged to Puyo and Kongju, to the Chollipo Arboretum, and to the
Pyonsan Peninsula area (between Chonju and Chongju, central sector, to
the west). This last program highlights two temples, Naesosa and Sonunsa,
both of which are in splendid coastal locations. The RAS tours in general
are arranged over two days—usually weekends—and nonmembers are
welcome to join if there is space available. You can write to the society

at Box 255, Seoul, for details of the programs. The street address is sixth floor, Christian Broadcasting Building, 136-46, Yonji-dong (Chong-no 5-ka), Chongno-ku, Seoul (Tel. 763-9483).

Within the area, it is sometimes possible to join "domestic" tours designed by local travel agents for Koreans to explore their own heritage. Your hotel manager can help you look into these, but the frequency of local buses and often short distances between attractions usually make it easy to put together your own programs.

For those who like sea cruises, there are a number of opportunities in the area for visiting off-shore islands. From Mokpo, in the southwest, you can take a ferry cruise to the island of Hongdo. It takes about eight hours, and the destination itself has little to offer, but the cruise is through the western section of the Tadohae National Sea Park. Some of the seascapes are spectacular, and you can find accommodations on nearby Taehuksando Island. From Mokpo, or Wando in the far south, you can also take a cruise to Chejudo.

WHAT TO SEE. Historic Sites. The West Plain and Coastal Area has an abundance of Paekche-era relics, particularly around the old capitals of Puyo and Kongju. The descriptive chapters for the northern section will give you details. The **Puyo Hill** is one of the major areas of interest—it has some beautiful Paekche pavilions, fortifications, and a shrine to honor three loyal supporters of the last Paekche king. In Puyo, also, there is a small park displaying two national treasures from a Paekche temple—an 11-foot-high Buddha image, and a five-story pagoda in a typical Paekche style. Near the town center of Kongju is a Paekche tomb that was only discovered in 1971. Although the tomb itself has had to be sealed against humidity, a replica is nearby. The treasures from the tomb, some 3,000 of them, are displayed in the Kongju Museum, and in the National Museum in Seoul.

The provincial capital of Chonju, in the central sector of the area, has a city gate, **Pungnammun,** which is a very fine example of Yi Dynasty design and engineering.

Parks. Within or on the outskirts of the whole area, there are 11 provincial and six national parks—two of them the only sea parks in the country. The most important of the parks are discussed with their particular attractions in the descriptive paragraphs of this chapter, but for convenience we'll list them again here.

Northern Sector. The Sosan Sea Coast national park; Toksan, Chilgapsan, and Taedunsan provincial parks; and the National Park of Kyeryongsan.

Central Sector. The Pyonsan, Sonunsan, Moaksan, and Maisan provincial parks; and the national parks of Naejangsan and Togyusan.

Southern Sector. The other national sea park, Tadohae, which sweeps around from the Hallyo Waterway in the Southeast Area; the Wolchulsan, Turyunsan, Mudungsan, and Chogyesan provincial parks; and the National Park of Chirisan.

All of the parks feature the rugged beauty of Korea's mountains, and, of course, the brilliance of the seasonal changes. However, because many of the parks are relatively isolated, they are spared the terrific popularity of their counterparts to the north and northeast. With the exception of

Chirisan, which has escalated in popularity since the opening of the Taegu-Kwangju Expressway, the hiking trails and special scenic spots of this area's parks will have fewer crowds and more peace and tranquility. However, tourist facilities are, in general, less developed.

Temples and Shrines. There are nearly 30 temples in the entire area, some with national treasures, and others that are among the largest, oldest, or most beautiful in the country. In general, it is the settings that make them especially spectacular. Korean temple architecture against a background of valley and hill is always exquisite. Even in peak season popularity, the temples are well worth exploring. Here are the most important in the area, and the closest major town for convenient access.

In Northern Sector. The **Hyonchungsa Shrine,** to honor Admiral Yi Sun-Shin, near Onyang, his birthplace; **Sudoksa Temple,** on the slopes of Toksan Mountain, west of Onyang; **Magoksa,** one of the best examples of traditional temple architecture in the country, just north of Kongju; **Koransa,** at the base of the famous Nakhwaam cliff ("Rock of the Falling Flowers") in Puyo; the **Kapsa** and **Tonghaksa temples** in the west of the Keryongsan National Park; and the **Kwanchoksa Temple** with its Unjin Miruk Buddha statue that's 1,000 years old, near Nonsan.

In Central Sector. Kumsansa Temple, which has some 10 cultural treasures including a Paekche pagoda, on Mt. Moaksan near Chonju; **Songwangsa Temple,** with its fine color murals, near Chonju; the fascinating **Tapsa** complex—not a temple but an enchanting series of pagodas made from piled-up stones by an eccentric hermit, in the Maisan provincial park; and the **Naejangsa** and **Paegyangsa temples,** in the Naejangsa National Park.

In Southern Sector. Wonhyosa and **Chungsimsa temples,** in the Mudungsan Park, Kwangju; **Songgwangsa Temple** in Chogyesan Park, which is one of Korea's largest temple complexes and has Western nuns and monks in permanent residence, easily reached from Kwangju; the **Chunhyang Shrine** in Namwon, to honor a Yi lady of remarkable fidelity; **Hwaomsa Temple,** among the oldest in Korea, and **Ssangyesa Temple,** both in the Chirisan National Park, and best reached from the town of Kurye.

Museums and Art Centers. As the area is rich in history, there are several museums, all with something different to show.

In Northern Sector. The **Onyang Folklore Museum,** 403–10, Kwongok-ri, Onyang; Tel. (0418) 42–6001. This is a private collection of over 14,000 exhibits, including paintings and crafts, designed to show the origin of Korean folk customs and the process of their development. The **Kongju National Museum,** 284-1, Chunghak-dong, Kongju; Tel. (0416) 54–2205, displays over 7,000 relics excavated from the tomb of the Paekche king Muryong. It is closed on Mondays. The **Puyo National Museum,** Kwanbuk-ri, Puyo; Tel. (0463) 33–8562, features Paekche relics, especially ceramics. It also is closed on Mondays.

In Central Sector. Chonju Municipal Museum, 3–102, Pungnam-dong; Tel. (0652) 84–2337. This has a general historical collection, open daily.

In Southern Sector. Kwangju National Museum, 83–3, Maegok-dong, Kwangju; Tel. (062) 55–7111. This houses the largest collection of Yuan-era ceramics ever excavated outside China, and treasures from Chollanamdo province including neolithic relics, Buddhist bells, and white porcelain. It is closed on Mondays. There is also a municipal museum in Kwangju displaying another 1,500 items, at 164, Unam-dong; Tel. (062) 56–9041. Tamyang, a small town north of Kwangju, has one of Korea's most unusual museums—the **Tamyang Bamboo Museum**, 87–2, Tamju, Tamyang-gun, Chollanamdo; Tel. (0684) 2–4111, which features the area's major cottage industry. Items displayed range from tiny pins to elaborate furniture. Also in the southern sector is a new art museum called the **Pau Memorial Hall,** on a slope of Mt. Wolchul in the town of Yongam. It is open year-round.

Botanical Gardens. The northern sector features two major botanical attractions— **Anmyondo Island,** noted for unusual plants, trees, and flowers, and its forests of camellias; and the **Chollipo Arboretum,** at the northern end of the Sosan sea park. This is a 200-acre plant sanctuary, owned and run by a resident foreigner who has spent years developing a spectacular collection of domestic and exotic flowers, shrubs, and trees. Visits by the general public are not encouraged, but people with a genuine interest in Oriental flora are welcome. There is an island in the southern sector, **Hongdo,** which is also noted for its forests of camellias. It is an eight-hour ferry trip from Mokpo to get there, however. It is possible to find simple accommodations and meals on the Taehuksando Island nearby.

SPORTS. Hiking predominates, because of all the mountain parks, but the **golf** enthusiast is also well accommodated. In the northern sector, you can play at **Togo,** Shinsong-ri, Songjang-myon, Asun-gun; Tel. (0418) 42–0271, Seoul office (02) 568–5231 at the 18-hole course attached to the resort called Paradise Dogo (see "Accommodations"), and at **Yuseong,** Pongmyong-dong, Chung-ku, Taejon; Tel. (042) 822–7103, Seoul office (02) 752–2568 near the hot springs west of Taejon (Central Area).

In the central sector, there is an 18-hole course at **Iri,** Tokki-dong; Tel. (0653) 856–2151, a town whose main importance is as a commercial rail terminus, a little northwest of Chonju.

In the southern sector, you play in **Kwangju,** Hapkang-ri, Okwa-myon, Koksong-gun; Tel. (062) 523–5533, where there are 18 holes. Although these are membership clubs, it is possible for foreign visitors to obtain playing privileges. You can also hire clubs and caddies.

BEACHES. There is a wide choice from north to south in the area. Apart from the supervised and protected areas, you will find many more secluded, sandy bays. Be guided by the Koreans, however, and swim where there are other people around. Officially designated areas are listed by sector. On the western fringe of the Sosan Sea Coast National Park, in the northern sector, we have **Chollipo, Mallipo,** and **Yonpo** (which is also popular for sailing). The next important beach is **Taechon,** probably the most popular in the entire West Plain and Coastal Area. There are basically two beaches here—the north is more Korean in flavor, with lots of inns, restaurants, and a very lively atmosphere. To the south is the beach that has a cluster of bungalows owned by Protestant missionaries. It is also possible to arrange accommodations here, but remember that the high summer season (mid-July to the end of August) is pretty crowded. A little south of Taechon is **Muchangpo.** Our central sector features **Sonyudo,** at an offshore island cluster, and **Pyonsan,** off the Pyonsan Peninsula. A little more south are **Tongho** and **Kyeman.** The southern sector has lots of beaches, including **Oedaldo** and **Kumho** near Mokpo; and **Songho,** to the west of Wando Island. There is another excellent stretch of beaches around **Yulpo,** a small coastal town to the south of Posong. Summer facilities at the designated areas are good. Beachside restaurants and snack bars mushroom overnight, and there are usually toilet facilities and showers. You won't find top-notch accommodations, although the *yogwan,* Korean inns, are both comfortable and plentiful. You will probably be happiest at Taechon, in the northern sector. It's easy to reach and used to catering to foreign guests.

HOT SPRINGS. There are three spas of note, all in the northern sector. **Onyang,** near the Folklore Museum and Admiral Yi's shrine, is known for its carburetted, alkaline waters (temperature 52° Fahrenheit). At nearby **Togo,** the waters are cooler, 27°, and sulphurous. **Toksan,** farther west, has waters noted for their radium content, apparently excellent for treating dermatological disorders. Water temperature here is 52°. Hotels and inns in the areas all offer access to mineral baths. There is another spa on the eastern edge of the northern sector, at **Yusong,** just to the west of the city of Taejon, covered in our chapter on the Central Area. The Yusong waters are radium, alkaline, and have a natural temperature of 55°, among the hottest in the country.

SHOPPING. The best shopping opportunities in this area are in the five main cities covered in our descriptive paragraphs—Onyang, Puyo, Kongju, Chonju, and Kwangju. Because of their size and importance as tourist centers, there are busy local markets in these places and an assortment of souvenir shops featuring the specialties of the area.

Chonju is well known as Korea's primary producer of traditional paper, called *hanji* in Korean. The paper is produced on the outskirts of the city at Huksokkol, about a 15-minute drive by taxi from the downtown area. Here you can see paper being made, and purchase a range of paper products. The **Chollabuk-do Handicrafts Cooperative,** downtown at 31–3 Chungang-dong, Chonju; Tel. (0652) 84–5921, also sells the paper crafts—fans, lanterns, and umbrellas, along with some excellent regional wood products.

Namwon is also known for its woodcrafts. Two places are recommended in this town near the entrance to Chirisan national park (on the Olympic Expressway that runs between Kwangju and Taegu); **Howonsa,** Tel. (0671) 625–3354, and **Haeshimdang,** Tel. 625–2274, are both in Namwon's Ssangyo-dong area, a short walk from the bus terminal. At these places you can watch the production process as well as buy.

Kwangju is the handicrafts center of Chollanamdo. A good area to browse is Hwarang-ka, near the Kwangju Police Station, which has over 20 galleries displaying and selling antique chests, paintings, pottery, and other craft items. For ceramics, try the **Ceramic Gallery of Cho Ki Jung,** at the **Chollanamdo Handicrafts Cooperative,** 58–79, Chang-dong, Tongku, Kwangju; Tel. (062) 222–1566.

To the north of Kwangju is Tamyang, the bamboo village, where market days are held every five days (usually the 2d, 7th, 12th, 17th, 22d, and 27th of each month). The sprawling market gives you the opportunity to see the full scope of Tamyang's artistry. Visit the unusual Bamboo Museum while you're there.

Finally, if you're in Mokpo, there are a number of interesting stores near the bus terminal, in Sang-dong. One recommended is the **Haeng Nam Sa Company,** Tel. (0631) 76–2112.

ANNUAL EVENTS. Special celebrations in the area are as follows:

Paekche Cultural Festival (Northern Sector). This is usually held in September or October (the date for 1993 was not yet confirmed at press time) in both Puyo and Kongju, the last capitals of the Paekche Dynasty. The celebrations include rituals honoring the ancient kings, loyal subjects, and court maidens, with processions and traditional music and dance performances.

Village Ritual of Unsan (Unsan Pyolshin) (Northern Sector). This festival is Korea's Intangible Cultural Asset No. 9., and is held to honor the spirits of legendary generals who fought for independence during the Paekche era. By tradition, the events take place at a shrine just outside Unsan. The festival usually takes place in March or April (the 1993 date was not confirmed).

Moyang Castle Festival (in Kochang, Central Sector). This is held in October to celebrate the completion of Moyang Castle, which was built using only female laborers. More than 5,000 women and girls parade in traditional costume on top of the castle wall, more than a mile around.

Chunhyang Festival (at Namwon, Southern Sector). Here again the date changes each year according to the lunar calendar, but the festival takes place around the same time as Buddha's Birthday, May 28 in 1993. The ceremonies take place at a shrine to the heroine Chunghyang, who was a model of feminine virtue. A major part of this event is the Pansori Contest, a competition to find who can sing the best narrative song.

USEFUL ADDRESSES AND TELEPHONE NUMBERS. Medical Attention. For any medical emergency, ask your hotel manager for assistance. In Kwangju, the **Chunnam University Hospital** is recommended (at Hak-dong, Tong-ku; Tel. 220–5114). In Puyo, there is **St. Joseph's Hospital** (at 261 Gua-ri; Tel. 836–2483), and in Chonju there is the **Presbyterian Hospital** (Tel. 86–4141).

Tourist Information. As is the situation for the other less tourism-oriented areas of Korea, printed matter on the West Plain and Coastal Area is limited. Visit the KNTC Information Center in Seoul (Tel. 757–0086) and collect the latest information before you leave. While you're in the area, the best source of information is your hotel manager. Souvenir stores and often, railway station bookstores will have maps.

CENTRAL AREA

A quick overall survey of the Central Area shows that the eastern limit is easily defined by the country's Central Rail Line. This runs from the eastern outskirts of Seoul on a southeast route through Chechon and Tanyang to Yongju, and then heads due south to Andong, and on into the Southeast Area and Kyongju. The southern border of the Central Area is a rather arbitrary line drawn from a point north of Taegu westward for about 38 miles, dropping a bit to include the national parks of Kayasan and Togyusan and then veering a little west again. The western boundary is formed mainly by the Seoul-Pusan Expressway, which heads north from Taejon.

The area encompasses parts of two provinces—the bulk of Chungchong-pukdo and the western half of Kyongsanpukdo—plus snippets of two southern provinces at its lower edge.

The Taebaek Mountains run down through the Central Area, but the area is not entirely mountainous—the very center is made up of some vast stretches of rice fields.

The total Central Area is about 150 miles long from north to south, and some 100 miles wide. The area is not loaded with attractions, and most things that are worth exploring are around the edges, and easy to reach by road or rail. The exception is Sognisan National Park with its Popchusa Temple, which could be considered the centerpoint of the whole Central Area.

Excellent highways run around the edges of this area, and, in 1988, a new expressway opened that runs through the northwest corner, from Seoul to just north of Taejon, relieving some of the congestion on the present Kyongbu Expressway.

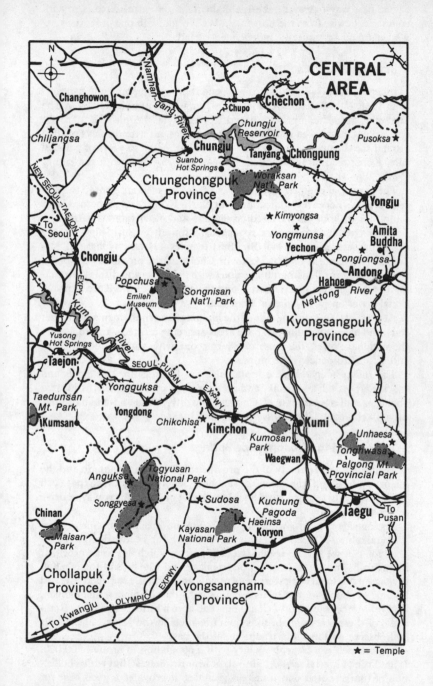

★ = Temple

The best way to outline the highlights of the Central Area is to work counterclockwise from the northwest. We'll begin with one of Korea's newest national "treasures," Independence Hall.

Independence Hall

Independence Hall was due to be opened with much pomp and pageantry in 1986, but a serious fire delayed its completion until a year later. The "national shrine" comprises a grand Korean-style "People's Hall" as the centerpoint, plus seven smaller exhibition rooms, all with displays created around the theme of independence from Japan. After 36 years of colonial rule, Korea won its independence on August 15, 1945, with the end of World War II.

The memorial complex also features a twin-tower monument to the Korean people's hopes for unification with North Korea, and numerous large sculptures to immortalize freedom fighters and other famous patriots.

Interior exhibits include a replica of Admiral Yi Sun-Shin's "turtle ship," miniatures of two lost Buddhist temples—Hwangnyongsa of Kyongju and Miruksa of Mt. Iksan in Chollapukdo province—historical weapons, and royal memorabilia, along with paintings and displays depicting the struggle for independence and the activities of the Korean provisional government in exile in Shanghai.

At present, the surroundings of the buildings and monuments are rather stark and bare, but numerous park areas are being created—one to feature the national flower, the Rose of Sharon, one with varieties of Bamboo, and a third to concentrate on pines.

The Independence Hall complex also has facilities for full meals and snacks, a post office, a bank, and an enormous parking lot. It is located about six miles southeast of Chonan, roughly a one-and-one-half-hour drive from Seoul. The admission fee is W1,000.

Taejon and the Yusong Hot Springs

Taejon is the capital city of the province of Chungchongnamdo and the major railhead on the Seoul-Pusan and Seoul-Kwangju-Mokpo-Yosu lines. It is easily reached from Seoul by the Kyongbu Expressway, a drive of about two hours.

Just outside the city's western suburbs are the Yusong Hot Springs (radium, alkaline, 55° Fahrenheit), ranked among the best in Korea. From here you can see Mt. Kyeryongsan (2,772 feet), which has some excellent hiking trails and a couple of famous monasteries. The hills of today's Kyeryongsan National Park were once remote and virtually impenetrable and became the home of numerous religious cults that combined Shamanism, Buddhism, the teachings of Confucius, and even a little Christianity. Remnants of these sects remain today, and hamlets in the Kyeryongsan hills still observe customs and traditions of the past.

Taejon itself is a large, busy city with a population of around 700,000. It has little of special scenic, cultural, or historic interest, but with a collection of tourist hotels and transport facilities, it provides a good base for exploration of the surrounding areas.

Sognisan National Park and the Popchusa Temple

The national park is about a one-hour drive northeast of Taejon, and takes about three hours by car directly from Seoul. The name translates to "escape from the vulgar," and the park-resort has become one of the most popular excursions in the Central Area. The park's village of Sogni-dong is the starting point for hikes to some 20 or so temples and pavilions that are scattered among the hills. The peak of Sogni Mountain is called Munjangdae, and Koreans will tell you that if you reach the top, you will not have to go to purgatory as you have suffered enough. Though somewhat strenuous, the climb is exhilarating for its spectacular mountain views.

On the drive toward the park, you will pass the most beloved pine tree in the country. It is said to be 1,000 years old, and to have raised its branches for King Sejo (who reigned from 1456 to 1468) to pass beneath. The tree's politeness was rewarded with the bestowing of a rank equivalent to that of a cabinet minister. Today the tree is caged for protection.

Nearby is the private Emileh Museum, owned by Dr. Zo Zayong, one of the leading authorities on Korean folk art. The collection comprises over 8,000 items, including folk paintings, roof tiles, and masks.

The central feature of the park is its Popchusa Temple, which dates from the sixth century and has been one of the most important in the country. The complex houses three national treasures—a five-storied pagoda (the only one of its type left in Korea), a carved stone lantern supported by twin lions, and a stone cistern shaped like an open lotus flower. These and other lanterns, pillars, stone images, and reliefs all date back to the Silla period.

The temple is most noted for a modern addition: a 75-foot concrete image of the Miruk Buddha (Buddha of the Future), the largest in the country, which was completed in 1964. It makes up in size for what it lacks in ancient grace.

You can reach the temple by a short walk through forest, and there are some pleasant spots for a picnic. However, as mentioned earlier, Sognisan is a most popular excursion point and you could meet crowds on weekends and holidays. The nearby village has a good hotel (see "Accommodations") and numerous small inns and restaurants. A special local delicacy is mountain mushrooms, definitely worth trying.

Kimchon and the Chikchisa Temple

Kimchon is a town on the Kyongbu Expressway, midway between Taejon and Taegu. It's the departure point for the temple of Chikchisa, which is an easy four-mile taxi ride from Kimchon, and is located on the southeastern slope of Mt. Hwangaksan, a popular destination for day-trippers and weekend hikers. Because of its popularity, Chikchisa is rarely serene, but does offer rare pleasures in its paintings, which hang on just about every available wall, and its shrines, which are filled with finely carved statues. Apart from the beauty of the buildings themselves, which blend glorious combinations of blue, magenta, and gold, Chikchisa is noted for the brilliant blue tiles of its main sanctuary, some 1,000 small statuettes of the Buddha as a baby, and the support pillars of the main gate, which are reputed to be 1,000 years old.

According to legend, the temple was established by the monk Ado, who introduced Buddhism to the Silla kingdom during the fifth century. It was apparently rebuilt by the Silla priest Chajang during the seventh century, and was completely destroyed during the Japanese invasions of the late sixteenth century. Of the 15 major buildings today, the oldest date to the reconstruction of 1602.

Chikchisa is one of several temples associated with Samyong Taesa, born in 1544, who was both a Buddhist saint and a military hero. His study of Zen at Chikchisa led to his attainment of enlightenment, and he became chief priest of the temple in 1574. He later became a disciple of Sosan, the most prominent Korean Buddhist master of the time, and led Sosan's warrior monks in battles against the Japanese. After playing a key role in the conclusion of hostilities, Samyong retired to the nearby Haeinsa Temple, in the Kayasan Mountains, where he died in 1610.

To the east of Kimchon is Mt. Kumosan, another popular park with hikers (also mentioned in the *East Coastal Area* chapter), and to the southwest is Mt. Togyusan, on the old fortified frontier that separated the three ancient kingdoms of Koguryo, Silla, and Paekche. This national park has numerous hiking trails and the remains of a few historic temples. Both Anguksa and Songgyesa temples are known for their scenic locations rather than their cultural importance.

Andong, the Village of Hahoe, and Yongju

This eastern fringe of the Central Area is celebrated as a stronghold of Korean Confucianism, and there are many places in the Andong-Yechon-Yongju area that reflect a reluctance to give up the past. Traditional Korea survives in its purest forms here, probably because the area was spared the ravages of the Mongol, Japanese, and Manchu invasions.

Let's begin with Andong, the ancestral home of the aristocratic Kwon Clan, which, although extensively modernized, retains some of the gracious old mansions of the Yi Dynasty gentry. To the east of the town is a large reservoir, recently developed as a recreational park. Nearby is a cluster of buildings, some up to 300 years old, that were moved here before the reservoir area was flooded. Styles range from simple thatched cottages to an elaborate villa, and the atmosphere is pleasantly authentic. On the way here, you can stop at a Silla-era brick pagoda, the oldest and largest in Korea. It is seven stories high and engraved with images of fierce temple guardians.

You can take a bus ride and a short walk northeast of Andong to the Tosan Sowon, a Confucian academy founded in the mid-sixteenth century by Yi Toegye, probably Korea's greatest scholar. The wisdom of Confucius is no longer taught here, but you can visit the main lecture hall, see wooden plates that were used for printing lessons, and see some relics of the founder. His descendents still live in a wooden Yi Dynasty house behind the school.

About 10 miles to Andong's northwest is the Pongjongsa Temple, which has four designated treasures, and wooden structures that are believed to be among the oldest in Korea. Just a few miles north of Andong, on the road to Yongju, is an awesome Amita Buddha, dating back to the Koryo Dynasty (935–1392). The robe and hands are carved into a giant granite boulder; the head and hair are carved in two separate pieces of rock, set into place on top.

The hamlet of Hahoe is located along the Naktong-gang River, about a 30-minute drive to the southwest of Andong. Little has changed here since the early days of the Yi Dynasty, and the people like it that way. The name Hahoe means "enfolded by the river," and it is this isolation by water that has prevented the village from becoming modernized. Some comforts prevail, such as refrigerators and the ubiquitous television sets, but the only modern building is a school. Some of the houses date back over 500 years, and the village has been designated for cultural preservation. Foreigners are rare in Hahoe, and you should be sensitive to the fact that this village is real, not one that has been created for tourism.

Hahoe is where one of Korea's masked dance rituals was developed during the Yi Dynasty. Though primarily religious, based on Shamanist rituals, the dances served as a vent for the many grievances of the common people about restrictions placed on them by the nobility. Some early Hahoe masks are still preserved today. The mask dance is one of the cultural highlights at the annual Andong Folk Festival (the 1993 date was not confirmed at press time, but it usually takes place in September).

Yongju is about 20 miles north of Andong and is also a seat of Confucian teaching, with values retained and reflected in the city's life today. Like Andong with its Hahoe Village, Yongju has a nearby site that is not easy to get to, but well worth taking the trouble. A one-hour bumpy bus ride from the center of Yongju will take you to Pusoksa, the Floating Rock Temple, which has a number of treasures unique in the country. The main hall, Muryangsujon (the Hall of Eternal Life), is the oldest surviving wooden structure in Korea, dating from the fourteenth century. Also from the Koryo period is a nine-foot seated figure of the Amita Buddha, entirely made of clay and covered with lacquer and gilt. It is the only one of its kind in Korea. Some of Korea's oldest Buddhist mural paintings can also be seen at this temple.

The temple gets its name from a charming legend woven around the temple's founder, the high priest Uisang, who returned from China with teachings of Hwaom Buddhism, and the love of a youth, Myohwa ("Delicate Flower"). It is said that her spirit transformed itself into a massive boulder to protect him and his temple from harm. This "floating rock" balances outside the Main Hall today. Later, the legend continues, Myohwa took the form of a stone dragon, which burrowed beneath the temple to put its head at the altar and its tail some 60 feet away by a stone lantern. Recent scientific excavations near the lantern revealed part of a rock with etchings in a scalelike pattern. The excavations have been discontinued.

Tanyang, Chungju, and Cruises

Continuing our sweep through the Central Area, we turn westward from Yongju on the short ride to Tanyang. This is an area noted for its "eight natural beauty scenes," each created by the sculpturing effects of water. Over many thousands of years, water has eroded the limestone that forms the area's geological underpinning, creating superb combinations of falling water and weird rock formations in scenic settings. These eight scenic wonders are located within a seven-mile radius of the center of town, along the upper stream of the Namhan-gang River (South Han River).

The Tanyang area is dotted with limestone caves, two of which are impressive enough to warrant tourist attention. The Kossidonggul Cave is near the small town of Kaktong, some 30 miles northeast of Tanyang, a pretty drive along a winding local road that follows the course of the river. The geological stratum of the cave, which is over a mile long, is believed to have been formed some 400–500 million years ago. It is named after a particular Ko family who took shelter there during the Japanese invasion in the late sixteenth century. Closer to town is the Kosudonggul Cave, less than a mile from the city center, which is known as "the underground palace" because of its magnificent stalactites.

About 25 miles to the west of Tanyang is Chungju, almost at the top of the Central Area. The surrounding area is famous for Korea's first fertilizer plants, the country's only talc mine, and the production of a very high grade of tobacco. Popular sights near the city are the Tangumdae scenic area, where a famous Silla musician named Uruk trained in musical techniques, and the pretty Chungnyolsa Shrine. Today, Chunju area's most popular tourist draws are the Chungju Dam and Reservoir. A man-made lake now stretches some 32 miles between Chungju and the outskirts of Tanyang, and various spots have been turned into recreational areas for waterskiing, boating, and fishing. A number of sleek, air-conditioned cruise boats ply the route between Chungju and Shintanyang, the western suburb of Tanyang, with stops at the centers of most tourist interests. These include a stop at the northern edge of the Woraksan National Park, which offers access to an impressive 30-foot stone Miruk Buddha, and the Suanbo Hot Springs. Because of their high radium content, the springs are reputed to have remarkable curative powers for the treatment of dermatological disorders. The cruise is also one of the best ways to see the "Cluster of Cultural Assets" at Chongpung, and the Tanyangpalgyong— the eight scenic wonders of the Tanyang area.

PRACTICAL INFORMATION FOR
CENTRAL AREA

WHEN TO GO. The best seasons here are spring, summer, and fall. In the mountains that run down through the center of the area you will, of course, find cooler temperatures whatever the season, and especially severe winters.

HOW TO GET THERE. The area is served only by bus and train, but very comprehensively. Here are your choices for reaching the main cities and towns:

To Taejon (in the east of the area). From Seoul. **By train** from Seoul Station, with some 58 departures a day by superexpress (Saemaul), air-conditioned express (mugunghwa), and ordinary express (Tongil). The superexpress (departing 16 times daily) takes around one hour, 30 minutes, and costs W8,500 first class and W6,200 economy. For information, call the foreigners' ticket counters at the stations—Seoul (02) 392–7811, Taejon (042) 253–7788. **By express bus,** from Seoul's Express Bus Terminal in Kangnam, a one-hour, 50-minute ride, departing every five to 10 minutes, 6 A.M. to 8:30 P.M. (W2,910). For express bus information in Seoul, call 535–4151.

To Yusong (the hot springs, and an entry point to the Mt. Kyeryongsan National Park). From Seoul, **by express bus** from the Kangnam Terminal, a two-hour ride, departing every 30 minutes, 6 A.M. to 8:30 P.M. (W2,960). Access to Yusong is easier from Taejon, **by intercity bus,** a drive of just 30 minutes with frequent departures.

To Mt. Sognisan National Park. From Seoul. **By express bus** from the Kangnam Terminal to Poun, entrance of Mt. Sognisan, a two-hour, 30-minute ride, departing every one hour, 30 minutes, 7:30 A.M. to 6:30 P.M. (W3,720). From Taejon. **By suburban bus,** a one-hour, 30-minute ride, departing every 20 minutes, 6:20 A.M. to 8:10 P.M. (W1,950).

To Kimchon (to visit the Chikchisa Temple, Mt. Kumosan Park, or the Mt. Togyu National Park). From Seoul. **By train** from Seoul Station (air-conditioned express or ordinary express), a three-hour ride, with departures every 15 minutes between 6:10 A.M. and 11:55 P.M. daily. **By express bus,** from the Kangnam Terminal, a three-hour ride, departing every one hour, 10 minutes, 7 A.M. to 6 P.M. (W4,280). From Kimchom to Chikchisa takes about 20 minutes by suburban bus, with departures every nine minutes between 6:20 A.M. and 7:20 P.M.

To Andong (in the east). From Seoul. **By train,** air-conditioned express from Chongnyangni Station, a five-hour ride, departing six times daily between 9 A.M. and 9 P.M. **By local bus,** from Seoul's Dongseoul Terminal, a four-hour, 30-minute ride, with departures every 30 minutes, 6 A.M. to 6:20 P.M. From Kimchon. **By suburban bus,** a three-hour, 30-minute ride, departing every 40 minutes, 6:25 A.M. to 7:00 P.M. (W2,900).

To Yongju (north of Andong, and departure point for the Pusoksa Temple). From Seoul. **By train,** air-conditioned express from Chongnyangni

Station, with departures six times daily between 9 A.M. and 9 P.M. **By local bus,** from Seoul's Dongseoul Terminal, a four-hour, 20-minute ride, with departures every hour, 6:20 A.M. to 5:40 P.M. (W6,260). To the Pusoksa Temple from Yongju is a one-hour **suburban bus** ride, with departures several times a day.

To Tanyang. From Seoul. **By train,** air-conditioned express from Chongnyangni Station (same departure schedule as to Yongju farther to the southeast). **By local bus,** from the Dongseoul Terminal, a three-hour, 30-minute ride on the same route and schedule as Yongju, for a fare of W4,690.

To Chungju (west of Tanyang). From Seoul. **By local bus** from Dongseoul Terminal, a one-hour, 50-minute ride, with departures every 15 minutes, 6 A.M. to 8:20 P.M. (W3,210).

To Suanbo Hot Springs (near Chungju). From Seoul. **By local bus** from the Dongseoul Terminal, a two-hour, 20-minute ride, with departures every hour, 6:30 A.M. to 6:40 P.M. (W3,810). From Chungju. **By suburban bus,** a 40-minute ride, with departures every 20 minutes, 6 A.M. to 8 P.M.

HOW TO GET AROUND. The fringes of the Central Area, which offer the most tourist attractions, are well served by local **trains** and **buses.** A good tourist map will show you the rail lines, most of which are served by air-conditioned express and/or ordinary express trains, plus the slower Pidulgi ("Pigeon") trains. There is also a rail line running out of Seoul eastward to Wonju, which then turns south and splits at Chupo into two branch lines that run south down each side of this area. The western branch runs through Chungju and Chongju to Taejon, and then eastward to Yongdong and Kimchon, most of which have attractions. The eastern branch makes stops at Tanyang, Yongju, and Andong before meandering southward out of the area.

Suburban buses are excellent for getting from town to town, or town to park, spa, or temple. Distances within the area are short, roads range from good to excellent (very few are unpaved), and the bus frequencies are impressive.

Taxis are good value here, as they are elsewhere in Korea, and are among the most convenient ways of getting around. Language undoubtedly will be a problem, but you can ask a member of your hotel staff to write out your destinations in Korean. A taxi for the day should cost you in the area of W50,000, less if you're very clever with bargaining, and more if you're visiting in the peak holiday season or on a public holiday.

In the main center of Taejon it is relatively easy to rent a **car,** with a driver if you prefer. Two agencies are recommended: *Hyundai Rent-a-Car* (Tel. 535–6040), and *Chungnam* (Tel. 533–0104). It is sometimes possible to rent cars in the other towns in the Central Area—your hotel information desk will be able to provide current details.

Between Chungju and Tanyang it is possible to travel by water along the Chungju Reservoir. You can travel by modern cruise **boat** from Chungju to Worak, on the northern edge of the Woraksan National Park (seven-and-one-half miles, W1,230), and then from Worak to Shintanyang (32 miles, W5,350), the western suburb of Tanyang. An alternative is a cruise from Chungju to Shintanyang, or the reverse (33 miles, W5,460). Departures are frequent, and the scenery along the way is splendid.

ACCOMMODATIONS. The largest city in the area is Taejon, the provincial capital of Chungchongnamdo. Tourist hotels are few in the entire area—there are only five in Taejon, for example, and only one of these is officially classified as first class. However, there are excellent *yogwan*, Korean inns, and this area provides some excellent opportunities to enjoy the local flavor of the country. In Andong and Yongju, for example, you will be exploring areas where the old Confucian traditions are still very much a way of life, and staying in a local inn will complement your sightseeing experiences.

You can also check around the borders of this area on your tourist map for an adjacent town that might provide accommodations more convenient than the hotels listed below. Two such nearby possibilities are suggested— Taegu (The Southeast), from which you can explore the southeast corner of this Central Area; and Kongju or Puyo (West Plain and Coastal Area), for visiting the western side.

Hotel accommodations for a double or twin room will cost in the area of W50,000 to W70,000 for *1st class;* W30,000 to W50,000 for *2d* and *3d class.* The hotels indicated are all recommended for foreign visitors. Do bear in mind, however, that styles of service and facilities do not, in general, match the standards of Seoul, and English is not spoken as frequently.

Credit card abbreviations used are American Express, AE; Diner's Club, DC; MasterCard, MC; and Visa, V.

In Taejon

Yoo Soung Tourist. *1st class.* 480, Pongmyong-dong, Chung-ku, Taejon, Chungchongnamdo; Tel. (042) 822–0811. 140 rooms. A good collection of facilities including Western and Korean restaurants, a coffee shop, nightclub, sauna and mineral-spring baths, and an outdoor swimming pool. Credit cards: AE, DC, MC, V.

Dae Jon Tourist. *2d class.* 20–16 Won-dong, Tong-ku, Taejon, Chungchongnamdo; Tel. (042) 273–8131. 52 rooms, Western and Korean restaurants, and a nightclub. Credit cards: AE, DC, MC, V.

Joong Ang. *2d class.* 318, Chung-dong, Tong-ku, Taejon, Chungchongnamdo; Tel. (042) 253–8801, Fax. (042) 253–8801. 59 rooms, Western and Korean restaurants, a coffee shop, and a nightclub. Credit cards: AE, DC, V.

Mu Gung Hwa Tourist. *3d class.* 213–2, Pongmyong-dong, Chung-ku, Taejon, Chungchongnamdo; Tel. (042) 822–1234, Fax. (042) 822–1237. 62 rooms, Western and Korean restaurants, coffee shop, sauna and mineral-spring baths, and facilities for tennis. Credit cards: AE, DC, MC, V.

Royal Tourist. *3d class.* 202-5, Pongmyong-dong, Chung-ku, Taejon, Chunchangnamdo; Tel. (042) 822–0720. 43 rooms, Western and Korean restaurants, coffee shop, sauna, and hot-springs bath. Credit cards: AE, DC, MC.

At Sognisan National Park

Sognisan Tourist. *1st class.* 198, Sanae-ri, Naesongni-myon, Poun-gun, Chungchongbukdo; Tel. (0433) 42–5281, Seoul office (02) 738–8014. 122 rooms; location at the entrance to the Mt. Sognisan National Park. Western, Korean, and Japanese restaurants, a coffee shop, cocktail lounge, and a nightclub. There are outdoor facilities for golf and tennis. This hotel is popular not only for its proximity to the national park (and the Popchusa Temple), but also because it has the Central Area's only casino. Credit cards: AE, DC, MC, V.

At the Suanbo Resort, Onchon

(Southeast of Chungju, on the western edge of the Woraksan National Park, noted for its radium hot springs)

Suanbo Park. *2d class.* 838–1, Onchon-ri, Sangmo-myon, Chungwon-gun, Chungchongbukdo; Tel. (0441) 846–2331, Telex K25689, Fax. (0441) 846–3705. 84 rooms, Western and East Asian restaurants, a coffee shop, cocktail lounge, and a nightclub. The resort-style facilities include hot mineral baths, an indoor pool, golf practice area, and tennis courts. Credit cards: AE, DC, MC, V.

Suanbo Tourist. *2d class.* 291-1, Onchon-ri, Sangmo-myon, Chungwon-gun, Chungchongbukdo; Tel. (0441) 846–2311, Fax. (0441) 846–2315. 50 rooms and limited facilities. Both Western and Korean food are offered, along with a cocktail lounge, nightclub, sauna facilities, and the area's speciality, hot mineral baths. No credit cards.

Youth Hostels. Hanal Youth Hostel. This is one of two in the whole Central Area, at 730–1, Suanbo-onchon, Chongju, Chungwon-gun, Chungchongbukdo; Tel. (0441) 846–3151, Seoul office (02) 752–0803. There is a total of 80 rooms, most of them Korean-style, or with bunks for eight people. Dining facilities are limited to one general restaurant and a coffee shop, but there is also a nightclub, sauna, and hot mineral baths. No credit cards.

Songnisan Youth Hostel. 3–8, Sangpanri, Naesongni-myon, Poun-kun, Chungchongbukdo; Tel. (0433) 42–5211, Seoul office (02) 555–8437. This is the newest hostel in the area, but facilities are limited. No credit cards.

Chongju

This is a city of little tourist appeal at present, except as a base for visiting the attractions of the northwest corner of the Central Area. However, with the opening of an international airport in 1992, the town will doubtless gain importance. (Do not confuse this Chongju with the town of the same name in the West Plain Coastal Area.)

Chengju. *2d class.* 844–3, Pokdae-dong, Chongju, Chungchongbukdo; Tel. (0431) 64–2181, Fax. (0431) 66–8215. With 72 rooms, this hotel is located five minutes by taxi from the Chongju Express Bus Terminal. It features banquet rooms, a lounge, and a nightclub. Credit cards: MC, V.

RESTAURANTS AND NIGHTLIFE. Western-style dining is very much limited to the hotels (see above), and the quality/price ratio is generally not good. The best selection of food in all price ranges is Korean, and you should ask the hotel manager for his or her recommendations on dining outside your hotel. You will find the same limitations on evening entertainment—the "Western" nightclubs have a decidedly Korean flair, and you will probably have more fun (and spend far less money) in the local wine houses and beer halls. There is one, 24-hour **casino** in the area, at the Sognisan Hotel, 198, Sanae-ri, Naesongni-myon, Poun-gun, Chungchongbukdo; Tel. (0433) 42–5281.

TOURS. Tour opportunities for foreign visitors to the Central Area are limited, but it is certainly possible to join local bus trips to historic sites and scenic spots. Your hotel manager will be able to help you find out about such trips, and is also your best source of information about do-it-yourself tour programs.

With the opening of Independence Hall, about six miles southeast of Chonan, in the far northwest corner of the Central Area, a number of new tours have been developed, ranging from a few hours to a full day in length. These have been designed to include the Independence complex with other historic sites in the area, and there are a number of designated departure points. These include the folklore center in Chongpung (near Chungju), the Popchusa Temple in the Sognisan National Park, and the Independence complex itself. While the tours have been designed to show Koreans their own heritage, foreign visitors are welcome to join. Ask your hotel manager or at a tour desk for details.

Another interesting tour in the area is the boat cruise along the Chungju Reservoir, between Chungju and Tanyang, covered under the "How to Get Around" section above.

WHAT TO SEE. The Central Area's most important sights have been outlined in the descriptive section of this chapter. You should remember that the east of the Central Area overlaps the East Coastal section. This means that some of the sights discussed in the central and southern sectors of the East Coast are just as accessible from towns in the Central Area. A good example is Ondol Castle, well worth seeing, which falls into the East Coastal area but is really more accessible from Tanyang. At the same time, you can visit the Kossi Cave, mentioned in both our Central and East Coastal descriptions.

Temples. There are 17 temples in the Central Area, but three deserve special mention: **Popchusa,** in Mt. Sognisan National Park; **Chikchisa,** near the town of Kimchon; and **Pusoksa,** an hour's drive from Yongju. These all have historical importance, house national treasures, and have been outlined in the descriptive section of this chapter.

Parks. The three major national parks in the area are **Mt. Sognisan,** in the center; **Mt. Togyusan,** southwest of Kimchon; and **Mt. Woraksan,** near Chungju and Tanyang, to the south of the Chungju Reservoir. All have excellent hiking trails and important temples. Looking at your tourist map, you will see that the southern outskirts of the Central Area area have several other parks—Mt. Palgong, Mt. Kaya, and Mt. Kumo—all of which have been described in this and other chapters.

Museums. A new national museum opened in Chongju in late 1987, with exhibits focusing on relics excavated from the Chungchongbukdo Province area; Tel. (0431) 52–0710. Three halls concentrate on different periods: prehistoric (from the Paleolithic to the Iron ages), the Three Kingdoms era (37 B.C. to A.D. 935), and art and handicrafts from the Koryo and Yi dynasties (935–1910). The museum is closed on Mondays. The other notable museum in the Central Area is the private Emileh collection of folk art, near the Popchusa Temple in Sognisan. It is open from Wednesday through Sunday; Tel. (0433) 2–2955.

SPORTS. Hiking dominates in this region, but you'll also find a range of **water sports** around the Chungju Reservoir. Some of the resort hotels offer **tennis** facilities (see the "Accommodations" section). **Golf** in the northwest sector is excellent. There are a number of courses in the area of Yongin, and these have been outlined in the "Sports" section of *Practical Information for Seoul,* as they are all within easy distance of the capital city.

SHOPPING. There are no particular specialties of the Central Area, but you will find a number of general souvenir stores in the main hotels and at the village of the Mt. Sognisan National Park, for example. There are also plenty of local markets, and if you're in Chongju, you can visit the **Chungchongbukdo Handicrafts Cooperative,** at 28–11, Sokgyo-dong; Tel. (0431) 3–2984, which has the best collection of locally produced souvenirs and folk crafts.

CULTURAL EVENTS. The only annual celebration in the area is the **Andong Folk Festival,** held in the town of Andong (and the traditional village of Hahoe) usually in May or September. The three main events are the Chajonnori, or "War of Wagons," the Hahoe Mask Drama, and the "Girls Bridge-Crossing Game." Designated as Korea's Intangible Cultural Asset No. 24, the Chajonnori is the festival's main event. It is a "battle" between two teams, each with dozens of members. Each team manhandles a giant A-frame made of wood, with a warrior perched at the top. The two warriors try to dislodge each other, while the teams struggle to keep the A-frames from toppling. The Haehoe Mask Drama is a recreation of a ritual developed during the Yi Dynasty, when the common people donned masks to dance and air their grievances against the aristocracy. At press time, the date for the Andong Folk Festival in 1993 has not been confirmed.

National holidays and festivals are also celebrated throughout the area—the Buddhist temples are especially lovely when they are decorated for Buddha's Birthday, May 28, 1993.

USEFUL ADDRESSES AND TELEPHONE NUMBERS. Medical Attention. For any medical emergency, ask your hotel manager for assistance. In Taejon, the **Chungnam University Hospital** is recommended, in Taehung-dong, Chung-ku district; Tel. (042) 253–6831. In Andong you can go to the **Presbyterian Songsu Hospital,** Tel. (0571) 2–2621.

Tourist Information. Printed materials on the Central Area are limited. Check with the KNTC Information Center in Seoul for their latest pamphlets (Tel. 757–0086) before you head into the area. Souvenir stores and railway station bookstores will have maps.

FIVE-MINUTE KOREAN

No one will be expected to learn very much of any language in only five minutes, yet knowing a few words may go a long way toward developing mutual friendship, and appreciation. There are presently two romanization systems being used throughout Korea; the McCune-Reischauer system is the most popular. A romanization system attempts to spell out the Korean words in English letters as closely to their actual pronunciation as possible. If you are staying in Korea for some time it is recommended that you learn the *han'gul* alphabet, which is one of the simplest in the world. This of course will perfect your pronunciation without relying on romanization.

English	Korean
Yes	nae, ye
No	anee-oh
Thank You (for services rendered)	kamsa-hamnida
Thank You (most polite)	komap-sumnida
Hello (calling attention)	yoboseyo
Hello (polite greeting)	annyong-hashimnika
My name is_____	na-ui irum-un _____imnida
May I have your name?	irum-ee mooawt-shimnika?
Pardon me	mian-hamnida
I'm sorry	shillye-hamnida
Goodbye (your leaving)	anyong-ee kyeshipshio
Goodbye (others leaving)	anyong-ee kashipshio
What is the price?	awlma-imnika?
Please give me (buying)	chushipshio
It's expensive	pi-samnida
It's not expensive	an-pi-samnida
It's all right	Kwenchon-sumnida
Where is it?	awdee issumnika?
Where is the telephone?	chonwha-ga awdee issumnika?
Where is the toilet?	hwajangshil-ye awdee issumnika?
Please wait a moment	chamkanman kidaryo chushipshio
I don't speak Korean	hanguk-mal mott-hamnida
I am an American	megook-saram imnida
bus	basu
Where is the bus stop?	basu chongujang-ee awdee issumnika?
taxi	taekshi
Please take me to_____	_____-ro kapshida
train	kicha
Does this (bus or train) go to_____?	eegots-un_____-ro kamnika?
train station	yok
subway station	chihachol yok
Where is Pusan station?	Pusan yok-ee awdee issumnika?
airport	pihaengee-jang
Please go straight	kochang-kapshida
Please go right	orun-chokuro-kapshida
Please go left	hwen-chokuro-kapshida
Please stop here	sewo-chushipshio
Let's go	kapshida

Let's hurry and go	balee-kapshida
Please go slowly	chonchon-hee kapshida
What time is it?	meeyot-shi imnika?
How old are you?	meeyot-sal imnika?
I have some money	dawun-ee chokum issumnida
I would like to have. . . .	. . . chuseyo
May I have tea?	hongcha chuseyo?
May I have coffee?	kopee chuseyo?
It is beautiful	arumdap-sumnida
You are pretty (to a child)	eepuda
tomorrow	naeil
Will it rain tomorrow?	naeil pi-ga omnika?
It's good	chosumnida
Is it good?	chosumnika?
It's bad	Napumnida
hotel	hotel
Korean inn	yogwan
Where's a good inn?	awdee choun yogwan-ee issumnika?
Korean-style *ondal* room	awndal-pang
Do you have an inn room?	awndal-pang-ee issumnika?
policeman	kyongchal
Where's the police station?	kyongchalso-ga awdee issumnika?
What is that called?	moo-yot imnika?
I'm hungry	pae-ga kopumnida
I'm busy	papumnida
water (not for drinking)	mul
I'm frustrated	kolchi apumnida
Where's a restaurant?	shikdang-ee awdee-issumnika?
Please bring a (Korean) meal	shiksa chushipshio
barbecued beef meal	pulgogi
barbecued spareribs	kalbi
barley tea (water for drinking)	boricha
ginseng tea	insamcha
beer	maekju
milk	ooyu
May I have a Coca Cola?	kola chuseyo?
cigarettes	tambae

(Note there are two number systems, Chinese and Korean)

one	ill (hana)
two	ee (twoul)
three	sam (set)
four	sa (net)
five	oh (tasawt)
six	yuk (yawsawt)
seven	chil (illgawp)
eight	pal (yawdul)
nine	koo (ahhope)
ten	ship (yawl)
fifteen	ship-oh (yawl-tasawt)
twenty	ee-ship
fifty	oh-ship
one hundred	paek
two hundred	ee-paek
one thousand	chon
three thousand	sam-chon
ten thousand	man

thirteen thousand	man-sam-chon
fifty thousand	oh-man
one hundred thousand	ship-man

Index

Fodor's Travel Guides

U.S. Guides

Alaska

Arizona

Boston

California

Cape Cod, Martha's
Vineyard, Nantucket

The Carolinas & the
Georgia Coast

Chicago

Disney World & the
Orlando Area

Florida

Hawaii

Las Vegas, Reno,
Tahoe

Los Angeles

Maine, Vermont,
New Hampshire

Maui

Miami & the Keys

New England

New Orleans

New York City

Pacific North Coast

Philadelphia & the
Pennsylvania Dutch
Country

San Diego

San Francisco

Santa Fe, Taos,
Albuquerque

Seattle & Vancouver

The South

The U.S. & British
Virgin Islands

The Upper Great
Lakes Region

USA

Vacations in New York
State

Vacations on the
Jersey Shore

Virginia & Maryland

Waikiki

Washington, D.C.

Foreign Guides

Acapulco, Ixtapa,
Zihuatanejo

Australia & New
Zealand

Austria

The Bahamas

Baja & Mexico's
Pacific Coast Resorts

Barbados

Berlin

Bermuda

Brazil

Budapest

Budget Europe

Canada

Cancun, Cozumel,
Yucatan Penisula

Caribbean

Central America

China

Costa Rica, Belize,
Guatemala

Czechoslovakia

Eastern Europe

Egypt

Euro Disney

Europe

Europe's Great Cities

France

Germany

Great Britain

Greece

The Himalayan
Countries

Hong Kong

India

Ireland

Israel

Italy

Italy's Great Cities

Japan

Kenya & Tanzania

Korea

London

Madrid & Barcelona

Mexico

Montreal &
Quebec City

Morocco

The Netherlands
Belgium &
Luxembourg

New Zealand

Norway

Nova Scotia, Prince
Edward Island &
New Brunswick

Paris

Portugal

Rome

Russia & the Baltic
Countries

Scandinavia

Scotland

Singapore

South America

Southeast Asia

South Pacific

Spain

Sweden

Switzerland

Thailand

Tokyo

Toronto

Turkey

Vienna & the Danube
Valley

Yugoslavia

Special Series

Fodor's Affordables

Affordable Europe

Affordable France

Affordable Germany

Affordable Great
Britain

Affordable Italy

**Fodor's Bed &
Breakfast and
Country Inns Guides**

California

Mid-Atlantic Region

New England

The Pacific Northwest

The South

The West Coast

The Upper Great
Lakes Region

Canada's Great
Country Inns

Cottages, B&Bs and
Country Inns of
England and Wales

The Berkeley Guides

On the Loose in
California

On the Loose in
Eastern Europe

On the Loose in
Mexico

On the Loose in the
Pacific Northwest &
Alaska

**Fodor's Exploring
Guides**

Exploring California

Exploring Florida

Exploring France

Exploring Germany

Exploring Paris

Exploring Rome

Exploring Spain

Exploring Thailand

Fodor's Flashmaps

New York

Washington, D.C.

Fodor's Pocket Guides

Pocket Bahamas

Pocket Jamaica

Pocket London

Pocket New York
City

Pocket Paris

Pocket Puerto Rico

Pocket San Francisco

Pocket Washington,
D.C.

Fodor's Sports

Cycling

Hiking

Running

Sailing

The Insider's Guide
to the Best Canadian
Skiing

**Fodor's Three-In-Ones
(guidebook, language
cassette, and phrase
book)**

France

Germany

Italy

Mexico

Spain

**Fodor's
Special-Interest
Guides**

Cruises and Ports
of Call

Disney World & the
Orlando Area

Euro Disney

Healthy Escapes

London Companion

Skiing in the USA
& Canada

Sunday in New York

**Fodor's Touring
Guides**

Touring Europe

Touring USA:
Eastern Edition

Touring USA:
Western Edition

**Fodor's Vacation
Planners**

Great American
Vacations

National Parks of the
West

**The Wall Street
Journal Guides to
Business Travel**

Europe

International Cities

Pacific Rim

USA & Canada

WHEREVER
YOU TRAVEL,
$\mathcal{H}$ELP IS NEVER
FAR AWAY.

From planning your trip to providing travel assistance along the way, American Express® Travel Service Offices* are always there to help.

Korea

Global Tours
293-84 Yon-Dong
Cheju Shi, Cheju Do
64-46-8801

Global Tours
152 Kumnamno 5-Ga
Kwangju
62-225-2535

Global Tours
1-187 Taepyong No. 1-Ga
Daegu
53-423-0693

Global Tours
83-1 Chungang-Dong
Pusan
51-469-456

Global Tours
1031-6 Chuan-Dong
Inchon
32-868-6860

Global Tours
120 Namdaemunro 5-Ga
Seoul
2-777-9921

Global Tours
23-2 Unhaeng-Dong
Taejon
42-252-7225